THE
MARK TWAIN
ANTHOLOGY

THE
MARK TWAIN
ANTHOLOGY

Great Writers on

His Life and Works

EDITED BY SHELLEY FISHER FISHKIN

A SPECIAL PUBLICATION OF
The Library of America

Some of the material in this volume is reprinted with the
permission of holders of copyright and publishing rights.
Acknowledgments are on page 481.

Distributed to the trade by Putnam Group (USA) Inc. and in
Canada by Penguin Books Canada, Ltd.

Library of Congress Control Number: 2009939907

ISBN: 978-1-59853-065-0

The Library of America—199s

First Printing

Printed in the United States of America

Contents

Introduction   *xv*

Twain Matters: A Sampler   *1*

David Ross Locke
FROM New Books (1869)   *13*

Mark Twain
Memoranda: An Entertaining Article (1870)   *18*

Thérèse Bentzon
FROM Les Humoristes Américains: Mark Twain
   (The American Humorists: Mark Twain) (1872)   *24*

Eduard Engel
FROM Mark Twain: Ein Amerikanischer "Humorist"
   (Mark Twain: An American "Humorist") (1880)   *30*
FROM Mark Twain (1897)   *39*

Lafcadio Hearn
Mark Twain on the Mississippi (1883)   *42*

José Martí
FROM Escenas Norteamericanas
   (North American Scenes) (1884, 1890)   *48*

Henry Gauthier-Villars
FROM *Mark Twain* (1884)   *57*

Hamlin Garland
Mark Twain's Latest (1890)   *61*

Rudyard Kipling
An Interview with Mark Twain (1890)   *66*

Andrew Lang
On the Art of Mark Twain (1891)   *78*

Theodor Herzl
FROM Mark Twain in Paris (1894)   *83*

William Dean Howells
Mark Twain: An Inquiry (1901)   *88*

Ángel Guerra
FROM Prólogo: *Mark Twain, Cuentos Escogidos*
(Prologue to *Mark Twain: Selected Tales*) (1903)   *105*

Livia Bruni
FROM L'Umorismo Americano: Mark Twain
(American Humor: Mark Twain) (1905)   *108*

George Bernard Shaw
Letter to Samuel L. Clemens (1907)   *113*

Marina Tsvetaeva
Книги в красном переплёте
(Books Bound in Red) (1910)   *115*

Johannes V. Jensen
Mark Twain (1910)   *117*

George Ade
Mark Twain as Our Emissary (1910)   *121*

G. K. Chesterton
Mark Twain (1910)   *127*

Jesús Castellanos
FROM Mark Twain (1910)   *133*

George Soule
Mark Twain Protests (1916)   *137*

H. L. Mencken
FROM Mark Twain (1919)   *142*

Maks Erik
FROM ‏שלום-עליכם און מארק טווען.‏
(Sholem Aleichem and Mark Twain:
Notes on the Eighth Anniversary
of Sholem Aleichem's Death) (1924) *151*

Helen Keller
Our Mark Twain (1929) *159*

Lu Xun
FROM 《夏娃日记》小引
(A Short Introduction to "Eve's Diary") (1931) *173*

Jorge Luis Borges
Una Vindicación de Mark Twain
(A Vindication of Mark Twain) (1935) *177*

Theodore Dreiser
Mark the Double Twain (1935) *182*

Sterling Brown
FROM *The Negro in American Fiction* (1937) *195*

Grant Wood
My Debt to Mark Twain (1937) *200*

George Orwell
Mark Twain—the Licensed Jester (1943) *205*

Bernard DeVoto
FROM Introduction to *The Portable Mark Twain* (1946) *212*

Leslie Fiedler
Come Back to the Raft Ag'in, Huck Honey! (1948) *226*

T. S. Eliot
Introduction to *Huckleberry Finn* (1950) *234*

W. H. Auden
Huck and Oliver (1953) *246*

Ralph Ellison
Twentieth-Century Fiction and
the Black Mask of Humanity (1953)   *253*

Wallace Stegner
Yarn-Spinner in the American Vein (1957)   *271*

Mike Gold
Twain in the Slums (1959)   *275*

Yan Bereznitsky
FROM Mark Twain on the Bed of Procrustes (1959)   *278*
FROM The Question Is Significantly More
Profound: A Letter to Charles Neider (1960)   *280*

Lao She
FROM Mark Twain: Exposer of
the "Dollar Empire" (1960)   *283*

Edward Field
Mark Twain and Sholem Aleichem (1963)   *289*

Abel Startsev
FROM Марк Твен и Америка
(Mark Twain in America) (1963)   *293*

Kenzaburō Ōe
FROM アメリカ旅行者の夢—地獄にゆくハックルベリィ・フィン
(An American Traveler's Dreams—
Huckleberry Finn Who Goes to Hell) (1966)   *297*

John Seelye
FROM *The True Adventures of Huckleberry Finn* (1970)   *307*

Robert Penn Warren
Last Laugh (1978)   *314*

Norman Mailer
Huck Finn, Alive at 100 (1984)   *318*

David Carkeet
FROM *I Been There Before* (1985)   *325*

Chuck Jones
FROM *Chuck Amuck: The Life and Times
of an Animated Cartoonist* (1989)   329

David Bradley
Introduction to *How to Tell a Story
and Other Essays* (1996)   334

E. L. Doctorow
Introduction to *The Adventures of Tom Sawyer* (1996)   363

Hal Holbrook
Introduction to *Mark Twain's Speeches* (1996)   374

Erica Jong
Introduction to *1601 and Is Shakespeare Dead?*:
"Deliberate Lewdness" and the Lure
of Immortality (1996)   386

Ursula K. Le Guin
Introduction to *The Diaries of Adam and Eve*:
Reading Young, Reading Old (1996)   397

Toni Morrison
Introduction to *Adventures of
Huckleberry Finn* (1996)   408

Gore Vidal
Introduction to *Following the Equator
and Anti-Imperialist Essays* (1996)   420

Kurt Vonnegut
Some Comments on Mark Twain's *A Connecticut
Yankee in King Arthur's Court* by Kurt
Vonnegut at the Age of Seventy-Two (1996)   431

Ralph Wiley
FROM What's Up with Mad Mark Twain? (1996)   436

Dick Gregory
FROM *Callus on My Soul* (with Shelia P. Moss) (2000)   445

Ron Powers
What Hath Happened to
"The War-Prayer"? (2006)   *449*

Michael Blakemore
Is He Alive? (2008)   *454*

Min Jin Lee
Money as an American Character
and the Legacy of Permission: Or How
Mark Twain Taught Me That It Was
Okay to Talk About Money (2009)   *458*

Roy Blount Jr.
America's Original Superstar (2008)   *467*

Sources and Acknowledgments   *481*

Index of Works by Mark Twain   *490*

List of Illustrations

Pen-and-ink drawing of Mark Twain
    by Otto Schneider, 1906   11

Pencil sketch of Mark Twain
    by Samuel Johnson Woolf, 1906   104

Ink drawing by Jean Cocteau, 1958   199

"The American Lion of St. Mark's,"
    by William H. Walker, 1901   292

Chuck Jones:
    "Mark my words, this is my dearest friend," 1989   330
    "The Coyote—Mark Twain discovered
        him first," 1989   331
    "Boy meets protagonist," 1989   332

Charcoal sketch of Mark Twain
    by James Montgomery Flagg, 1949   372

Bronze relief portrait of Mark Twain
    by Barry Moser, 1985–86   477

Introduction

During his lifetime, Mark Twain was already one of the most famous and beloved writers in the world, and in the hundred years since his death, unlike so many once popular writers, the breadth of his appeal has never abated. *The Mark Twain Anthology* provides eloquent evidence of Twain's enduring influence by bringing together the words of scores of writers from his time to the present. They are an astonishingly diverse group and what they find in Twain's writing is equally diverse. The range of their responses is all the more remarkable because Twain is not on the surface a difficult writer, but on the contrary apparently welcoming and universally accessible.

Some readers have chosen to take him at face value as a humorous entertainer; others, early and late, have discerned darker and more troubling levels in his work. For some he was an exemplar of American values, for others a harsh critic of American injustices and overreaching. Few have argued with his unique importance as a stylist who drew his strength from the American vernacular voices, changing both American and world literature in the process. The writers represented in this anthology—novelists, poets, journalists, and others—frequently acknowledge his immense importance in their own development, as guide, goad, and gadfly.

William Faulkner called him "the first truly American writer," while Eugene O'Neill dubbed him "the true father of American literature" and Ernest Hemingway claimed that "all modern American literature comes from one book by Mark Twain called *Huckleberry Finn*." Faulkner, O'Neill, Hemingway, and countless others admired Twain as a pioneer in transforming the rough, raw material of American life and American speech into transcendent art. They marveled at the art Twain wrought from the speech of ordinary people—speech that in previous appearances in literature had most often been treated with ridicule. Jorge Luis Borges maintained that in *Huckleberry Finn* "for the first time an American writer used the language of America without affectation." Time and time again Twain defied readers' expectations, forging unforgettable narratives from voices and from lives that had not been the stuff of literature before. As he blasted through the constraints that had previously shackled both the style and content of American literature, Twain cleared a space for a new-world modernity that was intoxicatingly fresh and exciting. As William Dean Howells observed, "He saunters out into the trim world of letters, and lounges across its neatly kept paths, and walks about on the grass at will, in spite of all the signs that have been put up from the beginning of literature, warning people of dangers and penalties for the slightest trespass."

From the breezy slang and deadpan humor that peppered his earliest comic sketches to the unmistakably American characters who populated his fiction, Twain's writings introduced readers around the world to American personalities speaking in distinctively American cadences. H. L. Mencken wrote in 1917: "His humor was American. His incurable Philistinism was American. His very English was American. Above all, he was an American in his curious mixture of sentimentality and cynicism, his mingling of romanticist and iconoclast. *English Traits* might have been written by any one of half a dozen Germans. The tales of Poe, printed as translations from the French, would have deceived even Frenchmen. . . . But in *Huckleberry Finn*, in *A Connecticut Yankee* and in most of the short sketches there is a quality that is unmistakably and overwhelmingly national. They belong to our country and our time quite as obviously as the skyscraper or the quick lunch counter." George Bernard Shaw wrote to Twain in 1907 that "the future historian of America will find your work as indispensable to him as a French historian finds the political tracts of Voltaire," while British historian George Trevelyan asserted in the *Overland Monthly* in 1929 that Mark Twain "did more than any other man to make plain people in England understand plain people in America." In 1899 *The Times of London* called Twain "Ambassador at Large of the U.S.A." For readers the world over, his writings provided a window on American life available nowhere else.

As "American" as it was, however, Twain's work spoke to writers across the globe, shaping a range of other nations' literary traditions in the process. Twain's dazzling experiments with the vernacular inspired writers around the world to create art out of the language spoken by their own countrymen, from Lu Xun, widely viewed as the founder of modern Chinese literature to Johannes V. Jensen, considered the father of modern Danish literature. Joseph Conrad often thought of *Life on the Mississippi* when he commanded a steamer on the Congo, while Borges used it as a source for the book in which he made his debut as a storyteller. Kenzaburō Ōe cited *Huckleberry Finn* as the book that spoke to his condition so powerfully in war-torn Japan that it inspired him to write his first novel.

"Every book by Mark Twain was so different from the one preceding that comparisons were impossible," George Ade once observed. Each time critics thought they had him pegged, Twain set out in a new direction. While *The Innocents Abroad* might be seen as extending some of the comic gambits of the early sketches in the book that preceded it (*The Celebrated Jumping Frog of Calaveras County, and Other Sketches*), *Roughing It* struck out for new territory, as did *The Gilded Age*, *Tom Sawyer*, *A Tramp Abroad*, *The Prince and the Pauper*, *Life on the Mississippi*, *Huckleberry Finn*, *Connecticut Yankee*, *Pudd'nhead Wilson*, and *Joan of Arc*. One might strain to find common threads, to be sure—but those threads might stretch to the breaking point if asked to extend, as well, to such provocative late works as *To the Person Sitting in Darkness* and *What Is Man?* The dizzying range of Mark Twain's experiments (some more successful than others), the vastly different styles, forms, genres, goals, and audiences that he embraced, made (and make) him impossible to categorize—a fact that helps explain his appeal to scholars who devote their lives to him: one can't be bored by a writer who is actually so many different authors in one skin.

Multifaceted and complex, Mark Twain appealed to a broad range of writers drawn to him for a multitude of reasons. Some responded to the "unquenchable verve" of Twain's humor, as Thérèse Bentzon had put it—humor that Theodor Herzl found "immense, overpowering, and shattering" and that G. K. Chesterton called "truly mountainous and almost apocalyptic." Theodore Dreiser had no use for Twain the humorist, but esteemed Twain the deterministic philosopher who wrote the anonymously published *What Is Man?*, the Twain who meditated on "the meaning or absence of it in life." Dreiser also valued the Twain who penned the little-known Rabelaisian *1601—Conversation as It Was By the Social Fireside in the Time of the Tudors*, but refused to say why: "The initiated will understand. All others must inquire," he wrote. (Erica Jong appreciated *1601* as well, but unlike Dreiser was quite willing to say why: she argued persuasively that *1601* shows Twain "sneaking up on the muse so she would not be forewarned and escape," freeing his imagination to write a book as boldly transgressive as the novel he began that same summer: *Huckleberry Finn*.)

It was not Twain's humor or his philosophical musings that appealed to writers such as José Martí, Amiri Baraka, Langston Hughes, and Ralph Wiley, but rather his deft and dead-on social critique, sometimes searing and direct, sometimes subtly oblique and allusive. When José Martí read *A Connecticut Yankee in King Arthur's Court*, he was so moved by Twain's depiction of "the vileness of those who would climb atop their fellow man, feed upon his misery, and drink from his misfortune" that he wanted to "set off for Hartford to shake his hand"; Twain's treatment of race relations in *Pudd'nhead Wilson* led Amiri Baraka to call it "a wild book . . . I've never seen anything so strong," and prompted Langston Hughes to call it "as contemporary as Little Rock." Meanwhile, Ralph Wiley, in his 1996 *Dark Witness* admired the "brilliance" of the "controlled and telling imagery" with which Twain riffs on racism, American-style, in "Chapter 12, 'Jim Standing Siege,'" of *Tom Sawyer Abroad*. Wiley may be alone in finding brilliance in a book generally viewed as an embarrassing failure on Twain's part—but even skeptical readers might be forced to acknowledge the startling resonances of the scene to which Wiley draws our attention: "In this sequel to *Huck Finn*," Wiley wrote, "Twain finds a plausible way—plausible, within the absurd burlesque he weaves to hide it—to have Jim, the mild ex-slave, holding a small American flag while striking poses, then standing on his head while *perched on the head of the Sphinx!* as Tom and Huck sail by in a hot-air balloon, getting 'effects and perspectives and proportions.'" Wiley called Twain's writing "the literary equivalent of the best blues and jazz."

As a number of writers in this book eloquently demonstrate, it is in *Adventures of Huckleberry Finn* (a book deeply indebted to the African-American voices Twain listened to with admiration all his life) that Twain's critique of American racism coalesces most powerfully. It is also the book that secured Twain a berth on the honor shelf of world literature alongside such giants as Cervantes, Molière, Tolstoy, and Shakespeare. *Huckleberry Finn* was called "a masterpiece" as early as 1891, when Scottish writer Andrew Lang referred to it by that term in the *London Illustrated News*. Hemingway proclaimed it the source of "all modern American literature" in 1935, and T. S. Eliot called it "a masterpiece" in 1950. But although scores of writers and critics from the 1890s to the present may agree about *Huckleberry Finn*'s importance, they have valued it for a range of different reasons.

In 1937 in *The Negro in American Fiction*, poet and critic Sterling Brown singled out *Huckleberry Finn* for its depiction of "the callousness of the South to the Negro," conveyed "without preaching, but impellingly," and lauded Twain for the truth, the humor, and the sensitivity with which he crafted Jim, a slave whose dream was to get to a free state and work and save to buy his wife and then "to buy their children, or get an abolitionist to steal them." Brown wrote that "Jim is the best example in nineteenth-century fiction of the average Negro slave (not the tragic mulatto or noble savage), illiterate, superstitious, yet clinging to his hope for freedom, to his love for his own. And he is completely believable, whether arguing that Frenchmen should talk like people, or doing most of the work on the raft. . . ." In the decades following Brown's remarks, Jim would recede as a focus of writers' attention when they wrote about *Huckleberry Finn*; he would most often be displaced by a concern with the style of the book, the power of the river that ran through it, or the moral dilemma faced by Huck. But Brown's focus on Jim prefigures a tendency from the 1990s to today to view Jim, rather than Huck, as the hero of the novel, and to understand the novel as a satire on what Brown had called "the callousness" of the South—and of the nation—to its Black citizens. (Unfortunately, a number of writers who should know better—including Ernest Hemingway, Leslie Fiedler, and Norman Mailer—made the mistake of referring to Jim as "Nigger Jim." Twain never did—and never would have.)

From mid-century through the end of the Cold War, writers who championed *Huckleberry Finn* often invoked the unappeasable power of the "river-god" (T. S. Eliot's term) as an organizing force in the novel, and echoed Eliot's praise for the freshness of the novel's language. (In a speech in 1953, Eliot called the author of *Huckleberry Finn* "one of those writers, of whom there are not a great many in any literature, who have discovered a new way of writing, valid not only for themselves but for others.") They also held up Huck's decision late in the novel not to return Jim to his owner as a triumph of individual autonomy, an example of one human being rejecting the false morality of his society, an act that made the book gratifyingly "subversive." It was a stance that held special appeal to an avowedly democratic nation waging a Cold War against an enemy ready to absorb the individual into the collective. It also appealed to a nation that was taking belated steps to move beyond its Jim Crow past. As Kenneth Lynn observed, in the decades after World War II, as critics and readers gradually reached the conclusion that "the ancient pattern of discrimination against Negroes was morally indefensible," they often misread Huck as "renouncing his membership in a society that condoned slavery because they themselves did not wish to live in a segregationist nation." Huck never actually condemns slavery or renounces his membership in a society that condones it; but his failure to realize that he is right and that his society is wrong forces readers to ask the very questions Huck never asked himself, and to come up with answers to them on their own.

As writers and critics who came of age during the Civil Rights Movement wrestled with making sense of the troubling, burlesque "evasion sequence" with which the novel ends, new interpretations of the book began to emerge. The final section of *Huckleberry Finn*—which revolves around Tom Sawyer's bizarre maneuvers to free a slave who, it turns out, is already free—increasingly came to be understood as a satire on the ways in which the United States botched the enterprise of freeing the slaves. Toni Morrison observed in 1996 that in addition to the publication of *Huckleberry Finn* "the 1880s saw the collapse of civil rights for blacks," a sign that the country wanted "to bury the combustible issues Twain raised in his novel." "The nation, as well as Tom Sawyer," Morrison wrote, "was deferring Jim's freedom in agonizing play." Morrison's reading and others like it remind us that *Huckleberry Finn* dramatizes, perhaps as only a work of art can, both the spectacular boldness of our national experiment and the spectacular mess we made of that experiment for so much of our history.

Until relatively recently, readers in the U.S. were likely to be unfamiliar with the Mark Twain that writers in China and the Soviet Union had been praising for much of the 20th century. While most Americans encountered a tame and (in Maxwell Geismar's phrase) "castrated" Twain, writers in China like Lao She and in the Soviet Union like Yan Bereznitzky and Abel Startsev focused on a Twain unafraid to launch salvos at the hypocrisy and failings of the country that he loved. In a 1960 speech in Beijing commemorating the 50th anniversary of Twain's death, Lao She, one of the leading Chinese writers of the 20th century, celebrated the Mark Twain who in 1868 had published an article called "Treaty with China" in the *New York Tribune*, an article that to this day relatively few Americans have ever read, detailing (not for the only time in Twain's work) injustices inflicted on the Chinese in California. Lao She also lauded the Twain who wrote, in 1900, on the eve of China's invasion by allied Western powers: "It is all China now and my sympathies are with the Chinese. . . . I hope they will drive all the foreigners out and keep them out for good." (Twain's views on this subject led President Theodore Roosevelt to call him a "prize idiot" in 1901.) Yan Bereznitsky, writing in *Liturnaya Gazeta* in 1960 faulted the selections made by Charles Neider in his 1959 edition of *Mark Twain's Autobiography*, charging that Neider had allowed previously unpublished "inoffensive trifles" such as "Twain's meditations on baldness, on the value of hair-washing," to displace Twain's "indignant notes about the predatory wars which the United States carried on half a century ago" or his critiques of the "knights and henchmen of American expansionism." The Twain that Abel Startsev valued in his 1963 book, Марк Твен и Америка (*Mark Twain in America*) was a Twain whose love for his country forced him to blast the "racists and lynchers" of whom he wrote in the dystopian fantasy "The United States of Lyncherdom."

The publication of Jim Zwick's *Mark Twain's Weapons of Satire: Anti-Imperialist Writings on the Philippine-American War* in 1992 did much to help Americans rediscover this side of Twain and set in motion a reevaluation that continues in the 21st century. In 1996 Gore Vidal expressed his admiration for the anti-imperialist, anti-racist Twain these writers had celebrated, the author of works such as *To the Person Sitting in Darkness*. After seeing their country tell the Filipinos that "strictly for their own good, we would have to kill one or two hundred thousand men, women and children in order to make their country into an American-style democracy," most Americans, Vidal writes, were "happy to follow the exuberant lead of the prime architect of empire, Theodore Roosevelt. . . . But then suddenly Mark Twain quite forgot that he was *the* American writer and erupted, all fire and lava." Like Vidal, Ron Powers respects the Mark Twain who dared to criticize his country when it was wrong (an obligation that in Twain's view the true patriot incurred): "'The War-Prayer,'" Powers wrote in 2006, "taken in sum with Mark Twain's other polemic essays of the 1900s, form the Rosetta Stone of dissent from American imperialist folly." But this more radical Twain was largely unknown to most Americans for most of the 20th century—unless they had read Philip Foner's *Mark Twain, Social Critic* (1958) or Maxwell Geismar's *Mark Twain: An American Prophet* (1970). Or unless they had seen one of Hal Holbrook's stunning performances of his highly popular one-man show, *Mark Twain Tonight!* For half a century Holbrook's meticulous and engaging interpretations on stage of Twain's words (including much material from pieces published only after Twain's death) have given voice to a side of

Twain that Twain himself could not show the public during his lifetime, helping him come to life as a social critic in our time.

Mark Twain was not immune to criticism; from the start of his career he got his share of brickbats as well as bouquets from other writers. Sometimes he was taken to task for crudity and irreverence—the English novelist Henry Harland called Twain a "shrewd, clear-headed barbarian," whose "terrible inability to respect what he cannot understand" made it possible for him to crack his "dreadful jokes at the expense of things that to the majority of civilized mankind are sacrosanct." Later critics were more likely to complain that he did not go far enough: "Twain never attacks established beliefs in a way that is likely to get him intro trouble," wrote George Orwell in 1943, evidently unaware of those occasions when Twain *did* get into trouble for such attacks in his last decade. Even Twain's greatest admirers were not blind to his flaws. Bernard DeVoto wrote of the "savage vindictiveness" of which Twain was capable, while Wallace Stegner noted that Twain "fell much too frequently into triviality and improvisation."

But during his lifetime and beyond, any discussion of Twain's failings was overshadowed by the abiding sense of affection shared by everyone from the world's leading intellectuals to the millions of ordinary citizens who read and loved his books. William James wrote Josiah Royce from Florence in 1892: "Mark Twain is here for the winter in a villa outside of town, hard at work writing something or other. I have seen him a couple of times—a fine, soft-fibred little fellow with the perversest twang and drawl, but very human and good. I should think that one might grow very fond of him, and wish he'd come and live in Cambridge." As Thomas Edison remarked around 1908, "An American loves his family. If he has any love left over for some other person, he generally selects Mark Twain."

This book could easily have been at least two or three times longer than it is. Indeed, early drafts of it *were*, and I found the process of making the required cuts painful. I sought a mix of the usual suspects and fresh faces. I hope that the eclectic group assembled here conveys a sense of the range of writers who responded to Twain and the variety of forms their responses took.

The Mark Twain Anthology collects for the first time in one place a series of key responses by Black writers to Twain's treatment of race and racism—commentaries dating from 1937 to 2000 from Sterling Brown, Ralph Ellison, David Bradley, Toni Morrison, Ralph Wiley, and Dick Gregory, along with briefer remarks by Richard Wright, Langston Hughes, Amiri Baraka, and Richard Pryor. The book includes poems about Twain by Robert Penn Warren and Edward Field; excerpts from novels by John Seelye and David Carkeet in which Huck and Twain himself (respectively) have a chance to respond to the scholars who've spent years poring over their books; and comments on Twain from four U.S. Presidents (Theodore Roosevelt, Franklin Delano Roosevelt, Harry S. Truman, and Barack Obama). Two of the essays in this book have never previously been published: one by the award-winning director Michael Blakemore on the "surreal comic energy" of the play by Twain that he directed in its 2007 debut on Broadway, and the other by best-selling Korean-American novelist Min Jin Lee, author of *Free Food for Millionaires*, about how Twain gave her permission to write about money.

The Mark Twain Anthology includes personal commentaries documenting the role Twain played in inspiring David Bradley to become the kind of writer he became, and prompting Grant Wood to become the kind of painter he became. It features little-known sketches and portraits of Twain by prominent artists—including a charcoal sketch by James Montgomery Flagg (creator of the "Uncle Sam Wants You" poster); a pen-and-ink drawing by French writer and artist Jean Cocteau; a bas-relief bronze portrait by master illustrator and engraver Barry Moser, and sketches by animator Chuck Jones (of "Wile E. Coyote," "Roadrunner," and "Bugs Bunny" fame). The book also includes stories of personal encounters with Twain—such as Rudyard Kipling's account of his trek from Allahabad, India, to Elmira, New York, to interview his hero; or Helen Keller's moving description of an evening she spent in Twain's home in Redding, Connecticut, "listening" to Twain read *Eve's Diary* with "my elbow on the arm of his chair so that my fingers could rest lightly on his lips." ("His pleasant drawl was music to my touch," Keller writes. But things got confusing—as well as covered with ash—when he "began gesticulating with his pipe." From then on, her teacher "spelled the words into my right hand, while I looked at Mr. Clemens with my left, touching his face and hands and the book, following his gestures and every changing expression.")

Although the cultural conversation about Mark Twain most familiar to likely readers of this book has been conducted in English, writers have been responding to Mark Twain in languages other than English for at least 138 years. Indeed, the first book devoted to Mark Twain published anywhere, in any language, was a French volume published in Paris in 1884 by a 24-year-old Henry Gauthier-Villars (best known today for having been the controversial first husband of the writer Colette, whom he met five years later). It is a pleasure to present 16 pieces about Mark Twain by writers from Europe, Asia, and Latin America that were originally published in Chinese, Danish, French, German, Italian, Japanese, Russian, Spanish, and Yiddish and (aside from a few excerpts) that have been unavailable in English until now. These translations—done expressly for *The Mark Twain Anthology*—yielded some surprises. Who would guess, for example, from Twain's dyspeptic response to his earliest French readers, that his work was greeted with such enthusiasm and appreciation in that country? And is it not intriguing that the Cuban patriot José Martí, who would call his most widely reprinted essay "Nuestra América," or "Our America," affectionately referred to the author of *Connecticut Yankee* as "Nuestro Mark Twain," or "Our Mark Twain"?

Previously untranslated pieces include essays by Nobel Laureates from Denmark and Japan, by two of Cuba's most prominent public intellectuals, and by Argentina's most celebrated author; a famous Chinese writer's preface to the first book by Twain published in China; a poem by a major Russian poet; commentaries by respected writers from Germany, Italy, Spain, and the Soviet Union; and an article from a Yiddish newspaper in Vilna that serves as a poignant reminder of the vibrant intellectual culture that once thrived in Yiddish-speaking communities in Eastern Europe. All of these contributions help us understand the contexts in which Twain was read around the world. For instance, William Dean Howells was probably the first to compare *Connecticut Yankee* with *Don Quixote*, in a review the month after the book was published; but now we can extend our inquiry into what the two may or may not have in common by factoring in comments that José Martí made on this topic the same month as Howells' review—as well as what Ángel Guerra, a member of Spain's Generation of 1898, said on the subject a little over a decade later. All told, some 40 percent of the selections in *The Mark Twain Anthology* are by non-American writers.

The general organizing principle of this book is chronology, a principle violated on only a handful of occasions. One is when two works by one author are included (as is the case with José Martí, for example); in that case, the date of the first selection determines the placement of both pieces. Another comes at the end of the book. Although Roy Blount's 2008 essay appeared in print some nine months before Min Jin Lee wrote her previously unpublished one, his survey of Twain's entire career seemed an appropriate way to conclude this anthology. Reprising many of the themes raised by others in this volume, Blount examines the ways in which Mark Twain put humor and wit to use in the service of social justice, exploring how Twain "skewered the powerful, mocked the pious and helped change a nation." His essay reminds us just how many of the issues that Mark Twain addressed are issues we continue to grapple with today. Dick Gregory probably put it best: Mark Twain "was so far ahead of his time that he shouldn't even be talked about on the same day as other people."

I hope the chorus of these writers in conversation with Twain's works across time will send readers back to the works themselves—works that speak to the 21st century with as much "unquenchable verve" as they did to readers in the century in which he was born, and the century in which he left us.

—*Shelley Fisher Fishkin*
2009

Twain Matters: A Sampler

"Mark Twain's *Connecticut Yankee in King Arthur's Court* . . . was not worth the writing. Mark Twain, though a real genius, who has done admirable work in his line, is a man wholly without cultivation and without any real historical knowledge. . . . There is nothing cheaper than to sneer at and belittle the great men and great deeds and great thoughts of a bygone time."
Theodore Roosevelt, in a letter to his son Kermit, 1907

"Did you know, Mr. President, that the slogan of your administration was used by Twain in the *Connecticut Yankee*?"
"Yes, for it was there that I obtained the phrase. You recall the Yankee saying that he was in a country where a right to say how the country should be governed was restricted to six persons in each thousand of his population. He found himself, so to speak, a stockholder in a corporation where nine hundred and ninety-four of its members furnished all the money, and did all the work, and the other six elected themselves a permanent board of direction and took all the profits. And so he came to the logical and inescapable conclusion that what the nine hundred and ninety-four dupes needed was a new deal; I felt the same way about conditions in America as the Yankee did about those in ancient Britain. . . . I freely acknowledge my debt to Mark Twain."
Franklin Roosevelt, in an interview with Cyril Clemens, 1936

"Mark Twain said, in an inscription I have always had on my desk, 'Always do right. It will please some people, and astonish the rest.'"
Harry Truman, address to Americans for Democratic Action, 1952

"Of course, precisely because America isn't perfect, precisely because our ideals constantly demand more from us, patriotism can never be defined as loyalty to any particular leader or government or policy. As Mark Twain, that greatest of American satirists and proud son of Missouri, once wrote, 'Patriotism is supporting your country all the time, and your government when it deserves it.' Now we may hope that our leaders and our government stand up for our ideals, and there are many times in our history when that's occurred. But when our laws, our leaders or our government are out of alignment with our ideals, then the dissent of ordinary Americans may prove to be one of the truest expressions of patriotism."
Barack Obama, campaign speech in Independence, Missouri, 2008

"I have never known [Mr. Clemens] to be stirred up on any one question as he was on that of the cruel treatment of the natives in the Congo Free State. In his letter to Leopold, the late King of the Belgians, in his own inimitable way he did a service in calling to the attention of the world the cruelties practiced upon the black natives of the Congo that had far-reaching results. I saw him several times in connection with his efforts to bring about reforms in the Congo Free State, and he never seemed to tire of talking on the subject and planning for better conditions."

Booker T. Washington, North American Review, *1910*

"Twain hid his conflict in satire and wept in private over the brutalities and the injustices of his civilization."

Richard Wright, unpublished manuscript, circa 1935–37

"It is this treatment of race that makes *Pudd'nhead Wilson* as contemporary as Little Rock, and Mark Twain as modern as Faulkner, although Twain died when Faulkner was in knee pants."

Langston Hughes, introduction to Pudd'nhead Wilson, *1959*

"Nobody calls Twain's *Pudd'nhead Wilson* a novel of racial protest, but the comment it makes on what they call race relations is pretty strong. It's a wild book. I've never seen anything so strong."

LeRoi Jones (Amiri Baraka), interview in the San Francisco Chronicle, *1964*

"Seriously, though, two things people throughout history have held in common are hatred and humor. I am proud that, like Mark Twain, I have been able to use humor to lessen people's hatred."

Richard Pryor, on receiving the first Mark Twain Prize at the Kennedy Center, 1998

"I think he mainly misses fire: he might have been something: he comes near to being something: but he never arrives."

Walt Whitman, in conversation with
Horace Traubel, Camden, 1889

"An American loves his family. If he has any love left over for some other person, he generally selects Mark Twain."

Thomas Edison, as quoted by Mark Twain
in a speech at the Lotos Club, 1908

"Mark Twain, who is as deep and as broad as the Mississippi River and the Mississippi river is as deep and as broad as a river possibly could be which makes Mark Twain the pleasantest and most wonderful thing he did and the Mississippi ever might try."

Gertrude Stein, notes made during
a trip to St. Louis, undated

"Mark Twain is the true father of all American literature."

Eugene O'Neill,
letter to Cyril Clemens, 1935

"As a Nobel Prize winner I cannot but regret that the award was never given to Mark Twain."

Ernest Hemingway, speaking in Stockholm, 1954

"Of course Mark Twain is all of our grandfather."

William Faulkner, speech at
Washington and Lee University, 1958

"If you do not know the latest book by Twain, *The Adventures of Tom Sawyer*, it would be a pleasure for me to make you a little present of it."

> *Friedrich Nietzsche, letter to Franz and Ida Overbeck, 1879*

"The maid is permitted to do what she pleases in this room, but she must never touch those plants, and never touch those books on the table by the candle—with those books I read myself to sleep every night."

> *Charles Darwin, on* The Innocents Abroad *and* Tom Sawyer, *undated*

"Mark Twain was always a divine amateur."

> *Arnold Bennett*, London Bookman, *1910*

"Often I thought of [*Life on the Mississippi*] and of Twain while I was in command of a steamer in the Congo and stood straining in the night looking for snags."

> *Joseph Conrad, interview in* Mentor, *1924*

"Mark Twain did more than any other man to make plain people in England understand plain people in America."

> *G. M. Trevelyan*, Overland Monthly and Out West Magazine, *1929*

"The brutal fact is that Mark Twain never cared a cuss about us. We [Canadians] were not free and enlightened enough to be Americans: and not benighted and medieval enough to be Europeans. But still, it doesn't matter. We all loved Mark Twain and read his books. One-sided love lasts best."

> *Stephen Leacock*, Queen's Quarterly, *1935*

"If Mr. Clemens cannot think of something better to tell our pure-minded lads and lasses, he had better stop writing for them."

Louisa May Alcott, on Adventures of Huckleberry Finn,
Critic, *1885*

"All modern American literature comes from one book by Mark Twain called *Huckleberry Finn*. If you read it you must stop where the Nigger Jim is stolen from the boys. That is the real end. The rest is just cheating. But it's the best book we've had. All American writing comes from that. There was nothing before. There has been nothing as good since."

Ernest Hemingway, Green Hills of Africa, *1935*

"If Mark Twain had not had the unfortunate notion of bringing in that boring little muttonhead, Tom Sawyer, to ruin the last few chapters, [*Huckleberry Finn*] would have been faultless."

W. Somerset Maugham,
The Saturday Evening Post, *1940*

"*The Ordeal of Mark Twain* by a bothered and bothering American of the psychoanalyzing 30s has succeeded in bothering me a bit . . . Down in the river Huck Finn sits, watching the light come. It is a lovely fresh passage in a book I enjoy less than *Tom Sawyer*. How foolish it seems to put the writer through an ordeal while one is in contact with such a passage."

*E. M. Forster, on the 1933 revised edition of Van Wyck Brooks'
study of Twain in his commonplace book, 1943*

"To read it [*Huckleberry Finn*] young is like planting a tree young—each year adds a new growth ring of meaning, and the book is as little likely as the tree to become dull."

Lionel Trilling, The Liberal Imagination, *1951*

"Twain, at least in *Huckleberry Finn*, reveals himself to be one of those writers, of whom there are not a great many in any literature, who have discovered a new way of writing, valid not only for themselves but for others."

T. S. Eliot, speech at Washington University, St. Louis, 1953

"So if the ideal of achieving a true political equality eludes us in reality—
as it continues to do—there is still available that fictional vision of an ideal
democracy in which the actual combines with the ideal and gives us rep-
resentations of a state of things in which the highly placed and the lowly,
the black and the white, the Northerner and Southerner, the native-born
and the immigrant combine to tell us of transcendent truth and possibilities such as those discovered when Mark Twain set Huck and Jim afloat
on the raft."

Ralph Ellison, introduction to
the 30th Anniversary Edition
of Invisible Man, *1982*

"A lot of snotty academics have spent a lot of time and wasted a lot of
journal ink criticizing the ending of *Huckleberry Finn*. But I notice none
of them has been able to suggest, much less write, a better ending. Two
actually tried—and failed. They all failed for the same reason that
Twain wrote the ending as he did. America has never been able to write
a better ending. America has never been able to write any ending at
all."

David Bradley, speech at Drake University, 1995

"There is not one use of 'nigger' in *Huck Finn* that I consider inauthen-
tic, and I am hard to please that way."

Ralph Wiley, Dark Witness, *1996*

"We have not had a writer as devoted to seeking out truth and outing
lies. *Huck Finn* is a great book because it tells the truth about the
human condition in a way that delights us. It is a great work of our
national literature because, more than any other book before or since,
it locates itself squarely on our National Dilemma, which is: How can
anyone be truly free in a country as violent and stupid as ours? The
book still lives, because the question does."

George Saunders, introduction to Adventures
of Huckleberry Finn, *2001*

"The truth about Mark is that he was a colossus, that he stood head and shoulders above his country and his time, that even the combined pull of Puritanism without and Philistinism within could not bring him down to the national level."

H. L. Mencken, The Smart Set, *1917*

"His real self, the artist, in short, could not develop, and yet, repressed as it was, it prevented him from becoming whole-heartedly anything else."

Van Wyck Brooks, The Ordeal of Mark Twain, *1920*

"THERE IS ONE THING THAT OUGHT TO BE ELIMINATED IN THIS COUNTRY AND THAT IS EVERY TIME SOMEBODY GETS A LAUGH OF SOME SMALL DIMENSIONS, WHY HE IS CALLED THE MODERN MARK TWAIN."

Will Rogers, telegram to the
Hannibal Courier-Post, *1925*

"[Mark Twain] was simply too popular for his own good, with both of the important publics of his time—the masses and the genteel school. He was overfed with praise and starved for understanding; the ponderous machinery of exploitation drew him in and he was processed."

Dwight Macdonald, The New Yorker, *1960*

"Mark Twain was the most notorious spy in the house of the American oligarchy. He, more than any other American writer, historian, scholar, politician or statesman, deserved the fame and the honor of being the greatest traitor to his class."

Maxwell Geismar, Scanlan's Monthly, *1970*

"He was a madman, but he was right."

John Gardner on Mark Twain, interview, 1977

"The rugged truth of the sketch leaves all other stories of slave life infinitely far behind, and reveals a gift in the author for the simple, dramatic report of reality which we have seen equaled in no other American writer."

> *William Dean Howells on Mark Twain's*
> *"A True Story,"* The Atlantic Monthly, *1875*

"Its wildest extravagance is the break and fling from a deep feeling, a wrath with some folly which disquiets him worse than other men, a personal hatred for some humbug or pretension that embitters him beyond anything but laughter."

> *William Dean Howells on* A Tramp Abroad,
> The Atlantic Monthly, *1880*

"When I think how purely and wholly American it is, I am a little puzzled at its universal acceptance."

> *William Dean Howells on Mark Twain's humor,*
> Century Magazine, *1882*

"I warn the reader that if he leaves out of the account an indignant sense of right and wrong, a scorn for all affectation and pretence, an ardent hate of meanness and injustice, he will come indefinitely short of knowing Mark Twain."

> *William Dean Howells,*
> Century Magazine, *1882*

"Of all the literary men I have known he was the most unliterary in his make and manner. I do not know whether he had any acquaintance with Latin, but I believe not the least; German he knew pretty well, and Italian enough late in life to have fun with it; but he used English in all its alien derivations as if it were native to his own air, as if it had come up out of American, out of Missourian ground. His style was what we know, for good and for bad, but his manner, if I may difference the two, was as entirely his own as if no one had ever written before. I have noted before this how he was not enslaved to the consecutiveness in writing which the rest of us try to keep chained to. That is, he wrote as he thought, and as all men think, without sequence, without an eye to what went before or should come after. If something beyond or beside what he was saying occurred to him, he invited it into his page, and made it as much at home there as the nature of it would suffer him."

* * *

"The part of him that was Western in his Southwestern origin Clemens kept to the end, but he was the most desouthernized Southerner I ever knew. No man more perfectly sensed and more entirely abhorred slavery, and no one has ever poured such scorn upon the second-hand, Walter-Scotticized, pseudo-chivalry of the Southern ideal. He held himself responsible for the wrong which the white race had done the black race in slavery, and he explained, in paying the way of a negro student through Yale, that he was doing it as his part of the reparation due from every white to every black man. He said he had never seen this student, nor ever wished to see him or know his name; it was quite enough that he was a negro. About that time a colored cadet was expelled from West Point for some point of conduct "unbecoming an officer and gentleman," and there was the usual shabby philosophy in a portion of the press to the effect that a negro could never feel the claim of honor. The man was fifteen parts white, but, 'Oh yes,' Clemens said, with bitter irony, 'it was that one part black that undid him.' It made him a 'nigger' and incapable of being a gentleman. It was to blame for the whole thing. The fifteen parts white were guiltless."

* * *

"Clemens was entirely satisfied with the result of the Civil War, and he was eager to have its facts and meanings brought out at once in history. He ridiculed the notion, held by many, that 'it was not yet time' to philosophize the events of the great struggle; that we must 'wait till its passions had cooled,' and 'the clouds of strife had cleared away.' He maintained that the time would never come when we should see its motives and men and deeds more clearly, and that now, now, was the hour to ascertain them in lasting verity. Picturesquely and dramatically he portrayed the imbecility of deferring the inquiry at any point to the distance of future years when inevitably the facts would begin to put on fable."

* * *

"Emerson, Longfellow, Lowell, Holmes—I knew them all and all the rest of our sages, poets, seers, critics, humorists; they were like one another and like other literary men; but Clemens was sole, incomparable, the Lincoln of our literature."

William Dean Howells, My Mark Twain, *1910*

"Why don't people understand that Mark Twain is not merely a great humorist? He's a very remarkable fellow in a very different way."

Thomas Hardy at a dinner
with William Dean Howells in 1883

"Mark Twain is here for the winter in a villa outside the town, hard at work writing something or other. I have seen him a couple of times—a fine, soft-fibred little fellow with the perversest twang and drawl, but very human and good. I should think that one might grow very fond of him, and wish he'd come and live in Cambridge."

William James, letter to Josiah Royce, Florence, 1892

"He is very much in the same position as myself. He has to put matters in such a way as to make people who would otherwise hang him believe he is joking."

George Bernard Shaw, in a letter to
Archibald Henderson, 1907

"He spoke like one who used words fresh from the mint with the sheen of their minting still upon them."

Hamlin Garland, North American Review, *1910*

"I was astonished at the princely grace of his greeting when my mother introduced me. I might have been the Lord Mayor instead of a scared child."

Max Eastman, Harper's, *1938*

"Mark Twain. A natural—a man who learned to write the way a river pilot learns the feel of a channel."

Wright Morris, "The Available Past: Mark Twain," 1958

"To the end he remained as much an enigma and prodigy to himself as he was to the thousands at the Brick Presbyterian Church in New York who filed past the casket, topped with a single wreath of laurel, where he lay in a white suit."

Justin Kaplan, Mr. Clemens and Mark Twain, *1966*

Pen-and-ink drawing of Mark Twain by Otto Schneider, dated May 5, 1906. Inscribed: "It is not best to use our morals weekdays, Edward, it gets them out of repair for Sundays. Your friend Mark Twain" *Mark Twain Papers (Bancroft Library, University of California)*

David Ross Locke

Journalist and political satirist David Ross Locke (1833–1888) was best known by the pseudonym "Petroleum V. Nasby," the name of a fictional character he invented. "Nasby" was a self-confident, ignorant, opinionated, racist blowhard—a pro-Confederate postmaster who erupted (the V. stood for Vesuvius) in hundreds of letters that appeared in newspapers in the 1860s and 1870s, many of which were collected into best-selling books. Locke also gave lectures as "Nasby" across the country. Abraham Lincoln was one of his biggest fans. Mark Twain was another. Twain recalled in 1898 that Locke had been given a company to command during the Civil War and was about to leave for the front when the governor of Ohio wisely "refused to sign Nasby's commission and ordered him to stay at home. He said that in the field Nasby would be only one soldier, handling one sword, but at home with his pen he was an army—with artillery! Nasby obeyed and went on writing his electric letters." Twain heard "Nasby" give his famous "Cussed Be Canaan" lecture in Hartford in 1868 and described it as "a volleying and sustained discharge of bullseye hits, with the slave power and its Northern apologists for target." "Nasby" exemplified for Twain, years before Twain came into his own as a writer, the explosive potential of satire. Indeed, he may well have had "Nasby" in mind when he wrote that "against the assault of Laughter, nothing can stand." It is quite likely that, on a subliminal level at least, seeds of Pap Finn may have been planted in Twain's mind as he witnessed Locke's success at using the persona of an offensive, uneducated, unapologetic bigot to get his more genteel readers to reject their own bigotry. The admiration Twain had for Locke as a satirist must have made him all the more pleased by the appreciation Locke expressed for Twain's satire in this glowing review of Twain's first travel book, published in the *Toledo Blade* (a newspaper Locke ran and for which he wrote the editorial content). Locke was Twain's ideal reader—and reviewer.

FROM

New Books

In the year of our Lord 1867, a company of persons of both sexes, who desired to see something of the world, chartered the steamer *Quaker City* for a voyage to Europe, the Holy Land,

and such other parts of the globe as could be reached by water that they desired to see. One of the company was SAM'L L. CLEMENS (Mark Twain) and to his going the world is indebted for one of the queerest, profoundest, most entertaining, and most instructive books of travel and record of experience ever printed.

MARK TWAIN never wrote a stupid or common-place paper. From the beginning of his career, to the present, everything that bears his name contains wit, humor and philosophy, the three elements mixed in such exact proportions as to make it difficult to decide in which class he is to be placed. A close observer, and possessing rare facility of expression, with the happiest faculty of reproducing upon paper the men he meets and the things he sees, he has furnished the reading public with more amusement and instruction combined than the entire brood of American "humorists," from the first to the last. His first book, *The Jumping Frog*, is full of genius. The picture of the garrulous old man talking, in an everlasting monotone, of "Thish yer Smiley," is inimitable, and "The Biography of the Bad Little Boy named Jim, who *didn't* come to Grief," is the most effective thrust at the humbuggery over-zealous men use in maintenance of a good thing, that has ever fallen under our notice. We mention these specimens of MR. CLEMENS' handiwork because they are entirely dissimilar. One is pure fun without a purpose, save to photograph character; the other is fun with a purpose. We prefer, of course, the wit that accomplishes something more than the amusement of the reader, but we would not have him stop producing either.

The Innocents Abroad is a remarkable book. From the first page to the last it is gemmed with good things.

* * *

The account of the experience of the knot of congenial spirits who did Italy with Twain, with guides, is amusing enough. The party in making the regular rounds, determined to crush the professional guide by doubting everything, and by betraying no enthusiasm whatever. At Genoa: "'Come wis me, genteelmen, come! I show you ze letter writing by Christopher Colombo! write it himself! write it wis his own hand!—come!'"

The guide unlocked the repository, and spread the document before the party, dancing with delight. Not a manifestation of enthusiasm or even of interest. The "Doctor," one of the party, examined it deliberately, and perused it over and over:

"Ah—Ferguson—what—what did you say was the name of the party who wrote this?"

"Christopher Colombo! ze great Christopher Colombo!"

Another deliberate examination.

"Ah—did he write it himself, or—or how?"

"He write it himself!—Christopher Colombo! he's own hand-writing, write by himself!"

Then the doctor laid the document down and said:

"Why, I have seen boys in America only fourteen years old that could write better that that."

"But zis is ze great Christo—"

"I don't care who it is! It's the worst writing I ever saw. Now you musn't think you can impose on us because we are strangers. We are not fools, by a good deal. If you have got any specimens of penmanship of real merit, trot them out!—and if you haven't, drive on!"

The poor guide attempted to get up some interest in an Egyptian mummy, but it was no use. The doctor's unimpassioned inquiry as to the name of the gentleman, and his request to have a nice, fresh corpse brought out, so completely crushed him that he was from that time the meekest and mildest of men.

*   *   *

We have not space for further extracts. Mr. CLEMENS' book is a complete departure from precedent. Instead of giving the reader extracts from guide books, and describing things that have been described a thousand times, he has written his impressions of a most interesting journey, describing that which was of enough importance to describe, and nothing else. He has given us the manners, customs and habits of the people he saw—has demolished a hundred, more or less, of humbugs and impositions, and all in a fresh, breezy, crispy way that makes his book as entertaining as it is instructive. There is descriptive writing in it of high character, there is humor, and satire; it is, in short, a most enjoyable, most entertaining book, which he who reads will take up gladly and lay down reluctantly. We are under obligations to Mark Twain therefore.

Toledo Blade, 1869

Mark Twain

The first travel book by Mark Twain (Samuel Clemens) (1835–1910), *The Innocents Abroad*, was garnering largely positive reviews from newspapers across the United States when Twain read in the *Boston Advertiser* that in October 1870, "a solemn, serious critique" of the English edition of his book had just appeared in the London *Saturday Review*. Twain could not resist writing a parody of what a humorless, literal-minded review of his book might look like and publishing it in the December issue of *The Galaxy* in the "Memoranda" section that he edited—supposedly reprinted from the London journal. He confessed to the hoax in the next issue, writing that "the idea of such a literary breakfast by a stolid, ponderous British ogre of the quill was too much for a naturally weak virtue, and I went home and burlesqued it—revelled in it, I may say. I never saw a copy of the real 'Saturday Review' criticism until after my burlesque was written and mailed to the printer." The real review must have been a bit of a letdown. It contained no exasperated fulminations about "the insolence, the impertinence, the presumption, the mendacity, and, above all, the majestic ignorance of this author." Although the English critic did acknowledge that the reader of the review might be persuaded that "Mr. Twain is a very offensive specimen of the vulgarest kind of Yankee," he added, "And yet, to say the truth, we have a kind of liking for him. There is a frankness and originality about his remarks which is pleasanter than the mere repetition of stale raptures." Before Twain owned up to his hoax, several American publications were fooled. In his confession Twain gleefully quoted the "happy, chirping confidence" with which the *Cincinnati Enquirer* had announced: "Even Mark Twain has been taken in by an English review of his 'Innocents Abroad.' Mark Twain is by no means a coarse humorist, but the Englishman's humor is so much finer than his, that he mistakes it for solid earnest." Twain resolved that in the future, "when I write an article which I know to be good, but which I may have reason to fear will not, in some quarters, be considered to amount to much, coming from an American, I will aver that an Englishman wrote it and that it is copied from a London journal. And then I will occupy a back seat and enjoy the cordial applause."

Memoranda: An Entertaining Article

I take the following paragraph from an article in the Boston "Advertiser":

> An English Critic on Mark Twain.—Perhaps the most successful flights of the humor of Mark Twain have been descriptions of the persons who did not appreciate his humor at all. We have become familiar with the Californians who were thrilled with terror by his burlesque of a newspaper reporter's way of telling a story, and we have heard of the Pennsylvania clergyman who sadly returned his "Innocents Abroad" to the book-agent with the remark that "the man who could shed tears over the tomb of Adam must be an idiot." But Mark Twain may now add a much more glorious instance to his string of trophies. The "Saturday Review," in its number of October 8, reviews his book of travels, which has been republished in England, and reviews it seriously. We can imagine the delight of the humorist in reading this tribute to his power; and indeed it is so amusing in itself that he can hardly do better than reproduce the article in full in his next monthly Memoranda.

[Publishing the above paragraph thus, gives me a sort of authority for reproducing the "Saturday Review's" article in full in these pages. I dearly wanted to do it, for I cannot write anything half so delicious myself. If I had a cast-iron dog that could read this English criticism and preserve his austerity, I would drive him off the doorstep.—Editor Memoranda.]

[From the London Saturday Review.]

REVIEWS OF NEW BOOKS.

The Innocents Abroad. A Book of Travels. By Mark Twain. London: Hotten, publisher. 1870.

Lord Macaulay died too soon. We never felt this so deeply as when we finished the last chapter of the above-named extravagant work. Macaulay died too soon—for none but he could mete out complete and comprehensive justice to the insolence, the impertinence, the presumption, the mendacity, and, above all, the majestic ignorance of this author.

To say that the "Innocents Abroad" is a curious book, would be to use the faintest language—would be to speak of the Matterhorn as a neat elevation, or of Niagara as being "nice" or "pretty." "Curious" is too tame a word wherewith to describe the imposing insanity of this work. There is no word that is large enough or long enough. Let us, therefore, photograph a passing glimpse of book and author, and trust the rest to the reader. Let the cultivated English student of human nature picture to himself this Mark Twain as a person capable of doing the following-described things—and not only doing them, but with incredible innocence *printing them* calmly and tranquilly in a book. For instance:

He states that he entered a hair-dresser's in Paris to get shaved, and the first "rake" the barber gave with his razor it *loosened his "hide" and lifted him out of the chair*.

This is unquestionably exaggerated. In Florence he was so annoyed by beggars that he pretends to have seized and eaten one in a frantic spirit of revenge. There is of course no truth in this. He gives at full length a theatrical programme seventeen or eighteen hundred years old, which he professes to have found in the ruins of the Coliseum, among the dirt and mould and rubbish. It is a sufficient comment upon this statement to remark that even a cast-iron programme would not have lasted so long under such circumstances. In Greece he plainly betrays both fright and flight upon one occasion, but with frozen effrontery puts the latter in this falsely tame form: "We *sidled* toward the Piræus." "Sidled," indeed! He does not hesitate to intimate that at Ephesus, when his mule strayed from the proper course, he got down, took him under his arm, carried him to the road again, pointed him right, remounted, and went to sleep contentedly till it was time to restore the beast to the path once more. He states that a growing youth among his ship's passengers was in the constant habit of appeasing his hunger with soap and oakum between meals. In Palestine he tells of ants that came eleven miles to spend the summer in the desert and brought their provisions with them; yet he shows by his description of the country that the feat was an impossibility. He mentions, as if it were the most commonplace of matters, that he cut a Moslem in two in broad daylight in Jerusalem, with Godfrey de Bouillon's sword, and would have shed more blood *if he had had a graveyard of his own*. These statements are unworthy a moment's attention. Mr. Twain or any other foreigner who did such a thing in Jerusalem would be mobbed, and would infallibly lose his life. But why go on? Why repeat more of his audacious and exasperating falsehoods? Let us close fittingly with this one: he affirms that "in the mosque of St. Sophia at Constantinople I got my feet so stuck up with a complication of gums, slime, and general impurity, that *I wore out more than two thousand pair of bootjacks* getting my boots off that night, and even then some Christian hide peeled off with them." It is monstrous. Such statements are simply *lies*—there is no other name for them. Will the reader longer marvel at the brutal ignorance that pervades the American nation when we tell him that we are informed upon perfectly good authority that this extravagant compilation of falsehoods, this exhaustless mine of stupendous lies, this "Innocents Abroad," has actually been adopted by the schools and colleges of several of the States as a text-book!

But if his falsehoods are distressing, his innocence and his ignorance are enough to make one burn the book and despise the author. In one place he was so appalled at the sudden spectacle of a murdered man, unveiled by the moonlight, that he jumped out of window, going through sash and all, and then remarks with the most childlike simplicity that he "was not scared, but was considerably agitated." It puts us out of patience to note that the simpleton is densely unconscious that Lucrezia Borgia ever existed off the stage. He is vulgarly ignorant of all foreign languages, but is frank enough to criticise the Italians' use of their own tongue. He says they spell the name of their great painter "Vinci, but pronounce it Vinchy"—and then adds with a naïveté possible only to helpless ignorance, "*foreigners always spell better than they pronounce*." In another place he commits the bald absurdity of putting the phrase "tare an ouns" into an Italian's mouth. In Rome he unhesitatingly believes the legend that St. Philip Neri's heart was so inflamed with divine love that it burst his ribs—believes it wholly because an author with a learned list of university degrees strung after his name endorses it—"otherwise," says this gentle idiot, "I should have felt a curiosity to know what Philip had for dinner." Our author makes a long, fatiguing journey to the Grotto del Cane on purpose to test its poisoning powers on a dog—got elaborately ready for the experiment, and then discovered that he had no dog. A wiser person would have kept such a thing discreetly to himself, but with this harmless creature everything comes out. He hurts his foot in a rut two thousand years old in exhumed Pompeii, and presently, when staring at one of the cinder-like corpses unearthed in the next square, conceives the idea that may be it is the remains of the ancient Street Commissioner, and straightway his horror softens down to a sort of chirpy contentment with the condition of things. In Damascus he visits the well of Ananias, three thousand years old, and is as surprised and delighted as a child to find that the water is "as pure and fresh as if the well had been dug yesterday." In the Holy Land he gags desperately at the hard Arabic and Hebrew Biblical names, and finally concludes to call them Baldwinsville, Williamsburgh, and so on, "*for convenience of spelling!*"

We have thus spoken freely of this man's stupefying simplicity and innocence, but we cannot deal similarly with his colossal ignorance. We do not know where to begin. And if we knew where to begin, we certainly would not know where to leave off. We will give one specimen, and one only. He did not know, until he got to Rome, that Michael Angelo was dead! And then, instead of crawling away and hiding his shameful ignorance somewhere, he proceeds to express a pious, grateful sort of satisfaction that he is gone and out of his troubles!

No, the reader may seek out the author's exhibitions of his uncultivation for himself. The book is absolutely dangerous, considering the magnitude and variety of its misstatements, and the convincing confidence with which they are made. And yet it is a text-book in the schools of America.

The poor blunderer mouses among the sublime creations of the Old Masters, trying to acquire the elegant proficiency in art-knowledge, which he has a groping sort of comprehension is a proper thing for the travelled man to be able to display. But what is the manner of his study? And what is the progress he achieves? To what extent does he familiarize himself with the great pictures of Italy, and what degree of appreciation does he arrive at? Read:

> When we see a monk going about with a lion and looking up into heaven, we know that that is St. Mark. When we see a monk with a book and a pen, looking tranquilly up to heaven, trying to think of a word, we know that that is St. Matthew. When we see a monk sitting on a rock, looking tranquilly up to heaven, with a human skull beside him, and without other baggage, we know that that is St. Jerome. Because we know that he always went flying light in the matter of baggage. When we see other monks looking tranquilly up to heaven, but having no trade-mark, we always ask who those parties are. We do this because we humbly wish to learn.

He then enumerates the thousands and thousands of copies of these several pictures which he has seen, and adds with accustomed simplicity that he feels encouraged to believe that when he has seen "SOME MORE" of each, and had a larger experience, he will eventually "begin to take an absorbing interest in them"—the vulgar boor.

That we have shown this to be a remarkable book, we think no one will deny. That it is a pernicious book to place in the hands of the confiding and uninformed, we think we have also shown. That the book is a deliberate and wicked creation of a diseased mind, is apparent upon every page. Having placed our judgment thus upon record, let us close with what charity we can, by remarking that even in this volume there is some good to be found; for whenever the author talks of his own country and lets Europe alone, he never fails to make himself interesting; and not only interesting, but instructive. No one can read without benefit his occasional chapters and paragraphs, about life in the gold and silver mines of California and Nevada; about the Indians of the plains and deserts of the West, and their cannibalism; about the raising of vegetables in kegs of gunpowder by the aid of two or three teaspoonfuls of guano; about the moving of small farms from place to place at night in wheelbarrows to avoid taxes; and about a sort of cows and mules in the Humboldt mines, that climb down chimneys and disturb the people at night. These matters are not only new, but are well worth knowing.* It is a pity the author did not put in more of the same kind. His book is well written and is exceedingly entertaining, and so it just barely escaped being quite valuable also.

*Yes, I calculated they were pretty new. I invented them myself.— Mark Twain.

The Galaxy, 1870

Thérèse Bentzon

Thérèse Bentzon (Mme. Marie-Thérèse Blanc) (1840–1907) was a sophisticated French woman of letters with a strong classical education who wrote these comments on Mark Twain as part of a series she published on American humorists in *Revue de Deux Mondes* in 1872 under the name "Th. Bentzon." (Bentzon was her mother's maiden name. She also published journalism under the pen name "Théodore Bentzon," choosing to present herself as a male author, a choice that her friend and mentor George Sand had made as well.) The lengthy article included Bentzon's own translation of Twain's "Jumping Frog" story in its entirety, in addition to her extended analysis of *The Innocents Abroad*. Irked by what he considered the rather supercilious tone she took in this piece, Mark Twain responded by writing a hilarious response entitled "THE 'JUMPING FROG' IN ENGLISH. THEN IN FRENCH. THEN CLAWED BACK INTO A CIVILIZED LANGUAGE ONCE MORE, BY PATIENT AND UNREMUNERATED TOIL." which he published in *Sketches, New and Old* in 1875. Twain's preface to the volume refers to his piece as restoring the story "to the English tongue after martyrdom in the French." To prove that Bentzon's translation "is no more like the Jumping Frog when he gets through with it than I am like a meridian of longitude," Twain provides an atrociously garbled literal retranslation back into English that draws its fun from the differences between English and French grammar. That same year, Bentzon panned his novel *The Gilded Age* (written with Charles Dudley Warner) in *Revue de Deux Mondes* as "curious and incoherent." The authors, she opined, were not up to the challenge of interpreting the great tableau of the American scene. Bentzon took on the challenge of interpreting America herself when she toured the country in 1893, reporting on the condition of women for *Revue de Deux Mondes*. Her travel journals, published in 1896, became a best seller in France.

FROM

Les Humoristes Américains: Mark Twain
(The American Humorists: Mark Twain)

The country that has produced Voltaire, Rabelais, the *Pamphlets of Courrier* and the *Persian Letters* [of Montesquieu] has certainly no cause to envy any other in terms of light-hearted and stinging mockery or of joyous wit: we have, by general agreement, pushed to the highest degree the fine art of banter; it is nonetheless true that *humor*, while it comes from wit, whose home country is France, remains so foreign to us that up to now we have not been able either to translate or define a word of it. It is the oscillation between laughter and tears—it is the joke of a man who even while joking keeps a serious expression, that is how one best explains that mixture of verve and melancholy, of grace and brutality, of malice and reverie, of skepticism and tenderness, that gives a particular flavor to the genius of Shakespeare and Byron, the talent of Sterne, Heine and Richter. *Humor* is like a reflection of human life, rich in unexpected and rough contrasts; it thus captures our imagination and gets on our nerves, ready to wear them out quite fast when it is French nerves and imagination, refined, demanding, lined with good taste, hostile to dissonances. . . . However ingenious it may be, *humor*, at least that which is defined as literary humor, seems to us a sort of disease native to stormy climates. . . . English humor, generally lugubrious, warms our heart; the profundities of German humor often strike us as heavy and obscure. It is curious from this point of view to study American humorists and to note the transformations that this literary form has undergone, the result of habits of mind imported, acclimatized and *uncivilized* in the New World.

"The Jumping Frog" of Mark Twain must be cited first as one of the most popular, indeed classic, pieces of this type. Yet it is quite difficult for us to understand, in reading this story, the *roars of laughter* [English in original] that it has brought "in Australia and India, in New York and London," the numerous editions that have appeared of it, the title of "inimitable" that it has been granted by admiring critics in the English press. Let us try to judge it by the translation that I have made of it, which attempts to capture as much as possible the mocking tone of the original. . . . [Her translation of "Jumping Frog" follows.]

"The Jumping Frog" is just the first of several brief sketches which make up a volume. All of them are suffused with the same inoffensive cheerfulness: the sorrows of Aurelie, whose fiancé, disfigured by smallpox, deprived by successive accidents of the use of his arms and legs, and finally scalped by Indians, such that she is no longer quite sure how much of him remains to be loved—a set of slapstick ways to cure a cold—the story of a horse who no longer wishes to walk—the killing of Julius Caesar "localized," such as a Roman newspaper, *The Daily Evening Fasces*, might have reported it on the day of the murder, all that draws from the same spring of jovial irony, petulance and *animal spirits* [English in original] and all that is enough to entertain mightily a young people who do not make a point of being blasé. It is obvious that Mark Twain's first celebrity came from the new cities, the mining towns of California. . . .

There is a striking connection between the man's works and his physical appearance: nothing refined or delicate, complete ignorance of tact, good taste, and all the qualities that sprout only in the soil of an advanced civilization—on the other hand, a lively imagination, a superabundance of energy, a cheerfulness by turns naïve, honest, carefree, and sanguine, lots of good-natured mockery, a primitive vigor, an eccentricity in invention, and an originality of style altogether incomparable. Mark Twain possesses to the nth degree the temperament that his compatriots describe as *jolly, bluffy, telling, queer* [English in original], all quite untranslatable terms; droll, comic, clownish—such words give only a feeble idea of them. Such unquenchable verve often lacks lightness—you can't expect ale to have the froth of champagne—but at least it is not licentious. . . .

In spring 1867, a marvelously perfect version of the common pleasure trip was organized in New York. A steamboat would leave from the city in the summer, head across the Atlantic into the Mediterranean, stop successively on the coasts of Spain, France, Italy, Turkey, Greece, Egypt and Syria, then bring all the travelers back home at the beginning of winter, for a bargain price of $1250 (around 6300 francs). By this point, Mark Twain's wealth had increased: the editor of the Nevada *Territorial Enterprise* was living in San Francisco, and was taken throughout America for one of the great masters of the new California literature. He signed up his already famous name alongside that of three ministers, eight doctors, sixteen ladies, and several military and naval officers, all of whom made up the passenger list, and at the start of June the *Quaker City* weighed anchor. From this voyage have appeared two volumes, *The Innocents Abroad* (New York to Naples) and *The New Pilgrim's Progress* (which includes the excursions in Greece, Syria and the Holy Land). It is the first that is the most interesting for our purposes. What is the opinion that this innocent, as he calls himself, brings back from Old Europe, as he arrives without previous education, without preconceived ideas or admiration, without any kind of biases—without any of the prejudices that we absorb with our mother's milk, as it were—but with the simple resolve to view things as they really are and ready to put all his wit and intelligence at the service of his curiosity? He knows nothing of the world but the mountains of his home country, the slopes brutally pocked by the miner's pick, and the giant villages where all the citizens are equally handy with a gun or a fist; he wishes to compare these new societies with our outmoded aristocracies, that extraordinary natural landscape wrapped in gold with our fertile countryside, those freshly made buildings with our historic ruins, America's most splendid industry with the art of which he knows nothing.

Well, really! One might note that one of Montesquieu's Persians, Voltaire's Hurons, or even one of Mme. De Graffigny's simple Peruvians judges European civilization more sensibly than a real American from San Francisco. The reason is that it is not enough to have wit or even a natural sense of taste to appreciate works of art and to form a proper aesthetic opinion; nothing replaces experience. Hawthorne proved this, Hawthorne, one of the most complex, refined, and cultivated talents that America has ever produced. Hawthorne, who instead became attached to the Old World by his profound knowledge of the secret ills of the soul, his exquisite sensibility and aristocratic temperament. Hawthorne is no longer himself when he speaks to us of Italy; he hesitates, he gropes around in those judgments of his that are normally so firm and refined; he makes mistakes at each moment. If this is what we get even from Hawthorne, then what heresies must a young literary pioneer from the new America commit, one full of brio and instinct, democratic, practical, ready to make fun of anything not familiar and ready to be wounded in his deepest patriotic pride by anything too radically different from the ways of his home country! He admits it: the railway platforms, the great roads, the boulevards, the warehouses, the markets interest him more than a hundred galleries of priceless art, because he can understand the former, while for the latter he has neither education, experience or standards of comparison to judge; but for natural beauty he shows himself a sensitive and intelligent observer. . . .

It is a humorist's right to be extravagant; still, a little good sense, however carefully concealed, should shine a bit through the paradox. Even when Heinrich Heine (I never get tired of quoting this master on the subject of *humor*) makes fun of the Gods of Olympus the most nimbly, we know that whatever fun he has mocking Venus as a tart, his soul, whatever the blasphemies of his mouth, prostrates itself in pious admiration before the statue of Venus de Milo. In contrast, Mark Twain is the protestant who rises up against the pagan cult of broken marble, and the democrat who rejects all medieval poetry.

The Innocents at Home and *Roughing It* are bursting with the same kind of anecdotes, which demonstrate the happy impossibility of extinguishing, even under the influence of gold fever, the tender feelings and fundamental needs of the heart. Mark Twain tells these stories with a savage charm and a moving simplicity which are difficult to render. What is most impossible to translate, and what is the main value of these colorful tales, is the original and mordant style, the idiomatic language, a strange and often picturesque mixture of neologism, dialect and what the Americans call *slang* [English in original]. English remains his mother tongue, and an essential one, to be sure, but an old wet nurse of a mother tongue whose teats frequently dry up; they can only express European civilization, and are caught up short when faced with the overabundance of ideas, inventions and discoveries of which America is so proud. To describe new things, one must have new words; onto the old stock have been grafted various rather disfigured borrowings, more or less corrupt, made from the varied dialects which the immigrants coming from all quarters of the world have granted their adopted homeland. . . . Out of this mix-up of languages have

shot up, like so many new shoots, new, energetic, bold and ingenious expressions. . . . [T]he most vulgar temerities of a Mark
Twain still shock us; but soon we will grow accustomed to an
American language whose savory spiciness should not be sneezed
at, even as we await the more delicate and revealing qualities
which time will surely bring it.

Translated by Greg Robinson
Revue des Deux Mondes, 1872

Eduard Engel

Eduard Engel (1851–1938), an influential German novelist, critic, and philologist, wrote about Mark Twain on several occasions, reviewing his books as they came out in *Magazin für die Literatur des Auslandes*, a German periodical devoted to foreign literature which he edited, and in his history of American literature. At first Engel finds aspects of *The Innocents Abroad* to be crude and formulaic; but he later changes his mind and calls Twain's "eye for the ridiculous" in his first travel book "wonderful." Twain's works had been appearing in German translations since the early 1870s, and by the 1890s they were popular among ordinary citizens and the elite. During a visit to Germany, Twain himself was stunned to hear both the Kaiser and the *portier* of his lodging house praise *Life on the Mississippi* in virtually the same terms on the same evening. Engel, whose two dozen books include a number of novellas as well as popular literary histories, was also a distinguished philologist who fought tirelessly for the purification of the German language—a fact that makes his enthusiastic response to Twain's "The Awful German Language" particularly interesting. Despite Engel's status as the leading defender of the purity of German, in 1933 the Nazis denounced him, suppressed his books, and stripped him of his pension because he was a Jew.

FROM

Mark Twain: Ein Amerikanischer "Humorist"
(Mark Twain: An American "Humorist")

With every travel narrative I read, my conviction grows that there is scarcely a better way to gain immortal ridiculousness than to publish a travel narrative. I explicitly exclude the useful guides called Baedeker, Meyer, Murray, Joanne, etc. from my condemnation, i.e. if they limit themselves to simply relating how many square miles this province measures, how high that church tower is, how old an ugly town hall is or how much an unpleasant tunnel has cost. As soon as they get involved with the psychology of nations they belong to the eternally incorrigible crowd of fibbing know-it-alls who believe that one gets to know a nation the same way one learns to count from one to ten in a foreign language. . . . One only has to remember how variable and often contradictory even the judgments of citizens of a certain nation toward its own character are in order to imagine the full monstrosity of the impertinence with which a foreigner, who travels for his own enjoyment, after only four weeks assumes to give an unshakable verdict about a country whose language he often does not even know! Mark Twain himself says at one point quite correctly that the German language is so difficult it takes thirty years to learn it. And yet, he has never realized that one has to beware of judging, after a stay of thirty days, a country whose language—after all only one expression of intellectual life—is already that inaccessible.

But there is an even more dangerous category of modern fellow men: the "humorous" authors of travel narratives. In Germany, this species only flourishes where German humor as such is given a humble shelter: in the feuilletons of political newspapers. . . . The humorous travel jesters sprawl the most exuberantly in North America. Someone who has "done Europe"—as they say—in eight weeks sits down, writes a book of at least 400 pages with critical examinations of the German military, French politics, the character of the Swiss, the art of the Italians, social and political perspectives of the Russians; seasons his banalities with some antics, called humor in America, finds of course a publisher and benevolent critics (who will follow his example the next year), and the fame of the American humorist is secured—for ten years.

Mark Twain is a peculiar example of the general rule about how the writing of travel narratives can spoil the best man. He unquestionably has wit, good humor, imaginativeness, a sharp sense of the ridiculous—in others; more recently even style; and still only in one book has he accomplished an achievement as a writer in which everyone can rejoice with unclouded amusement: *The Adventures of Tom Sawyer*—*not* a travel narrative. If the muses are in favor of Mark Twain, they will not allow him to cross the Atlantic again. The kind of humor with which his travels have supplied him may be American—but then it is to be lamented that American humor will not soon gain citizenship within world literature.

The recipe of Mark Twain's humor at the expense of Europe is quite simple: One only has to lack the slightest idea of anything one may see that is beautiful, venerable or has evolved out of traditions and in spite of that declare bluntly: all of this is nonsense, "*trash*," "*swindle*,"—and there you go—"*that is the humor of it*," foolproof, isn't it? Also a German reporter who came to America could easily produce a humorous travel narrative using this recipe.

The reader is sometimes seized by terror of the Iroquois-like ignorance, the truly brilliant empty-headedness regarding anything that we infirm Europeans label wonderful accomplishments of a millennia-old culture. One does not dare to believe it—one always thinks: Oh, he must be just joking around. But Twain is dead serious about his Indian barbarism. Calling Raphael an ass and Titian a beast is a mere trifle to him—but that is so incredibly humorous, isn't it? At least American newspapers and magazines, from time to time even an English journal in a misguided hour, assure us that this is the acme of up-to-date American humor. Oh, could we instead still have good old Washington Irving, who was not exceedingly ingenious but a little less Iroquois-like.

Mark Twain is the proof of the truth beautifully articulated by a Prussian secretary: "Ignorance is a precious godsend but one must not abuse it."—Mark Twain (Samuel Clemens by his given name) has had a hard childhood full of privations; according to a reliable source, he was pilot of a Mississippi steamboat or something of that kind and has therefore not had leisure to complete the regular education of a gentleman. Later he became apprentice to a printer, typesetter, proofreader, reporter, editor—as is not uncommon in America. I am far from esteeming him less because of that than he—nevertheless—deserves; on the contrary. However, he did have the misfortune to cross the ocean in his younger years, at a time when he was part of a great editorial staff and thus wrote his *Innocents Abroad* for the multitude of thousands of newspaper readers. American newspapers may be the highest incarnation of what daily papers should be but they are—and I am daily confirmed in that belief—the one manifestation of the human mind that has the least to do with literature. American magazines are their own genre, a very good one, actually. Had Mark Twain been able to completely follow the inspirations of his unquestionable talent, had he not been compelled to bow to the "taste" of the American newspaper readers, *The Innocents Abroad* might have become—yes it would probably have become—an enduring masterpiece of Anglo-Saxon humor, whereas it is now merely a thoroughly irritating book. Irritating because a member of the guild of men of letters could commit such horrible crudities—and even more because alongside those crudities we find the loveliest, wittiest, funniest jokes, of a kind that even Dickens hardly quarried in such originality.

Innocents Abroad ("Die Arglosen auf Reisen" ["The Artless Travelers"] says Mr. Moritz Busch, "Yankees im Ausland" [" Yankees Abroad"] I would suggest) was published in 1868 [sic] and made the author famous in America and England and rich as well. The book originated in a group journey of Yankees (male as well as female) to Europe and the Holy Land on a ship hired for this purpose. The enterprise had been initiated with the greatest fanfares of American advertising. It was said that the most prestigious members of American society would take part in it, Mrs. Harriet Beecher Stowe, for instance, with her famous brother Mr. Henry Ward Beecher, a former president of the United States, General Sheridan etc., etc.; a strict selection was supposed to be conducted among the applications that were naturally expected in immense numbers and everything was to be done to assure that the group of passengers would be "very select." In the end, as Mark Twain makes drastically clear, any applicant with 1,250 Dollars to spare was received happily and the most famous figure aboard the *Quaker City* was in fact an actual "Commissioner of the United States of America to Europe, Asia and Africa." This respectable gentleman traveled on behalf of the Smithsonian Institution in Washington in order to complete its scientific collection.

The community of Yankees assembled on board was a rather uplifting one. According to Mark Twain, its majority consisted of perfect idiots, in whom a combination of incredible ignorance, the usual portion of Anglo-Saxon pietism, and the respective amount of indelicacy formed a lovely whole. Mark

Twain and a few of the other younger participants on this pilgrimage to the Holy Land are the only reasonably enjoyable people on board. As long as Mark Twain limits himself to relating the often really witty incidents he and his companions experience, mostly because of their ignorance in regard to everything that is not American, he is in his element. Thus, his depiction of the terrible embarrassment when the group has to pay a bill of about 23,000 reis in the Azores, for instance, is a jewel. He also gains my highest esteem through his drastic way of stopping the Cicerones' silly explanations. But why do these ladies and gentlemen need such people, who are—as is well-known—able to spoil the good humor of the best-tempered traveler, at all? Yet there are hundreds of thousands of Americans who due to their absolute ignorance of foreign languages are dependent on that nuisance and form their opinion of the "character of a nation" accordingly. The story of the Englishman who, after a short stop in Calais, where he had been served by a red-haired waiter, wrote in his diary, "In France, all men have red hair," may be fictional but he is still a symbol of the way in which most tourists form their ethnographic opinions.

However, Mark Twain's habit of ridiculing the works of art he sees during his travels is unforgivable. First, the reader believes for the benefit of the author that he is only joking and that the joke actually conceals the honest admiration of an educated man. But the reader is absolutely mistaken; when Mark Twain mocks Leonardo da Vinci, Raphael, Titian, Dürer, and other masters with words I do not want to reproduce, he does so *ex plenitudine cordis*, out of the depths of his absolute ignorance. It may not be a crime to lack a feeling for art but it is a crime to then have one's cheeky remarks printed and to fill a whole generation of readers with the same "know-nothing" contempt toward anything they do not understand. We are not born with the ability to admire a beautiful painting, to listen to a piece of classical music or to understand an accomplished piece of poetry as we are born with the ability to eat and digest. We have to painstakingly acquire it. The Sioux and Iroquois of Mark Twain's homeland, for example, have no sense of the beauty of sunrises and sunsets or of the rustling of the forests—even that must be learned. But if, like Mark Twain, one has not the slightest idea of all those things that the civilized world quite deliberately praises as revelations of beauty, one is wise to hold one's tongue and write rather about the life of Yankees, about the follies of those people with whom one has dealt for years, to sharpen one's wit on things one understands and thus preserve one's reputation as a tactful writer—and as a gentleman. Why has Mark Twain not taken that golden word, found in his own *Innocents Abroad*, more to heart: "The gentle reader will never, never know what a consummate ass he can become, until he goes abroad."

Still, the author can be excused to some degree. At every turn he faces his fellow countrymen's false, hypocritical enthusiasm for things of which they are, like him, notoriously ignorant—absolutely ignorant. When, for instance, he relates a long series of stereotypical exclamations which the herds of American tourists utter in front of Leonardo da Vinci's *Last Supper*:

"Oh wonderful!"

"Such expression!"

"Such grace of attitude!"

"Such dignity!"

"Such faultless drawing!"

"Such matchless colouring!"

"Such feeling!"

"What delicacy of touch!"

one cannot resent the fact that the devil of opposition awakes in him and incites him to the most blasphemous outbursts. Actually, his humor is most biting when it turns against the American "snob" or "shoddy," who, after staying for a month in France, spoils his English with bits of awful French, who says "Parry" instead of "Paris" and who enlists in hotel registers, even beyond France as "W. L. Ainsworth, *travailleur* (for 'traveler'), Etats Unis." If there was a German Mark Twain, he would find similar curiosities committed by ladies of the landed gentry from Mecklenburg or by master tailors from Berlin who absolutely want to appear as thoroughbred Frenchmen in the hotel registers of German-speaking Switzerland.

The Adventures of Tom Sawyer is a book of much higher caliber. Tom Sawyer is an American boy of indeterminate age—I'd put him at 14 or so—who plays all sorts of ridiculous pranks, frightening his sweet old aunt to death at least once a week, who succeeds in attending his own funeral in the best of health, and in the end acquires a genuine treasure of purest gold in the most astonishing way. The descriptions of the lives of a band of good-for-nothing boys—as all of us once were—is so charmingly ac-curate and based on such precise observations of the lives of children, that I cannot understand why Mark Twain is con-stantly being referred to as the author of *The Innocents Abroad* rather than of *Tom Sawyer*. This peculiar book is, in a sense, comparable to *Little Women* by Miss Alcott, but has the advan-tage of being shorter by more than half. I would place it at least on a level with the famous *Story of a Bad Boy* by Aldrich and the best of Bret Harte.

Mark Twain's most recent work is *A Tramp Abroad*, a humor-ous description of a journey through Germany and Switzerland. It shows a fortunate improvement in the nature of the author; crudities are far less frequent and not as overwhelming in their dimensions than in *The Innocents Abroad*. Passages in which the dry but jovial American humor unfolds, however, are more nu-merous and better dispersed. Admittedly, as in other works, Mark Twain's humor at times happens to become so subtle that regular mortals—and even people with a sense for jokes—fail to recognize it or take it for crude silliness. The fate of Mark Twain's humor is similar to that of the flea in the Brother Grimm's fairy tale, which in a contest for the king's daughter jumped so high that the others' gazes could not follow it and which thus did not gain the due reward for its efforts.

A German reader will most of the time enjoy reading the first volume, which deals with the journey through the south of Ger-many. Many things, seen through the eyes of a foreign specta-tor, will appear to him in an entirely new light. Most obliged to Mark Twain, however, are the German students, in particular the Heidelberg corps. By mere chance, the American got in touch with Heidelberg student life and he sketches it with so much enthusiasm and also so much good will towards some of its outgrowths as probably no one who is not a student and not even a German has done before. His description of an official duel is a small masterpiece.

*   *   *

But the best Mark Twain has ever accomplished is his appendix to this book [*A Tramp Abroad*] titled "The Awful German Language." Here ignorance, good humor, and wit form such a strange mixture that when reading it one really does not know if one should get angry or laugh. I preferred the latter and advise any reader of this appendix to do the same. For, after all, the author knows not what he does. Moreover, out of his mouth—as out of the mouth of children and sucklings—come some truths quite worth taking to heart. Here's Mark Twain's description of the structure of an average German sentence:

> There are ten parts of speech, and they are all troublesome. An average sentence, in a German newspaper, is a sublime and impressive curiosity; it occupies a quarter of a column; it contains all the ten parts of speech—not in regular order, but mixed; it is built mainly of compound words constructed by the writer on the spot, and not to be found in any dictionary—six or seven words compacted into one, without joint or seam—that is, without hyphens; it treats of fourteen or fifteen different subjects, each inclosed in a parenthesis of its own, with here and there extra parentheses which reinclose three or four of the minor parentheses, making pens within pens: finally, all the parentheses and reparentheses are massed together between a couple of king-parentheses, one of which is placed in the first line of the majestic sentence and the other in the middle of the last line of it—after which comes the VERB, and you find out for the first time what the man has been talking about; and after the verb—merely by way of ornament, as far as I can make out—the writer shovels in "haben sind gewesen gehabt haben geworden sein," or words to that effect, and the monument is finished.

*   *   *

Well, a leopard just cannot change its spots. If our eloquent classics have not been able to bestow on our syntax more logical structures and clearer word order, we will now have to humbly restrict ourselves to using that ill-famed tool called the German language for a couple more centuries.

There is a sad truth in another one of Mark Twain's remarks.

> We have the parenthesis disease in our literature, too; and one may see cases of it every day in our books and newspapers: but with us it is the mark and sign of an unpracticed writer or a cloudy intellect, whereas with the Germans it is doubtless the mark and sign of a practiced pen and of the presence of that sort of luminous intellectual fog which stands for clearness among these people. For surely it is not clearness—it necessarily can't be clearness. Even a jury would have penetration enough to discover that.

He considers our compound tenses, which sometimes dissolve again into their original parts, as, for instance, "ich will abreisen" [I want to depart], another stumbling block: "Er reiste nach einigem Bedenken etc. etc.—*ab*."* Well, concerning this, as is well-known, a reform, if you want to call it one, is on its way; if Mark Twain visits Germany again in another ten years, I may be allowed to write with impunity: "es vorbereitet sich eine Reform."[†]

Declining German nouns bothers Mark Twain just as much as distinguishing between the three grammatical genders with regard to sexless objects. He proposes the following remedies: abolition of the dative case (at least in the north of Germany this is promptly attended to), moving the verb up further to the front—I'm very sorry, that is impossible,—distributing the sexes according to the will of the Creator, consequently "die Weib," "die Mädchen," the removal of conglomerates of verbs, abolition of parentheses, and eventually the introduction of certain (in his opinion) strong English words instead of the "colorless" German ones. This is because Mark Twain has discovered that the German language sounds too mild, he misses words that are similarly onomatopoetic as "crash, storm, thunder, cry, battle, hell!" Up to now, we have been of the opinion that "Krach" is just as strong as "crash," "Sturm" much louder than "storm" (with an almost silent r!), and that "Donner" rumbles much more than "thunder" etc. But this only proves how willful one's ears can be, especially if one plugs them against anything foreign.

*   *   *

Mark Twain is a still relatively young man. He will have enough time to write more mature works. He should only—at least as far as his literary works go—remain in America and take care to use his powerful humor to judge things and people he knows. If he does so, one will gladly forgive him youthful transgressions like *The Innocents Abroad*.

Translator's notes
*cf. Twain: he DE—after kissing his mother and sisters, and once more pressing to his bosom his adored Gretchen, who, dressed in simple white muslin, with a single tuberose in the ample folds of her rich brown hair, had tottered feebly down the stairs, still pale from the terror and excitement of the past evening, but longing to lay her poor aching head yet once again upon the breast of him whom she loved more dearly than life itself, PARTED.]
†Engel here changes "hier bereitet sich bekanntlich eine Reform, wenn man's so nennen will, vor" to "es vorbereitet sich eine Reform"—which is by the way still unacceptable today.

Translated by Valerie Bopp
Magazin für die Literatur des Auslandes, 1880

FROM

Mark Twain

We certainly have to acknowledge Mark Twain (born in 1835 in Florida, Missouri) as the prime American humorist. He was christened Samuel Clemens and took "Mark Twain" from his job as a pilot on a Mississippi steamboat in his youth: While fathoming, a sailor would shout "Mark one!—Mark twain," etc. It is self-evident that he is not ashamed of this career: One of his best—and incidentally more serious—works, *Life on the Mississippi* (1883), commemorates his earlier, eventful occupation.

Mark Twain is the writer without any prejudices, who, as a real

American, jokes about and judges European people and customs. He does so as free from any presuppositions as if he was facing the inhabitants of the moon. The limitless simple-mindedness— a mask he consciously puts on, of course—with which he utters the queerest things in a serious way, makes even professional melancholics laugh. What comedy there was for a writer to get from the folly of humanity, Mark Twain got. His first longer work was *The Innocents Abroad* (1867), the description of a journey through Europe and Palestine, taken by a group of Americans. Already in this work, he showed his wonderful talent, an eye for the ridiculous. While reading Twain, one's facial muscles are constantly twitching; one is temporarily ashamed of being wonderfully amused by these queer things; one may resist the urge to laugh for several minutes, but then, there is no way out: The author has captivated us and we feel that it is no sign of tastelessness to laugh about the ridiculous.

Even more comical is *A Tramp Abroad* (1880), one of the funniest works of Twain's age. I want to mention here that Mark Twain's humor is never more appealing than in the chapters that deal with Germany. The description of student life in Heidelberg with its duels and immediately after that the send-up of duels in France—these are climaxes of this hilarious book. No German reader with the smallest sense of humor will be seriously angry with Twain for the funny appendix "The Awful German Language."

A third travel narrative by Mark Twain, *Roughing It* (1872), describes a journey from New York to Nevada, which he took with his brother before the construction of the Pacific Railroad. Some of it reminds the reader of Bret Harte; what Twain lacks is the ability to remain serious for more than five minutes. He cannot stand sentimentality at all. If he catches himself being sentimental, he is the first one to laugh at himself.

Since Mark Twain started changing his subjects from year to year with astonishing miscellaneousness, one cannot call him merely an author of comic travel narratives. First there is the children's story *Tom Sawyer* (1876), which also captivates adults, the description of a pack of naughty boys, a book full of sensitive understanding of the mind of children. Then there is the "historical novel": *The Prince and the Pauper* (1880), a completely new genre as Mark Twain turns history upside-down and aims only at depicting the spirit of the age. With baffling roguishness, he says in the preface: "It may have happened, it may not have happened: but it *could* have happened." *A Yankee at the Court of King Arthur* (1889) and *Joan of Arc* (1894) belong to the same genre.

Translated by Valerie Bopp
Geschichte der Nordamerikanischen Literatur, 1897

Lafcadio Hearn

Lafcadio Hearn (1850–1904), at the time he wrote this review of Mark Twain's *Life on the Mississippi*, was known for his impressionistic sketches of New Orleans. Born in Lefcada, Greece, and educated in Dublin, Ireland, Hearn moved to the United States at age 19. After working as a newspaper reporter for several years in Cincinnati, he went to New Orleans in 1877. For the next decade he wrote prolifically about the city in articles published in local newspapers and popular national monthlies. Hearn so indelibly shaped Americans' understanding of the city's cuisine, folklore, and local color that he was widely credited with having "invented" New Orleans. He is probably best known today for the books of Japanese folklore and legends he collected after his move to Japan in 1890.

Mark Twain on the Mississippi

"*Life on the Mississippi*," Mark Twain's new production, is a large volume of more than six hundred pages,—much resembling in form the famous "*Innocents Abroad*," and "*Roughing It*." Like those highly successful books, "*Life on the Mississippi*" has been illustrated with humorous engravings, the spirit of which will be appreciated by all familiar with the picturesque features of American river-life. A number of the early chapters are already familiar to readers of the *Atlantic*,—having been contributed to that periodical several years ago; but their interest has been greatly augmented, and their verisimilitude emphasized, by the drawings which now accompany them. The past and present types of steamboatmen are portrayed with a certain rough and lively humor in thorough keeping with the text.

Notwithstanding its lively spirit of fun, the volume is a more serious creation by far than "*The Innocents Abroad*;" and in some respects seems to us the most solid book that Mark Twain has written. Certainly the first two hundred and fifty pages possess a large historical value; and will be referred to in future years as trustworthy paintings of manners, customs, and social phases which have already been much changed, and will doubtless, before another generation, belong altogether to the past. But in addition to reminiscences of the old-time river-life, and the curious multitude of incidents and amusing experiences, one finds that the author has taken pains to collect and set forth almost every important fact connected with the Mississippi River—historical or geographical. These positive data rather gain than lose in weight by their humorous presentation; and it may safely be said that many persons who may read the opening chapters will obtain from them a better knowledge of what the Mississippi is, than they could gain by laborious study of physical geographies. When one finds upon page 25 the statement that "*nearly the whole of that one thousand three hundred miles of old Mississippi River which La Salle floated down in his canoe, two hundred years ago, is good solid dry land now*"—one gains a juster idea of the river's eccentricities than the perusal of many volumes of solid and statistical reports could give. Within less than five pages an astonishing variety of information is given in similarly compressed shape;—the whole natural history of the river, (its importance, its fickleness, its capacities of construction or destruction) is presented in a brief series of ingeniously epitomized paragraphs which, once read, will not easily be forgotten.

The most delightful part of the book is included in the autobiographical chapters—in the history of the author's early experience as a pilot's apprentice. These pages are full of laughing vividness, and paint the brighter side of old-fashioned river-life with such a delicate exaggeration of saliencies as that by which the peculiarities of English habits fifty years ago are perpetuated for us by the early artists of *Punch*. But there is a kernel of curious fact in every richly-flavored incident of humor. Here the book is absolutely unique;—it contains the only realistic history of piloting on the Mississippi in existence, and written by perhaps the only author of the century whose genius is thoroughly adapted to the subject treated. Indeed, one must have followed for years some peculiar river-calling in order to comprehend what steamboat life is, and appreciate its various presentations of tragedy, comedy, and poetry—to all of which we find ample justice done in the book before us. It is the sum of the experience of years; and no little art has been shown in selecting specimens from such a range of memoirs. The old-time flatboatmen and raftsmen—so famous in Mississippi River history—are capitally drawn; and we have a rare sketch of the lordly pilots of ante-bellum days, who drew their $250 or more per month, and were idolized by the fair of numberless little river-towns. Not less interesting is the brief history of the Pilots' Association in those days—an imperious monopoly which sustained many furious campaigns against steamboat owners, and almost invariably won the fight at last by dint of certain ingenious devices pleasantly recounted in Chapter XV.

Mark Twain's humor being of the most typically American sort, and rich in that imaginative quality which an ingenious foreign critic has compared to "sheet lightning, flashing over half a world at once," has won him that literary reputation in Europe formerly held by Artemus Ward. Ward is now old-fashioned; Twain occupies a far larger transatlantic position. His stories have been widely translated; and within the past six months we have seen as many of his sketches "done into French," for the Paris *Figaro*. Much of the dialectic fun was necessarily lost in the transmutation; but otherwise the comic element survived admirably in the French—a language especially well suited to the exaggerations of American humor. We fancy that the present work will have a larger success in Europe than its illustrated predecessors; for it is more novel in its character, and even more thoroughly American in its fun, and withal, more historically valuable. Others have described the frontier life sketched in "*Roughing It*," and the days of '49; but no other has ever touched the subject of Mississippi life except in ballads or brief stories.

The last three hundred pages are devoted to the Mississippi Life of to-day as compared with that of before the war;—they represent the result of the author's Southern trip during the last inundation. This part of his history opens with the recital of a pleasant personal adventure, in which the author attempted to play impolite with an old pilot too sharp to be caught, who tells a wonderful yarn about a dredge-boat, which he calls by another name:—

"An alligator boat? What's it for?"
"To dredge out alligators with."

"Are they so thick as to be troublesome?"

"Well, not now, because the government keeps them down. But they used to be. Not everywhere, but in favorite places, here and there, where the river is wide and shoal—like Plum Point and Stack Island and so on—places they call alligator beds."

"Did they actually impede navigation?"

"Years ago, yes, in very low water; there was hardly a trip, then, that we didn't get aground on alligators."

Finally, after a most interesting history of "alligator pilots," Mark Twain's mask is torn off, and he is put to the wheel in expiation of his attempt at mystification. He finds that even after twenty-one years he has not forgotten how to manage a steamboat; but the river has so changed in the long interval that portions of its ante-bellum geography are no longer recognizable. He wants to go ashore subsequently, and so informs the captain:—

"Go ashore where?"

"Napoleon."

The captain laughed; but seeing that I was not in a jovial mood, stopped that and said,—

"But you are serious?"

"Serious? I certainly am."

The captain glanced up at the pilot-house and said,—

"He wants to get off at Napoleon!"

"*Napoleon?*"

"That's what he says."

"Great Cæsar's ghost!"

Uncle Mumford approached along the deck. The captain said:

"Uncle, here's a friend of yours wants to get off at Napoleon!"

"Well, by—!"

I said,—

"Come, what is all this about? Can't a man go ashore at Napoleon if he wants to?"

"Why, hang it, don't you know? There isn't any Napoleon
any more. Hasn't been for years and years. The Arkansas
River burst through it, tore it all to rags, and emptied it into
the Mississippi!"

This spirit of fun never flags, even to the end of the book; but
every page of humor is underlaid by some solid truth, often
more or less grim, and bearing important witness for one side of
that now vastly agitated subject—The Mississippi River Question. Here the reader will find a startling account of the changes
of the Mississippi since the era of our civil war.

We have already published extracts from the chapter on New
Orleans; but the author has given a great deal more space to our
city and its features than the aforesaid extracts would suggest.
Here and there he pokes some sharp fun at New Orleans' peculiarities,—especially regarding funerals and undertakers; but
there is no malice in the satire and nobody is badly hurt. Some
pleasant reminiscences of his visit appear,—his acquaintance
with George W. Cable and others; and THE TIMES-DEMOCRAT
must acknowledge the handsome compliments paid to it
throughout the volume, besides the republication in the appendix of Mr. Whitney's correspondence during the relief trip of
the Susie B. in March 1882.

New Orleans Times Democrat, 1883

José Martí

José Martí (1853–1895), Cuban writer and national hero, is celebrated as an innovative poet and gifted orator, as an idealistic political leader and the father of the Cuban revolution, and as a martyr who tragically lost his life in the struggle to make Cuba an independent, democratic nation. Martí can also be credited with having been the first writer to popularize Mark Twain's work in the Spanish-speaking world. (Ivan A. Schulman notes that although other 19th-century American writers such as Emerson, Whitman, Poe, Hawthorne, and Longfellow were recognized names among the cultivated reading public in Spanish America during the last quarter of that century, Mark Twain was not; only one brief mention of Twain in a Latin American periodical has come to light before Martí began writing about him.) Martí referred to Twain a number of times during his exile in the U.S. in the 1880s and 1890s. He first mentioned him in an 1880 article he wrote in English for the New York *Hour*: "There is, among the Americans, an excellent writer, the humorist Mark Twain." He added some positive comments about *A Tramp Abroad*, particularly Twain's humorous dissection of what Martí called the "mastodonic composition of German words" (in the piece we know as "The Awful German Language"). In 1884, Martí attended a reading by Mark Twain and George Washington Cable where he heard Twain read selections from *A Tramp Abroad* and from a new book due out shortly, *Adventures of Huckleberry Finn*. In a letter to the editor of *La Nación* (Buenos Aires) Martí praised the unaffected freshness of Twain's prose and expressed admiration for the ways in which Twain's satire "clarifies with a certain picaresque innocence, the contradictions, baseness and hypocrisy of ordinary people" in a manner that causes people to "laugh at themselves." Martí made a brief reference to Twain in a letter to *La Nación* in 1887, praising his "literary originality" and observing that "he is noted for his satirical take on the relationship between Americans and Europeans." But everything that Martí had written about Twain previously was pallid and tame compared to his response to *A Connecticut Yankee in King Arthur's Court*. "There are paragraphs in Twain's book that make me want to set off for Hartford to shake his hand," Martí wrote *La Nación* in 1890, just a little over a month after the book was published. Martí clearly recognized that Twain was committed, as a writer and as a citizen of a democracy, to values that Martí shared: both men rejected the claims of aristocracy to deference and legitimacy; both abhorred injustice; both sympathized with the downtrodden and disempowered; both disdained writing that was pretentious and affected. Martí clearly saw in Twain a kindred spirit: in a letter to *La Nación* in 1890, the writer who would entitle his most widely reprinted essay "*Nuestra América*," or "Our America," referred to the author of *Connecticut Yankee* as "*Nuestro Mark Twain*," or "Our Mark Twain."

FROM

Escenas Norteamericanas
(North American Scenes)

The good people of New York, the native sort who are more astute than lavish, those who make a show of their moderation and healthiness, filled a lecture hall yesterday where two of the most famous writers of the United States appeared to talk and read some of their work. *Mark Twain* is the pen name of one, whose real name is Samuel Clemens. George Cable was the other, a New Orleans Pérez Galdós, like him meticulous, laborious, and given to pathos. They are not the children of books, but of Nature. Those bookstore men of letters are like the younger siblings of literature, and like the light reflected in mirrors. A soul must bleed under the words.

These are no longer the blockheads and inexpressive faces of the streets: an elegant sobriety is noticeable in the clothes, there is light in the faces; in the heads there is that size, variety, and character associated with the range of intellectual occupations. The best of New York has come to the hall. The night when the celebrated humorist and the perspicacious novelist of the South read is not to be missed. *Mark Twain* writes humorous books, bursting with satire, in which the comical does not depend on the portrayal of ridiculous and exaggerated people, but rather shines its light, with a certain picaresque innocence, on the contradictions, baseness, and hypocrisy of ordinary people, and contrasts, with consummate art, what they pretend to be thinking and feeling, with what they actually think and feel. But he does it in such an easygoing manner, and with so little air of pedantry, that people laugh to see themselves surprised in their innermost selves, like a child who in the moment of stealing strawberries from the basket catches sight of his mother regarding him tenderly. His ideas come to him directly from life; and although you can see the literary skill very well in his books, he is not one to trim, snip, and fashion his ideas to appear cultivated, as if any woman in finery for a formal ball were more beautiful than Venus de Milo.

Where else but from excessive affectation comes that evasion or distortion of what one sees for oneself, out of an urge to demonstrate one's knowledge of what others have said? It is good to know what people are saying and take advantage of this knowledge; but since all that is a record of its day, it will not survive for future ages. Let each observe for himself, write for himself, look into himself for light, and probe Nature within himself and all around him.

Literature lives from impressions more than expressions. Rubbish, rubbish! All these stuffed phrases, all these historical appraisals, all these literary adornments, what do they leave in the reader except the presumption that the writer is a know-it-all? In literature one ought to be not a Narcissus but a missionary. One should not write in order to show off and fan like a peacock one's enormous tail; rather, one should write for the good of one's neighbor, to utter, as if rendering up something that has been entrusted, what Nature has put within one. Motifs, abominable and sensational motifs have become popular in literature as in music.

One man spins phrases out of another man's inspiration, and dilutes, inflates, and gilds it. The ideas of the age pass through the air, because each age has its atmosphere of ideas: you gather them in a literary spoonful, and present them, plucked and pompous, without the verve, color, and sweep of living ideas that spring, like a bird surprised in its nest, from every wound in the heart, from every long night of the mind that finally brings it down.

Literature is now an occupation for gilders; it urgently needs to be an occupation for miners. The hands hurt more, but you extract, with strong hands, pure metal. There are more than enough ornamentalists and executors of other's wills. In spite of his fame in the world of letters, *Mark Twain* is not a major light, but he shines with his own light, which is a rare quality today, and he deserves his fame, which is great, in Europe and America. Unlike the young gentlemen of our pampered regions, who are given beautiful wives, houses, and carriages the moment they emerge from the classroom in their scarlet university robes, Mark Twain was not hand-fed from a silver spoon.

He began as a printer. Adventure spoke into his ear, and he became a man of the sea: he still carries it in his fresh and ruddy face. On the Mississippi he adopted his pen name because he was captivated by the words when he first heard them: "Mark twain," the leadsman's voice would often call out, meaning "at two fathoms." He not only began, with his mocking self-assurance, to tell tales of what he saw in the world and to draw from the outward man the true man within, he sealed it with the Mississippi shout: "*Mark Twain.*" Later, he traveled as his brother's secretary through the mining country, where people sleep on top of a gold vein and wake with a dagger in the chest.

He has been in the burning workshops where the country was forged: with those who make mistakes, with those who fall in love, with those who rob, with those who live in solitude and people it, and with those who build. He liked to wander, and once he had seen man in one place, he took his leave, longing to see him in another. He has the habit of squinting, as if to see better, or so others do not guess his thoughts by his expression. He knows men, and the trouble they take to hide or disguise their defects; and he loves to tell things so that the real man—hypocritical, servile, cowardly, wanton—drops from the last line of his story like a puppet from the hands of the clown who toyed with it. And he peeps out from his phrase to watch him fall.

He sketches in charcoal, but with quick and firm lines. He understands the power of adjectives, the adjectives that economize on phrases, and he loads up a character with them in such a way that the person begins to walk as if he were alive. By dint of observation, he has gained confidence in description. There are credulous and ardent spirits who see everything in the light of their own flames, and through their own clouds, nonsensical, exaggerated or deformed, false or confused: there are other spirits, like that of *Mark Twain*, incredulous from pure experience and made tranquil, perhaps by suffering: and these spirits see things in their natural proportion, even if at times, as the defect of their quality, they are unable to conjecture about the winged aspect of things. His travel books have made him famous, and earned him four hundred thousand dollars. He tells his jokes like someone who doesn't want to tell them, and he tells them without intending to hurt anyone.

He does not like to show himself, lest people conceal themselves from him and hide their character which, like a good hunter, he stirs up and watches closely. He must have, and I believe he does, the incurable melancholy of those who know humans profoundly. He married a rich woman, and he has been in the Sandwich Islands and all through Europe, Egypt, and Palestine. The foolish and the hypocritical inevitably inspire his pen. His wit gets its originality and roughness from his own life. He exercised it for a long time among common people and he must have blended right in with them from the way the people peep out from all his pages. There is more de Kock than Chamfort in him. But more than either of them, he has an exquisite sense of nature, which, had he painted it with a more delicate brush, would have engendered many illustrious copies. His own joking and mocking persona diminishes his vivid paintings.

If you don't want to go to see Athens at night, you don't have to go after you read the picture Mark Twain paints of it, for he shows it exactly as it is: nor will you need to go to the Pyramids. He undertakes to tell how, on top of one of them, he bet a guide that he could climb down, get to the top of the next pyramid, and come back to where they were in ten minutes. And the speedy Arab breaks into a run: Twain paints him going down with long strides, unleashes him across the burning plain, you see him as a dog, you see him as a dove, I saw him as a fly, now you don't see him, you see a black dot ascending the far pyramid, he goes up, arrives, waves, comes down, running again, reaches the base of the pyramid, and is back like the wind at the top once more to win the bet, not even ten minutes have passed. In just twenty lines Mark Twain has told this, and even though he doesn't describe it point by point, he sees the magnificent solitude, the burning sun, the great pyramids, the distance between them, the whirling sand, the burnoose floating in air.

He writes novels that are not yet fully shaped. He recounts, as if reluctantly and in haste, incidents of his life or episodes in his works; he comes out from the wings seeming bored and hesitant, he reads his story to the public as he might to his own children, to amuse them and be rid of them. To the humor of his ideas he adds that produced irresistibly by the contrast between his comic pictures and exaggerated descriptions and the peevish, nasal, and imperturbable tone in which he recites them. He doesn't attain his full effect in short jokes, instead he expands and stretches them out; his piquancy is not in the felicitousness of his expression, which can seem excessive when he tries too hard or overextends himself, but in the justice of his criticism, and his way of juxtaposing appearances and feelings. To turn up somewhere and wander about has always served him well and given him pleasure, and the titles of his best books reveal this method and tendency: *The Innocents Abroad*, *The Innocents at Home*, *A Tramp Abroad*. And of course he always carries with him a most ingenious slingshot.

At times, with an acrobat's skill, he can set a cascade of jokes dancing on top of an atom. The *Figaro* of Paris enjoys his books, and translates and celebrates them: not for their refinement of style—for he knows his people and refinement is not what they want—but for the subtlety of observation. He combs his white mane; the eyes betray experience, profundity, and roguishness; the nose, long and aquiline, presides over a martial mustache; otherwise his face, of a healthy color, is clean-shaven: he tilts his head forward with a scrutinizing glance, and his back is raised as if he had decided to shrug his shoulders forever. Such is *Mark Twain*, or Samuel Clemens, the most outstanding North American humorist.

Translated by Edward M. Test
La Nación (Buenos Aires), 1884–85

———

Chivalric romances are in vogue now because, apart from *Don Quixote*, nothing better has been said about them and nothing has thrashed them more innovatively and effectively than the book by the powerful, prescient, and incensed humorist Mark Twain. Twain lives in his castle because his house in the town of Hartford surrounded by oak trees and bordered by a lake looks like a castle; but he earned it with his brains, depicting the rowdy characters he had seen with his own eyes in frontier camps, mines, rivers and brawls in *Roughing It*, and in his *Innocents Abroad* and *A Tramp Abroad*, where his comic misadventures from London to Cairo gave plenty to laugh about. Although back then his style was unpolished and he smoked cheap tobacco, already these books showed glimpses of a man capable of seeing for himself, with judgment purified by a long and deep sorrow, and a love for the afflicted. Moved by the chaos around him, the injustice that exasperates him, and the privileged classes who are beginning to rise on the backs of the poor, Twain wrote at last the more cultured and effortless *Connecticut Yankee in King Arthur's Court*, where through the simple device of contrasting the free Yankee and the Knights of the Round Table, he makes evident—with an anger that sometimes borders on the sublime—the vileness of those who would climb atop their fellow man, feed upon his misery, and drink from his misfortune. He handles his subject with such skill—a skill that requires more than copying the prominent elements of that epoch, that age of kings and bishops, villagers and serfs—that a picture emerges of that which is starting to be seen in the United States today: virtuous men who are scourged by whips, armed by nature with only solitude and hunger, men who go forth with a pen for a lance and a book for a shield to topple the money castles of the new aristocracy. There are paragraphs in Twain's book that make me want to set off for Hartford to shake his hand. Twain has taken it upon himself to rally men and men will thank him for it. *Don Quixote* will have its rightful place in libraries and the *Yankee* alongside it. Both contain shields and visors and they resemble each other in the magnificence of their mockery. But *Don Quixote* is what it is, a wise and painful depiction of the life of man, while *Yankee*, fueled by indignation, is a cowboy-style battle with lasso and revolver, like that of its hero against Lagramor, for the good of the common, free man, his majesty and his glory. The plot fits in a thimble: the foreman of a factory gets into a fight with an insubordinate worker, receives a blow to the head from which he passes out. He wakes up, with his modern Yankee know-how and resourcefulness, in a court in which all scientific knowledge is embodied in Merlin, Heaven's vault is the miter, the morality of the kingdom is to be found in Lancelot and Guinevere's love, and government amounts to the will of the powerful King Arthur. Oh, that tour of the disguised King, and the Yankee—who had defeated Merlin and become the King's First Minister—through the towns of the serfs and the fields of the peasants, the hills of the infamous castle covered in gallows, the plague-infested house cursed by the Church, and a chain of serfs sold at auction! That tournament in which "the Boss," wearing everyday clothes and riding his prairie nag with no weapons other than the pistol in his belt and his lasso in the air, topples the towering armor-clad knight riding towards him who turns out to be the great Lagramor, Merlin's nephew, and who falls on his back, scattering metal shards, arms and legs in the air, neck in the lasso and rear-end in the sand! That electrified place, where "the Boss" and his fifty-two boys, fifty-two innocents, defeat with never-before-seen maneuvers and true miracles the twenty-five thousand knights in armor. And his language, the jewel of Yankee-dom!

Twain takes all that is typical and expressive from the vernacular, and speaks with the Boss in Yankee, and with Merlin and Arthur in the archaic language of the Chronicles.

The language is literary, of course, but at the same time energetic and natural, and it's clear Twain preferred short words to long ones, native words to latinates; he strove to use words as the bones of ideas, rather than their dress. The effect is sharp as a pencil. There's something spider-like in the style, made of strong silk, through which the spider flees after wounding its victim, half-laughing, half-fearing the results.

The author behind the book does not detract from its charm when he shows up at an unlikely moment, or stops the action so that the audience may hear his sarcastic and clever remarks. A useful book it is, because although it is humorous, as it is said to be, it was written after having cried. . . .

Translated by Rubén Builes and Cintia Santana
La Nación (Buenos Aires), 1890

Henry Gauthier-Villars

The first book devoted to Mark Twain published anywhere, in any language, was published in Paris by a 25-year-old French law student named Henry Gauthier-Villars in 1884. His family's publishing house published *Mark Twain* not long after Gauthier-Villars had presented it as a lecture sponsored by the Conférence Olivaint, the oldest student organization in France. Gauthier-Villars (1859–1931), who often (but not on this occasion) published under the pen name "Willy," would later become famous as a flamboyant journalist, novelist, and music critic. Today, however, he is best known for having been the controversial first husband of the French writer Colette, whom he married in 1893—and whose first novel, *Claudine at School*, he published under his own name in 1900. Although Gauthier-Villars opens his book by complimenting Thérèse Bentzon on her translations of Twain, he then proceeds to provide new translations of his own—not just of familiar tales Bentzon had translated earlier like "The Jumping Frog" (Gauthier-Villars' translation is a bit more fast-paced and colloquial than Bentzon's), but also of a piece that to this day has attracted almost no critical attention, "The Judge's 'Spirited Woman'" (which appears in *Sketches, New and Old*), a work that is not comic at all: it focuses on a Mexican woman (whom Twain clearly admires) who takes the law into her own hands in an American courtroom when it becomes clear that justice will not be done. Other pieces Gauthier-Villars discusses include "How I Edited an Agricultural Paper" and "The Story of the Bad Little Boy." He shows an appreciation of the moral dimensions of Twain's work—of the ideas of justice and goodness that his humor slyly conveys and also of the fresh vitality of his prose. Gauthier-Villars has little use for the "refined stylists" then in vogue in France who "compose a sentence with the minute labor of a mosaicist," with results that are "tangled-up" and "precious." He regrets their disdain for the "gaiety, spontaneity," and "literary good health" so abundant in the work of Mark Twain. In the years that followed his publication of *Mark Twain*, Gauthier-Villars occasionally published under "Jim Smiley"—the name of the gambling-obsessed figure central to Mark Twain's "Jumping Frog" story.

Mark Twain

I would like to try and show you, dear readers, in the field of wit, there is at least one area, that of humor, that seems to have been forbidden to us French, and on which we have never even timidly set foot. It is true that we are masters in the difficult art of keeping balance and grace in gaiety; our national literature prides itself on containing all the different forms of laughter, and whoever tried to list the great French comics would be forced to make an enumeration as vast as that of the great Homer, enumerating, in round terms, the ships of the principal Greek chiefs united to avenge the honor of the unfortunate Menelaus. In this formidable army of laughter, the chiefs are well-known, and all the neighboring peoples admire, without being able to match, the smiling skepticism of Montaigne, the broad jokes of Rabelais, the cruel buffoonery of Satyre Menipée, the disheveled verve of Régnier, the irresistible *vis comica* of Moliere, the cynical sniggering of Voltaire, the rebellious liveliness of Montesquieu, the stormy mockery of Beaumarchais, the painstaking irony of Paul-Louis Courier, even the charming blooming of Labiche of the wild character of the intransigent pamphleteers that Noumea has brought us.

Still, in this litany of names, which I could make even longer, have I been able to touch on a single author, just one, who was really and truly, entirely, fundamentally, humorous? I do not think so. We do not have any humorists, and we are inclined to consider humor, that prodigal son of the stray minds of the northern people, as barbarous, whether it comes from across the English Channel or the Rhine. . . .

There remains young America and its completely new literature, since the authors of the Old World have nothing more to satisfy our jaded minds, and here is a first-rate writer who has not taken from the Germans either their mysticism or their brutality, and who even leaves to the English their jolts of convulsive laughter and black depression; he will not ever lose himself in the foggy ruminations of Jean-Paul; he will not tarry either in the lovingly stroked descriptions of tea prepared at just the right

temperature that try the patience of the French in insurmount-
able terror! No! He is lively, jovial, incisive, and his bold irony
deserves to focus, at least for a moment, our easily distracted
attention. Hello then, charming writer with no model or imi-
tator! I bid you welcome among us, newcomer with endless
verve; the sound of the hurrahs you have raised has already
crossed the ocean. We have been waiting for you, for we are
tired of the grubby woes that have taken over too many of our
countrymen. We have not forgotten that "Laughter is the best
medicine" and we want to learn American humor from you,
the cheerful Yankee with the ringing laugh, the inimitable
Mark Twain! . . .

Samuel Langhorne Clemens, better known under the pen
name of Mark Twain, was born in Florida in 1835, and like most
of his countrymen, has led a singularly hectic life. He was in
turn a printer, gold miner, journalist, riverboat pilot on the Mississippi, he got married, he served as secretary to his brother,
government agent in Nevada, traveled through Palestine, the
Hawaiian Islands, Greece, and France, and all that without ever
losing, through all the strokes of chance in this capricious existence, his observant humor and his robust spirit. Like Heine
who made "little songs from his great sorrows," Mark Twain has
brought to life in his stories the thousand adventures he has
experienced, as he is one of those people who has lived a lot and
remembered a lot. His images of the Mississippi abound in *The
Gilded Age*. *The Eye Openers*, *Screamers*, *Roughing It* are full of
comedic and touching stories inspired by his life as a miner; his
travel diaries, collected under the title *The Innocents Abroad* and
The New Pilgrim's Progress, have raised a storm of controversy,
and now the short stint he did with his brother has given us an
amusing tale, *My Late Senatorial Secretaryship*. We might credit
his former work as an editor (a wonderful job, incidentally) as
being very useful to him in inspiring a worthy and uncommon
respect for the rules of punctuation.

All these works have had the most resounding success, and
Mark Twain's reputation, just starting here in France, extends to
the most remote English and American colonies. His books are
the joy of the poor dockworkers in London and the recreation

of the Indian Army officer buffeted by tropical fevers. They conquer the boredom of the passenger who is shut up in a railroad coach for seven days along the strip of metal 3,786 miles long that connects New York and San Francisco. They often make the walls of squatters' cabins lost in the middle of the Australian wilderness shake with bolts of laughter. . . .

For such readers, subtle analysis, delicacy of thought, and refinements of style would be a closed book. Mark Twain is content to tell them stories, with an original clownishness, which he himself calls, without false modesty, "Good Things, Immensely Funny Sayings and Stories That Will Bring a Smile Upon the Gruffest Countenance." These merry fancies do not all have the same weight, some are merely funny jokes, of a somewhat childish disposition, whose sole aim is to make the reader laugh; while in others, by contrast, have a moral that comes out from the story and most often, is not to be sneezed at. That is the case, for example, of one of the most popular pieces of Mark Twain, *The Celebrated Jumping Frog of Calaveras County.*

In this odd little story, Twain wanted to ridicule the gambling fever infecting America: horse races, Congressional elections, dogfights and cockfights are all fine occasions for wagering vast sums; in the church as in the boxing ring, the bets go on. . . .

I do not intend to attribute to this piece of light literature more importance than it possesses, and I hope I have avoided, at least in part, the narrow-minded spirit of the commentator of whom it was said "Nothing is more absurd than a passionate idiot who digs into himself." Still, despite all my desire not to delve too deeply into things, I cannot help finding real merits to these jokes, an unpretentious cheeriness of which the *Jumping Frog* is the classic example. And just think of how amusing, under the weight of their native slang, the original versions of these stories must be, free of the translation that covers their lively originality with a leaden overcoat. Be aware that the old Italian saying *traduttore, traditore* is especially true when applied to Mark Twain—to translate him is to betray him. Gerard de Nerval, who knew what he was doing, called the translation of Heinrich Heine's verses "stuffed moonlight" (*clair de lune empaillé*). One can only guess what name he would bestow on the translations of Mark Twain, which cannot capture the joyous temerity of the American prose, or the joyous eccentricity of the expressions Twain creates from whole cloth, or the sharp edges of the humor to which the original use of slang adds irresistible comedy.

Translated by Greg Robinson
Mark Twain, 1884

Hamlin Garland

Hamlin Garland (1860–1940), journalist, novelist, short-story writer, and poet, grew up on various homesteads across the Midwest and went to Boston with hopes of launching a literary career. Garland admired Mark Twain from an early age: he recalled that a teacher had rebuked him for praising *Roughing It* too enthusiastically in a school essay. In a tribute to Twain that he published in the *North American Review* the year of Samuel Clemens' death, he proudly claimed Twain as a fellow Midwestern writer: "No amount of Old World contact could destroy his quaint drawl, and not all his reading nor his acquired personal knowledge of other writers could conventionalize his method. He remained the mid-Western American and literary democrat to the last." Garland wrote the review that follows the year before he had his own first literary success, *Main-Travelled Roads*, a collection of stories. (The book we know as *A Connecticut Yankee in King Arthur's Court* was published in Britain under the title *A Yankee at the Court of King Arthur*, and as *A Yankee in the Court of King Arthur* in some early American editions as well—including the one Garland read when he wrote this review.)

Mark Twain's Latest

It is probable that the general public will be decidedly taken by surprise by Mark Twain's "Yankee in the Court of King Arthur," because of the spirit of reform which animates the book. "Mark Twain as a reformer" will seem strange indeed, and yet to those who know him well it will only be familiar things made public. Our genial humorist in his private life is a man of wide and ready sympathy, with a democracy of the most pronounced kind, hating all shams and loving truth and all sincerity.

This book is curiously complex, not at all the simple, fanciful tale it sets out to be. It is first of all the most powerful presentation of the "sunny side" of chivalry. With really wonderful power, grotesque yet graphic, it shows the actualities of an age, at which we should shudder, and at which we would shudder had not the chroniclers lied to us and everywhere deceived us by covering up its realities of violence.

It is the reverse side of the web of romance woven by Scott and his disciples. It tells us of the slave and the "freeman" (?) of the day. It shows or hints at (words refuse to express) "le droit de seigneur."

He tells us how ruthless these "glorious knights of the round table" were when dealing with the peasants. He gives curious details of actual services required, etc. His thoughts about the freemen of the time, which he expresses through the Yankee, are worth giving in his own words as an illustration of the spirit of democracy that pervades the book. He says:

> And here where these freemen assembled in the early morning to work on their lord the bishop's road three days each—gratis; every head of a family and every son of a family three days each gratis, and a day or so added for their servants. Why, it was like reading about France and the French, before the memorable and blessed revolution, which swept a thousand years of such villainy away in one swift tidal wave of blood—one: a settlement of that hoary debt in the proportion of half a drop of blood for each hogshead of it that had been pressed by slow tortures out of that people in the weary stretch of ten centuries of wrong and shame and misery, the like of which was not to be mated but in hell. There were two "reigns of terror," if we would but remember it and consider it; the one wrought in murder in hot passion, the other in heartless cold blood; the one lasted mere months, the other had lasted a thousand years; the one inflicted death upon ten thousand persons, the other upon one hundred million; but our shudders are all for the horrors of the minor terror, the momentary terror, so to speak; whereas, what is the horror of swift death by the axe compared with life-long death from hunger, cold, insult, cruelty and heart break? What is swift death by lightning compared with death by slow fire at the stake? A city cemetery could contain the coffins filled by that brief terror which we have all been so diligently taught to shiver at and mourn over; but all France could hardly contain the coffins filled by that older and real terror—that unspeakably bitter and awful terror

which none of us have been taught to see in its vastness or pity as it deserves.

Such writing as this will be new to many people, and especially notable in a funny book, for the book is funny, that's the best part of its powerful attack. It is like Don Quixote, only more modern, more human, more certain in certain directions. The humor a little more savage. It is the modern man's comment.

But, besides being an attack upon the chivalry of the past and all relics of it still surviving, it is also a comment equally striking and definite on the present. It is another manifestation of the growing discontent with conditions which we are getting to see as hideously opposite to genuine altruistic industrialism.

The Yankee in the court of King Arthur pauses to talk of things in the far off nineteenth century, from which he has been ruthlessly snatched, and reads nineteenth century people a lesson in political science. "The citizen," he says, "who thinks he sees that the commonwealth's political clothes are worn out, and yet holds his peace and does not agitate for a new suit is disloyal—he is a traitor. That he may be the only one who thinks he sees this decay, does not excuse him; it is his duty to agitate any way, and it is the duty of the others to vote him down if they do not see the matter as he does." But the Yankee believed in accomplishing political reforms by appropriate means. Applying his own lesson to himself he says:

> Here I was in a country where the right to say how the country should be governed was restricted to six persons in each thousand of its population. For the nine hundred and ninety-four to express dissatisfaction with the regnant system and propose to change it, would have made the whole six to shudder as one man, it would have been so disloyal, so dishonorable, such putrid black treason. So to speak, I was to become a stockholder in a corporation where nine hundred and ninety-four of its members furnished all the money and did all the work, and the other six elected themselves a permanent board of direction and took all the dividends. It seemed to me that what the nine hundred and

ninety-four dupes needed was a new deal. The thing that would have best suited the circus side of my nature would have been to resign the boss-ship and get up an insurrection and turn it into a revolution; but I knew that the Jack Cade or the Wat Tyler who tries such a thing without first educating his materials up to revolution grade is almost absolutely certain to get left. I had never been accustomed to getting left, even if I do say it myself. Wherefore, the deal which had been for some time working into shape in my mind was of a quite different pattern from the Cade-Tyler sort.

As relates to the age of chivalry, the finest portions—and they are thrillingly sweet and strong—are those relating to the mental and moral changes which came to king Arthur as he left his throne, and wearing the thrall's coarse garments took his way with "the base" through the kingdom, studying dungeons and slavery as it really was and when with the pox-smitten girl in his arms he steps before us we are ready to exclaim with the Yankee, "he was truly great now."

This is, perhaps, the highest note struck in the book, and it is a genuine surprise, even to those who have known something of the growing humanity of the author. It is impossible to overestimate the significance of that one passage. It has many phases. Here was a man who had fought for Christ all his life, and only now came to the point of really living the life his master taught. What a commentary on today! When the churches are "so busy teaching the divinity of Christ they forget his humanity."

This book is distinctively the book of a radical. Like the latest (and perhaps greatest) book of W. D. Howells, it is a profound criticism of present thought and present social conditions. It is generally full of the reform spirit, and specifically the author advocates the land for the people. He is helped out in definiteness by Mr. Daniel Beard, who illustrates the book superbly, and who is known as a "single tax man" among his brother artists. One of the most striking of the illustrations is the one showing the result of "free natural opportunity." Another is the eclipse of the "divine right of kings," by "the land for the people."

It is not without reason that this book has been called one of the most significant publications of the year. When a humorist of the power of Mr. Clemens turns the laugh on the conservative element so markedly as in this book, the land reform is shown to have passed out of its preliminary stages. It is an earnest, determined assault along practical and peaceful lines. And the still further importance of this book lies in the fact that it will be read by a class of people hardly reached otherwise: people who will read to laugh, and pause in their laughing to think.

Boston Evening Transcript, 1890

Rudyard Kipling

Rudyard Kipling (1865–1936), born to British parents in Mumbai, was a 23-year-old journalist working for a newspaper in Allahabad, India, when he traveled to Elmira, New York, in 1889 to conduct this interview with Mark Twain. Although he enjoyed meeting Kipling, at the time Twain had no idea who he was. Soon after, however, Twain would become an admirer of Kipling's books, often reading selections from them aloud to his family and friends. The two men stayed in touch and got together when their travels made it possible. In 1895, Twain wrote Kipling: "It is reported that you are about to visit India. This has moved me to journey to that far country in order that I may unload from my conscience a debt long due you. Years ago you came from India to Elmira to visit me, as you said at the time. It has always been my purpose to return that visit and that great compliment some day. I shall arrive next January and you must be ready. I shall come riding my ayah with his tusks adorned with silver bells and ribbons and escorted by a troop of native howdahs richly clad and mounted upon a herd of wild bungalows; and you must be on hand with a few bottles of ghee, for I shall be thirsty." Twain and Kipling both received honorary degrees in a ceremony at Oxford in 1907.

An Interview with Mark Twain

You are a contemptible lot, over yonder. Some of you are Commissioners, and some Lieutenant-Governors, and some have the V. C., and a few are privileged to walk about the Mall arm in arm with the Viceroy; but *I* have seen Mark Twain this golden morning, have shaken his hand, and smoked a cigar—no, two cigars—with him, and talked with him for more than two hours! Understand clearly that I do not despise you; indeed, I don't. I am only very sorry for you, from the Viceroy downward. To soothe your envy and to prove that I still regard you as my equals, I will tell you all about it.

They said in Buffalo that he was in Hartford, Conn.; and again they said "perchance he is gone upon a journey to Portland"; and a big, fat drummer vowed that he knew the great man intimately, and that Mark was spending the summer in Europe—

which information so upset me that I embarked upon the wrong train, and was incontinently turned out by the conductor three-quarters of a mile from the station, amid the wilderness of railway tracks. Have you ever, encumbered with great-coat and valise, tried to dodge diversely-minded locomotives when the sun was shining in your eyes? But I forgot that you have not seen Mark Twain, you people of no account!

Saved from the jaws of the cowcatcher, me wandering devious a stranger met.

"Elmira is the place. Elmira in the State of New York—this State, not two hundred miles away;" and he added, perfectly unnecessarily, "Slide, Kelley, slide."

I slid on the West Shore line, I slid till midnight, and they dumped me down at the door of a frowzy hotel in Elmira. Yes, they knew all about "that man Clemens," but reckoned he was not in town; had gone East somewhere. I had better possess my soul in patience till the morrow, and then dig up the "man Clemens'" brother-in-law, who was interested in coal.

The idea of chasing half a dozen relatives in addition to Mark Twain up and down a city of thirty thousand inhabitants kept me awake. Morning revealed Elmira, whose streets were desolated by railway tracks, and whose suburbs were given up to the manufacture of door-sashes and window-frames. It was surrounded by pleasant, fat, little hills, rimmed with timber and topped with cultivation. The Chemung River flowed generally up and down the town, and had just finished flooding a few of the main streets.

The hotel-man and the telephone-man assured me that the much-desired brother-in-law was out of town, and no one seemed to know where "the man Clemens" abode. Later on I discovered that he had not summered in that place for more than nineteen seasons, and so was comparatively a new arrival.

A friendly policeman volunteered the news that he had seen Twain or "some one very like him" driving a buggy the day before. This gave me a delightful sense of nearness. Fancy living in a town where you could see the author of *Tom Sawyer*, or "some one very like him," jolting over the pavements in a buggy!

"He lives out yonder at East Hill," said the policeman; "three miles from here."

Then the chase began—in a hired hack, up an awful hill, where sunflowers blossomed by the roadside, and crops waved, and *Harper's Magazine* cows stood in eligible and commanding attitudes knee-deep in clover, all ready to be transferred to photogravure. The great man must have been persecuted by outsiders aforetime, and fled up the hill for refuge.

Presently the driver stopped at a miserable, little, white wood shanty, and demanded "Mister Clemens."

"I know he's a big-bug and all that," he explained, "but you can never tell what sort of notions those sort of men take into their heads to live in, anyways."

There rose up a young lady who was sketching thistle-tops and goldenrod, amid a plentiful supply of both, and set the pilgrimage on the right path.

"It's a pretty Gothic house on the left-hand side a little way farther on."

"Gothic h——," said the driver. "Very few of the city hacks take this drive, specially if they know they are coming out here," and he glared at me savagely.

It was a very pretty house, anything but Gothic, clothed with ivy, standing in a very big compound, and fronted by a verandah full of chairs and hammocks. The roof of the verandah was a trellis-work of creepers, and the sun peeping through moved on the shining boards below.

Decidedly this remote place was an ideal one for work, if a man could work among these soft airs and the murmur of the long-eared crops.

Appeared suddenly a lady used to dealing with rampageous outsiders. "Mr. Clemens has just walked downtown. He is at his brother-in-law's house."

Then he was within shouting distance, after all, and the chase had not been in vain. With speed I fled, and the driver, skidding the wheel and swearing audibly, arrived at the bottom of that hill without accidents. It was in the pause that followed between ringing the brother-in-law's bell and getting an answer that it occurred to me for the first time Mark Twain might possibly have other engagements than the entertainment of escaped lunatics from India, be they never so full of admiration. And in another man's house—anyhow, what had I come to do or say? Suppose the drawing-room should be full of people,—suppose a baby were sick, how was I to explain that I only wanted to shake hands with him?

Then things happened somewhat in this order. A big, darkened drawing-room; a huge chair; a man with eyes, a mane of grizzled hair, a brown mustache covering a mouth as delicate as a woman's, a strong, square hand shaking mine, and the slowest, calmest, levellest voice in all the world saying:—

"Well, you think you owe me something, and you've come to tell me so. That's what I call squaring a debt handsomely."

"Piff!" from a cob-pipe (I always said that a Missouri meerschaum was the best smoking in the world), and, behold! Mark Twain had curled himself up in the big armchair, and I was smoking reverently, as befits one in the presence of his superior.

The thing that struck me first was that he was an elderly man; yet, after a minute's thought, I perceived that it was otherwise, and in five minutes, the eyes looking at me, I saw that the grey hair was an accident of the most trivial. He was quite young. I was shaking his hand. I was smoking his cigar, and I was hearing him talk—this man I had learned to love and admire fourteen thousand miles away.

Reading his books, I had striven to get an idea of his personality, and all my preconceived notions were wrong and beneath the reality. Blessed is the man who finds no disillusion when he is brought face to face with a revered writer. That was a moment to be remembered; the landing of a twelve-pound salmon was nothing to it. I had hooked Mark Twain, and he was treating me as though under certain circumstances I might be an equal.

About this time I became aware that he was discussing the copyright question. Here, so far as I remember, is what he said. Attend to the words of the oracle through this unworthy medium transmitted. You will never be able to imagine the long, slow surge of the drawl, and the deadly gravity of the countenance, the quaint pucker of the body, one foot thrown over the arm of the chair, the yellow pipe clinched in one corner of the mouth, and the right hand casually caressing the square chin:—

"Copyright? Some men have morals, and some men have—other things. I presume a publisher is a man. He is not born. He is created—by circumstances. Some publishers have morals. Mine have. They pay me for the English productions of my books. When you hear men talking of Bret Harte's works and other works and my books being pirated, ask them to be sure of their facts. I think they'll find the books are paid for. It was ever thus.

"I remember an unprincipled and formidable publisher. Perhaps he's dead now. He used to take my short stories—I can't call it steal or pirate them. It was beyond these things altogether. He took my stories one at a time and made a book of it. If I wrote an essay on dentistry or theology or any little thing of that kind—just an essay that long (he indicated half an inch on his finger), any sort of essay—that publisher would amend and improve my essay.

"He would get another man to write some more to it or cut it about exactly as his needs required. Then he would publish a book called *Dentistry by Mark Twain*, that little essay and some other things not mine added. Theology would make another book, and so on. I do not consider that fair. It's an insult. But he's dead now, I think. I didn't kill him.

"There is a great deal of nonsense talked about international copyright. The proper way to treat a copyright is to make it exactly like real-estate in every way.

"It will settle itself under these conditions. If Congress were to bring in a law that a man's life was not to extend over a hundred and sixty years, somebody would laugh. That law wouldn't concern anybody. The man would be out of the jurisdiction of the court. A term of years in copyright comes to exactly the same thing. No law can make a book live or cause it to die before the appointed time.

"Tottletown, Cal., was a new town, with a population of three thousand—banks, fire-brigade, brick buildings, and all the modern improvements. It lived, it flourished, and it disappeared. To-day no man can put his foot on any remnant of Tottletown, Cal. It's dead. London continues to exist. Bill Smith, author of a book read for the next year or so, is real-estate in Tottletown. William Shakespeare, whose works are extensively read, is real-estate in London. Let Bill Smith, equally with Mr. Shakespeare now deceased, have as complete a control over his copyright as he would over his real-estate. Let him gamble it away, drink it away, or—give it to the church. Let his heirs and assigns treat it in the same manner.

"Every now and again I go up to Washington, sitting on a board to drive that sort of view into Congress. Congress takes its arguments against international copyright delivered ready made, and—Congress isn't very strong. I put the real-estate view of the case before one of the Senators.

"He said: 'Suppose a man has written a book that will live for ever?'

"I said: 'Neither you nor I will ever live to see that man, but we'll assume it. What then?'

"He said: 'I want to protect the world against that man's heirs and assigns, working under your theory.'

"I said: 'You think that all the world has no commercial sense. The book that will live for ever can't be artificially kept up at inflated prices. There will always be very expensive editions of it and cheap ones issuing side by side.'

"Take the case of Sir Walter Scott's novels," Mark Twain continued, turning to me. "When the copyright notes protected them, I bought editions as expensive as I could afford, because I liked them. At the same time the same firm were selling editions that a cat might buy. They had their real estate, and not being fools, recognized that one portion of the plot could be worked as a gold mine, another as a vegetable garden, and another as a marble quarry. Do you see?"

What I saw with the greatest clearness was Mark Twain being forced to fight for the simple proposition that a man has as much right to the work of his brains (think of the heresy of it!) as to the labour of his hands. When the old lion roars, the young whelps growl. I growled assentingly, and the talk ran on from books in general to his own in particular.

Growing bold, and feeling that I had a few hundred thousand folk at my back, I demanded whether Tom Sawyer married

Judge Thatcher's daughter and whether we were ever going to hear of Tom Sawyer as a man.

"I haven't decided," quoth Mark Twain, getting up, filling his pipe, and walking up and down the room in his slippers. "I have a notion of writing the sequel to *Tom Sawyer* in two ways. In one I would make him rise to great honour and go to Congress, and in the other I should hang him. Then the friends and enemies of the book could take their choice."

Here I lost my reverence completely, and protested against any theory of the sort, because, to me at least, Tom Sawyer was real.

"Oh, he *is* real," said Mark Twain. "He's all the boys that I have known or recollect; but that would be a good way of ending the book"; then, turning round, "because, when you come to think of it, neither religion, training, nor education avails anything against the force of circumstances that drive a man. Suppose we took the next four and twenty years of Tom Sawyer's life, and gave a little joggle to the circumstances that controlled him. He would, logically and according to the joggle, turn out a rip or an angel."

"Do you believe that, then?"

"I think so. Isn't it what you call Kismet?"

"Yes; but don't give him two joggles and show the result, because he isn't your property any more. He belongs to us."

He laughed—a large, wholesome laugh—and this began a dissertation on the rights of a man to do what he liked with his own creations, which being a matter of purely professional interest, I will mercifully omit.

Returning to the big chair, he, speaking of truth and the like in literature, said that an autobiography was the one work in which a man, against his own will and in spite of his utmost striving to the contrary, revealed himself in his true light to the world.

"A good deal of your life on the Mississippi is autobiographical, isn't it?" I asked.

"As near as it can be—when a man is writing to a book and about himself. But in genuine autobiography, I believe it is impossible for a man to tell the truth about himself or to avoid impressing the reader with the truth about himself.

"I made an experiment once. I got a friend of mine—a man painfully given to speak the truth on all occasions—a man who wouldn't dream of telling a lie—and I made him write his autobiography for his own amusement and mine. He did it. The manuscript would have made an octavo volume, but—good, honest man that he was—in every single detail of his life that I knew about he turned out, on paper, a formidable liar. He could not help himself.

"It is not in human nature to write the truth about itself. None the less the reader gets a general impression from an autobiography whether the man is a fraud or a good man. The reader can't give his reasons any more than a man can explain why a woman struck him as being lovely when he doesn't remember her hair, eyes, teeth, or figure. And the impression that the reader gets is a correct one."

"Do you ever intend to write an autobiography?"

"If I do, it will be as other men have done—with the most earnest desire to make myself out to be the better man in every little business that has been to my discredit; and I shall fail, like the others, to make my readers believe anything except the truth."

This naturally led to a discussion on conscience. Then said Mark Twain, and his words are mighty and to be remembered:—

"Your conscience is a nuisance. A conscience is like a child. If you pet it and play with it and let it have everything that it wants, it becomes spoiled and intrudes on all your amusements and most of your griefs. Treat your conscience as you would treat anything else. When it is rebellious, spank it—be severe with it, argue with it, prevent it from coming to play with you at all hours, and you will secure a good conscience; that is to say, a properly trained one. A spoiled one simply destroys all the pleasure in life. I think I have reduced mine to order. At least, I haven't heard from it for some time. Perhaps I have killed it from over-severity. It's wrong to kill a child, but, in spite of all I have said, a conscience differs from a child in many ways. Perhaps it's best when it's dead."

Here he told me a little—such things as a man may tell a stranger—of his early life and upbringing, and in what manner he had been influenced for good by the example of his parents. He spoke always through his eyes, a light under the heavy eyebrows; anon crossing the room with a step as light as a girl's, to show me some book or other; then resuming his walk up and down the room, puffing at the cob pipe. I would have given much for nerve enough to demand the gift of that pipe—value, five cents when new. I understood why certain savage tribes ardently desired the liver of brave men slain in combat. That pipe would have given me, perhaps, a hint of his keen insight into the souls of men. But he never laid it aside within stealing reach.

Once, indeed, he put his hand on my shoulder. It was an investiture of the Star of India, blue silk, trumpets, and diamond-studded jewel, all complete. If hereafter, in the changes and chances of this mortal life, I fall to cureless ruin, I will tell the superintendent of the workhouse that Mark Twain once put his hand on my shoulder; and he shall give me a room to myself and a double allowance of paupers' tobacco.

"I never read novels myself," said he, "except when the popular persecution forces me to—when people plague me to know what I think of the last book that every one is reading."

"And how did the latest persecution affect you?"

"Robert?" said he, interrogatively.

I nodded.

"I read it, of course, for the workmanship. That made me think I had neglected novels too long—that there might be a good many books as graceful in style somewhere on the shelves; so I began a course of novel reading. I have dropped it now; it did not amuse me. But as regards Robert, the effect on me was exactly as though a singer of street ballads were to hear excellent music from a church organ. I didn't stop to ask whether the music was legitimate or necessary. I listened, and I liked what I heard. I am speaking of the grace and beauty of the style.

"You see," he went on, "every man has his private opinion about a book. But that is my private opinion. If I had lived in the beginning of things, I should have looked around the township to see what popular opinion thought of the murder of Abel before I openly condemned Cain. I should have had my private opinion, of course, but I shouldn't have expressed it until I had felt the way.

You have my private opinion about that book. I don't know what my public ones are exactly. They won't upset the earth."

He recurled himself into the chair and talked of other things.

"I spend nine months of the year at Hartford. I have long ago satisfied myself that there is no hope of doing much work during those nine months. People come in and call. They call at all hours, about everything in the world. One day I thought I would keep a list of interruptions. It began this way:—

"A man came and would see no one but Mr. Clemens. He was an agent for photogravure reproductions of Salon pictures. I very seldom use Salon pictures in my books.

"After that man another man, who refused to see any one but Mr. Clemens, came to make me write to Washington about something. I saw him. I saw a third man, then a fourth. By this time it was noon. I had grown tired of keeping the list. I wished to rest.

"But the fifth man was the only one of the crowd with a card of his own. He sent up his card. 'Ben Koontz, Hannibal, Mo.' I was raised in Hannibal. Ben was an old schoolmate of mine. Consequently I threw the house wide open and rushed with both hands out at a big, fat, heavy man, who was not the Ben I had ever known—nor anything like him.

"'But *is* it you, Ben?' I said. 'You've altered in the last thousand years.'

"The fat man said: 'Well, I'm not Koontz exactly, but I met him down in Missouri, and he told me to be sure and call on you, and he gave me his card, and'—here he acted the little scene for my benefit—'if you can wait a minute till I can get out the circulars—I'm not Koontz exactly, but I'm travelling with the fullest line of rods you ever saw.'"

"And what happened?" I asked breathlessly.

"I shut the door. He was not Ben Koontz—exactly—not my old school-fellow, but I had shaken him by both hands in love, and . . . I had been bearded by a lightning-rod man in my own house.

"As I was saying, I do very little work in Hartford. I come here for three months every year, and I work four or five hours a day in a study down the garden of that little house on the hill. Of course, I do not object to two or three interruptions. When a man is in the full swing of his work these little things do not affect him. Eight or ten or twenty interruptions retard composition."

I was burning to ask him all manner of impertinent questions, as to which of his works he himself preferred, and so forth; but, standing in awe of his eyes, I dared not. He spoke on, and I listened, grovelling.

It was a question of mental equipment that was on the carpet, and I am still wondering whether he meant what he said.

"Personally I never care for fiction or story-books. What I like to read about are facts and statistics of any kind. If they are only facts about the raising of radishes, they interest me. Just now, for instance, before you came in"—he pointed to an encyclopædia on the shelves—"I was reading an article about 'Mathematics.' Perfectly pure mathematics.

"My own knowledge of mathematics stops at 'twelve times twelve,' but I enjoyed that article immensely. I didn't understand a word of it; but facts, or what a man believes to be facts, are always delightful. That mathematical fellow believed in his facts. So do I. Get your facts first, and"—the voice dies away to an almost inaudible drone—"then you can distort 'em as much as you please."

Bearing this precious advice in my bosom, I left; the great man assuring me with gentle kindness that I had not interrupted him in the least. Once outside the door, I yearned to go back and ask some questions—it was easy enough to think of them now—but his time was his own, though his books belonged to me.

I should have ample time to look back to that meeting across the graves of the days. But it was sad to think of the things he had not spoken about.

In San Francisco the men of *The Call* told me many legends of Mark's apprenticeship in their paper five and twenty years ago; how he was a reporter delightfully incapable of reporting according to the needs of the day. He preferred, so they said, to coil himself into a heap and meditate until the last minute. Then he would produce copy bearing no sort of relationship to his legitimate work—copy that made the editor swear horribly, and the readers of *The Call* ask for more.

I should like to have heard Mark's version of that, with some stories of his joyous and variegated past. He has been journeyman printer (in those days he wandered from the banks of the Missouri even to Philadelphia), pilot cub and full-blown pilot, soldier of the South (that was for three weeks only), private secretary to a Lieutenant-Governor of Nevada (that displeased him), miner, editor, special correspondent in the Sandwich Islands, and the Lord only knows what else. If so experienced a man could by any means be made drunk, it would be a glorious thing to fill him up with composite liquors, and, in the language of his own country, "let him retrospect." But these eyes will never see that orgy fit for the gods!

The Pioneer (Allahabad), 1890
Reprinted in *From Sea to Sea: Letters of Travel*, 1913

Andrew Lang

The publication of *A Connecticut Yankee* in Britain led critics who condemned it as "a lamentable failure" to dismiss Mark Twain's earlier work as unworthy of attention as well. These harsh responses prompted Twain to write to his friend Andrew Lang (1844–1912), collector of folklore and fairy tales, poet, novelist, critic, and historian, asking him to be his advocate before the public. Twain complained, "The critic assumes every time that if a book doesn't meet the cultivated-class standard it isn't valuable. . . . I have never tried, in even one single little instance, to help cultivate the cultivated classes. I was not equipped for it either by native gifts or training. And I never had any ambition in that direction, but always hunted for bigger game—the masses. I have seldom deliberately tried to instruct them, but I have done my best to entertain them. . . . My audience is dumb; it has no voice in print, and so I cannot know whether I have won its approval or only got its censure." He asked Lang to urge critics to formulate standards whereby work like Twain's—not geared to the "cultivated classes"—might be judged: "No voice can reach further than yours in a case of this kind or carry greater weight of authority." Lang's response was the article that follows. His stated goal was not to persuade readers of the "cultivated class" that Twain was "an impeccable artist." But Lang did warn them that they ignored *Huckleberry Finn*—a book he confidently called "the great American novel"—at their peril.

On the Art of Mark Twain

The duty of self-examination is frequently urged upon us by moralists. No doubt we should self-examine our minds as well as our conduct now and then, especially when we have passed the age in which we are constantly examined by other people. When I attempt to conduct this delicate inquiry I am puzzled and alarmed at finding that I am losing Culture. I am backsliding, I have not final perseverance, unless indeed it is Culture that is backsliding and getting on to the wrong lines. For I ought to be cultured: it is my own fault if I have not got Culture.

I have been educated till I nearly dropped; I have lived with the earliest Apostles of Culture, in the days when Chippendale was first a name to conjure with, and Japanese art came in like a raging lion, and Ronsard was the favourite poet, and Mr. William Morris was a poet too, and blue and green were the only wear, and the name of Paradise was Camelot. To be sure, I cannot say that I took all this quite seriously, but "we too have played" at it, and know all about it. Generally speaking, I have kept up with Culture. I can talk (if desired) about Sainte-Beuve, and Mérimée, and Félicien Rops; I could rhyme "Ballades," when they were "in," and knew what a *pantoom* was. I am acquainted with the scholia on the Venetus A. I have a pretty taste in Greek gems. I have got beyond the stage of thinking Mr. Cobden Sanderson a greater binder than Bauzonnet. With practice I believe I could do an epigram of Meleager's into a bad imitation of a sonnet by Joachim du Bellay, or a sonnet of Bellay's into a bad imitation of a Greek epigram. I could pass an examination in the works of M. Paul Bourget. And yet I have not Culture. My works are but a tinkling brass, because I have not Culture. For Culture has got into new regions where I cannot enter, and, what is perhaps worse, I find myself delighting in a great many things which are under the ban of Culture.

This is a dreadful position, which makes a man feel like one of those Liberal politicians who are always "sitting on the fence," and who follow their party, if follow it they do, with the reluctant acquiescence of the prophet's donkey. Not that I *do* follow it. I cannot rave with pleasure over Tolstoi, especially as he admits that "The Kreutzer Sonata" is not "only his fun" but a kind of Manifesto. I have tried Hartmann, and I prefer Plato. I don't like poems by young ladies in which the verses neither scan nor rhyme, and the constructions are all linguistically impossible. I am shaky about Blake, though I am stalwart about Mr. Rudyard Kipling.

This is not the worst of it. Culture has hardly a new idol but I long to hurl things at it. Culture can scarcely burn anything, but I am impelled to sacrifice to that same. I am coming to suspect that the majority of Culture's modern disciples are a mere crowd of very slimly educated people, who have no natural taste or impulse; who do not really know the best things in literature; who have a feverish desire to admire the newest thing, to follow the latest artistic fashion; who prate about "style" without the faintest acquaintance with the ancient examples of style, in Greek, French, or English; who talk about the classics and criticise the classical critics and poets, without being able to read a line of them in the original. Nothing of the natural man is left in these people; their intellectual equipment is made up of ignorant vanity, and eager desire of novelty, and a yearning to be in the fashion.

Take, for example—and we have been a long time in coming to him—Mark Twain. If you praise him among persons of Culture, they cannot believe that you are serious. They call him a Barbarian. They won't hear of him, they hurry from the subject; they pass by on the other side of the way. Now I do not mean to assert that Mark Twain is 'an impeccable artist,' but he is just as far from being a mere coarse buffoon. Like other people, he has his limitations. Even Mr. Gladstone, for instance, does not shine as a Biblical critic, nor Mark Twain as a critic of Italian art nor as a guide to the Holy Land. I have abstained from reading his work on an American at the Court of King Arthur, because here Mark Twain is not, and cannot be, at the proper point of view. He has not the knowledge which would enable him to be a sound critic of the ideal of the Middle Ages. An Arthurian Knight in New York or in Washington would find as much to blame, and justly, as a Yankee at Camelot. Let it be admitted that Mark Twain often and often sins against good taste, that some of his waggeries are mechanical, that his books are full of passages which were only good enough for the corner of a newspaper.

If the critics are right who think that art should so far imitate nature as to leave things at loose ends, as it were, not pursuing events to their conclusions, even here 'Huckleberry Finn' should satisfy them. It is the story of the flight down the Mississippi of a white boy and a runaway slave. The stream takes them through the fringes of life on the riverside; they pass feuds and murders of men, and towns full of homicidal loafers, and are intermingled with the affairs of families, and meet friends whom they would wish to be friends always. But the current carries them on: they leave the murders unavenged, the lovers in full flight;

the friends they lose for ever; we do not know, any more than in reality we would know, 'what became of them all.' They do not return, as in novels, and narrate their later adventures.

As to the truth of the life described, the life in little innocent towns, the religion, the Southern lawlessness, the feuds, the lynchings, only persons who have known this changed world can say if it be truly painted, but it looks like the very truth, like an historical document. Already "Huckleberry Finn" is an historical novel, and more valuable, perhaps, to the historian than "Uncle Tom's Cabin," for it is written without partisanship, and without "a purpose." The drawing of character seems to be admirable, unsurpassed in its kind. By putting the tale in the mouth of the chief actor, Huck, Mark Twain was enabled to give it a seriousness not common in his work, and to abstain from comment. Nothing can be more true and more humorous than the narrative of this outcast boy, with a heart naturally good, with a conscience torn between the teachings of his world about slavery and the promptings of his nature. In one point Mark Twain is Homeric, probably without knowing it. In the Odyssey, Odysseus frequently tells a false tale about himself, to account for his appearance and position when disguised on his own island. He shows extraordinary fertility and appropriateness of invention, wherein he is equaled by the feigned tales of Huckleberry Finn. The casual characters met on the way are masterly: the woman who detects Huck in a girl's dress; the fighting families of Shepherdson and Grangerford; the homicidal Colonel Sherborne, who cruelly shoots old Boggs, and superbly quells the mob of would-be lynchers; the various old aunts and uncles; the negro Jim; the two wandering impostors; the hateful father of Huck himself. Then Huck's compliment to Miss Mary Jane, whom he thought of afterwards "a many and a many million times," how excellent it is! "In my opinion she had more sand in her than any girl I ever see; in my opinion she was just full of sand. It sounds like flattery, but it ain't no flattery. And when it comes to beauty—and goodness, too—she lays over them all." No novel has better touches of natural description; the starlit nights on the great river, the storms, the whole landscape, the sketches of little rotting towns, of the woods, of the cotton-fields, are simple, natural, and visible to the mind's eye. The story, to be sure, ends by lapsing into burlesque, when Tom Sawyer insists on freeing the slave whom he knows to be free already, in a manner accordant with "the best authorities." But even the burlesque is redeemed by Tom's real unconscious heroism. There are defects of taste, or passages that to us seem deficient in taste, but the book remains a nearly flawless gem of romance and of humour. The world appreciates it, no doubt, but "cultured critics" are probably unaware of its singular value. A two-shilling novel by Mark Twain, with an ugly picture on the cover, "has no show," as Huck might say, and the great American novel has escaped the eyes of those who watch to see this new planet swim into their ken. And will Mark Twain never write such another? One is enough for him to live by, and for our gratitude, but not enough for our desire.

The Critic (London), 1891

Theodor Herzl

Budapest-born Theodor Herzl (1860–1904), who would become known as the "father of Zionism," was covering the Dreyfus trial in 1894 as the Paris correspondent of the liberal Vienna newspaper *Neue Freie Presse* when he wrote this article about a reading he heard Mark Twain give at the British embassy. That same year, Herzl wrote a play entitled *Das Neue Ghetto* (*The New Ghetto*), which explored Viennese anti-Semitism, and which he hoped would lead to greater tolerance and mutual respect between Jews and Christians. Twain saw the play when it had its premiere in Vienna in 1898, and was so impressed that he immediately began translating it into English. The outbreak of the Spanish-American War, however, created an atmosphere in New York City in which only war-themed plays had much chance of success, so Twain put aside his translation and never finished it.

FROM
Mark Twain in Paris

Here he comes, the most famous jester of two hemispheres. He shakes hands with an old man, who bursts into laughter and whose face lights up with joy. I am sure that all Mark Twain said to him was "good evening," but could one imagine Mark Twain uttering a word that wasn't funny? Well, it is he. A smallish, slim, somewhat slovenly looking man, with artistic grey locks, a thick moustache hanging under a hooked nose, a blank gaze, flabby cheeks, and a pointed chin. This is Mr. Clemens (as he is known in civil life), but I pictured Mark Twain to myself differently; I cannot say how, but not like this—of course, I am not blaming him for it. The outstanding features in that face are his eyebrows—splendid, energetic, bushy, protruding eyebrows that twirl upwards and which indicate at once both the good and the stinging nature in Mark Twain.

His humour is something immense, overpowering, and shattering—great chunks of humour intended for a people that doesn't smile. Once an Englishman makes up his mind to laugh, he means to do so wholeheartedly; he lets himself go, and he laughs until his sides split. And it is this little man who is responsible for this huge laughter wherever the English tongue is spoken, reaching the widest field.

*　　*　　*

It is well worth studying Mark Twain's audience in this elegant hall of Her Majesty's Embassy to see with what respect Mr. Clemens is received, with what respect and veneration. He is indeed a remarkable reader, but Mark Twain's subjects are not suitable for his reading. He makes of them something totally different from what they are intended to be, and it is really funny in itself to see how he spoils his remarkable pieces by his remarkable reading. He is an artist in writing and a master in recitation, but one is nevertheless disappointed because this is not how one pictured his style, which is coarse, dry, surly, with an occasional twinkle under his primeval eyebrows. Little Mr. Clemens is far too sharp and clever, and he seems, strangely enough, bent on obtaining more effect from the reading than from the work itself. I can only surmise that he must be much in demand as a reader and that he has acquired the actor's mannerisms. The more one listens to him, the more one's suspicions grow, and one is inclined to think that every movement is carefully studied, however natural he may actually be—for he is naturalness itself. His very slips are striking for they tend to illustrate the taste of those for whom his mannerisms are assumed. The public want value for their money, and if they pay for a recital, there has to be something in it. This explains why everything is so thickly laid on and so realistically portrayed, why he makes such unnecessary gesticulations when he has not already slipped his hand into his waistcoat pocket, and it also explains why he acts the comedian. Whenever he would express surprise, he staggers backwards, even jumps about, and when he wants to show embarrassment, he rubs his nose, his mouth, and his clean-shaven cheeks. Finally, he scratches his head, and I regret having to record that this gave rise to some annoyance to the public who consisted mainly of English people, unaccustomed to such American familiarity.

*　　*　　*

A certain Samuel Clemens declared here in a bar at No. 7, Rue Montmarte, in the presence of several Americans, that he would see himself hanged if he could not recite Mark Twain's sketches better than any one else. This reached the ears of Lord Dufferin, who took it to be a challenge, and he would certainly have been ashamed of himself had he not taken it up. Advantage was then taken of a charitable occasion in order to give Samuel Clemens an opportunity of proving his claim.

I listened to Samuel Clemens and I will not conceal here my opinion, and there is no reason why I should. Samuel Clemens does not know how to recite Mark Twain's sketches. He may delude the drunkards of Rue Montmarte, but he can't mislead anyone who knows what recitation means. This fellow Samuel Clemens promised to give a reading, but it was anything but a semblance of a reading. The metal spectacles on his nose mean nothing at all, anyone can put metal spectacles on his nose; but to give a recital, why, that is something totally different. Samuel Clemens chose a sketch which is included in Mark Twain's book, "The 1,000,000 Pound Note."

* * *

Samuel Clemens read two other sketches which were much the best, one about the absurdities of the German language and the other about interviews. Everyone is acquainted with the comic side of the German language, and people have laughed themselves silly over split verbs, and isn't it really funny that there should be three articles: der, die, das? Mark Twain, too, hits at the German grammar and pokes fun at it. Foreigners are funny, aren't they? In German, "woman" is neuter, and so on. Here my praise ends, and I want to deal with the sketch about the interviewer. I really can't stand people making fun of my profession, and those who do would be incapable of jotting down on paper five lines fit to print. Mark Twain may be forgiven because he is master of our craft, even though he favoured his own fame to that of others. Ours is a profession that depends on the way it is carried out.

I waited for Samuel Clemens at the exit and I addressed a few kindly words to him: "Clemens, old boy," I said, "I don't want to be personal, but you simply lied when you claimed to be the best reader of Mark Twain. This sort of fraud can only be played on ignorant or genteel folk. Do take on another job. What about boot cleaning? I shall certainly not let you give another reading anywhere else. Mind you, should I ever get to know that you intend to do so, then I shall see to it that I am there, and I must already express my sympathy to you in advance for any injuries which a Medical Police Officer may subsequently testify that you have sustained. I reckon it would mean the loss of an eye, a few teeth, and one or two broken ribs."

We then shook hands and went our ways. I think he must have taken my hint.

Written in 1894, first published in 1903
Translated by Alexander Behr
Mark Twain Quarterly, 1951

William Dean Howells

The remarkable friendship between William Dean Howells (1837–1920) and Mark Twain began when they met in Boston in 1869 in the office of James T. Fields, the editor of the *Atlantic Monthly*. Twain, then 34, had come to thank Fields for the anonymous review the *Atlantic* had published of *The Innocents Abroad* celebrating the book's "delicious impudence." Fields introduced him to the reviewer, a 32-year-old assistant editor named William Dean Howells who, like Twain, hailed from the Midwest. The friendship that began that day ended only with Twain's death over 40 years later. Howells became a confidante, sounding board, sometime collaborator, boon companion, and sage adviser. Howells, who was editor of the *Atlantic Monthly* from 1871 to 1881, accepted Twain's first publication in that prestigious journal—"A True Story, Repeated Word for Word as I Heard It"—in 1874. He continued to review Twain's books as they came out in the *Atlantic* and later in *Harper's*. In 1910 Howells published a volume of reminiscences entitled *My Mark Twain*, a highly personal landmark appraisal of the late author's career. Howells' insightful reviews did much to shape Twain's reputation. In the *Atlantic* in 1872 Howells lauded the "kaleidoscopic succession" of glimpses into the West that *Roughing It* provided, applauding the ways in which "excursions and digressions of all kinds are the very woof of it" with a result that was "not less than triumphant." Writing in the *Atlantic* on *Sketches, New and Old* in 1875, Howells said of "A True Story," "The rugged truth of the sketch leaves all other stories of slave life infinitely far behind, and reveals a gift in the author for the simple, dramatic report of reality which we have seen equaled in no other American writer." In his review of *A Connecticut Yankee* in *Harper's* in 1890 he made the point that "there are passages in which we see the noble of Arthur's day who fattened on the blood and sweat of his bondmen is one in essence with the capitalist" of the present day "who grows rich on the labor of his underpaid wagemen." Howells wrote to Twain in 1899 that "I want to get a chance to somehow write a paper about you, and set myself before posterity as a friend who valued you aright in your own time." Howells got that chance when (on the publication of a uniform edition of Mark Twain's works) he wrote the essay included here; it was the most astute appreciation of Twain's style, method, and achievement published in his lifetime. It could not have appeared at a more opportune moment, for the February 1901 issue of the *North American Review* also contained a contribution from Twain himself: "To the Person Sitting in Darkness." A scorching attack on imperialists of all stripes and the Christian missionaries who gave theological cover to their rapacity and hypocrisy, Twain's essay about the Philippine-American War was his most controversial publication yet. It sparked a firestorm of denunciations from the press. Howells' essay reminded the public that the man whom newspapers across the country were now vilifying as a "traitor" was the same author his countrymen loved, who had added freshness and originality to writing in America, and who was held in a "luminous" regard abroad that "no other American author has enjoyed." He alerted readers of the *North American Review* of a point he would argue even more forcefully in *My Mark Twain*: an "ethic sense" had been at the core of Twain's writings from the start; a seriousness had always hovered not far under the surface of the "drollery."

Mark Twain: An Inquiry

I.

So far as I know Mr. Clemens is the first writer to use in extended writing the fashion we all use in thinking, and to set down the thing that comes into his mind without fear or favor of the thing that went before, or the thing that may be about to follow. I, for instance, in putting this paper together, am anxious to observe some sort of logical order, to discipline such impressions and notions as I have of the subject into a coherent body which shall march column-wise to a conclusion obvious if not inevitable from the start. But Mr. Clemens, if he were writing it, would not be anxious to do any such thing. He would take whatever offered itself to his hand out of that mystical chaos, that divine ragbag, which we call the mind, and leave the reader to look after relevancies and sequences for himself. These there might be, but not of that hard and fast sort which I am eager to lay hold of, and the result would at least be satisfactory to the author, who would have shifted the whole responsibility to the reader, with whom it belongs, at least as much as with the author. In other words, Mr. Clemens uses in work on the larger scale the method of the elder essayists, and you know no more where you are going to bring up in "The Innocents Abroad" or "Following the Equator" than in an essay of Montaigne. The end you arrive at is the end of the book, and you reach it amused but edified, and sorry for nothing but to be there. You have noted the author's thoughts, but not his order of thinking; he has not attempted to trace the threads of association between the things that have followed one another; his reason, not his logic, has convinced you, or rather it has persuaded you, for you have not been brought under conviction. It is not certain that this method is of design with Mr. Clemens; that might spoil it; and possibly he will be as much surprised as any one to know that it is his method. It is imaginable that he pursues it from no wish but to have pleasure of his work, and not to fatigue either himself or his reader; and his method may be the secret of his vast popularity, but it cannot be the whole secret of it. Any one may compose a scrap-book, and offer it to the public with nothing of Mark Twain's good fortune. Everything seems to depend upon the nature of the scraps, after all; his scraps might have been consecutively arranged, in a studied order, and still have immensely pleased; but there is no doubt that people like things that have at least the appearance of not having been drilled into line. Life itself has that sort of appearance as it goes on; it is an essay with moments of drama in it rather than a drama; it is a lesson, with the precepts appearing haphazard, and not precept upon precept; it is a school, but not always a schoolroom; it is a temple, but the priests are not always in their sacerdotal robes; sometimes they are eating the sacrifice behind the altar and pouring the libations for the god through the channels of their dusty old throats. An instinct of something chaotic, ironic, empiric in the order of experience seems to have been the inspiration of our humorist's art, and what finally remains with the reader, after all the joking and laughing, is not merely the feeling of having had a mighty good time, but the conviction that he has got the worth of his money. He has not gone through the six hundred pages of "The Innocents Abroad" or "Following the Equator" without having learned more of the world as the writer saw it than any but the rarest traveller is able to show for his travel; and possibly with his average practical American public, which was his first tribunal, and must always be his court of final appeal, Mark Twain justified himself for being so delightful by being so instructive. If this bold notion is admissible, it seems the moment to say that no writer ever imparted information more inoffensively.

But his great charm is his absolute freedom in a region where most of us are fettered and shackled by immemorial convention. He saunters out into the trim world of letters, and lounges across its neatly kept paths, and walks about on the grass at will, in spite of all the signs that have been put up from the beginning of literature, warning people of dangers and penalties for the slightest trespass.

One of the characteristics I observe in him is his single-minded use of words, which he employs as Grant did to express the plain, straight meaning their common acceptance has given them, with no regard to their structural significance or their philological implications. He writes English as if it were a primitive and not a derivative language, without Gothic or Latin or Greek behind it, or German and French beside it. The result is the English in which the most vital works of English literature are cast, rather than the English of Milton, and Thackeray, and Mr. Henry James. I do not say that the English of the authors last named is less than vital, but only that it is not the most vital. It is scholarly and conscious; it knows who its grandfather was; it has the refinement and subtlety of an old patriciate. You will not have with it the widest suggestion, the largest human feeling, or perhaps the loftiest reach of imagination, but you will have the keen joy that exquisite artistry in words can alone impart, and that you will not have in Mark Twain. What you will have in him is a style which is as personal, as biographical as the style of any one who has written, and expresses a civilization whose courage of the chances, the preferences, the duties, is not the measure of its essential modesty. It has a thing to say, and it says it in the word that may be the first, or second, or third choice, but will not be the instrument of the most fastidious ear, the most delicate and exacting sense, though it will be the word that surely and strongly conveys intention from the author's mind to the reader's. It is the Abraham Lincolnian word, not the Charles Sumnerian; it is American, Western.

II.

Now that Mark Twain has become a fame so world-wide, we should be in some danger of forgetting, but for his help, how entirely American he is, and we have already forgotten, perhaps, how truly Western he is, though his work, from first to last, is always reminding us of the fact. But here I should like to distinguish. It is not alone in its generous humor, with more honest laughter in it than humor ever had in the world till now, that his work is so Western. Any one who has really known the West (and really to know it one must have lived it), is aware of the profoundly serious, the almost tragical strain which is the fundamental tone in the movement of such music as it has. Up to a certain point, in the presence of the mystery which we call life, it trusts and hopes and laughs; beyond that it doubts and fears, but it does not cry. It is more likely to laugh again, and in the work of Mark Twain there is little of the pathos which is supposed to be the ally of humor, little suffusion of apt tears from the smiling eyes. It is too sincere for that sort of play; and if after the doubting and the fearing it laughs again, it is with a suggestion of that resentment which youth feels when the disillusion from its trust and hope comes, and which is the grim second mind of the West in the presence of the mystery. It is not so much the race effect as the region effect; it is not the Anglo-American finding expression; it is the Westerner, who is not more thoroughly the creature of circumstances, of conditions, but far more dramatically their creature, than any prior man. He found himself placed in them and under them, so near to a world in which the natural and primitive was obsolete, that while he could not escape them, neither could he help challenging them. The inventions, the appliances, the improvements of the modern world invaded the hoary eld of his rivers and forests and prairies, and while he was still a pioneer, a hunter, a trapper, he found himself confronted with the financier, the scholar, the gentleman. They seemed to him, with the world they represented, at first very droll, and he laughed. Then they set him thinking, and as he never was afraid of anything, he thought over the whole field, and demanded explanations of all his prepossessions, of equality, of humanity, of representative government and revealed religion. When they had not their answers ready, without accepting the conventions of the modern world as solutions or in any manner final, he laughed again, not mockingly, but patiently, compassionately. Such, or somewhat like this, was the genesis and evolution of Mark Twain.

Missouri was Western, but it was also Southern, not only in the institution of slavery, to the custom and acceptance of which Mark Twain was born and bred without any applied doubt of its divinity, but in the peculiar social civilization of the older South from which his native State was settled. It would be reaching too far out to claim that American humor, of the now prevailing Western type, is of Southern origin, but without staying to attempt it I will say that I think the fact could be established; and I think one of the most notably Southern traits of Mark Twain's humor is its power of seeing the fun of Southern seriousness, but this vision did not come to him till after his liberation from neighborhood in the vaster far West. He was the first, if not the only man of his section, to betray a consciousness of the grotesque absurdities in the Southern inversion of the civilized ideals in behalf of slavery, which must have them upside down in order to walk over them safely. No American of Northern birth or breeding could have imagined the spiritual struggle of Huck Finn in deciding to help the negro Jim to his freedom, even though he should be forever despised as a negro thief in his native town, and perhaps eternally lost through the blackness of his sin. No Northerner could have come so close to the heart of a Kentucky feud, and revealed it so perfectly, with the whimsicality playing through its carnage, or could have so brought us into the presence of the sardonic comi-tragedy of the squalid little river town where the storekeeping magnate shoots down his drunken tormentor in the arms of the drunkard's daughter, and then cows with bitter mockery the mob that comes to lynch him. The strict religiosity compatible in the Southwest with savage precepts of conduct is something that could make itself known in its amusing contrast only to the native Southwesterner, and the

revolt against it is as constant in Mark Twain as the enmity to
New England orthodoxy is in Dr. Holmes. But he does not take
it with such serious resentment as Dr. Holmes is apt to take his
inherited Puritanism, and it may be therefore that he is able to
do it more perfect justice, and impart it more absolutely. At any
rate, there are no more vital passages in his fiction than those
which embody character as it is affected for good as well as evil
by the severity of the local Sunday-schooling and church-going.

III.

I find myself, in spite of the discipline I intend for this paper,
speaking first of the fiction, which by no means came first in
Mark Twain's literary development. It is true that his beginnings
were in short sketches, more or less inventive, and studies of life
in which he let his imagination play freely; but it was not till he
had written "Tom Sawyer" that he could be called a novelist.
Even now I think he should rather be called a romancer, though
such a book as "Huckleberry Finn" takes itself out of the order
of romance and places itself with the great things in picaresque
fiction. Still it is more poetic than picaresque, and of a deeper
psychology. The probable and credible soul that the author di-
vines in the son of the town drunkard is one which we might
each own brother, and the art which portrays this nature at first
hand in the person and language of the hero, without pose or
affectation, is fine art. In the boy's history the author's fancy
works realistically to an end as high as it has reached elsewhere,
if not higher; and I who like "The Connecticut Yankee at King
Arthur's Court" so much have half a mind to give my whole
heart to "Huckleberry Finn."

Both "Huckleberry Finn" and "Tom Sawyer" wander in episodes loosely related to the main story, but they are of a closer
and more logical advance from the beginning to the end than
the fiction which preceded them, and which I had almost forgotten to name before them. We owe to "The Gilded Age" a
type in Colonel Mulberry Sellers which is as likely to endure as
any fictitious character of our time. It embodies the sort of
Americanism which survived through the Civil War, and characterized in its boundlessly credulous, fearlessly adventurous,

unconsciously burlesque excess the period of political and economic expansion which followed the war. Colonel Sellers was,
in some rough sort, the America of that day, which already
seems so remote, and is best imaginable through him. Yet the
story itself was of the fortuitous structure of what may be called
the autobiographical books, such as "The Innocents Abroad"
and "Roughing It." Its desultory and accidental character was
heightened by the cooperation of Mr. Clemens's fellow humorist, Charles Dudley Warner, and such coherence as it had was
weakened by the diverse qualities of their minds and their irreconcilable ideals in literature. These never combined to a sole
effect or to any variety of effects that left the reader very clear
what the story was all about; and yet from the cloudy solution
was precipitated at least one character which, as I have said,
seems of as lasting substance and lasting significance as any
which the American imagination has evolved from the American environment.

If Colonel Sellers is Mr. Clemens's supreme invention, as it
seems to me, I think that his "The Connecticut Yankee" is his
greatest achievement in the way of a greatly imagined and sym-
metrically developed romance. Of all the fanciful schemes in
fiction it pleases me most, and I give myself with absolute delight to its notion of a keen East Hartford Yankee finding himself, by a retroactionary spell, at the court of King Arthur of
Britain, and becoming part of the sixth century with all the customs and ideas of the nineteenth in him and about him. The
field for humanizing satire which this scheme opens is illimit-
able; but the ultimate achievement, the last poignant touch, the
most exquisite triumph of the book, is the return of the Yankee
to his own century, with his look across the gulf of the ages, at
the period of which he had been a part and his vision of the sixth-
century woman he had loved holding their child in her arms.

It is a great fancy, transcending in æsthetic beauty the invention in "The Prince and Pauper," with all the delightful and affecting implications of that charming fable, and excelling the
heartrending story in which Joan of Arc lives and prophesies
and triumphs and suffers. She is, indeed, realized to the modern
sense as few figures of the past have been realized in fiction; and

is none the less of her time and of all time because her supposititious historian is so recurrently of ours. After Sellers, and Huck Finn, and Tom Sawyer, and the Connecticut Yankee she is the author's finest creation; and if he had succeeded in portraying no other woman nature, he would have approved himself its fit interpreter in her. I do not think he succeeds so often with that nature as with the boy nature or the man nature, apparently because it does not interest him so much. He will not trouble himself to make women talk like women at all times; oftentimes they talk too much like him, though the simple, homely sort express themselves after their kind; and Mark Twain does not always write men's dialogue so well as he might. He is apt to burlesque the lighter colloquiality, and it is only in the more serious and most tragical junctures that his people utter themselves with veracious simplicity and dignity. That great, burly fancy of his is always tempting him to the exaggeration which is the condition of so much of his personal humor, but which when it invades the drama spoils the illusion. The illusion renews itself in the great moments, but I wish it could be kept intact in the small, and I blame him that he does not rule his fancy better. His imagination is always dramatic in its conceptions, but not always in its expressions; the talk of his people is often inadequate caricature in the ordinary exigencies, and his art contents itself with makeshift in the minor action. Even in "Huck Finn," so admirably proportioned and honestly studied, you find a piece of lawless extravagance hurled in, like the episode of the two strolling actors in the flat-boat; their broad burlesque is redeemed by their final tragedy—a prodigiously real and moving passage—but the friend of the book cannot help wishing the burlesque was not there. One laughs and then despises oneself for laughing, and this is not what Mark Twain often makes you do. There are things in him that shock, and more things that we think shocking, but this may not be so much because of their nature as because of our want of naturalness; they wound our conventions rather than our convictions. As most women are more the subjects of convention than men, his humor is not for most women; but I have a theory that when women like it they like it far beyond men. Its very excess must satisfy that demand of their insatiate nerves for something that there is enough of; but I offer this conjecture with instant readiness to withdraw it under correction. What I feel rather surer of is that there is something finally feminine in the inconsequence of his ratiocination, and his beautiful confidence that we shall be able to follow him to his conclusion in all those turnings and twistings and leaps and bounds, by which his mind carries itself to any point but that he seems aiming at. Men, in fact, are born of women, and possibly Mark Twain owes his literary method to the colloquial style of some far ancestress who was more concerned in getting there, and amusing herself on the way, than in ordering her steps.

Possibly also it is to this ancestress that he owes the instinct of right and wrong which keeps him clear as to the conditions that formed him and their injustice. Slavery in a small Missouri River town could not have been the dignified and patriarchal institution which Southerners of the older South are fond of remembering or imagining. In the second generation from Virginia ancestry of this sort, Mark Twain was born to the common necessity of looking out for himself, and while making himself practically of another order of things he felt whatever was fine in the old and could regard whatever was ugly and absurd more tolerantly, more humorously than those who bequeathed him their enmity to it. Fortunately for him, and for us who were to enjoy his humor, he came to his intellectual consciousness in a world so large and free and safe that he could be fair to any wrong while seeing the right so unfailingly; and nothing is finer in him than his gentleness with the error which is simply passive and negative. He gets fun out of it, of course, but he deals almost tenderly with it, and hoards his violence for the superstitions and traditions which are arrogant and active. His pictures of that old river town, Southwestern life, with its faded and tattered aristocratic ideals and its squalid democratic realities, are pathetic, while they are so unsparingly true and so inapologetically and unaffectedly faithful.

The West, when it began to put itself into literature, could do so without the sense, or the apparent sense, of any older or politer world outside of it; whereas the East was always looking fearfully over its shoulder at Europe, and anxious to account for itself as well as represent itself. No such anxiety as this entered Mark Twain's mind, and it is not claiming too much for the Western influence upon American literature to say that the final liberation of the East from this anxiety is due to the West, and to its ignorant courage or its indifference to its difference from the rest of the world. It would not claim to be superior, as the South did, but it could claim to be humanly equal, or rather it would make no claim at all, but would simply be, and what it was, show itself without holding itself responsible for not being something else.

The Western boy of forty or fifty years ago grew up so close to the primeval woods or fields that their inarticulate poetry became part of his being, and he was apt to deal simply and uncritically with literature when he turned to it, as he dealt with nature. He took what he wanted, and left what he did not like; he used it for the playground, not the workshop of his spirit. Something like this I find true of Mark Twain in peculiar and uncommon measure. I do not see any proof in his books that he wished at any time to produce literature, or that he wished to reproduce life. When filled up with an experience that deeply interested him, or when provoked by some injustice or absurdity that intensely moved him, he burst forth, and the outbreak might be altogether humorous, but it was more likely to be humorous with a groundswell of seriousness carrying it profoundly forward. In all there is something curiously, not very definably, elemental, which again seems to me Western. He behaves himself as if he were the first man who was ever up against the proposition in hand. He deals as newly, for instance, with the relations of Shelley to his wife, and with as personal and direct an indignation as if they had never attracted critical attention before; and this is the mind or the mood which he brings to all literature. Life is another affair with him; it is not a discovery, not a surprise; every one else knows how it is; but here is a new world, and he explores it with a ramping joy, and shouts for the reader to come on and see how, in spite of all the lies about it, it is the same old world of men and women, with really nothing in it but their passions and prejudices and hypocrisies. At heart he was always deeply and essentially romantic, and once must have expected life itself to be a fairy dream. When it did not turn out so he found it tremendously amusing still, and his expectation not the least amusing thing in it, but without rancor, without grudge or bitterness in his disillusion, so that his latest word is as sweet as his first. He is deeply and essentially romantic in his literary conceptions, but when it comes to working them out he is helplessly literal and real; he is the impassioned lover, the helpless slave of the concrete. For this reason, for his wish, his necessity, first to ascertain his facts, his logic is as irresistible as his laugh.

IV.

All life seems, when he began to find it out, to have the look of a vast joke, whether the joke was on him or on his fellow beings, or if it may be expressed without any irreverence, on their common creator. But it was never wholly a joke, and it was not long before his literature began to own its pathos. The sense of this is not very apparent in "Innocents Abroad," but in "Roughing It" we began to be distinctly aware of it, and in the successive books it is constantly imminent, not as a clutch at the heartstrings, but as a demand of common justice, common sense, the feeling of proportion. It is not sympathy with the under dog merely as under dog that moves Mark Twain; for the under dog is sometimes rightfully under. But the probability is that it is wrongfully under, and has a claim to your inquiry into the case which you cannot ignore without atrocity. Mark Twain never ignores it; I know nothing finer in him than his perception that in this curiously contrived mechanism men suffer for their sorrows rather oftener than they suffer for their sins; and when they suffer for their sorrows they have a right not only to our pity, but to our help. He always gives his help, even when he seems to leave the pity to others, and it may be safely said that no writer has dealt with so many phases of life with more unfailing justice. There is no real telling how any one comes to be what he is; all speculation concerning the fact is more or less impudent or futile conjecture; but it is conceivable that Mark Twain took from his early environment the custom of clairvoyance in things in which most humorists are purblind, and that, being always in the presence of the under dog, he came to feel for him as under with him. If the knowledge and vision of slavery did not tinge all life with potential tragedy, perhaps it was this which lighted in the future humorist the indignation at injustice which glows in his page. His indignation relieves itself as often as not in a laugh; injustice is the most ridiculous thing in the world, after all, and indignation with it feels its own absurdity.

It is supposable, if not more than supposable, that the ludicrous incongruity of a slave-holding democracy nurtured upon the Declaration of Independence, and the comical spectacle of white labor owning black labor, had something to do in quickening the sense of contrast which is the mountain of humor or is said to be so. But not to drive too hard a conjecture which must remain conjecture, we may reasonably hope to find in the untrammelled, the almost unconditional life of the later and farther West, with its individualism limited by nothing but individualism, the outside causes of the first overflow of the spring. We are so fond of classification, which we think is somehow interpretation, that one cannot resist the temptation it holds out in the case of the most unclassifiable things; and I must yield so far as to note that the earliest form of Mark Twain's work is characteristic of the greater part of it. The method used in "Innocents Abroad" and in "Roughing It" is the method used in "Life on the Mississippi," in "A Tramp Abroad" and in "Following the Equator," which constitute in bulk a good half of all his writings, as they express his dominant æsthetics. If he had written the fictions alone, we should have had to recognize a rare inventive talent, a great imagination and dramatic force; but I think it must be allowed that the personal books named overshadow the fictions. They have the qualities that give character to the fictions, and they have advantages that the fictions have not and that no fiction can have. In them, under cover of his pseudonym, we come directly into the presence of the author, which is what the reader is always longing and seeking to do; but unless the novelist is a conscienceless and tasteless recreant to the terms of his art, he cannot admit the reader to his intimacy. The personal books of Mark Twain have not only the charm of the essay's inconsequent and desultory method, in which invention, fact, reflection and philosophy wander in after one another in any following that happens, but they are of an immediate and most informal hospitality which admits you at once to the author's confidence, and makes you frankly welcome not only to his thought, but to his way of thinking. He takes no trouble in the matter, and he asks you to take none. All that he requires is that you will have common sense, and be able to tell a joke when you see it. Otherwise the whole furnishing of his mental mansion is at your service, to make such use as you can of it, but he will not be always directing your course or requiring you to enjoy yourself in this or that order.

In the case of the fictions he conceives that his first affair is to tell a story, and a story when you are once launched upon it does not admit of deviation without some hurt to itself. In Mark Twain's novels, whether they are for boys or for men, the episodes are only those that illustrate the main narrative or relate to it, though he might have allowed himself somewhat larger latitude in the old-fashioned tradition which he has oftenest observed in them. When it comes to the critical writings, which again are personal, and which, whether they are criticisms of literature or of life, are always so striking, he is quite relentlessly logical and coherent. Here there is no lounging or sauntering, with entertaining or edifying digressions. The object is in view from the first, and the reasoning is straightforwardly to it throughout. This is as notable in the admirable paper on the Jews, or on the Austrian situation, as in that on Harriet Shelley or that on Cooper's novels. The facts are first ascertained with a conscience uncommon in critical writing of any kind, and then they are handled with vigor and precision till the polemic is over. It does not so much matter whether you agree with the critic or not; what you have to own is that here is a man of strong convictions, clear ideas and ardent sentiments, based mainly upon common sense of extraordinary depth and breadth.

V.

In fact, what finally appeals to you in Mark Twain, and what may hereafter be his peril with his readers, is his common sense. It is well to eat humble pie when one comes to it at the *table d'hôte* of life, and I wish here to offer my brother literary men a piece of it that I never refuse myself. It is true that other men do not really expect much common sense of us, whether we are poets or novelists or humorists. They may enjoy our company, and they may like us or pity us, but they do not take us very seriously, and they would as soon we were fools as not if we will only divert or comfort or inspire them. Especially if we are humorists do they doubt our practical wisdom; they are apt at first sight to take our sense for a part of the joke, and the humorist who convinces them that he is a man of as much sense as any of them, and possibly more, is in the parlous case of having given them hostages for seriousness which he may not finally be able to redeem.

I should say in the haste to which every inquiry of this sort seems subject that this was precisely the case with Mark Twain. The exceptional observer must have known from the beginning that he was a thinker of courageous originality and penetrating sagacity, even when he seemed to be joking; but in the process of time it has come to such a pass with him that the wayfaring man can hardly shirk knowledge of the fact. The fact is thrown into sudden and picturesque relief by his return to his country after a lapse of time long enough to have let a new generation grow up in knowledge of him. The projection of his reputation against a background of foreign appreciation, more or less luminous, such as no other American author has enjoyed, has little or nothing to do with his acceptance on the new terms. Those poor Germans, Austrians, Englishmen and Frenchmen who have been, from time to time in the last ten years, trying to show their esteem for his peculiar gifts could never come as close to the heart of his humor as we could; we might well doubt if they could fathom all his wisdom, which begins and ends in his humor; and if ever they seemed to chance upon his full significance, we naturally felt a kind of grudge, when we could not call it their luck, and suspected him of being less significant in the given instances than they supposed. The danger which he now runs with us is neither heightened nor lessened by the spread of his fame, but is an effect from intrinsic causes. Possibly it might not have been so great if he had come back comparatively forgotten; it is certain only that in coming back more remembered than ever, he confronts a generation which began to know him not merely by his personal books and his fiction, but by those criticisms of life and literature which have more recently attested his interest in the graver and weightier things.

Graver and weightier, people call them, but whether they are really more important than the lighter things, I am by no means sure. What I am amused with, independently of the final truth, is the possibility that his newer audience will exact this serious mood of Mr. Clemens, whereas we of his older world only suffered it, and were of a high conceit with our liberality in allowing a humorist sometimes to be a philosopher. Some of us, indeed, not to be invidiously specific as to whom, were always aware of potentialities in him, which he seemed to hold in check, or to trust doubtfully to his reader as if he thought they might be thought part of the joke. Looking back over his work now, the later reader would probably be able to point out to earlier readers the evidence of a constant growth in the direction of something like recognized authority in matters of public import, especially those that were subject to the action of the public conscience as well as the public interest, until now hardly any man writing upon such matters is heard so willingly by all sorts of men. All of us, for instance, have read somewhat of the conditions in South Africa which have eventuated in the present effort of certain British politicians to destroy two free Republics in the interest of certain British speculators; but I doubt if we have found the case anywhere so well stated as in the closing chapters of Mark Twain's "Following the Equator." His estimate of the military character of the belligerents on either side is of the prophetic cast which can come only from the thorough assimilation of accomplished facts; and in those passages the student of the actual war can spell its anticipative history. It is by such handling of such questions, unpremeditated and almost casual as it seems, that Mark Twain has won his claim to be heard on any public matter, and achieved the odd sort of primacy which he now enjoys.

But it would be rather awful if the general recognition of his prophetic function should implicate the renunciation of the humor that has endeared him to mankind. It would be well for his younger following to beware of reversing the error of the elder, and taking everything in earnest, as these once took nothing in earnest from him. To reverse that error would not be always to find his true meaning, and perhaps we shall best arrive at this by shunning each other's mistakes. In the light of the more modern appreciation, we elders may be able to see some things seriously that we once thought pure drolling, and from our experience his younger admirers may learn to receive as drolling some things that they might otherwise accept as preaching. What we all should wish to do is to keep Mark Twain what he has always been: a comic force unique in the power of charming us out of our cares and troubles, united with as potent an ethic sense of the duties, public and private, which no man denies in himself without being false to other men. I think we may hope for the best he can do to help us deserve our self-respect, without forming Mark Twain societies to read philanthropic meanings into his jokes or studying the Jumping Frog as the allegory of an imperializing Republic. I trust the time may be far distant when the Meditation at the Tomb of Adam shall be memorized and declaimed by ingenuous youth as a mystical appeal for human solidarity.

North American Review, 1901

Pencil sketch of Mark Twain by Samuel Johnson Woolf, 1906. From S. J. Woolf, *Drawn from Life* (New York and London: Whittlesey House, 1932)

Ángel Guerra

Ángel Guerra (José Betancort Cabrera) (1874–1950) was a member of the Generation of 1898, a group of Spanish writers who sought to regenerate their culture and society. Guerra was a prominent journalist in Madrid known for his sharp social critiques as well as his novels, poetry, and comic operas. This essay was his prologue to a collection of translated short stories by Mark Twain published in Spain. The stories that piqued his interest, and that he writes about here, include "The Story of the Bad Little Boy" and "The Story of the Good Little Boy." Guerra may have had occasion to recall the challenges these two stories posed to conventional ideas of morality, and reward and punishment, years later during his six-year stint as director of prisons in Spain, when he strove to reform the penal system by paying greater attention to prisoner education and preparation for re-entry into society.

FROM

Prólogo: *Mark Twain Cuentos Escogidos*
(Prologue to *Mark Twain: Selected Tales*)

The truth is that nobody, neither Saxons nor Germans, has learned to laugh and cry at the same time like our Cervantes. The gentleman from La Mancha is the symbol of the eternal ups and downs of life, the strange marriage of happy and painful adventures that mark the enterprises of men. Nobody has achieved the level of humor that he reached. One would say that in those admirable pages, to the pleasure of the muses and the astonishment of readers, pain laughs and laughter cries. Hand in hand, these two human sentiments walk together and become one. What reader of Cervantes could trace the border that separates them?

* * *

The art of the humorist must encompass the ideas of a thinker. It is difficult and balanced. . . . Are there ideas that seem indestructible? The humorist mocks them and shows how fragile they are. Are there sentiments reputed to be solid? He shows how easily they can be subverted. Revealed through humor, the heroes of legend are audacious clods; those the public thinks of as wicked show themselves to be men with heart, true heroes, just as sanctity proves to be egoism and genius madness; everything subverted and spoiled.

Illogical, they demonstrate implacable logic; violators of established laws, they behave as if they upheld them. But at bottom, the contradiction warns us that everything is false, and surrenders to its own sorrow.

There is nothing in consciousness or in life that is invulnerable like the heel of Achilles. The social laws we respect are our own invention; the ideas we revere as inviolable were born from the *sport* of human thought, which then turned them into its tyrant.

Such is the reasoning of humor, and with great virtuosity of expression it raises this critical spirit to the level of literary art. It seems a trivial, monstrous, extravagant art, and yet it is strong, great-hearted, moralizing and combative.

Of all those who cultivate it, I know of none superior to Mark Twain. His work is admirable and his reputation universal. All that I have read from his pen is of the purest and most genuine Anglo-Saxon humor. It is sober, caustic, and pleasant, without any tendency toward frightful visions. Its meditations divert and do not elicit shudders. But at bottom it is cruel and bitter. He is a philosopher whose speech imitates the wild dreaminess of a poet.

*   *   *

I know many of Mark Twain's stories from having read them before; others by leafing through them now.

None has failed to teach me something.

Mark Twain's stories cheer the heart of the reader, make him laugh a good healthy laugh; but after reading them, the spirit is detained for a moment playing with a mischievous idea that continues to twist around inside it, and joviality little by little turns meditative.

To give a living demonstration that in this world everything is topsy-turvy, and that in the struggle for existence, the more ignorant a man is, the more money and fame he acquires, Twain tells us how he edited an agricultural periodical without understanding anything of that science. He wrote notable nonsense: that the guano is a beautiful bird, or that turnips suffer terribly because they are not gathered by shaking them from the tree; but the magazine sold and made money. Are not those who have failed in art the ones who wield the most authority and power in the republic of letters?

*   *   *

And what about social morality, cataloguing instances and classifying them?

Jim is a bad boy; his actions are reprehensible in terms of morality and custom, and his guilt ought to lead to punishment; but the reality of life demonstrates the contrary, giving him good fortune for every blameworthy act, while Jacob Blivens, the good boy, who always acts in accordance with established moral principles, sees all his efforts turn out badly; he expects to be recompensed for his virtue and is always amazed to discover that life rewards him with misfortune.

*   *   *

In this careful amalgamation of the burlesque and the tragic, the macabre and the laughable, the ironic and the sentimental, Mark Twain artfully produces a humor that is thoroughly salutary and comforting.

Translated by Edward M. Test
Prólogo, Mark Twain: Cuentos Escogidos, 1912

Livia Bruni

Livia Bruni was an Italian writer who published a volume of her translations of Mark Twain's stories in 1906. She had previously included some of her translations of Twain's work in this appreciative article about him that appeared in the journal *Nuova Antologia* the year before. Rather than take offense at Twain's negative descriptions of Italy in *The Innocents Abroad*, Bruni credits him with not being completely wrong about her country. When Bruni was writing this article, Twain had just moved to Florence for his wife's health. Livy Clemens died there in June 1904. There is sad irony in the hope that Bruni expressed, at the close of her article, that the "green tranquility of the Florentine villa where he is presently residing" will inspire him to be creative and productive. Twain's stay in Florence turned out to be one of the grimmest periods of his life.

FROM

L'Umorismo Americano: Mark Twain
(American Humor: Mark Twain)

A certain variety of light, good-hearted and spirited sarcasm, often present in many British and American writers, and in a few German writers, constitutes what is called humor. This English word, that no other language has as yet made its own, only adding the derivatives *umorismo* and *umorista*, evokes in our minds the grateful memory of many pages of Sterne and Dickens, of Douglas Jerrold and Charles Browne, of John Habberton and Mark Twain, to touch on the youngest and most recent.

Humor does not have the sparkling effervescence of French wit . . . nor is it an expression of the frank joy which can be found in Boccaccio and Berni, and in so many pages of the inexhaustible Rabelais.

Humor, instead, is something finer, more philosophical and above all more suggestive, always slightly sarcastic and often accompanied by an involuntary feeling of quiet sadness. The humorist knows how to capture the comic, ridiculous aspect of a weakness, an idiosyncrasy, a moral aberration, and quietly ridicules it, maintaining a calm composure that serves to intensify the effect of the joke.

There is no literary treatise to define this kind of wit; indeed, it would be exceedingly difficult. For how can you analyze the subtle magic that makes you smile when reading certain scenes of Shakespeare, certain pages of Cervantes, or of Manzoni? Instead, definitions abound for that which the French call *esprit* and the English wit. For Samuel Johnson, wit is a faculty of the mind that unexpectedly combines dissimilar ideas. In his discussion of Berni, Peruzzi observes that the main quality of his work is the genius with which Berni finds resemblances between entirely different things, and the felicitous use of unusual metaphors and comparisons, sometimes sublime and sometimes ridiculous when considered in connection with the subject they refer to.

But the humorist is not content with these artifices alone. His objective is not to surprise us with unexpected associations of labored brillance, but to conquer us gradually. He knows how to deceive us into thinking at first that what he says is serious, only later to make us laugh without our being able to see how he did it.

It is here that American writers prove to be imaginatively at the height of their inventive powers. They display an almost childish joy together with a quizzical good humor that delights in exaggeration, in impossibilities, in endless oddities, an infinite art of not expressing the thought at once, but of veiling it subtly, with the underlying intent of engaging both the subject and the reader of his discourse.

Take for example, the following passage where Mark Twain describes the life of the people of Civitavecchia as it used to be, and fortunately no longer is. (This passage comes from the second half of chapter 25.) [of *Innocents Abroad*]

This Civita Vecchia is the finest nest of dirt, vermin and ignorance we have found yet, except that African perdition they call Tangier, which is just like it. The people here live in alleys two yards wide, which have a smell about them which is peculiar but not entertaining. It is well the alleys are not wider, because they hold as much smell now as a person can stand, and of course, if they were wider they would hold more, and then the people would die. These alleys are paved with stone, and carpeted with deceased cats, and decayed rags, and decomposed vegetable-tops, and remnants of old boots, all soaked with dish-water, and the people sit around on stools and enjoy it. They are indo-lent, as a general thing, and yet have few pastimes. They work two or three hours at a time, but not hard, and then they knock off and catch flies. This does not require any tal-ent, because they only have to grab—if they do not get the one they are after, they get another. It is all the same to them. They have no partialities. Whichever one they get is the one they want. They have other kinds of insects, but it does not make them arrogant. They are very quiet, unpre-tending people. They have more of these kind of things than other communities, but they do not boast.

One thing to bear in mind about Anglo-Saxon humor is that it is always wholesome and not obscene. In Italy and France, wit is too often based on obscenity. True humor avoids low-cut dresses and lewd expressions because they are vulgar. The most gifted, prolific, and well known American humorist is Mark Twain.

*   *   *

Considering that Twain had no classical education, that he led a simple life in backward surroundings, that he had abso-lutely no preparation for the new unknown territory in which he found himself, the unexpected reactions of his unworldly mind to the wonders of European culture are understandable. Most of the time Mark Twain felt like a fish out of water, and after hundreds of pages full of lively descriptions of the natural beauty of the countries he visited, which he was most sensitive to, it becomes clear that he has decided not to be surprised by anything. Major works of art left him cold; he was unmoved by historical memoirs; he often took issue with accepted beliefs, and I agree with Bentzon who states that often what Mark Twain has to say about his travels is much more amusing than he could have realized.

In addition to their being a financial success for the author, both books are extremely interesting and fully deserve the praise they have received and continue to receive.

Clemens' literary productivity was indeed remarkable, and his vein inexhaustible. Sketches, lectures, travel writings, newspaper articles all flowed readily from his pen, but the best works are the autobiographical sketches like *Innocents Abroad*, *Life on the Mississippi*, and *Roughing It*. . . . It is not difficult to imagine the unusual characters and odd episodes that he was able to observe. With calm and cheerful philosophy, he describes life outside the law and without social conventions. Quakers and Indians, Mormons and gold prospectors, soldiers and ministers, swindlers and murderers, journalists and Negroes all parade freely in his pages among lively descriptions of mines and valleys, remote sierras and snow-covered mountain peaks, virgin forests and isolated mountain lakes, whose quiet beauty sets vibrating in the humorist's style that poetic note that we all feel at times echoing in our soul.

Needless to say Mark Twain's jokes are never licentious. His wit never shines at the expense of modesty, nor offends any belief, which is no small merit these days.

*   *   *

Twain's international reputation is all the more surprising because his works are not easily translated. The strength of his writing is due mainly to his use of colorful idioms and words that had only recently entered into the spoken language, not to mention a vibrant, edgy style which loses its effectiveness when rendered in a foreign language.

*   *   *

Despite a late start, by traveling frequently and maintaining contact with all that European intellectual life had to offer, Twain has become remarkably well-informed; and, always the democrat, his mind has become more liberal toward all that is not North American. In fact, many of his most biting remarks are send-ups of American prejudices. He is, perhaps, no longer so smug and haughty in his disdain of present-day Europe, which despite its many weaknesses does have some advantages over the United States: life in Europe may be less lucrative, but there is less turmoil and less intellectual and emotional frustration. At present, Europe has a real fascination for Twain, especially France and Italy. And to think how he mistreated Italians in his early travel writings! But maybe he wasn't all that wrong, given the miserable situation of our country! Now he has made amends, and the new nation has all his sympathy. Since he is never idle, we shall soon see if, in green tranquility of the Florentine villa where he is presently residing, he will be inspired by beautiful, delicate Florence. If so, we hope his inspiration will be as it was in the past, bold and merry, and without too many sociological or technical theses.

We are happy to conclude these lines by saying that he has the honor of having remained an enthusiast for liberty, truth, and justice, a staunch enemy of every kind of oppression, and that such sentiments have inspired hundreds of generous pages and justly procured for him the sympathies of countless people of every country, every faith, and every political party: the highest praise and the ultimate reward of a conscience as honest and an activity as tireless as his.

Translated by Patricia Thompson Rizzo
Nuova Antologia (Rome), 1905

George Bernard Shaw

Playwright and critic George Bernard Shaw (1856–1950) was introduced to Mark Twain in London in 1907. Twain had come to England to receive an honorary degree from Oxford, and he had taken
the same boat and train as Archibald Henderson, Shaw's biographer,
who introduced the two writers at the railroad station where they
bantered for the benefit of the crowd of journalists that surrounded
them. Shaw invited Twain to have lunch at his flat in Adelphi Terrace a week or two later. Twain was immediately taken with Shaw—
"that brilliant Irishman," as he later referred to him—and the two
became fast friends. "Shaw is a pleasant man," Twain wrote in an
autobiographical dictation, "simple, direct, sincere, animated; but
self-possessed, sane, and evenly poised, acute, engaging, compan-
ionable, and quite destitute of affectation. I liked him." Shaw wrote
to Henderson that "I consider Mark Twain America's greatest writer
by far." Shaw observed that Twain "had a complete gift of intimacy
which enabled us to treat one another as if we had known one another
all our lives, as indeed I had known him through his early books,
which I had read and revelled in before I was twelve years old."

Letter to Samuel L. Clemens

10 Adelphi Terrace WC
3rd July 1907

My dear Mark Twain—not to say Dr Clemens (though I
have always regarded Clemens as mere raw material—
might have been your brother or your uncle)

Just a line to excuse myself for running away today. A domestic bargain was made to the effect that I should not keep you all
to myself; so I cleared out to give Charlotte & Max a good turn.
I had my reward at the dentist's.

I meant to ask you whether you had ever met William Morris. I wont ask you now, because it would put you to the trouble
of answering this letter; so let it stand over until I look you up
in America. But what put it into my head was this. Once, when
I was in Morris's house, a superior anti-Dickens sort of man
(sort of man that thinks Dickens no gentleman) was annoyed

by Morris disparaging Thackeray. With studied gentleness he asked whether Morris could name a greater master of English. Morris promptly said "Mark Twain." This delighted me extremely, as it was my own opinion; and I then found that Morris was an incurable Huckfinomaniac. This was the more remarkable, as Morris would have regarded the Yankee at the Court of King Arthur as blasphemy, and would have blown your head off for implying that the contemporaries of Joan of Arc could touch your own contemporaries in villainy.

I am persuaded that the future historian of America will find your works as indispensable to him as a French historian finds the political tracts of Voltaire. I tell you so because I am the author of a play [*John Bull's Other Island*] in which a priest says "Telling the truth's the funniest joke in the world," a piece of wisdom which you helped to teach me.

yours ever
G. Bernard Shaw

Marina Tsvetaeva

Marina Tsvetaeva (1892–1941) is now regarded as one of the best Russian poets of the 20th century—certainly one of the most original poets of her era and a writer who helped carve out new roles for women in the arts in the Soviet Union. Tsvetaeva's work, which was not well regarded by Stalin, began to be rehabilitated only in the 1960s. Her Moscow childhood was punctuated by frequent and often violent family arguments, and her poetic aspirations were belittled and discouraged. During these stressful years the family set of Mark Twain's works—books bound in red cloth—were key to her escape into the world of her imagination. In 1908 she studied literature at the Sorbonne and became aware of the dramatic innovations that the Russian symbolist poets were developing. She wrote "Books Bound in Red" in 1909 and included it in her first book of poems, *Evening Album* (Vechernii Al'bom), which she published herself. Tsvataeva went on to write plays in verse, narrative poems, novellas, and ten collections of lyric poems, some of the best known of which are satirical. Her work was admired by poets such as Osip Mandelstam, Boris Pasternak, Rainer Maria Rilke, Anna Akhmatova, and Joseph Brodsky. Dmitri Shostakovich set six of Tsvetaeva's poems to music.

Книги в красном переплёте
(Books Bound In Red)

From paradise of children's lives
You're sending me a farewell greeting,
Friends who never betrayed
In frayed red bindings.
Each time my homework was complete
I would hurry off to meet you again.
"It's late!"—"Oh Mama, just ten lines!" . . .
And happily Mama was forgetful.
Light glitters on the chandelier . . .
How good to sit with a book at home!
Listening to Grieg, Schumann, and Kui
I learnt about the fate of Tom.

It's getting dark . . . The air is fresh . . .
Tom is happy with Becky and full of faith.
And Joe the Indian with a torch
Is wandering in the cave's darkness . . .
A graveyard . . . Owl's prophetic hoot . . .
(I'm scared!) Coming over tussocks
Is the prim widow's foster child
Who lives in a barrel like Diogenes.
Sun's throne room is getting light,
A crown over a slender boy . . .
Look: pauper! Lord! He uttered,
"Wait, I'm the heir to the throne!"
Lost in the dark who came from it.
Britain's fate is sad . . .
—Oh why can't I fall asleep again
Under the lamp among red books?
O golden times,
Where one's gaze is brave and clear!
O golden names
Huck Finn, Tom Sawyer, Prince and Pauper!

Translated by Yuri Tretyakov
Evening Album (Vechernii Al'bom), 1910

Johannes V. Jensen

Danish novelist, poet, and essayist Johannes V. Jensen (1873–1950) is often considered the first great modern Danish author. Three decades after he wrote this essay on Mark Twain, which ran as an editorial in the Copenhagen newspaper *Politiken* just after Twain's death, Jensen won the Nobel Prize in Literature. The citation recognized "the rare strength and fertility of his poetic imagination," combined with "an intellectual curiosity of wide scope and a bold, freshly creative style." Like Twain, Jensen worked as a journalist for many years, and also traveled widely, to Asia and to the United States. It is not surprising that he particularly valued Twain's travel books about Europe—although he thought they were a bit marred by the "sticky American parochialism" that still adhered to them. It was the *vitality* of Twain's work above all that held the greatest appeal for Jensen. Indeed, he prided himself on having imparted something akin to that vitality to his own country's literature: "After extensive journeys to the East, to Malaya and China, and several visits to the United States, I inspired a change in the Danish literature and press by introducing English and American vigour, which was to replace the then dominant trend of decadent Gallicism."

Mark Twain

With Mark Twain we have lost one of the most distinctive figures of our time, and he takes with him an America which already is no longer. But in his works, in which culture and lack of culture wrestle in a gallant mind, there are concerns that will survive.

So far he is certainly *not* forgotten. We all have our own Mark Twain, just as we presumably at one time had our own Wessel, possibly without our having read either one. They are both among the great joking hoaxers, whose stories are in the air, and whose characters become legends. "Mark Twain"—when his name is invoked, who does not feel an irresistible urge to retell one of his anecdotes, and in the reflection of his comic wit, to enjoy the triumph when people laugh? There is deadly, lethal material in Mark Twain's humor, for we can all die from laughing. With all his devilish skepticism he was, however, so sound and so adversely positive that his laughter always soothes, never harms.

In Europe it is, I believe, a common misunderstanding to consider Mark Twain a lightweight wag, the incarnation of the Yankee's rude and ludicrous mood, such as it is demonstrated in a bar with a pioneer's May-fly joke. It is gone the moment the glass is empty and everybody has left. Mark Twain was more. He was actually a moralist and his preferences set up guideposts. That he himself thought he was reaching profound depths in his art is revealed when he portentously and "heavily armed" acts the part of the teacher of ethics in the most rigid and least-read periodicals in America. On those occasions he is insufferable and really has nothing to communicate—because that is not his style. Mark Twain did not become a moralist by preaching to us, but by what he disparaged.

He belongs, nevertheless, among those who have a great gift. As a talented performer, he reminds us of the clown in the circus who rakes in laughter just by entering, and yet is the most accomplished acrobat in the ring. Personally, Mark Twain also had, particularly in his final years, enough of the circus appearance to look like an artiste from the good old days. He was easygoing, but true genius was hidden in the performer's *Hamadryas* mask. He had the ancient, indomitable, true wit, the virile stare, which characterizes Mephistopheles, as Goethe described him.

Without space for quotations it is not easy to show the nature and value of Mark Twain's humor. If we skip over the purely entertaining features, which are the best known and, by the way, often excel in an absolutely brilliant exuberance, you have to look for the weightiest expression of his mind in the far-roaming travel accounts that he published: *The Innocents Abroad, A Tramp Abroad*, etc. The way he, as an American, views Europe and the culture of the old world during his travels, which now actually were some time ago, is of considerable value. He is akin to Heine in his boldness and innate vigor. Mark Twain never poses as the spoiled Romantic writer; he is in truth *innocent* in observing the world, he does it firsthand and innocuously like a child; the emperor feels cold in his new clothes under his stare. His criticism of Europe would be classic, if it were not that a measure of sticky American parochialism adheres to it, a failing sense of spiritual values. He is at times labored and can be crude, but in other places how captivatingly cheerful and shamelessly provocative like a young devil! At the height of his genius he is beautiful, eternal youth radiates from his forehead, and as such he will enter the tradition.

It does not pay to label others with one word; but what is not said briefly is not said at all—*vitality* is the word that almost fully covers Mark Twain's nature. There is something singularly rested and awake about him, he rears, challenges, he is new, and there is a new world around him. His essence is a new beginning. It has its origin in the social atmosphere in America, where in a new way they have found an impressive vigor, such as that of Theodore Roosevelt, unencumbered by "tradition."

In Mark Twain breathing as a free citizen has released a keen sense of life itself: he is brimming with life. In high spirits, which are not much different from what a young colt enjoys, he takes his position on all the Methuselah-old, acrimonious, and pitiful things that mankind is superstitious enough to keep dragging about. He himself is too delighted to start stewing in wretchedness and he has too much common sense to expect the world to be different. In this way his mind develops, nourished by a healthy background and contempt for authority, the unrelenting attack, the exaggeration and understatement, the punishment and pardon at the same time, as nature itself has it, all the "American" humor that expresses itself by accepting things as they are, but whose innermost strength is elasticity, a permanently repeated self-correction, as life continues.

In spite of his inclination to see humor in all contradictions, Mark Twain retained a manly, respectable, praiseworthy attitude throughout his life; few ostentatious and seriously earnest men can claim his discipline and uprightness. Well-known is the display of strength with which, it seems for the second time, he lost his fortune and, although already an old man, undertook to earn a new one; as it is, you do sense that the situation shaped the speed and quantity of the writing he produced. But the courage and the free citizen's need for self-reliance do not fail. In the Jester hides a Job.

What will have a lasting value among Mark Twain's writings is difficult to say. All of his work may still be read throughout with more than an antiquarian profit. And when his time and the types he revealed in his humor are faded memories, it will not be forgotten that he cleared the way for a new time and new people.

The trail-blazing pioneer often becomes the victim of the change he himself initiated. Should you come to think less of Mark Twain's humor, after your mind has been enriched by it—well, then it has not been in vain, after all!

Mark Twain has also contributed significantly to the cultural history of America by writing on the social atmosphere in the middle of the 19th century, in the West, among tough, carefree pioneers; here he enters literary tradition, while Bret Harte, the sentimentalist, drops out of it. The description Mark Twain gives us of the Mississippi has the ring of a classic, it is permeated by knowledge and it is imperishable in its Herodotian sense of the place and the people that inspired the memory.

It was here that, as a very young river pilot, he heard his pen name, when a leadsman at the line sounded "mark twain," which means two fathoms' depth. His real name was Samuel Clemens.

And now that he has boarded his final vessel on that broad and silent river, it is also "Mark Twain" that the ferryman must shout, as the boat approaches the other bank. Under that name the man, who has entertained and enlightened so many and in his way is irreplaceable, has passed into immortality.

Translated by Jan Norby Gretlund
Politiken (Copenhagen), 1910

George Ade

The American columnist, novelist, and playwright George Ade (1866–1944) is best remembered as a turn-of-the-century humorist from Indiana whose popular "fables in slang" transformed Midwestern manners into the stuff of genial social satire. Ade, who wrote a series of pieces for the *Chicago Record* from 1893 to 1900 filled with observations by alter-ego characters, is sometimes credited with having invented the modern newspaper column. Ade idolized Mark Twain and drew inspiration from him as he crafted his own brand of vernacular humor in the American heartland. (Twain admired Ade's work, writing to William Dean Howells after reading one of his novels, that Ade "flashes a character onto his page in a dozen words, you turn the leaf & there he stands, alive & breathing.") In 1904 Ade made Broadway history by being the first playwright to have three plays running simultaneously, the most successful of which, *The College Widow*, featured a high-spirited college football team at a school based on his alma mater, Purdue. Broadway audiences loved the energetic, slang-filled dialogue. A few years later when the play traveled to the Strand Theatre in London, the explanatory glossary of American slang handed out with the playbills failed to prevent English audiences from being hopelessly confused, and the play closed in a matter of weeks. Ade's appreciation of the remarkable response to Twain outside the United States in this article may well have been shaped by the difficulty Ade himself had when he tried to export his own brand of American humor from Broadway to the West End.

Mark Twain as Our Emissary

Mark Twain had a large following of admirers who came to regard themselves as his personal friends. Many of them he never met. Most of them never saw him. All of them felt a certain relationship and were flattered by it. Men and women in all parts of our outspread domain, the men especially, cherished a private affection for him. They called him by his first name, which is the surest proof of abiding fondness. Andrew Jackson was known as "Andy"; Abraham Lincoln was simply "Abe" to every soldier boy; and, as a later instance, we have "Teddy."

Some men settle down to a kinship with the shirt-sleeve contingent, even when they seem indifferent to the favor of the plain multitude.

Mark Twain never practised any of the wiles of the politician in order to be cheered at railway stations and have Chautauquas send for him. He did not seem over-anxious to meet the reporters, and he had a fine contempt for most of the orthodox traditions cherished by the people who loved him. Probably no other American could have lived abroad for so many years without being editorially branded as an expatriate. In some sections of our country it is safer to be an accomplice in homicide, or a stand-patter in politics, than it is to be an "expatriate." When Mr. Clemens chose to take up his residence in Vienna he incurred none of the criticism visited upon Mr. William Waldorf Astor. Every one hoped he would have a good time and learn the German language. Then when the word came back that he made his loafing headquarters in a place up an alley known as a *stube*, or a *rathskeller*, or something like that, all the women of the literary clubs, who kept his picture on the high pedestal with the candles burning in front of it, decided that *stube* meant "shrine." You may be sure that if they can find the place they will sink a bronze memorial tablet immediately above the main faucet.

Of course, the early books, such as "Innocents Abroad," "Roughing It," and "The Gilded Age" gave him an enormous vogue in every remote community visited by book-agents. The fact that people enjoyed reading these cheering volumes and preserved them in the bookcase and moved out some of the classics by E. P. Roe and Mrs. Southworth in order to make room for "Tom Sawyer" and "Huckleberry Finn," does not fully account for the evident and accepted popularity of Mark Twain. Other men wrote books that went into the bookcase but what one of them ever earned the special privilege of being hailed by his first name?

When a man has done his work for many years more or less under the supervising eye of the public, the public learns a good many facts about him that are in no way associated with his set and regular duties as a servant of the public. Out of the thousand-

and-one newspaper mentions and private bits of gossip and whispered words of inside information, even the busy man in the street comes to put an estimate on the real human qualities of each personage, and sometimes these estimates are surprisingly accurate, just as they are often sadly out of focus.

Joseph Jefferson had a place in the public esteem quite apart from that demanded by his skill as an actor. Players and readers of newspapers came to know in time that he was a kind and cheery old gentleman of blameless life, charitable in his estimates of professional associates, a modest devotee of the fine arts, an outdoor sportsman with the enthusiasm of a boy, and the chosen associate of a good many eminent citizens. When they spoke of "Joe" Jefferson in warmth and kindness, it was not because he played "Rip Van Winkle" so beautifully, but because the light of his private goodness had filtered through the mystery surrounding every popular actor. William H. Crane is another veteran of the stage who holds the regard of the public. It knows him as a comedian, and also it knows him as the kind of man we should like to invite up to our house to meet the "folks." The sororities throb with a feeling of sisterhood for Miss Maude Adams because the girls feel sure that she is gracious and charming and altogether "nice."

Mark Twain would have stood very well with the assorted grades making up what is generally known as the "great public" even if he had done his work in a box and passed it out through a knot-hole. Any one who knew our homely neighbors as he knew them and could tell about them in loving candor, so that we laughed at them and warmed up to them at the same time, simply had to be "all right." Being prejudiced in his favor, we knew that if he wanted to wear his hair in a mop and adopt white clothing and talk with a drawl, no one would dare to suggest that he was affecting the picturesque. He was big enough to be different. Any special privilege was his without the asking. Having earned 100 per cent. of our homage he didn't have to strain for new effects.

His devotion to the members of his family and the heroic performance in connection with the debts of the publishing house undoubtedly helped to strengthen the general regard for him. Also, the older generation, having heard him lecture, could say that they had "met" him. Every one who sat within the soothing presence of the drawl, waiting to be chirked up on every second sentence with a half-concealed stroke of drollery, was for all time a witness to the inimitable charm of the man and the story-teller.

The knowledge of his unaffected democracy became general. No doubt the housewives loved him for his outspoken devotion to home-cooking. Has any one told in public the anecdote of his tribute to an humble item in the bill of fare? It was at a dinner party in Washington. Senator Hearst was giving the dinner, and Mark Twain was the guest of honor. Here were two transplanted westerners who knew more about roughing it than ever appeared in a book. As the high-priced food was being served to them, they talked longingly of the old-fashioned cookery of Missouri. The Senator wondered if there was any real corned beef and cabbage left in the world. Mark Twain spoke up in praise of the many old-time dishes, reaching his climax when he declared that, in his opinion, "Bacon would improve the flavor of an angel!"

Furthermore is it not possible that much of the tremendous liking for Mark Twain grew out of his success in establishing our credit abroad? Any American who can invade Europe and command respectful attention is entitled to triumphal arches when he arrives home. Our dread and fear of foreign criticism are still most acute. Mrs. Trollope and Captain Marryat lacerated our feelings long ago. Dickens came over to have our choicest wild flowers strewn in his pathway and then went home to scourge us until we shrieked with pain. Kipling had fun with us, and for years after that we trembled at his approach. George Bernard Shaw peppers away at long range and the "London Spectator" grows peevish every time it looks out of the window and sees a drove of Cook tourists madly spending their money.

It is a terrible shock to the simple inlander, who has fed upon Congressional oratory and provincial editorials, when he discovers that in certain European capitals the name "American" is almost a term of reproach. The first-time-over citizen from Spudville or Alfalfa Center indicates his protest by wearing a flag on his coat and inviting those who sit in darkness to come over and see what kind of trams are run on the Burlington. The lady, whose voice comes from a point directly between the eyes, seeks to correct all erroneous impressions by going to the table d'hote with fewer clothes and more jewels than any one had reason to expect. These two are not as frequently to be seen as they were twenty years ago but they are still gleefully held up by our critics as being "typical."

Probably they are outnumbered nowadays by the apologetic kind,—those who approach the English accent with trembling determination and who, after ordering in French, put a finger on the printed line so that the waiter may be in on the secret.

There are Americans who live abroad and speak of their native land in shameful whispers. Another kind is an explainer. He becomes fretful and involved in the attempt to make it clear to some Englishman with a cold and fish-like eye that, as a matter of fact, the lynchings are scattered over a large territory, and Tammany has nothing whatever to do with the United States Senate, and the millionaire does not crawl into the presence of his wife and daughters, and Morgan never can be King, and citizens of St. Louis are not in danger of being hooked by moose. After he gets through the Englishman says "Really?" and the painful incident is closed.

Every man is handicapped and hobbled when he gets out of his own bailiwick. The American is at a special disadvantage in Europe. If he cannot adapt himself to strange customs and social regulations, he thinks that he will be set down as an ignoramus. If he tries to nullify or override them he may be regarded as a boor or a barbarian. Once in a while an American, finding himself beset by unfamiliar conditions, follows the simple policy of not trying to assimilate new rules or oppose them, and merely goes ahead in his own way, conducting himself as a human being possessed of the usual number of faculties. This odd performance may be counted upon to excite wonder and admiration. Benjamin Franklin tried it out long ago and became the sensation of Europe. General Grant and Colonel Roosevelt got along comfortably in all sorts of foreign complications merely by refusing to put on disguises and to be play-actors. But Mark Twain was probably the best of our emissaries. He never waved the starry banner and at the same time he never went around begging forgiveness. He knew the faults of his home people and he understood intimately and with a family knowledge all of their good qualities and groping intentions and half-formed plans for big things in the future; but apparently he did not think it necessary to justify all of his private beliefs to men who lived five thousand miles away from Hannibal, Missouri. He had been in all parts of the world and had made a calm and unbiased estimate of the relative values of men and institutions. Probably he came to know that all had been cut from one piece and then trimmed variously. He carried with him the same placid habits of life that sufficed him in Connecticut and because he was what he pretended to be, the hypercritical foreigners doted upon him and the Americans at home, glad to flatter themselves, said, "Why, certainly, he's one of us."

Century Magazine, 1910

G. K. Chesterton

G. K. Chesterton (1874–1936) was the author of some 80 books on subjects ranging from philosophy to detective fiction to biography as well as hundreds of poems, stories, and essays. Recognized as a master of wit, Chesterton was particularly qualified to analyze the dynamics of the humor he found in the work of Mark Twain. "Wit," he wrote in the piece included here, "requires an intellectual athleticism, because it is akin to logic." He added that "wit is a sword; it is meant to make people feel the point as well as see it. All honest people saw the point of Mark Twain's wit. Not a few dishonest people felt it." The distinction Chesterton drew between "Mark Twain" and "Samuel Clemens" in this essay anticipated by over half a century an approach that would be central to Justin Kaplan's 1967 Pulitzer Prize–winning biography, *Mr. Clemens and Mark Twain.*

Mark Twain

We are always told that there is something specially sinister in the death of a great jester. I am not so sure about the point myself, seeing that so many thousand human beings, diplomatists, financiers, kings, bankers, and founders of philosophies, are engaged in functions far more ultimately fruitless and frivolous than really making the smallest schoolboy laugh. If the death of a clown makes pantomimes for a moment tragic, it is also true that the death of a statesman makes statesmanship for a moment highly comic; the irony cuts both ways. But in the case of the great man whom Englishmen and Americans must now join in lamenting (not because they are all Anglo-Saxons, but because they can all admire good literature written in English)—in the case of Mark Twain there is a particular cause which at once emphasises and complicates this contrast between the comic and the serious. The point I mean is this: that while Mark Twain's literary merits were very much of the uproarious and topsy-turvy kind, his personal merits were very much of the stoical or even puritanical kind. While irresponsibility was the energy in his writings, an almost excessive responsibility was the energy in his character. The artistic European might feel that he was, perhaps, too comic when he was comic; but such a European would also feel that he was too serious when he was serious.

The wit of Mark Twain was avowedly and utterly of the extravagant order. It had that quality of mad logic carried further and further into the void, a quality in which many strange civilisations are at one. It is a system of extremes, and all extremes meet in it; thus houses piled one on top of the other is the idea of a flat in New York and of a pagoda in Pekin. Mark Twain was a master of this mad lucidity. He was a wit rather than a humorist; but I do not mean by this (as so many modern people will certainly fancy) that he was something less than a humorist. Possibly, I think, he was something more than a humorist. Humour, a subtle relish for the small incongruities of society, is a thing that exists in many somewhat low society types, in many snobs and in some sneaks. Like the sense of music, it is exquisite and ethereal; but, like the sense of music, it can exist (somehow or other) in utter blackguards or even in utter blockheads; just as one often meets a fool who can really play the fiddle, so one often meets a fool who can really play the fool. But wit is a more manly exercise than fiddling or fooling; wit requires an intellectual athleticism, because it is akin to logic. A wit must have something of the same running, working, and staying power as a mathematician or a metaphysician. Moreover, wit is a fighting thing and a working thing. A man may enjoy humour all by himself; he may see a joke when no one else sees it; he may see the point and avoid it. But wit is a sword; it is meant to make people feel the point as well as see it. All honest people saw the point of Mark Twain's wit. Not a few dishonest people felt it.

But though it was wit it was wild wit, as wild as the pagoda in China or the other pagodas in New York. It was progressive, and the joke went forward by arithmetical progression. In all those excruciating tales of his, which in our youth made us animally ill with laughing, the idea always consisted in carrying some small fact or notion to more and more frantic lengths of deduction. If a man's hat was as high as a house Mark Twain would think of some way of calling it twenty times higher than a house. If his hat was smashed as flat as a pancake Mark Twain would invent some startling and happy metaphor to prove that it was smashed twenty times flatter than a pancake. His splendid explosive little stories, such as that which describes how he edited an agricultural paper, or that which explains how he tried to decipher a letter from Horace Greeley, have one tremendous essential of great art. I mean that the excitement mounts up perpetually; they grow more and more comic, as a tragedy should grow more and more tragic. The rack, tragic or comic, goes round until something breaks inside a man. In tragedy it is his heart, or, perhaps, his stiff neck. In farce I do not quite know what it is—perhaps his funnybone is dislocated; perhaps his skull is slightly cracked.

Anyhow, the humour or wit of Mark Twain was of this ascending and exaggerative order. As such it was truly mountainous, and almost apocalyptic. No writer of modern English, perhaps, has had such a genius for making the cow jump over the moon; that is, for lifting the heaviest and most solemn absurdity high up into the most starry adventures. He was never at a loss for a simile or a parable, and they were never, strictly speaking, nonsense. They were rather a kind of incredible sense. They were not suddenly inconsequent, like Lewis Carroll; rather they were unbearably consequent, and seemed capable of producing new consequences for ever. Even that fantastic irreverence and fantastic ignorance which sometimes marked his dealings with elements he insufficiently understood were never abrupt departures, but only elaborate deductions from his idea. It was quite logical that when told that a saint's heart had burst his ribs he should ask what the saint had had for dinner. It was quite logical that his delightful musician, when asked to play music appropriate to the Prodigal Son, should play, "We all get blind drunk when Johnny comes marching home." These are things of real wit, like that of Voltaire; though they are not uttered with the old French restraint, but with a new American extravagance. Voltaire is to them as the Rhone is to Niagara; not inferior in quality, but merely in quantity, for Niagara is not only one of the violences, but almost one of the vulgarities, of Nature. The laughter of Mark Twain was literally like Niagara.

Such was Mark Twain; such was not Samuel Clemens. His lonely figure stands up in strange solitude and severity against the confusion and extravagance of the background of his works. The virtues which we have all now to regret in their return to God were specially virtues rather of the restrained than of the riotous or sympathetic order. We know, indeed, that he rose from the ranks, in the sense that he was poor and pugnacious in a rich and pugnacious society; that he came of Southern folk, served with the heroic Southern armies, but that the greater part of his life was such a scramble of incalculable successes and unavoidable failures as Stevenson has well described in the one convincing picture of a good American, Jim Pinkerton, in "The Wrecker." The words Stevenson used of Pinkerton might quite truly be used of Clemens: "He was stuffed full of manly virtues. Thrift and courage glowed in him." When his hair was white and his soul heavy with years an accident led him into liabilities which the law would have discharged by the ordinary arrangements of bankruptcy. The old man refused to accept the ordinary arrangements which the law allowed him. He set to work strenuously, writing and lecturing as if he were at the beginning of his life rather than at the end of it. He repaid his unrecognised and unlegal debt, and a little later he died. Thus the primary paradox is emphasised almost in the article of death; the man whom ten million people had adored as a tom-fool was too serious even for the expectation of his own creditors.

The credit of such glowing thrift and courage (to quote an admirable phrase again) must be ascribed to something or somebody; I will no longer disguise the dreadful fact that I ascribe it exactly where Mark Twain would have ascribed it. I ascribe it to the Republican virtue of America. Of course, if Mark Twain had said that in so many words, everybody in England would have thought he was making one of his best jokes; whereas, in truth, he would have been indulging in one of his worst pieces of seriousness. Somebody in an advanced Socialist paper that I saw the other day said that Mark Twain was a cynic. I suppose there never was a person so far removed from cynicism as Mark Twain. A cynic must at least mean a man who is flippant about serious things; about things that he thinks serious. Mark Twain was always serious to the verge of madness. He was not serious about St. Francis; he did not think St. Francis serious. He honestly supposed the marvels of St. Francis to be some ecclesiastical trick of Popes and Cardinals. He did not happen to know that the Franciscan movement was something much more certainly popular than the Revolution that rent America from England. He derided King Arthur's Court as something barbaric. He did not happen to know that the only reason why that dim and highly-dubious Court has made a half-entry into history is that it stood, if it ever stood at all, for the remnant of high civilisation against the base advance of barbarism. He did not happen to know that, in his time, St. Francis stood for the ballot-box. He did not happen to know that, in his time, King Arthur stood for the telephone. He could never quite get rid of the American idea that good sense and good government had begun quite a little while ago; and that the heavier a monumental stone was to lift the more lightly it might be thrown away. But all these limitations of his only re-emphasise the ultimate fact: he never laughed at a thing unless he thought it laughable. He was an American; that is, an unfathomably solemn man. Now all this is due to a definite thing, an historical thing, called Republican virtue. It *was* worth while to issue the Declaration of Independence if only that Mark Twain might declare his independence also.

In this the great humorist not only represents his country, but a big mistake about his country. The apparent clamour and complexity of America is very superficial; America is not really advanced or aggressively civilised. New York, Philadelphia, Chicago are jokes; just such tall jokes as Mark Twain would have made. American commerce is all one tall story; American commerce is a vast American lie. But the American lie is a very serious, separate, and authoritative institution, which could only exist among a singularly truthful people. Behind these extravagances, whether in words or wealth, whether in books or bricks, there remains a grave simplicity which is truly American. The genuine value of the Yankee is not his forwardness. Rather it is his backwardness that is the real beauty of the Yankee. There is in the depths of him the rural stillness of an intellectual backwater: he is a great rustic. The log-hut, and not the sky-scraper, is the American home. Therefore, despite the revolting vices of wealth and all the vulgarities of unhistorical individualism, there does remain in the Americans a certain average of virile virtues, equality, hard work, patriotism, and a plain ideality. Corrupt fatigue is uncommon; unclean despair is almost unknown. You could not have made Mark Twain even understand either of these things. He was radiant with a rectitude none the less noble for being slightly naïve; he carried everywhere those powerful platitudes that are like clubs of stone. With these he hammered Calvinism in his youth and Christian Science in his old age. But he was not an "advanced" thinker, not a mind in revolt; rather he was a conservative and rustic grandfather older than all such follies. But this strength in him and his country truly came from a great spirit which England resisted and has forgotten; the spirit which, when all is said, made it no nonsense to compare Washington to Cincinnatus; the austere love of liberty and of the ploughshare and the sword.

T. P.'s Weekly (London), 1910

Jesús Castellanos

Jesús Castellanos y Villageliú (1878–1912) was a Cuban journalist, fiction writer, and artist. In 1901 he began writing acclaimed humorous articles about Cuban political figures, accompanied by caricatures, for the Havana newspaper *La Discusión.* General Leonard Wood, the U.S. Military Governor of Cuba, was so offended by a political cartoon that Castellanos drew that represented the Cuban people as a crucified Jesus Christ between two thieves, Wood and President William McKinley, that he charged both Castellanos and the editor of *La Discusión* with criminal libel and had them briefly jailed. (Wood went on to become Governor General of the Philippines, where his brutality earned him Mark Twain's bitter contempt.) Castellanos, known for being honest, independent, and outspoken, did not hesitate to criticize the United States when he felt such criticism was warranted—or to defend it against critics when he felt such a defense was called for. He took issue with the United States for discriminating against Japanese children in California schools. But when an Argentine writer urged all South American republics to unite into one confederation to resist absorption by North America, Castellanos took him to task for not recognizing that the United States had done more to help Cuba in its struggle for independence than Argentina had. Castellanos is also recognized as a pioneer of Cuban fiction. His stories and novels focused on the lives of ordinary Cubans with a special sympathy for the poor. He addressed hypocrisy, dishonesty, and stupidity in politics and social relations, and on occasion his work centered on Afro-Cuban figures or African-American culture. In 1910, the year he wrote this piece on Mark Twain, Castellanos was elected the first director of the Academia Nacional de Artes y Letras, an organization which he helped to found to enhance the cultural and intellectual vitality of his country. For Castellanos, Mark Twain was a truly "American" writer in the *continental* sense of the word.

FROM
Mark Twain

O n the streets of New York, always crowded and always merry, when people speak of "a gentleman from Missouri" the reference is to a fine gentleman with an ample beard and wearing an ill-fitting suit, whom everyone makes the butt of the cruelest jokes in their repertoire. Nevertheless, a "gentleman from Missouri" has just died who laughed at the expense of all those practical men, and with laughter so irresistibly wholesome and contagious that it sounded throughout the entire planet, providing each reader a minute of true happiness and forgetfulness. Above all, this extravagant and imperturbable gentleman from Missouri was able to win what ought to be the ultimate prize for men of heart: to hear himself called—as perhaps neither Longfellow and Washington Irving ever did—the national author.

Mark Twain's immense aura of popularity came from the most powerful element that a writer of imagination could have at his disposal: a profound knowledge of the American people such as only a photographer could have from the outside, and only a mother from the inside. Of the multitude of writers of all languages who have given their impressions of this admirable new type of humanity, simple and mutable like radium, there is only one in all the continent who can call himself truly American; no one else has presented such astonishing discoveries of expression, feeling, ideas, language, as this great joker without philosophical pretensions. Any reader of *Huckleberry Finn* already knows this modern figure of a man, who with the impassiveness of the Sphinx roars with the laughter of a child; a compound of the rudeness of emerald Ireland, of powerful English pride, and of hazy and remote German romanticism. And the design of a history that in a short time has greedily piled up great deeds will be explained as the reason for that ferocious industrialism, and why lynchings and philanthropic millionaires can flourish there side by side. Remington, with his drawings of the mines and the prairies of the Far West captured for future generations one distinct type of American; Charles Dana Gibson dressed him in bright flannels and set him promenading through the beaches and clubs of the East. Between them is Mark Twain, presenting through sixty years of bantering jokes and travels throughout the Union, from San Francisco to Boston, the whole parade of this strange conglomerate which, in sum, does honor and gives comfort to humanity.

This note in memory of the master who has left us does not need to be an attempt at biography. Everyone knows the life of Samuel Langhorne Clemens; everyone knows he was a "self-made" man; that, like many American writers, from Benjamin Franklin to William Dean Howells, he began as a typesetter; that his life was a nomadic trek not devoid of sorrows which he concealed out of consideration for his public; that, in the end, he died fairly poor, asking to be buried like a young maiden in a white coffin, still laughing, always laughing like Beaumarchais' Figaro "for fear of being obliged to weep."

In Mark Twain's humor there was nevertheless no bitterness. Far from him were the literary nettles of Thackeray or the Span-iard Bartrina, writers humorous only in name. His wit is clean, healthy, almost childish; he cannot be charged with the sin of punning, or of describing anything that chaste ears should not hear. His strength resides in his imagination; his work abounds in unexpected thrusts and an indeterminable and delicious some-thing in his way of saying things precisely as they are not. Clearly this is nothing other than the definition of irony; but in Twain such wordplay, now much in style, is accompanied by a certain element of jocose satire. Mark Twain does not jeer at or suffer anything, and it is precisely this seeming Panglossianism that re-fines the enchantment of his stories. Read, for example, his fa-mous *Celebrated Jumping Frog of Calaveras County* or, lighter fare, his sketches *Politic Economy* or *Why I Am Dying*—these last have been translated into Spanish—and you will see how easily and spontaneously they can make you not only smile but break into the roaring laughter of our village grandparents, simply by the diabolical power of seriousness in diction and monstrousness in comparison that he was able to combine so cunningly.

*   *   *

It is interesting to note that Mark Twain was never obliged to resort to life's arduous difficulties to compose his vast body of work. Like almost all the great humorists, his jokes have com-mented on his life, and the magic of his form lets us forgive these personal exhibitions. Charles Dickens and Alphonse Daudet contented themselves with giving us impressions of

their childhoods in two masterpieces. Mark Twain has repeatedly recounted his own history from childhood to old age. *Tom
Sawyer*—which along with *Huckleberry Finn* is the work of his
that will last through the centuries—constitutes his autobiography up to the point when he fled the country of his childhood.
Then come the years of adventure: the author smokes a great
pilot's pipe over the sea-green waves of a river; and the recollection of that wild youth produces *Life on the Mississippi*. When the
war is over—"where he was one-hundred times on the verge of
being a hero without ever being a hero"—he becomes a miner
in Nevada, with the aid of a brother who was a respected digni-
tary there; and this savage uprooting gives life through the years
to *Roughing It*, painted in colors whose only parallel can be
found in the celebrated *California Sketches* of Bret Harte. A trip
to Europe is the seed of *A Tramp Abroad*; a visit to London lives
on in *A Connecticut Yankee in King Arthur's Court*; a pilgrimage to
the Holy Land inspires the lightly blasphemous *The Innocents
Abroad*, an infallible antidote against every form of hypochon-
dria. Old now, with all his friends in the cemetery, he remembers, remembers still, and writes his full biography for the *North
American Review*. In short, he was a man, this was his life; both
are laid bare. Perhaps this meeting his public on its own level
was the talisman of his success.

The work of Mark Twain was compared during his lifetime
with that of Cervantes and Molière. Now that he is dead, once
the memory of his white dress coat and witty toasts between two
sips of champagne has passed, critics may rate him a little lower.
If the limit of injustice is reached and no one remembers that
the libraries contain a *Huckleberry Finn*, it will still serve as a
model to the young of every generation, to those who are hopeless and sad. For *Huckleberry Finn* arose from a life of perennial
spiritual health achieved through the sole stimulus of work, and
this old fighter of literature who was able to transform himself
from a "sage-brush reporter" into what the Yankees audaciously
call "a world-wide celebrity," will be a secular saint.

Translated by Edward M. Test
Los Optimistas, 1910

George Soule

"Mark Twain Protests" by American journalist and economist George Henry Soule (1887–1970) was a response to the publication of a strange little book "by Mark Twain" that was published posthumously in October 1916 under the title *The Mysterious Stranger: A Romance*. (It had also been serialized in *Harper's* from May to November of that year.) Twain's name may have been on the cover and title page, but the "fairy tale dipped in irony" was actually a novella that Twain's literary executor, Albert Bigelow Paine, and Harper editor Henry Duneka, patched together from manuscript fragments that Twain had left unfinished at his death. Twain's *Mysterious Stranger Manuscripts* in the form he left them have since been published by the Mark Twain Project. The material that Soule quotes in this review is from manuscript fragments by Twain known today as "The Chronicle of Young Satan" and "No. 44, The Mysterious Stranger," written between 1897 and 1900 while Twain lived in Vienna and London. Passages like the ones Soule quotes here startled a doting public that had come to view Twain in large part as an avuncular jester, ignoring or denying the darker, more troubling aspects of his work. Although written well before World War I, Twain's words, in Soule's view, spoke to the present in uncanny ways. The week this article appeared marked the end of the Somme offensive, the battle that cost over a million British, French, and German lives and resulted in just 12 kilometers of ground changing sides.

Mark Twain Protests

It is possible to say several foolish things upon discovering that the greatest American humorist wrote a book of pessimism, and most of them are being said. There are the melodramatic commonplaces about gaiety assumed to conceal sorrow, and the tragic character of the jester. There is the view which sees in the book merely a fable expounding a second-rate philosophy borrowed perhaps from Schopenhauer, and faulty because it is imperfectly borrowed. There are the pious utterances of the people who shake their heads and say what a pity it is that a man of so fine instincts should not have accepted the consolations of religion, and that the book is a final proof that no one can be really happy unless he is a Christian.

Any such categorical valuations falsify the earthy mould out of which such a book must have sprung, they violate the sensitive and honorable contact with the world which it represents. This is no Pagliacci among books, concerned in a bitter personal tragedy which has hid itself in laughter. It is not an allegory ingeniously told to illustrate a thesis formally apprehended. Rather than a groping refusal of religion, it is evidence of a thirst more strong than any revealed religion had power to assuage. It is not portentous at all, but a story by Mark Twain, familiar and American, in which he chooses not to amuse us but to tell us how he feels about men and women, and the world they live in.

"Eseldorf was a paradise for us boys." Enchantingly it begins, like a fairy story. Then appears the strange boy who says he is an angel, Satan by name, an unfallen nephew of the illustrious fiend. He makes for the boys' entertainment a toy village of living beings, destroys it by a thunderbolt, and then thins to the irridescence of a soap-bubble, bouncing along the turf till he vanishes. Satan is gay and beautiful, he plays blissful music on a strange, sweet instrument, he is lofty towards man, who amuses him; but on the whole he is indulgent. His cruelty to the little living creatures he made for his toy village seems inevitable. If one were all-powerful, celestial, could not suffer, what would such trifles matter, after all?

Cruelty does matter to the boys, however. The next time they see Satan they reproach him with the evil consequences of a mischievous attempt of his to help an old priest. Whose fault is it? replies the angel. Men are so stupid they cause most of their own misery. However, just to show you, I'll seriously try to help the people you're interested in. He goes ahead to do so, but of course the result is that people destroy their own happiness, or are deprived of it through envy, or are stoned and burned for witchcraft; and the only way Satan can really make anybody happy for long is to kill him or drive him mad.

Satan is fond of dogs and cattle, and objects when a cruel man is called a brute. A brute, he says, can never be so disgusting as a man. This is because man has that terrible thing, moral sense. "A sense whose function is to distinguish between right and wrong, with liberty to choose which of them he will do. Now what advantage can be got out of that? He is always choosing, and in nine cases out of ten he chooses the wrong. There shouldn't be any wrong; and without the moral sense there couldn't be any." To prove it he shows them the progress of the human race—largely a story of wars. "In five or six thousand years," says Satan, "five or six high civilizations have arisen, flourished, commanded the wonder of the world, then faded out and disappeared; and not one of them except the latest ever invented any sweeping and adequate way to kill people. They all did their best—to kill being the chiefest ambition of the human race and the earliest incident in its history—but only the Christian civilization has scored a triumph to be proud of. Two or three centuries from now it will be recognized that all the competent killers are Christians."

Satan spoke long before 1914, therefore his paragraph on war is worth quoting. "There never has been a just one, never an honorable one—on the part of an instigator of the war. . . . The loud little handful—as usual—will shout for the war. The pulpit will—warily and cautiously—object—at first; the great, big, dull bulk of the nation will rub its sleepy eyes and try to make out why there should be a war—and will say, earnestly and indignantly, 'It is unjust and dishonorable, and there is no necessity for it.' Then the handful will shout louder. A few fair men on the other side will argue and reason against the war with speech and pen, and at first will have a hearing and be applauded; but it will not last long; those others will outshout them, and presently the anti-war audiences will thin out and lose popularity. Before long you will see this curious thing: the speakers stoned from the platform, and free speech strangled by hordes of furious men who in their secret hearts are at one with those stoned speakers. . . . Next the statesmen will invent cheap lies, putting the blame upon the nation that is attacked, and every man will be glad of those conscience-soothing falsities, and will diligently study them, and refuse to examine any refutations of them: and thus he will by and by convince himself that war is just and will thank God for the better sleep he enjoys after this process of grotesque self-deception."

In the end Satan tells the boys that he himself does not exist; that he is a dream of man; that God, the world as it is, and the moral sense and the future life, and all the rest of it, is the dream of man—"a grotesque and foolish dream." "Dream other dreams, and better!"

Of course this may be pessimism. But on the other hand it may be satire from the courageous heart of a lover of mankind. If we hate cruelty, we must not blame it on a perfect God, but at least do as little of it ourselves as we may. Supernatural powers would not help us if we had them. And above all, let us not imagine a God, and then claim his solemn sanction for our cruelties.

Such a foreshortening conceals the intimate charm of the story—a fairy tale dipped in irony. It is nothing new to say that man is only a coward if he casts his burden on the Lord. But Mark Twain's way of saying it was genuine because he felt presently and in detail each other man's sorrow, and because he knew himself in honor responsible for his neighbor. There is not a person in the tale, however lightly touched, who is not made warm by his sympathy.

This is the sort of thing that comes straight from the soul of America. It is national in the sense that Tolstoy and Dostoevsky are national; it interprets the simplicity, the humanitarian aspirations, the reverence for the humble, the impatience of formalism, the hard-headed distrust of authority, the resolute sensitiveness, that have found a thousand cruder expressions on this continent in the last year. Those who have angrily shouted their doubts of America's intrinsic honor should go back and look in their Mark Twain. It is a very real honor they will find there.

The New Republic, 1916

H. L. Mencken

As a child Henry Louis Mencken (1880–1856) found *Huckleberry Finn* in his father's bookcase alongside tomes of a very different sort. "If I undertook to tell you the effect it had upon me," Mencken wrote in his memoir *Happy Days*, "my talk would sound frantic, and even delirious. Its impact was genuinely terrific." He considered his "discovery" of Mark Twain's novel to be "probably the most stupendous event of my whole life." A prolific writer himself, Mencken went on to become one of the most influential—and controversial—journalists and cultural critics in the nation. The "Sage of Baltimore," as he came to be known, began his career writing for Baltimore newspapers and soon took over the editorship of *The Smart Set* (with George Jean Nathan) and later *The American Mercury*. Walter Lippmann called him "the most powerful personal influence on this whole generation of educated people." Throughout his career Mencken led the charge to demolish the image many Americans had of Twain as a popular but unimportant writer and to secure a place for him in the canon of great American authors—and not just any place, but a spot at the top. As early as 1909, Mencken claimed that *Huckleberry Finn* alone was worth "the complete works of Poe, Hawthorne, Cooper, Holmes, Howells and James, with the entire literary output to date of Indiana, Pennsylvania and all the States south of the Potomac thrown in as makeweight." In Mencken's view (as he put it in the 1913 piece that follows) Twain was "the true father of our national literature, the first genuinely American artist of the blood royal." He added, "Instead of being a mere entertainer of the mob, he was in fact a literary artist of the very highest skill and sophistication" as well as "a destructive satirist of the utmost pungency and relentlessness . . ." But even for Mencken, Twain had his flaws: he faulted the author for his "intellectual timorousness, his abiding fear of his own ideas, his incurable cowardice in the face of public disapproval." Few would have accused the fearless and outspoken Mencken of "timorousness" or "cowardice" as he filled the void left by Twain's death as the nation's most "destructive satirist" and "bitter critic of American platitude and delusion." And yet, Mencken himself, perhaps taking a cue from his literary patron saint, left (as Twain had) instructions that some of his writings not be published until many decades after his death.

Mark Twain

In "The Curious Republic of Gondour," a small volume of
Mark Twain's early sketches, hitherto unpublished in book
form (*Boni-Liveright*), there is little that is of much intrinsic
value, but nevertheless it is agreeable to see the collection get
between covers, for even the slightest of Mark's work has its moments and should be accessible. He wrote these pieces during
the year 1870, some of them for the *Buffalo Express*, in which he
had lately acquired a proprietary interest, and the others for the
New York *Galaxy*, to which he began contributing a monthly
department in May, 1870. Some of the other things that he did
for the *Galaxy* are well known, for he reprinted them in "Sketches
Old and New." Yet others were done into a book by a Canadian
pirate named Backas, and this book was republished in London.
I doubt that the present volume has the *imprimatur* of the Clemens executors, or of the Harpers, who control the Mark Twain
copyrights. But what if it hasn't? Mark was too vast a figure in
the national letters to be edited after death by executors. Whatever he wrote, signed and published during his lifetime should
be decently in print today, that readers may judge it for themselves. If, in the exercise of an incomprehensible discretion, his
executors venture to suppress this or that, not as of legal right
but simply because it offends their susceptibilities, then it seems
to me competent for any other publisher to print it an he listeth.
In the present case, as I say, no lost masterpiece is revealed, but
nevertheless the stuff, in the main, is quite as good as that which
got into "Sketches Old and New." Incidentally, it shows an early
flowering of two qualities that marked the great humorist very
broadly in his later days, to wit, his curious weakness for the
gruesome and his unshakable moral passion—his high indignation at whatever he conceived to be wrong. No one familiar
with the Markian canon could possibly fail to recognize the
authorship of "A Reminiscence of the Back Settlements" and
"About Smells." Both the former, with its Rabelaisian sporting
with the idea of death, and the latter, with its furious onslaught

upon the Presbyterian Pecksniff, T. De Witt Talmage, are absolutely characteristic.

Such a collection, I repeat, has its uses, and it is a pity that it is not more extensive. The official edition of Mark, published by the Harpers, shows serious defects. For one thing, it is incomplete. For another thing, the binding is gaudy and inappropriate (though not, perhaps, so horribly hideous as the Mother Hubbard binding the Harpers put upon poor Dreiser). And for a third thing, most of the illustrations of the first editions are omitted. In a few cases this last is an improvement; the pictures in "Following the Equator," for example, were unspeakable. But just as certainly there is something lacking in "Huckleberry Finn" when it appears without the capital drawings of Kemble, and something lacking in "A Tramp Abroad" when any of those of Brown are omitted. It would be easy to reproduce all the original illustrations; it would restore to the earlier books something that is essential to their atmosphere. But it is not done. Neither is anything approaching fair progress being made with the publication of the things that Mark left in manuscript, particularly his autobiography. He himself, I believe, desired that parts of it remain unprinted for a long while—he once proposed to the Harpers a contract providing for its publication a century after his death—but certainly there are other parts that might be done forthwith. As for me, I also grow restive waiting for "Three Thousand Years Among the Microbes," several pages of which are printed by Albert Bigelow Paine in the appendix to his excellent biography, and for the Bessie dialogues, and for "Letters From the Earth," and for "The War Prayer," and above all, for "1601." The last-named was once privately printed and contraband copies are still occasionally circulated. Why not a decent edition of it? If the Comstocks are capable of sufficiently throttling their swinishness to permit the open publication and circulation of Walt Whitman's "A Woman Waits For Me," why shouldn't they consent to the printing of "1601"? Must it wait until some extraordinarily literate United States Senator reads it into the *Congressional Record*?

II

The older I grow the more I am convinced that Mark was, by long odds, the largest figure that ever reared itself out of the flat, damp prairie of American literature. He was great absolutely, but one must consider him relatively to get at the measure of his true greatness. Put him beside Emerson, or Whitman, or Hawthorne, or even Poe; he was palpably the superior of all of them. What ailed the whole quartette was a defective contact with their environment, an aloofness from the plain facts of life, a sort of incurable other-worldliness. Emerson was always half lost in the shadows; toward the end of his life they closed upon him completely. The ideas that he spoke for, in the main, were ideas borrowed from men in far lands, and for all his eloquence he never got into them any sense of their pressing importance to the men of his own country. He was the academic theorist *par excellence*. He inhabited a world of mystical abstractions. The very folks who yielded most readily to his soughing phrases were furthest from grasping their exact import; to this day he is chiefly the philosopher, not of men who think clearly and accurately, but of half-educated dolts whose thinking is all a mellow and witless booziness. A man of extraordinary mental equipment and of even more extraordinary nobility of character, he failed both as a great teacher and as a great artist because of his remoteness from the active, exigent life that he was a part of. Set here in the America of the nineteenth century, begirt by politics, railways and commercial enterprise (and no less by revivals, cuspidors and braggadocio), he carried on his inquiries in the manner of a medieval monk, and his conclusions showed all the nebulousness that one associates with the monkish character. To this day his speculations have had no appreciable influence upon American ways of thought. His only professed disciples, in fact, are the votaries of what is called the New Thought, and these idiots libel him quite as absurdly as the Methodists, say, burlesque Christ.

The intellectual foreignness and loneliness of Hawthorne, Whitman and Poe is scarcely less noticeable. They lived in the republic, but were anything but of it. Hawthorne concerned himself with psychological problems that were not only inordinately obscure and labored, but even archaic; his enterprise, in his chief work, might almost be called an attempt to psychoanalyze the dead. It would be ridiculous to say that there was anything in his books that was characteristic of his time and his country. The gusto of a man thoroughly at home in his surroundings was simply not in him, and it is surely not surprising to hear that while he was physically present in America he lived like a hermit, and that his only happiness was found abroad. Whitman was even more solitary. The democracy he dreamed of was simply a figment of his imagination; it had no more relation to the reality sprawling before him than the Sermon on the Mount has to the practical ethic of the average Christian ecclesiastic. His countrymen, recognizing the conflict, regarded him generally as a loafer and a scoundrel, and it was only after foreign enthusiasts began to cry him up that he emerged from the constant threat of going to jail. As for Poe, he was almost the complete antithesis of a great national artist. In the midst of the most sordid civilization ever seen on earth and in the face of a population of utter literalists, he devoted himself grandly to *héliogabalisme*. His countrymen, in the main, were quite unaware of his stature while he lived. They regarded Cooper and Irving as incomparably greater artists, and such eighth-raters as N. P. Willis as far cleverer men. When they went to the works of Poe at all they went to them as, a generation later, they went to Barnum's circus—that is, as to an entertainment fantastic and somehow discreditable—one to be enjoyed now and then, but not too often. The Baptist critic, Rufus W. Griswold, accurately expressed the national view; his judgment was not challenged for years. An American boy of 1848 who had conceived the ambition of becoming a second Poe would have been caned until his very pantaloons took fire.

At the bottom of this isolation of Poe and Whitman and Hawthorne and Emerson there was, of course, the dense ignorance of a nation in a very backward state of culture; a Beethoven or a Mozart or an El Greco, set down amid the same scenes, would have got the same cold shoulder. But the fault, obviously, was not all on one side; the men themselves lacked something. What that something was I have already indicated. It may be described briefly as responsiveness, observation, aliveness, a sense of reality, a joy in life. Around them roared a great show; it was dramatic, thrilling, unprecedented; above all, it was intensely amusing. And yet they were as unconscious of it as so many deaf men at a combat of brass bands. Only Whitman seemed to have the slightest notion that anything was going on—and Whitman mistook the show for a great sacrament, a cheap and gaudy circus for a sort of Second Coming of Christ. Well, such lofty detachment is not the habit of great artists. It was not the habit of Shakespeare, or of Cervantes, or of Goethe, or of Pushkin, or Thackeray, or of Balzac. More important to our present purpose, it was not the habit of Mark Twain. Mark was the first of our great national artists to be whole-heartedly and enthusiastically American. He was the first to immerse himself willingly and with gusto in the infinitely picturesque and brilliant life of his time and country. He was the first to understand the common man of his race, and to interpret him fairly, honestly and accurately. He was the first to project brilliantly, for the information and entertainment of all the world, the American point of view, the American philosophy of life, the American character, the American soul. He would have been a great artist, I believe, even on the high-flung plane of Emerson or Hawthorne. He would have been *konzertmeister* even among the *umbilicarii*. But being what he was, his greatness was enormously augmented. He stands today at the head of the line. He is the one indubitable glory of American letters.

III

The bitter, of course, goes with the sweet. To be an American is, unquestionably, to be the noblest, the grandest, the proudest mammal that ever hoofed the verdure of God's green footstool. Often, in the black abysm of the night, the thought that I am one awakens me like a blast of trumpets, and I am thrown into a cold sweat by contemplation of the fact. I shall cherish it on the scaffold; it will console me in hell. But, as I have said, there is no perfection under heaven, and so even an American has his small blemishes, his scarcely discernible weaknesses, his minute traces of vice and depravity. Mark, alas, had them: he was as thoroughly American as a Knight of Pythias, a Wheeling stogie or Prohibition. One might almost exhibit his effigy in a museum as the archetype of the *Homo Americanus*. And what were these stigmata that betrayed him? In chief, they were two in number, and both lay at the very foundation of his character. On the one hand, there was his immovable moral certainty, his firm belief that he knew what was right from what was wrong, and that all who differed from him were, in some obscure way, men of an inferior and sinister order. And on the other hand, there was his profound intellectual timorousness, his abiding fear of his own ideas, his incurable cowardice in the face of public disapproval. These two characteristics colored his whole thinking; they showed themselves in his every attitude and gesture. They were the visible signs of his limitation as an Emersonian Man Thinking, and they were the bright symbols of his nationality. He was great in every way that an American could be great, but when he came to the border of his Americanism he came to the end of his greatness.

The true Mark Twain is only partly on view in his actual books—that is, in his printed books. To get the rest of the portrait you must go to Paine's exhaustive and fascinating biography—a work so engrossing as a character study that, despite its three volumes and more than 1,700 pages, I have gone through it three times. The real Mark was not the amiable jester of the white dress suit, the newspaper interviews and the after-dinner speeches. He was not the somewhat heavy-handed satirist of "A Tramp Abroad" and "Tom Sawyer." He was not even the extraordinarily fine and delicate artist of "Joan of Arc" and "Huckleberry Finn." Nay, he was a different bird altogether—an intensely serious and even lugubrious man, an iconoclast of the most relentless sort, a man not so much amused by the spectacle of life as appalled by it, a pessimist to the last degree. Nothing could be more unsound than the Mark legend—the legend of the light-hearted and kindly old clown. Study the volumes of Paine and you will quickly discern its unsoundness. The real Mark was a man haunted to the point of distraction by the endless and meaningless tragedy of existence—a man whose thoughts turned to it constantly, in season and out of season.

And to think, with him, was to write; he was, for all his laziness, the most assiduous of scribblers; he piled up notes, sketches of books and articles, even whole books, about it, almost mountain high.

Well, why did these notes, sketches, articles and books get no further? Why do most of them remain unprinted, even today? You will find the answer in a prefatory note that Mark appended to "What Is Man?" published privately in 1905. I quote it in full:

> The studies for these papers were begun twenty-five or twenty-seven years ago. The papers were written seven years ago. I have examined them once or twice per year since and found them satisfactory. I have just examined them again, and am still satisfied that they speak the truth. Every thought in them has been thought (and accepted as unassailable truth) by millions upon millions of men—and concealed, kept private. Why did they not speak out? Because they dreaded (*and could not bear*) the disapproval of the people around them. Why have I not published? The same reason has restrained me, I think. I can find no other.

Imagine a man writing so honest and excellent a book, imagine him examining it and re-examining it and always finding it good—and yet holding off the printing of it for twenty-five years, and then issuing it timorously and behind the door, in an edition of 250 copies, none of them for sale! Even his death did not quench his fear. His executors, taking it over as part of his goods, withheld the book for five years more—and then printed it very discreetly, with the betraying preface omitted! Surely it would be impossible in the literature of any other civilized country since the Middle Ages to find anything to match that long hesitation. Here was a man of the highest dignity in the national letters, a man universally recognized to be their chief living adornment, and here was a book into which he had put the earnest convictions of his lifetime, a book carefully and deliberately written, a book representing him more accurately than any other, both as artist and as man—and yet it had to wait thirty-five years before it saw the light of day! An astounding affair, in all conscience—but thoroughly American, Messieurs, thoroughly American. Mark knew his countrymen. He knew their intense suspicion of ideas, their blind hatred of heterodoxy, their bitter way of dealing with dissenters. He knew how, their pruderies outraged, they would turn upon even the gaudiest hero and roll him in the mud. And knowing, he was afraid. He "dreaded the disapproval of the people around him." And part of that dread, I suspect, was peculiarly internal. In brief, Mark himself was also an American, and he shared the national horror of the unorthodox. His own speculations always half appalled him. He was not only afraid to utter what he believed; he was even a bit timorous about *believing* what he believed.

The weakness takes a good deal from his stature. It leaves him radiating a subtle flavor of the second-rate. With more courage, he would have gone a great deal further, and left a far deeper mark upon the intellectual history of his time. Not, perhaps, intrinsically as artist. He got as far in that direction as it is possible for a man of his training to go. "Huckleberry Finn" is a truly stupendous piece of work—perhaps the greatest novel ever written in English. And it would be difficult to surpass the sheer artistry of such things as "A Connecticut Yankee," "Captain Stormfield," "Joan of Arc" and parts of "A Tramp Abroad." But there is more to the making of literature than the mere depiction of human beings at their obscene follies; there is also the play of ideas. Mark had ideas that were clear, that were vigorous, and that had an immediate appositeness. True enough, most of them were not quite original. As Prof. Schoenemann, of Harvard, has lately demonstrated, he got the notion of "The Mysterious Stranger" from Adolf Wilbrandt's "Der Meister von Palmyra"; much of "What Is Man?" you will find in the forgotten harangues of Ingersoll; in other directions he borrowed right and left. But it is only necessary to read either of the books I have just mentioned to see how thoroughly he recast everything he wrote; how brilliantly it came to be marked by the charm of his own personality; how he got his own peculiar and unmatchable eloquence into the merest statement of it. When, entering these regions of his true faith, he yielded to a puerile timidity—when he sacrificed his conscience and his self-respect to the idiotic popularity that so often more than half dishonored him—then he not only did a cruel disservice to his own permanent fame, but inflicted genuine damage upon the national literature. He was greater than all the others because he was more American, but in this one way, at least, he was less than them for the same reason. . . .

Well, there he stands—a bit concealed, a bit false, but still a colossus. As I said at the start, I am inclined year by year to rate his achievement higher. In such a work as "Huckleberry Finn" there is something that vastly transcends the merit of all ordinary books. It has a merit that is special and extraordinary; it lifts itself above all hollow standards and criteria; it seems greater every time I read it. The books that gave Mark his first celebrity do not hold up so well. "The Jumping Frog" still wrings snickers, but, after all, it is commonplace at bottom; even an Ellis Parker Butler might have conceivably written it. "The Innocents Abroad," re-read today, is largely tedious. Its humors are artificial; its audacities are stale; its eloquence belongs to the fancy journalism of a past generation. Even "Tom Sawyer" and "A Tramp Abroad" have long stretches of flatness. But in "Huckleberry Finn," though he didn't know it at the time and never quite realized it, Mark found himself. There, working against the grain, heartily sick of the book before it was done, always putting it off until tomorrow, he hacked out a masterpiece that expands as year chases year. There, if I am not wrong, he produced the greatest work of the imagination that These States have yet seen.

The Smart Set, 1919

Maks Erik

Maks Erik (1898–1937), the pen name of Zalman Merkin, a literary historian and critic born in Sosnowiec, Poland, wrote the article excerpted here for *Tog*, a Yiddish daily newspaper in Vilna. Sholem Aleichem was the pen name of the Ukrainian-born popular Yiddish author Sholem Naumovich Rabinovich, who lived in the United States during the last decade of his life. By the time he published this piece in 1924, Erik had begun to make a name for himself as an expert on Yiddish literature. Subsequently he published a ground-breaking history of Yiddish literature and a textbook on Yiddish literature in the 19th century. At the start of his essay on Mark Twain and Sholem Aleichem, Erik refers to a meeting between the two writers in New York City. Did they actually meet? In her book *My Father, Sholem Aleichem*, Marie Waife-Goldberg describes a meeting that took place in 1906 at a reception for the Educational Alliance on the Lower East Side. She wrote that her father was introduced as the "Jewish Mark Twain" (a title accorded him by *The New York Times*), to which "Mark Twain graciously replied, 'Please tell him that I am the American Sholem Aleichem.'" This meeting may or may not have happened—but references to it have long appeared in writing on Sholem Aleichem both in English and Yiddish. In 1929 Erik took up research positions at institutions in Minsk and Kiev. He had moved to the Soviet Union under the assumption that Yiddish culture would thrive there. Sadly, he was mistaken. In 1936, during the first wave of persecution of Jewish cultural figures, he was arrested and sent to the *gulag*; he died there in 1937.

FROM

שלום-עליכם און מארק טוועין.

(Sholem Aleichem and Mark Twain: Notes on the Eighth Anniversary of Sholem Aleichem's Death)

Mark Twain and Sholem Aleichem crossed paths during their lifetimes; Zalmen Shneour relates this as a definite fact, in his booklet.[1] The American humorist is supposed to have said to his Jewish colleague, "I've heard, my friend, that you are the Jewish Mark Twain," to which Sholem Aleichem is supposed to have responded, "And I've heard that you are the American Sholem Aleichem."

It's striking, just how the life of each individual gets dissolved into symbols. I've never closely pondered or researched the life of, say, Knut Hamsun. Why bother? It was revealed in his novels, in his entire body of work—and the story of Hamsun's love, which is the story of his life, is forever "concealed" in its public disclosure through art. Having provided us with love à la Hamsun as a *type*, Hamsun has irretrievably engraved the prototype into our curious imaginations. Yet, I have always pondered Dostoevsky's life, which is dissolving into the realm of legend and from year to year gets ever more enveloped in myth, in interpretation, in something that demands commentary. And how many arguments have erupted over Tolstoy's life, which is and cannot help but be a commentary on his entire creative oeuvre?

The life of the humorist dissolves into anecdotes—but anecdotes, too, are symbols that beg for commentary.

The fact is that whoever ends up writing the great monograph about Sholem Aleichem will bring Twain and Sholem Aleichem together, face to face. When Twain died, Kuprin[2] wrote an article entitled, "Laughter Has Died," bringing to bear numerous serious and weighty proofs that were intended to demonstrate that the laughter of our age followed Twain into his grave. And even more proof could be offered to show that the laughter of Yiddish literature—Yiddish humor—died together with Sholem Aleichem, possibly for good.

They will need to be brought together and also measured against each other, because both were indubitably humorists, kings of humor. In the end, great humorists are a rare commodity. Dickens, Gogol, Twain, Sholem Aleichem—and the roster of great modern humorists is just about closed. (Chekhov's powerful creative force can in no way be regarded as humor. The smug Jerome[3] and the entire stable of English humorists—and who among the English lacks a sense of humor?—can easily be subsumed within the receptacle known as "Dickens.")

*   *   *

From the Fair reveals definite influences of Twain. In this connection it is important to point out that ultimately it is not **what** one makes one's own, but **why** and **how** this is done. Writing "the work of his works, the book of his books, the Song of Songs of his soul," as he emphatically—and with great hyperbole—calls what he intended to be his "autobiographical novel," Sholem Aleichem undoubtedly drew upon Mark Twain's classic *Tom Sawyer* as his model. He was evidently impressed by Twain's objectivity and the absolute absence of saccharine sentimentality in his children's works. The "how" emerged not very happily (by the way, I am familiar only with the first volume). *From the Fair* is not a biography—it is too drawn out for a biography and possesses a large number of chapters lacking even a minimal biographical value—and it is not a novel. Sholem Aleichem naïvely believed that by "speaking about oneself in the third person" he automatically created the distance that transformed him into a novelistic hero. (Incidentally, Sholem Aleichem rarely speaks about himself in the third person.) Viewed as a novel, the *Fair* lacks concentrated action; overall, the work is purely descriptive, with a minimal dynamic. Add to that the cheap sentimentality of the piece, the constant "pinch" of his own cheek—something that Sholem Aleichem was actually concerned about—and one is calmly able to accept the well-worn consensus that Sholem Aleichem's "work of his works, the book of his books, the Song of Songs of his soul" was *Motl the Cantor's Son*.

Be that as it may, the juxtaposition of Twain and Sholem Aleichem reveals few points of intersection; primarily it has to do with parallels.

Above all, analogies in their lives can be cited: Both suddenly became rich (Mark Twain was even a millionaire three times over) and both carelessly neglected their fortunes. Both married out of love and both did so in the face of the unyielding opposition of their future in-laws—with whom they eventually became reconciled. And both extolled the idyll of love that led them back to their childhood years, to Buzi and Shimek,[4] and to Tom and the daughter of Judge Thatcher (who was evidently modeled upon Twain's father-in-law).

The book about Sholem Aleichem's life is called *From the Fair*, and that is how Twain's *Roughing It* should also be translated—the same careless leaps in life from the tip of one wave to another.

There is also convergence between the literary-historical situations that they encountered.

Twain represents the continuation of Dickens, and Sholem Aleichem is the continuation of Mendele.[5]

Dickens is a grandiose mausoleum. He encompasses the boundaries of "Merry Old England," the good old, conservative, placid Victorian era. The significance of his works resides not in their vision of the future, in opening a door to a new age. Rather, they are hermetic and enchained to their own stagnant present. Dickens is thus a model, an organism, a world. This hermetic quality made it possible for him to be a novelist.

There is only one of Dickens' works that presages Twain: *The Pickwick Papers*, which is the only work by Dickens that is not a novel but rather a kaleidoscope, a cinema of types revolving around the ostensible motions of Pickwick's *diligence*. In this masterpiece of English humor one detects youth—and English humor is so little accustomed to youth.

There are pages in *The Pickwick Papers* where it seems as if Dickens' humor has burst out of its chains—unconstrained humor! Twain-esque pages! Because Twain is English humor grown young. America made it possible—burst from the chains of tradition from which Dickens never managed to liberate himself, to free himself from a stagnant and smug English philistinism and fling himself confidently forward, with his own momentum and at his own pace.

Dickens made it to the year 1870, by which time his works had become frozen in time. He remained stuck at the point where European life was progressing at an ever more rapid imperial pace, and was beginning kaleidoscopically to transform its own patterns of thinking. Twain rolled over the wave, always at the crest, dancing and cavorting and enjoying this improvised, airborne cradle.

Mendele, too, became thoroughly stuck in his ways and closed out the era of Jewish traditionalism. He was left helpless in the face of the image of the idler who led the residents of Kasrilevke into the wider world, while at the same time he stands as a funereal monument to the Vale of Tears of Glupsk.[6]

Whereas his "grandson" danced away the hours with the new tempest, deriving energy from it, living from its motion, and fashioning his life's work out of it.

By ceasing to live in an era that was passing, and by serving as witnesses to the gradual rise of a new epoch—this made novel-writing impossible for them. Such was both Twain's and Sholem Aleichem's nostalgia and such was their impotence. Twain portrayed the former way of life—as, for example, in his work of genius *Huckleberry Finn*—by slowing down the kaleidoscopic action, because in contrast to *Tom Sawyer* this is a memoiristic work and not a children's book. He slowed it down but did not bend it. By "kaleidoscope" I mean the spinning out of a volume that possesses only length and breadth. But a novel requires more depth and nuance, a curve to the line of the action.

The final attempt at a novel by Sholem Aleichem was *Wandering Stars*—and he was impotent to make the leap.

They were incapable of becoming novelists. So, what they were left with was the epic, colliding against the sheer dimensions of the construct and the breadth of the canvas.

And here, in the characteristics discussed up to this point, is where the analogy just about comes to an end.

They differ fundamentally in their relationship to the past in which they were raised. Yiddish critics have already shown that Sholem Aleichem made fullest use of the process of differentiation in Jewish life—the Jew's donning of new garments. His greatest works are "Menakhem Mendl," "Tevye," and "Motl the Cantor's Son": Jewish economic life in flux, the Jewish family, and finally, Jewish emigration. He always operates and speculates about the contrast in this transformation, about the mad rush of the new and old ways. For this reason, naïveté plays an exceptionally great role in Sholem Aleichem's comic technique. For naïveté is based on the quantitative contrast, on transposition, the difference between tone and resonance. Naïveté is not an absolute quality; it emerges only in the telling and comparing. This does not suffice for Sholem Aleichem: he has a tendency to get entangled in a play of contrasts. There is the contrast between the small-town mentality of Menakhem Mendl, which big-city ways penetrate only in a distorted manner. Then we come to a new plane of friction: the category of Quixotic, utterly intellectualizing naïveté, of an idée fixe standing between the hero and the surrounding world, creating a peculiar fog around him, with external phenomena seeping through in bizarre and outlandish ways. If that isn't enough, he places Menakhem Mendl between the two fires of Sheyne Sheyndl[7] and Yehupetz,[8] thereby reinforcing the already powerful planes of friction.

Incidentally, he did not have to search far: Jewish life supplied him with flags, decorations, and perspectives. It provided that tragic aftertaste to his laughter, even when he wasn't thinking about it (for example, in the *Menakhem Mendl* saga). But there, too, artistic expression can be found: Sholem Aleichem is completely tragic only very rarely.

He is tragic when he does not want to be so, subconsciously. When he wishes to be tragic he becomes melodramatic. By contrast, Twain seldom combines tragedy and comedy. There is a powerful scene in *Huck Finn* about the demise of two families divided by a blood feud. Twain's laughter is suddenly stilled, and the brutality of the facts is all that is heard. To a far greater degree than Sholem Aleichem he has mastered the deeply human art of keeping silent.

And Twain portrays the past as past. He smiles, he laughs, he idyll-izes—infrequently confronting the present, possibly because of the absence of those planes of friction that his Jewish colleague treated in abundance—and he is therefore compelled to resort so often to caricature and hyperbole, which occupy so small a place in Sholem Aleichem's technique.

Translator's Notes

[1] Zalman Shneour, *Sholem-Aleykhems ondeynken* (Berlin: Klal-farlag, 1923), p.40.

[2] Aleksandr Ivanovich Kuprin (1870–1938), dubbed the "Russian Kipling" by Vladimir Nabokov.

[3] Jerome K. Jerome (1859–1927), author of *Three Men in a Boat* and other humorous works.

[4] From Sholem Aleichem's short story "Song of Songs" ("Shir ha-shirim").

[5] Mendele Moykher-Sforim (Mendele the Book Peddler), narrator and literary persona of Sholem-Ya'akov Abramovitsh (1835–1917), Yiddish and Hebrew satirist, referred to by Sholem Aleichem as the *zeyde*, or grandfather of Yiddish literature. See Dan Miron, *A Traveler Disguised* (New York: Schocken, 1973; Syracuse: Syracuse University Press, 1996).

[6] The "idler," being Sholem Aleichem's character Menakhem Mendl, a native of the small town of Kasrilevke. Glupsk was the archetypal Jewish small town of Mendele Moykher-Sforim's works.

[7] Menakhem Mendl's tempestuous wife.

[8] The big city, with its tumult and its Bourse.

Translated by Zachary M. Baker
Tog (Vilna), 1924

Helen Keller

Helen Keller (1880–1968) met Mark Twain in 1894 at the home of their mutual friend, writer and editor Lawrence Hutton. Twain was entranced by the precocious 14-year-old deaf and blind girl and by her remarkable teacher, Anne Sullivan, whom he dubbed the "miracle worker." Twain played a key role in making it possible for Keller to go to college: he introduced her to Standard Oil magnate Henry Huttleston Rogers, who, with his wife, paid for Keller's expenses at Radcliffe. When she graduated in 1904, Keller was the first deaf and blind person in the world to earn a bachelor of arts degree. Keller learned to read English, French, German, and Latin in Braille, and went on to become an outspoken anti-war activist as well as an advocate for woman suffrage, birth control, socialism, and workers' rights—and the author of 12 books. Twain called her one of the two most remarkable people of the 19th century (the other was Napoleon). When Keller sent him a copy of the autobiography she published at age 22, Twain wrote her a warm letter of thanks, saying, "I must steal half a moment from my work to say how glad I am to have your book and how highly I value it, both for its own sake and as a remembrance of an affectionate friendship which has subsisted between us for nine years without a break and without a single act of violence that I can call to mind. I suppose there is nothing like it in heaven; and not likely to be, until we get there and show off. I often think of it with longing, and how they'll say, 'there they come—sit down in front.' I am practicing with a tin halo. You do the same." At the time she published her account (included here) of "the volcano of invective and ridicule" that Mark Twain heaped on the American massacre of Moros in the Philippines, Twain's opposition to his country's imperialist military exploits had been largely buried by his biographers. But Keller insisted on foregrounding the fact that "all his life he fought injustice wherever he saw it in the relations between man and man—in politics, in wars, in outrages against the natives of the Philippines, the Congo, and Panama," adding, "I loved his views on public affairs, they were so often the same as my own."

Our Mark Twain

One of the most memorable events of our Wrentham years was our visit to Mark Twain.

My memory of Mr. Clemens runs back to 1894, when he was vigorous, before the shadows began to gather. Such was the affection he inspired in my young heart that my love for him has deepened with the years. More than anyone else I have ever known except Dr. Alexander Graham Bell and my teacher, he aroused in me the feeling of mingled tenderness and awe. I saw him many times at my friend Mr. Lawrence Hutton's in New York, and later in Princeton, also at Mr. H. H. Rogers's and at his own home at 21 Fifth Avenue, and last of all at Stormfield, Connecticut. Now and then I received letters from him. We were both too busy to write often, but whenever events of importance in our lives occurred we wrote to each other about them.

I was fourteen years old when I first met Mr. Clemens—one Sunday afternoon when Miss Sullivan and I were the guests of Mr. and Mrs. Lawrence Hutton in New York. During the afternoon several celebrities dropped in, and among them Mr. Clemens. The instant I clasped his hand in mine, I knew that he was my friend. He made me laugh and feel thoroughly happy by telling some good stories, which I read from his lips. I have forgotten a great deal more than I remember, but I shall never forget how tender he was.

He knew with keen and sure intuition many things about me and how it felt to be blind and not to keep up with the swift ones—things that others learned slowly or not at all. He never embarrassed me by saying how terrible it is not to see, or how dull life must be, lived always in the dark. He wove about my dark walls romance and adventure, which made me feel happy and important. Once when Peter Dunne, the irrepressible Mr. Dooley, exclaimed: "God, how dull it must be for her, every day the same and every night the same as the day," he said, "You're damned wrong there; blindness is an exciting business, I tell you; if you don't believe it, get up some dark night on the wrong side of your bed when the house is on fire and try to find the door."

The next time I saw Mr. Clemens was in Princeton during a spring vacation when we were visiting the Huttons in their new home. We had many happy hours together at that time.

One evening in the library he lectured to a distinguished company—Woodrow Wilson was present—on the situation in the Philippines. We listened breathlessly. He described how six hundred Moros—men, women, and children—had taken refuge in an extinct crater bowl near Jolo, where they were caught in a trap and murdered, by order of General Leonard Wood. A few days afterwards, Col. Funston captured the patriot Aguinaldo by disguising his military marauders in the uniform of the enemy and pretending to be friends of Aguinaldo's officers. Upon these military exploits, Mr. Clemens poured out a volcano of invective and ridicule. Only those who heard him can know his deep fervour and the potency of his flaming words. All his life he fought injustice wherever he saw it in the relations between man and man—in politics, in wars, in outrages against the natives of the Philippines, the Congo, and Panama. I loved his views on public affairs, they were so often the same as my own.

He thought he was a cynic, but his cynicism did not make him indifferent to the sight of cruelty, unkindness, meanness, or pretentiousness. He would often say, "Helen, the world is full of unseeing eyes, vacant, staring, soulless eyes." He would work himself into a frenzy over dull acquiescence in any evil that could be remedied. True, sometimes it seemed as if he let loose all the artillery of Heaven against an intruding mouse but even then his "resplendent vocabulary" was a delight. Even when his ideas were quite wrong, they were expressed with such lucidity, conviction, and aggressiveness that one felt impelled to accept them—for the moment at least. One is almost persuaded to accept any idea which is well expressed.

He was interested in everything about me—my friends and little adventures and what I was writing. I loved him for his beautiful appreciation of my teacher's work. Of all the people who have written about me he is almost the only one who has realized the importance of Miss Sullivan in my life, who has appreciated her "brilliancy, penetration, wisdom, character, and the fine literary competences of her pen."

He often spoke tenderly of Mrs. Clemens and regretted that I had not known her.

"I am very lonely, sometimes, when I sit by the fire after my guests have departed," he used to say. "My thoughts trail away into the past. I think of Livy and Susie and I seem to be fumbling in the dark folds of confused dreams. I come upon memories of little intimate happenings of long ago that drop like stars into the silence. One day everything breaks and crumbles. It did the day Livy died." Mr. Clemens repeated with emotion and inexpressible tenderness the lines which he had carved on her tombstone:

> Warm summer sun,
> Shine kindly here;
> Warm Southern wind,
> Blow softly here;
> Green sod above,
> Lie light, lie light;
> Good night, dear heart,
> Good night, good night.

The year after her death he said to me, "This has been the saddest year I have ever known. If it were not that work brings forgetfulness, life would be intolerable." He expressed regret that he had not accomplished more. I exclaimed, "Why, Mr. Clemens, the whole world has crowned you. Already your name is linked with the greatest names in our history. Bernard Shaw compares your work with that of Voltaire, and Kipling has called you the American Cervantes."

"Ah, Helen, you have a honeyed tongue; but you don't understand. I have only amused people. Their laughter has submerged me."

There are writers who belong to the history of their nation's literature. Mark Twain is one of them. When we think of great Americans we think of him. He incorporated the age he lived in. To me he symbolizes the pioneer qualities—the large, free, unconventional, humorous point of view of men who sail new seas and blaze new trails through the wilderness. Mark Twain and the Mississippi River are inseparable in my mind. When I told him that *Life on the Mississippi* was my favourite story of adventure, he said, "That amazes me. It wouldn't have occurred to me that a woman would find such rough reading interesting. But I don't know much about women. It would be impossible for a person to know less about women than I do."

After some badinage back and forth about women, Mr. Clemens's manner changed. A sadness came into his voice. "Those were glorious days, the days on the Mississippi. They will come back no more, life has swallowed them up, and youth will come no more. They were days when the tide of life was high, when the heart was full of the sparkling wine of romance. There have been no other days like them."

It was just after he had read my book *The World I Live In*, that he sent a note to Wrentham saying, "I command you all three to come and spend a few days with me in Stormfield."

It was indeed the summons of a beloved king. His carriage met us at Redding station. If my memory serves me, it was in February; there was a light snow upon the Connecticut hills. It was a glorious five mile drive to Stormfield; little icicles hung from the edges of the leaves and there was a tang in the air of cedar and pine. We drove rapidly along the winding country roads, the horses were in high spirits. Mr. Macy kept reading signboards bearing the initials "M. T." As we approached the Italian villa on the very top of the hill, they told me he was standing on the verandah waiting. As the carriage rolled between the huge granite pillars, he waved his hand; they told me he was all in white and that his beautiful white hair glistened in the afternoon sunshine like the snow spray on the gray stones.

There was a bright fire on the hearth, and we breathed in the fragrance of pine and the orange pekoe tea. I scolded Mr. Clemens a little for coming out on the verandah without his hat; there was still a winter chill in the air. He seemed pleased that I thought about him in that way, and said rather wistfully, "It is not often these days that anyone notices when I am imprudent."

We were in the land of enchantment. We sat by the fire and had our tea and buttered toast and he insisted that I must have strawberry jam on my toast. We were the only guests. Miss Lyon, Mr. Clemens's secretary, presided over the tea table.

Mr. Clemens asked me if I would like to see the house, remarking that people found it more interesting than himself.

Out of the living room there was a large sunny, beautiful loggia, full of living plants and great jardinières filled with wild grasses, cat-tails, goldenrod, and thistles which had been gathered on the hills in the late fall. We returned through the living room to the dining room and out on to the pergola and back again to the house and into the billiard room, where Mr. Clemens said he spent his happiest hours. He was passionately fond of billiards, and very proud of the billiard table with which Mrs. H. H. Rogers had presented him. He said he would teach me to play.

I answered, "Oh, Mr. Clemens, it takes sight to play billiards."

"Yes," he teased, "but not the variety of billiards that Paine and Dunne and Rogers play. The blind couldn't play worse." Then upstairs to see Mr. Clemens's bedroom and examine the carved bedposts and catch a glimpse of the view out of the great windows before darkness closed in upon us.

"Try to picture, Helen, what we are seeing out of these windows. We are high up on a snow-covered hill. Beyond, are dense spruce and firwoods, other snow-clad hills and stone walls intersecting the landscape everywhere, and over all, the white wizardry of winter. It is a delight, this wild, free, fir-scented place."

Our suite of rooms was next to his. On the mantel-piece, suspended from a candlestick, was a card explaining to burglars where articles of value were in the room. There had recently been a burglary in the house, and Mr. Clemens explained that this was a precaution against being disturbed by intruders.

"Before I leave you," he said, "I want to show you Clara's room; it is the most beautiful apartment in the house."

He was not content until he had shown us the servants' quarters, and he would have taken us to the attic if Miss Lyon had not suggested that we leave it for another day. It was obvious that Mr. Clemens took great satisfaction in his unusual house.

He told us that it had been designed by the son of my lifelong friend, William Dean Howells. Delightfully he pointed out that the architecture was exactly suited to the natural surroundings, that the dark cedars and pines, which were always green, made a singularly beautiful setting for the white villa. Mr. Clemens particularly enjoyed the sunlight that came through the great windows and the glimpse of field and sky that could be seen through them.

"You observe," he said to us, "there are no pictures on the walls. Pictures in this house would be an impertinence. No artist, going to this window and looking out, has ever equalled that landscape."

We stayed in our room till dinner was announced. Dinner in Mr. Clemens's house was always a function where conversation was important; yes, more important than the food. It was a rule in that house that guests were relieved of the responsibility of conversation. Mr. Clemens said that his personal experience had taught him that you could not enjoy your dinner if the burden of finding something to say was weighing heavily upon you. He made it a rule, he said, to do all the talking in his own house, and expected when he was invited out that his hosts would do the same. He talked delightfully, audaciously, brilliantly. His talk was fragrant with tobacco and flamboyant with profanity. I adored him because he did not temper his conversation to any femininity. He was a playboy sometimes and on occasions liked to show off. He had a natural sense of the dramatic, and enjoyed posing as he talked. But in the core of him there was no make-believe. He never attempted to hide his light under a bushel. I think it was Goethe who said, "Only clods are modest." If that is true, then in the world there was not less of a clod than Mr. Clemens.

He ate very little himself, and invariably grew restless before the dinner was finished. He would get up in the midst of a sentence, walk round the table or up and down the long dining room, talking all the while. He would stop behind my chair, and ask me if there was anything I wanted; he would sometimes take a flower from a vase and if I happened to be able to identify it he showed his pleasure by describing in an exaggerated manner the powers that lie latent in our faculties, declaring that the ordinary human being had not scratched the surface of his brain. This line of observation usually led to a tirade upon the appalling stupidity of all normal human beings. Watching my teacher spelling to me, he drawled, "Can you spell into Helen's left hand and tell her the truth?" Sometimes the butler called his attention to a tempting dish, and he would sit down and eat.

To test my powers of observation, he would leave the room quietly and start the self-playing organ in the living room. My teacher told me how amusing it was to see him steal back to the dining room and watch stealthily for any manifestations on my part that the vibrations had reached my feet. I did not often feel the musical vibrations, as I believe the floor was tiled, which prevented the sound waves from reaching me, but I did sometimes feel the chord vibrations through the table. I was always glad when I did, because it made Mr. Clemens so happy.

We gathered about the warm hearth after dinner, and Mr. Clemens stood with his back to the fire talking to us. There he stood—our Mark Twain, our American, our humorist, the embodiment of our country. He seemed to have absorbed all America into himself. The great Mississippi River seemed forever flowing, flowing through his speech, through the shadowless white sands of thought. His voice seemed to say like the river, "Why hurry? Eternity is long; the ocean can wait." In reply to some expression of our admiration for the spaciousness and the beauty of the room, which was a combination of living room and library, he said with more enthusiasm than was his wont, "It suits me perfectly. I shall never live anywhere else in this world."

He was greatly interested when we told him that a friend of ours, Mr. W. S. Booth, had discovered an acrostic in the plays, sonnets, and poems usually attributed to Shakespeare, which revealed the author to be Francis Bacon. He was at first sceptical and inclined to be facetious at our expense. He attacked the subject vigorously, yet less than a month elapsed before he brought out a new book, *Is Shakespeare Dead?* in which he set out, with all his fire, to destroy the Shakespeare legend, but not, he said in a letter to me, with any hope of actually doing it.

"I wrote the booklet for pleasure—*not* in the expectation of convincing anybody that Shakespeare did not write Shakespeare. And don't you," he warned me, "write in any such expectation. Shakespeare, the Stratford tradesman, will still be the divine Shakespeare to our posterity a thousand years hence."

When the time came to say good night, Mr. Clemens led me to my room himself and told me that I would find cigars and a thermos bottle with Scotch whiskey, or Bourbon if I preferred it, in the bathroom. He told me that he spent the morning in bed writing, that his guests seldom saw him before lunch time, but if I felt like coming in to see him about ten-thirty, he would be delighted, for there were some things he would like to say to me when my Guardian Angel was not present.

About ten o'clock the next morning, he sent for me. He liked to do his literary work in bed, propped up among his snowy pillows looking very handsome in his dressing gown of rich silk, dictating his notes to a stenographer. He said if doing my work that way appealed to me, I might have half the bed, provided I maintained strict neutrality and did not talk. I told him the price was prohibitive, I could never yield woman's only prerogative, great as the temptation was.

It was a glorious bright day, and the sun streamed through the great windows. Mr. Clemens said if I did not feel inclined to work after lunch (which was by way of sarcasm, as he had previously remarked that I did not look industrious, and he believed that I had somebody to write my books for me), he would take a little walk with us and show us the "farm." He said he would not join us at lunch, as his doctor had put him on a strict diet. He appeared, however, just as dessert was being served. He said he had smelt the apple pie and could not resist. Miss Lyon protested timidly.

"Yes, I know; but fresh apple pie never killed anybody. But if Helen says I can't, I won't." I did not have the heart to say he couldn't, so we compromised on a very small piece, which was later augmented by a larger piece, after a pantomimic warning to the others not to betray him.

I suspected what was going on, and said, "Come, let us go before Mr. Clemens sends to the kitchen for another pie."

He said, "Tell her I suspected she was a psychic. That proves she is."

He put on a fur-lined greatcoat and fur cap, filled his pockets with cigars, and declared himself ready to start on the walk. He led me through the pergola, stopping to let me feel the cedars which stood guard at every step.

"The arches were intended for ramblers," he said, "but unfortunately they haven't bloomed this winter. I have spoken to the gardener about it, and I hope the next time you come we shall have roses blooming for you." He picked out a winding path which he thought I could follow easily. It was a delightful path, which lay between rocks and a saucy little brook that winter had not succeeded in binding with ice fetters. He asked Mr. Macy to tell me there was a tall white building across an intervening valley from where we were standing. "Tell her it's a church. It used to stand on this side of the brook; but the congregation moved it last summer when I told them I had no use for it. I had no idea that New England people were so accommodating. At that distance it is just what a church should be—serene and pure and mystical." We crossed the brook on a little rustic footbridge. He said it was a prehistoric bridge, and that the quiet brown pool underneath was the one celebrated in the Songs of Solomon. I quoted the passage he referred to: "Thine eyes like the fishpools in Heshbon, by the gate of Bath-rabbim." It was a joy being with him, holding his hand as he pointed out each lovely spot and told some charming untruth about it. He said, "The book of earth is wonderful. I wish I had time to read it. I think if I had begun in my youth, I might have got through the first chapter. But it's too late to do anything about it now."

We wandered on and on, forgetful of time and distance, beguiled by stream and meadow and seductive stone walls wearing their autumn draperies of red and gold vines a little dimmed by rain and snow, but still exquisitely beautiful. When we turned at last, and started to climb the hill, Mr. Clemens paused and stood gazing over the frosty New England valley, and said, "Age is like this, we stand on the summit and look back over the distance and time. Alas, how swift are the feet of the days of the years of youth." We realized that he was very tired. Mr. Macy suggested that he should return cross-lots and meet us on the road with a carriage. Mr. Clemens thought this a good idea, and agreed to pilot Mrs. Macy and me to the road, which he had every reason to suppose was just beyond that elephant of a hill. Our search for that road was a wonderful and fearsome adventure. It led through cow-paths, across ditches filled with ice-cold water into fields dotted with little islands of red and gold which rose gently out of the white snow. On closer inspection we found that they were composed of patches of dry goldenrod and huckleberry bushes. We picked our way through treacherously smiling cart roads. He said, "Every path leading out of this jungle dwindles into a squirrel track and runs up a tree." The cart roads proved to be ruts that ensnared our innocent feet. Mr. Clemens had the wary air of a discoverer as he turned and twisted between spreading branches of majestic pines and dwarfed hazel bushes. I remarked that we seemed to be away off our course. He answered, "This is the uncharted wilderness. We have wandered into the chaos that existed before Jehovah divided the waters from the land. The road is just over there," he asserted with conviction. "Yes," we murmured faintly, wondering how we should ever ford the roaring, tumbling imp of a stream which flung itself at us out of the hills. There was no doubt about it. The road was just there "where you see that rail fence." Prophecy deepened into happy certainty when we saw Mr. Macy and the coachman waiting for us. "Stay where you are," they shouted. In a few seconds they had dismembered the rail fence and were transporting it over the field. It did not take them long to construct a rough bridge, over which we safely crossed the Redding Rubicon, and sure enough, there was the narrow road of civilization winding up the hillside between stone walls and clustering sumachs and wild cherry trees on which little icicles were beginning to form like pendants. Half way down the drive Miss Lyon met us with tearful reproaches. Mr. Clemens mumbled weakly, "It has happened again—the woman tempted me."

I think I never enjoyed a walk more. Sweet is the memory of hours spent with a beloved companion. Even being lost with Mr. Clemens was delightful, although I was terribly distressed that he should be exerting himself beyond his strength. He said many beautiful things about Stormfield, for instance, "It is my Heaven. Its repose stills my restlessness. The view from every point is superb and perpetually changes from miracle to miracle, yet nature never runs short of new beauty and charm." I hope the report is not true that he came to hate the place and feel that he had been defrauded of the society of his fellow men. But I can understand that a temperament like Mr. Clemens's would grow weary of the solitude.

The last evening of our visit we sat around a blazing log fire, and Mr. Clemens asked me if I would like to have him read me "Eve's Diary." Of course I was delighted.

He asked, "How shall we manage it?"

"Oh, you will read aloud, and my teacher will spell your words into my hand."

He murmured, "I had thought you would read my lips."

"I should like to, of course; but I am afraid you will find it very wearisome. We'll start that way anyhow, and if it doesn't work, we'll try the other way." This was an experience, I am sure, no other person in the world had ever had.

"You know, Mr. Clemens," I reminded him, "that we are going home to-morrow, and you promised to put on your Oxford robe for me before I went."

"So, I did, Helen, and I will—I will do it now before I forget."

Miss Lyon brought the gorgeous scarlet robe which he had worn when England's oldest university conferred upon him the degree of Doctor of Letters. He put it on, and stood there in the fire light the embodiment of gracious majesty. He seemed pleased that I was impressed. He drew me towards him and kissed me on the brow, as a cardinal or pope or feudal monarch might have kissed a little child.

How I wish I could paint the picture of that evening! Mr. Clemens sat in his great armchair, dressed in his white serge suit, the flaming scarlet robe draping his shoulders, and his white hair gleaming and glistening in the light of the lamp which shone down on his head. In one hand he held "Eve's Diary" in a glorious red cover. In the other hand he held his pipe. "If it gets in the way," he said, "I'll give it up, but I feel embarrassed without it."

I sat down near him in a low chair, my elbow on the arm of his chair, so that my fingers could rest lightly on his lips. Mr. Macy lighted his cigar, and the play began. Everything went smoothly for a time. I had no difficulty getting the words from his lips. His pleasant drawl was music to my touch, but when he began gesticulating with his pipe, the actors in the drama got mixed up with the properties and there was confusion until the ashes were gathered into the fireplace. Then a new setting was arranged. Mrs. Macy came and sat beside me and spelled the words into my right hand, while I looked at Mr. Clemens with my left, touching his face and hands and the book, following his gestures and every changing expression. As the reading proceeded, we became utterly absorbed in the wistful, tender chronicle of our first parents. Surely the joy, the innocence, the opening mind of childhood are among life's most sacred mysteries, and if young Eve laughs she makes creation all the sweeter for her Heaven-born merriment. The beauty of Mr. Clemens's voice, when Eve sighed her love, and when Adam stood at her grave grieving bitterly saying "wheresoever she was, there was Eden" caused me to weep openly, and the others swallowed audibly. Every one of us felt the yearning homesickness in that cry of pain.

To one hampered and circumscribed as I am it was a wonderful experience to have a friend like Mr. Clemens. I recall many talks with him about human affairs. He never made me feel that my opinions were worthless, as so many people do. He knew that we do not think with eyes and ears, and that our capacity for thought is not measured by five senses. He kept me always in mind while he talked, and he treated me like a competent human being. That is why I loved him.

Perhaps my strongest impression of him was that of sorrow. There was about him the air of one who had suffered greatly. Whenever I touched his face his expression was sad, even when he was telling a funny story. He smiled, not with the mouth but with his mind—a gesture of the soul rather than of the face. His voice was truly wonderful. To my touch, it was deep, resonant. He had the power of modulating it so as to suggest the most delicate shades of meaning and he spoke so deliberately that I could get almost every word with my fingers on his lips. Ah, how sweet and poignant the memory of his soft slow speech playing over my listening fingers. His words seemed to take strange lovely shapes on my hands. His own hands were wonderfully mobile and changeable under the influence of emotion. It has been said that life has treated me harshly; and sometimes I have complained in my heart because many pleasures of human experience have been withheld from me, but when I recollect the treasure of friendship that has been bestowed upon me I withdraw all charges against life. If much has been denied me, much, very much has been given me. So long as the memory of certain beloved friends live in my heart I shall say that life is good.

The affluence of Mr. Clemens's mind impressed me vividly. His felicitous words gushed from it with the abundance of the Shasta Falls. Humour was on the surface, but in the centre of his nature was a passion for truth, harmony, beauty.

Once he remarked in his pensive, cynical way, "There is so little in life that is not pretence."

"There is beauty, Mr. Clemens."

"Yes, there is beauty, and beauty is the seed of spirit from which we grow the flowers that shall endure."

I did not realize until I began this sketch how extremely difficult it would be to recapture Mr. Clemens's happy phrases from my memory. I am afraid I should not have succeeded at all if I had not made a few notes after my conversation with him. But I believe I have never falsified a word or an emphasis of the spirit of his utterances.

Time passed at Stormfield as it passes everywhere else, and the day came when we had to say good-bye. The kindly white figure stood on the verandah waving us farewell, as he had waved his welcome when we arrived. Silently we watched the stately villa on the white hilltop fading into the purple distance. We said to each other sadly, "Shall we ever see him again?" And we never did. But we three knew that we had a picture of him in our hearts which would remain there forever. In my fingertips was graven the image of his dear face with its halo of shining white hair, and in my memory his drawling, marvellous voice will always vibrate.

I have visited Stormfield since Mark Twain's death. The

flowers still bloom; the breezes still whisper and sough in the cedars, which have grown statelier year by year; the birds still sing, they tell me. But for me the place is bereft of its lover. The last time I was there, the house was in ruins. Only the great chimney was standing, a charred pile of bricks in the bright autumn landscape.

I sat on the step where he had stood with me one day, my hand warm in his, thoughts of him, like shadowy presences, came and went, sweet with memory and with regret. Then I fancied I felt someone approaching me; I reached out, and a red geranium blossom met my touch! The leaves of the plant were covered with ashes, and even the sturdy stalk had been partly broken off by a chip of falling plaster. But there was the bright flower smiling at me out of the ashes. I thought it said to me, "Please don't grieve." I brought the plant home and set it in a sunny corner of my garden, where always it seems to say the same thing to me, "Please don't grieve." But I grieve, nevertheless.

Midstream: My Later Years, 1929

Lu Xun

Lu Xun (Zhou Shuren) (1881–1936) is widely viewed as the father of modern Chinese literature, the first author to write short stories and prose poems in the language everyday Chinese people actually speak, rather than in the traditional literary language. Lu Xun had gone to Japan to study medicine in his youth, which is where he had his first contact with Western learning and the English language. In the preface to his first collection of short stories, *Call to Arms* (1923), he explained that he gave up his medical studies after seeing an illustration showing a group of impassive Chinese onlookers witnessing the execution of a Chinese man accused of being a spy during the Russo-Japanese War. The callous apathy he saw on the faces of his countrymen in that image made him decide to focus on his people's spiritual ills rather than their physical ones; he turned his attention to writing satirical and ironic fiction and social commentary, and to translating Western fiction into Chinese. His 1918 story "A Madman's Diary" (where Zhou Shuren used the pen name Lu Xun for the first time) is thought to be the first story written in modern Chinese. In 1931 Lu Xun's two-year-old son found an old copy of *Eve's Diary* (1906) by Mark Twain in a pile of trash left by a Westerner who had just moved out of the house next door to his home in Shanghai. Lu Xun was entranced by both the text and Lester Ralph's striking illustrations. He sent a request to Li Lan to translate the book into Chinese, which she did. Lu Xun wrote the preface to the Chinese edition of *Eve's Diary*, which was first published in a limited edition later that year, the first book-length publication of Mark Twain's work in Chinese.

FROM

《夏娃日记》小引
A Short Introduction to "Eve's Diary"

Mark Twain, needless to say, is a famous humorist from last century to the start of this one. That can be learned by leafing through a history of American literature. Not only do his works make one laugh: even his pseudonym sounds a bit humorous.

His real name is Clemens (Samuel Langhorne Clemens,

173

(1835–1910). He used to be a riverboat pilot, and so took the call for measuring the depth of water as his pseudonym when his work was published. His works were very popular in his time, and he was considered a superb teller of funny stories. Yet the publication of his posthumous book *The Mysterious Stranger* clearly showed him to be a deep-seated misanthrope.

Laughing but full of bitterness. Why is that?

We all know the U.S. is the home of Edgar Allan Poe, N. Hawthorne and Walt Whitman. Unlike Twain, they are basically the same, within or without. But that's the story before the Civil War. Since then, Whitman was not able to sing his songs, because the U.S. had become an industrial society in which individuals had to be molded in one type, and the self could no longer be asserted. If one had dared to assert his self, he would have been the object of persecution. What the writers had learned then was not how one should develop his own individuality, but how one should write so that his writings could be liked and sold, and his reputation could rise. Even celebrities like Howells came to believe men of letters made themselves acceptable only by entertaining the multitudes. The wild and unsubmissive like Henry James, therefore, could hardly find any readership except in a foreign country, but some learned to tell funny stories, like Mark Twain.

Thus, Twain became a humorist in order to live, but he imbued humor with bitterness and sarcasm in order to show that he was not satisfied with that kind of life. This little bit of revolt, however, is enough to make the children of New Land[1] laugh and claim: Mark Twain is ours.

Eve's Diary, published in 1906, is a late work by Twain. True, it is no more than a sketch, but enough to show weakness in innocence and sarcasm in narration. It is like an American girl at that time, who, the author believes, could be the portrait of all women. They smiled, but their smile clearly indicated their loss of youth. Nevertheless, this was made less visible by the author's masterly hand, and was thus still a lively piece of work, not to mention the translator's faithful, simple and natural rendering so that people almost began to think that it wouldn't have been any better if Eve had kept her diary in Chinese.

The 50-some line drawing illustrations by Lester Ralph look soft but fresh. The layout easily reminds people of Ren Weichang's art pieces of the Chinese Qing Dynasty.[2] But his drawings are all about gods and noble-minded gentlemen, looking thin and weird, far from being healthy like Ralph's Adam and Eve, figures which are mind-clarifying and beneficial to Chinese eyes that have been used to the paintings of almond-eyed and sloping-shouldered beauties.

Translator's Notes
[1]New Land: The Soviet Union.
[2]Ren Weichang (1822–1857), family name as "Xiong," and first name "Weichang," born in Xiaoshan, Zhejiang Province, painter of the late Qing Dynasty.

Translated by Gongzhao Li
1931

Jorge Luis Borges

Argentinian writer Jorge Luis Borges (1899–1986) first read Mark Twain as a child and returned to him often as an adult. He mentions *Life on the Mississippi* as a source for his *Universal History of Infamy*, the book in which he made his debut as a storyteller, and which was published the same year he wrote this essay about Twain in *Sur*, Argentina's most important literary journal (a publication to which Borges contributed on a regular basis). In the piece that follows, written during the centennial of Mark Twain's birth, Borges took the occasion to rescue him from what he viewed as the outrageously reductive and wrongheaded interpretation put forth by the American critic Van Wyck Brooks in his 1920 study *The Ordeal of Mark Twain*, a book Borges describes below as "269 aggrieved octavo pages." (Borges was far from alone in his recoil from Brooks; the British writer E. M. Forster observed in his commonplace book in 1943, "*The Ordeal of Mark Twain* by a bothered and bothering American of the psychoanalyzing 30s has succeeded in bothering me a bit. . . .") In the brief survey of American literature Borges published in 1971, he reiterated and expanded on a point he makes here: referring to *Huckleberry Finn*, he wrote, "From this great book have arisen two others whose outline is the same, *Kim* (1901) by Kipling and *Don Segundo Sombra* (1926) by Ricardo Güiraldes. *Huckleberry Finn* was published in 1884; for the first time an American writer used the language of America without affectation." He closed by quoting a comment by the American critic John Mason Brown with which he agreed: "*Huckleberry Finn* taught the whole American novel to talk." When he was 83, Borges agreed to lecture at Washington University in St. Louis on the condition that his hosts take him to Mark Twain's hometown of Hannibal, Missouri. Frail and nearly blind, he insisted on making the two-hour trip. When he got there, it was clear that there was really only one thing he wanted to do: put his hand in the Mississippi River. The river, he said, was the essence of Twain's writing. He had to touch it to get closer to the "divine collaboration" of Mark Twain and the Mississippi that produced *Huckleberry Finn*.

Una Vindicación de Mark Twain
(A Vindication of Mark Twain)

On November 30, 1835, Mark Twain was born. Today, a hundred years after that date, we must vindicate his bright memory from two outrages that are similar and share a common origin: one, the idea that in his joyful work it is the moments of complaint or sarcasm that are fundamental; the other, the reduction of him to a symbol of the frustrated artist mutilated by an arid century and a brutal continent. Both errors have wide currency in his homeland; they must be denounced before they spread here as well. Their source must be Van Wyck Brooks' *The Ordeal of Mark Twain*.

In 269 aggrieved octavo pages, Van Wyck Brooks seeks to demonstrate that Mark Twain was a potential genius deformed by the dark Calvinism of the United States. Nothing more European and sophisticated than this notion; nothing, therefore, more tempting for an "advanced" New York intellectual. Nothing more in keeping, as well, with a certain international cliché. From the moment Charles Pierre Baudelaire expressed astonishment that Edgar Allan Poe could have been born in the state of Massachusetts, no one could be unaware that an American, whether novelist, musician or painter, can be that only despite America and in opposition to it. So goes the consensus, but is it true? Let us return to the most famous case, that of Edgar Allan Poe. It has been said an infinite number of times that this innovator was American only by an accident of birth, and could just as well have come from London or Upsala. I cannot agree. The terrible and humorous Poe is not only American but Yankee, both in the continuous precision and practicality of the various games he plays with obscurity, with cryptograms, and with verse, and in the gusto of those immense hoaxes that recall Barnum. (This trait persists in his descendents: note the mystagogical air and sensational typography in which M. Edmond Teste indulges himself.)

In the particular case of Mark Twain, one fact is indisputable. Mark Twain is only imaginable in America. We do not know,

and can never know, what America took from him. We know
that it gave him *Huckleberry Finn* and *Roughing It* and *The Innocents Abroad* and *Tom Sawyer* and the vast ineptitude of the
police who failed to notice the migratory White Elephant. Let
us reduce all his books to one and sum it up: *Mark Twain composed* Huckleberry Finn *in collaboration with that muddy and
American river, the Mississippi*. To deplore this divine collaboration, to speak of frustration and repression, is like lamenting
that the province of Buenos Aires so deformed the genius of
Hernández that he wrote *Martín Fierro*. I will not insist; Brooks'
depressing thesis has been splendidly annihilated by Bernard De
Voto, in his passionate and lucid book *Mark Twain's America*.

I move on to the second of the claims denounced above.
The grossest of the many temptations of the intellect, but also
the easiest and most widespread, is to say that a thing is the
opposite of what it seems to be. If the thing being defined is a
humorist, the inverted definition is inevitable, since the image
of a clown who laughs—*ridi, pagliaccio!*—is a sentimental obscenity somehow offensive to the soul. Not even the happy
and mythical Mickey Mouse has gone unscathed. I can attest
that I heard a Spanish poet, whose name I do not wish to recall, say: "That mouse worries me, he disturbs me, because I
sense in him the tragedy of the American people." No need to
add that in Mark Twain, the distinguished companion of "that
mouse," an identical tragedy has been "sensed." There are ex-
tenuating circumstances, I know. Twain's nihilism, his conception of the universe as a ceaseless and senseless mechanism, his
constant manufacturing of cynical or blasphemous maxims, his
vehement denial of Free Will, his warming to the idea of suicide, his study of "the cheapest and most practical way to finish off humanity once and for all," his fanatical atheism, his
cult of Fitzgerald's *Rubáiyát*, are undeniable. Likewise I am
well aware that for contemporaries of Freud, an author's most
enduring work consists of the gossip of his friends. As a man of
this singular twentieth century, it would be improper for me to
be unaware of these habits, and yet . . . If Mark Twain has any
exceptional claim on our memory, it is as a writer; if we look
for (and find) something in his many volumes, it is not pre-

cisely the tragic. Mark Twain—oh, recovered and almost paradoxical axiom!—was a humorist.

About Mark Twain's comic methods—as about those of Quevedo, Sterne, and Rabelais—an infinite number of things can be said. One fact, nevertheless, is indisputable: the essential value of novelty, and also of surprise. Mark Twain does not have many surprises left; we've been using him up since childhood, like Estanislao del Campo and Eduardo Wilde. It is difficult to be surprised by something one knows by heart. *The laughter is gone from it*, says Bernard De Voto of one of Mark Twain's first pages—and I am afraid that this confession, coming from an admirer, applies to his last pages as well. Let me advance a conjecture: purely verbal humor—the humor of accumulation and incongruence—pertains to oral rather than written literature. Three friends who see each other with any regularity end up elaborating a burlesque language of their own, a tradition of splendid allusions, a reworking and, as it were, invigoration of their jokes. A lone man does not practice these games. By definition, a reader is a man alone. (Daniel Defoe enumerates Robinson Crusoe's salvagings, his labors, his regimen, his hoods and goatskin umbrellas, his devout monologues, his lapses of foresight, his accomplishments in boatbuilding and pottery-making, even his dreams of York; but he says nothing of any pranks or roars of laughter in the face of the sea. Given that he is such a punctilious historian, we can infer that no such things occurred.)

If Mark Twain's fundamental nihilism has not played a large role in the reception of his work and of the enormous jubilation he engendered, barely a ghost remains to us. Why, then, burden the printing presses and the reader's time with this futile reminder? John Macy (on page 249 of *The Spirit of American Literature*) proposes a desperate course of action: "to recognize that this incorrigible joker is a powerful and original thinker." Agreed, but then what term will we reserve for William James or for Mr. Macy himself: "incorrigible joker" perhaps? What's more, I foresee that the knot is not so Gordian and that we can forego this task. Mark Twain (it is important to reiterate) wrote *Huckleberry Finn*, a book that by itself is enough to confer glory.

It is a book neither burlesque neither tragic, merely happy. *Happiness is better than mirth*, I read again in a letter by William Blake.

In the beginning of August 1934, I reviewed with Adelina del Carril the proofs of the English translation of *Don Segundo Sombra*. I then wrote a brief article, from which I extract this paragraph: "In these proofs, I have caught a glimpse of the gravitational pull and accent of another essential book of our America, Mark Twain's *Huckleberry Finn*. It too is the book of a journey and a friendship; but a friendship in which the boy does the guide's work, and the man does the adoring and blundering, and a journey through the ceaseless waters of the greatest river on earth. The friendship was imitated by Rudyard Kipling in his novel *Kim*: another great novel akin to *Don Segundo Sombra*." The book was published; Waldo Frank, in his preface, found the same parallel between *Don Segundo* and *Huck Finn*.

If I am not misled, novels are good in direct proportion to the interest that inspires in the author the characters' uniqueness and in inverse proportion to the intellectual or sentimental notions that guide him. In *Kim*, the "politics" is obvious; it is sufficient for me to recall that revealing apotheosis in which the author, to compensate and crown the arduous escapades of his hero, gives him a job as a spy. In Ricardo Güiraldes we divine a partisan agenda: to demonstrate that the job of a cowboy on the flat plain joined to Buenos Aires (the literati of the capital call it the Pampa) has much of the heroic about it. Mark Twain, by contrast, is divinely impartial. *Huckleberry Finn* wants nothing more than to reproduce some men and their destiny.

Translated by Geoffrey O'Brien
Sur, (Buenos Aires), 1935

Theodore Dreiser

Journalist, novelist, and essayist Theodore Dreiser (1871–1945) may be virtually alone for valuing Mark Twain above all as "the powerful and original and amazingly pessimistic thinker that he really was, and that several of his most distinguished contributions to American letters prove," as he puts it in "Mark the Double Twain." Dreiser's response to Twain went far beyond the idea that he was much more than a humorist. Dreiser—who was not known for his own sense of humor—had no use for Twain's humor at all, but celebrated him, instead, as a marvelously "gloomy and wholly mechanistic thinker." In Dreiser's view the humor interfered with Twain's being a great artist. It was the Twain who had written the anonymously published *What Is Man?* (1906) who most appealed to Dreiser. When he wrote the essay that follows, Dreiser was entranced by the writings of physiologist Jacques Loeb, who, basing his experiments on lower forms of life, argued that humans were merely machines. In *What Is Man?* one of the book's two characters argues for the same kind of mechanistic determinism. Dreiser also valued the dark pessimism of *The Mysterious Stranger* (a creation of Twain's editor and biographer, but which included material that Twain had written), and admired the quasi-pornographic, little-known *1601* (privately printed in 1882). Dreiser identified with the Twain that emerges in *What Is Man?*, *The Mysterious Stranger*, and *1601* because of his own attraction to the deterministic view that ultimately humans *were* the product of forces largely beyond their control, and because of his conviction that the pressure (financial and otherwise) to conform to conservative, provincial, puritanical standards of decorum acted as a straightjacket for American writers. Dreiser himself had been censored as a journalist in St. Louis when he tried to say positive things about an African-American opera singer, and as a journalist in Pittsburgh he had been told to avoid criticizing the local plutocracy; his novels *Sister Carrie* and *The "Genius"* had been censored because of his treatment of sex and morality. Having battled various forms of censorship all his life, Dreiser's own experience prepared him to bemoan what he saw as Twain's defensive self-censorship and to berate Americans for their disregard of the works by Mark Twain that Dreiser valued most.

Mark the Double Twain

A psychologic as well as literary enigma that has much troubled me, as it has many another who has surveyed American literature, is Mark Twain. Middle West American of quite humble Tennessee and Missouri village and farm backgrounds—with a few parent- and relative-owned slaves to complicate the picture—he remains to this hour, in the minds of most Americans, not the powerful and original and amazingly pessimistic thinker that he really was, and that several of his most distinguished contributions to American letters prove—but rather, and to this hour, the incorrigible and prolific joker and, at best, humorist who, up to the time of his death and since, has kept the world chuckling so continuously that it has not even now sobered sufficiently to detect in him the gloomy and wholly mechanistic thinker.

If, by chance, he had encountered Jacques Loeb!

If he had sensed the direction of scientific thought in the last twenty years!

As it is, for most, he remains the laughing, hoaxing biographer of Tom Sawyer and Huckleberry Finn, of Puddin' Head Wilson, and the American Claimant, rarely the critical and massive creator of *The Mysterious Stranger* (still sold as a Christmas book for children), and of *What Is Man?* which Loeb would have welcomed as an addition to his mechanistic biologic conclusions.

But how came this to be? Were there two Twains from the beginning, as one and another critic has asked since reading *What Is Man* and *The Mysterious Stranger*? I recall that so early as 1910, and in the editorial office of no less an institution than Harper and Brothers, then and still his publishers, I discovered that there were really two Twains writing—one who possessed great fame and acclaim for the body of work which everyone knew and approved of as wholesomely humorous, exposing little more than the minor or more forgivable flaws of American character—and another, the really not-at-all-known Twain who brought the most amazing and Rabelaisian stories of his own composition to the then publishing intermediaries of Harper and Brothers, F. A. Duneka, and Major F. G. Leigh, both of whom had, as they felt, to employ to the utmost their arts of discreet and yet firm diplomacy, in order, as they said, to "protect Mark" from the violent and fateful public conservatism of Americans, if not the world in general, should any of the things he was writing and bringing in ever reach them. In substantiation of which, I have in my possession a copy of *1601—Conversation as It Was by the Social Fireside in the Time of the Tudors*, with an Introduction by Albert Bigelow Paine, and quoted comments by David Gray, John Hay, and others. I do not need to say more than that. The initiated will understand. All others must inquire.

However, it is not this particular Rabelaisian extension of Twain's classic gift for paradox and exaggeration and horseplay in the field of humor, quite rampant in his day (Bill Nye, Petroleum V. Nasby, Josh Billings), but rather his much more publicly subdued—and I may add, frustrated—gift as well as mood for dark and devastating, and at the same time quite tender and sorrowing, meditation on the meaning or absence of it in life, plus a force and clarity of realistic presentation and criticism which has arrested me as it has many another. And not only in such published works as *Joan of Arc*, *The Man Who Corrupted Hadleyburg*, *The Mysterious Stranger*, and *What Is Man?* but in various paragraphs and critical summaries which are to be found in his later letters and his still unpublished autobiography, which, now that the twenty-five years stipulated by him before his death as the length of time which must elapse before it could be issued has elapsed, might well be given to the world.

But will it be? The volume published this year should show.

The financial interest or investment in his earlier conventional works and their reputation is still very great.

In the meantime, however, we have had *Joan of Arc*, which when published anonymously in 1895 was so different from the accepted work of Twain himself at the time that it was suggested by Twain that it be published under a nom de plume. As it was, he feared an unfavorable reaction, and before signing it wished to know what the result was to be. Had it proved unfavorable, it might have remained under a nom de plume until after his death. Yet, as different as it was, the general opinion was favorable, and so he acknowledged it. Only it never sold as did *Innocents Abroad*, or *Huckleberry Finn*, or *Tom Sawyer*.

Just the same, shortly thereafter (1898) he wrote, although he withheld from publication until 1916—six years after his death—two works entirely out of harmony with anything he had previously written: *The Mysterious Stranger* and *What Is Man?* In the meantime, that is between 1898 and 1911, when he died, while these other works were on the shelf, he published such volumes as *A Double-barrelled Detective Story*, *King Leopold's Soliloquy*, *Eve's Diary*, *Christian Science*, plus the much more daring, although much more humorous and therefore much safer, *The Man Who Corrupted Hadleyburg*—the first real break in his public humor, salving of a naughty, naughty world. Also, *Captain Stormfield's Visit to Heaven*, equally laughable. But with *What Is Man?* and *The Mysterious Stranger* out, although ignored, there still remain other things which will see the light—when? In this reactionary day? I doubt it.

But, in order not to delay you in this matter of forming an opinion for yourself, and to prove to you that he said things after his death that he never dared say in his life, I give you—and this from his autobiography not published until 1924, and *not* containing the full of his realistic comments on life and his day, which are still to come (1935)—this from a frontispage of his so-called autobiography, and in his own handwriting: "I am writing from the grave. On these terms only can a man be approximately frank. He cannot be straightly and unqualifiedly frank *either in the grave or out of it*." (The italics are mine.)

Next (also from Vol. I of his delayed autobiography):

> This is a world where you get nothing for nothing; where you pay value for everything you get and fifty per cent, and when it is gratitude you owe, you have to pay a thousand. In fact, gratitude is a debt which usually goes on accumulating, like blackmail; the more you pay, the more is exacted. In time you are made to realize that the kindness done you is become a curse, and you wish it had not happened.

And this:

> *Concerning man*—he is too large a subject to be treated as a whole; so I will merely discuss a detail or two of him at this time. I desire to contemplate him from this point of view—this premise; that he was not made for any useful purpose; for the reason that he hasn't served any; that he was most likely not even made *intentionally*; and that his working himself up out of the oyster bed to his present position was probably a matter of surprise and regret to the Creator. For his history, in all climes, all ages and all circumstances, furnishes oceans and continents of proof that of all the creatures that were made, he is the most detestable. Of the entire brood he is the only one—the solitary one—that possesses malice.
>
> That is the basest of all instincts, passions, vices—the most hateful. That one thing puts him below the rats, the grubs, the trichinae. He is the only creature that inflicts pain for sport, knowing it to *be* pain. But if the cat knows she is inflicting pain when she plays with the frightened mouse, then we must make an exception here; we must grant that in one detail man is the moral peer of the cat. All creatures kill—there seems to be no exception; but of the whole list, man is the only one that kills for fun; he is the only one that kills in malice, the only one that kills for revenge. Also—in all the list he is the only creature that has a nasty mind.
>
> Shall he be extolled for his noble qualities, for his gentleness, his sweetness, his amiability, his lovingness, his courage, his devotion, his patience, his fortitude, his prudence, the various charms and graces of his spirit? The other animals share all these with him, yet are free from the blacknesses and rottennesses of this character [pp. 7 and 8].

And this:

> There are certain sweet-smelling sugar-coated lies current in the world which all politic men have apparently tacitly conspired together to support and perpetuate. One of these is, that there is such a thing in the world as independence:

independence of thought, independence of opinion, independence of action. Another is, that the world loves to see independence—admires it, applauds it. Another is, that there is such a thing in the world as toleration—in religion, in politics, and such matters; and with it trains that already mentioned auxiliary lie that toleration is admired and applauded. Out of these trunk-lies spring many branch ones: to wit, the lie that not all men are slaves; the lie that men are glad when other men succeed; glad when they prosper; glad to see them reach lofty heights; sorry to see them fall again. And yet other branch lies: to wit, that there is heroism in man; that he is not mainly made up of malice and treachery; that he is sometimes not a coward; that there is something about him that ought to be perpetuated—in heaven or hell, or somewhere. And these and other branch lies, to wit: that conscience, man's moral medicine chest, is not only created by the Creator, but is put into man ready charged with the right and only true and authentic correctives of conduct— and the duplicate chest, with the self-same correctives, unchanged, unmodified, distributed to all nations and all epochs [pp. 8 and 9].

And yet one other branch lie: to wit, that I am I, and you are you; that we are units, individuals, and have natures of our own, instead of being the tail end of a tapeworm eternity of ancestors extending in linked procession back and back and back—to our source in the monkeys, with this so-called individuality of ours a decayed and rancid mush of inherited instincts and teachings derived, atom by atom, stench by stench, from the entire line of that sorry column, and not so much new and original matter in it as you could balance on a needle point and examine under a microscope. This makes well-nigh fantastic the suggestion that there can be such a thing as a personal, original, and responsible nature in a man, separable from that in him which is not original, and findable in such quantity as to enable the obesrver to say, this is a man, not a procession [p. 9].

And this:

> All the talk about tolerance, in anything or anywhere, is plainly a gentle lie. It does not exist. It is in no man's heart; but it unconsciously, and by moss-grown inherited habit, drivels and slobbers from all men's lips. Intolerance is everything for oneself, and nothing for the other person. The mainspring of man's nature is just that—selfishness [p. 13].

Of course, these are mere tidbits intended to arouse your curiosity, if any, in the major, if less-known phase of that very impressive genius. They are not as tender, not as sorrowful, not even as mordant or angry, as some of his more extended and devastating reflection. But the point, for this article, is that they move in the direction of what I am attempting to convey. *What Is Man?* is more far-reaching and cruel. In *The Mysterious Stranger* he has conceived life from the depths of a giant despair. What I am earnestly seeking to convey is that by no means has Mark Twain been properly evaluated. In America, as it is intellectually running even at this time, I doubt if he can be. There is, as I have said, a financial interest in his reputation *as is*, which has to be and will be (never fear) taken into consideration.

Next, for all the labors of Hollywood and the young anarchists of sex in literature and art, compositions such as *1601* and his yet unpublished short stories will await a secret and a numbered issue—if so much. And for all the revelation of the laboratories that point to a mechanistic universe and the entire determinist philosophy, never fear that *What Is Man?* or *The Mysterious Stranger* will be given either wide publicity or achieve serious mental consideration in America if elsewhere. And there are several reasons for that: dogmatic religion, as well as social and moral convictions on every hand—these latter lying entombed or enwombed in the first—and next, the never ending benightedness of the mass—schools or no schools, universities or no universities, biological and physical laboratories, or no biological and physical laboratories. I suspect that not only the Millikans but the Haldanes, and even the Julian Huxleys, would rise in revolt. And, as I say, you have only to consider the fate of Jacques Loeb, the most distinguished mental figure since Darwin, or rather his mechanistic data, to grasp what I mean. Do you know aught of his dozen volumes describing the mechanistic processes of life, as he unraveled them? I truly believe our present "Watch and Ward" guarded libraries will even shut their doors before they will distribute them.

What interests me, however, is this seeming duality of Twain, for, of course, there were not any two Mark Twains, just one. From the beginning, there was only the conventionally environed Twain who did not arrive, for instance, at the reading of Pepys's *Diary* until he was forty, and whose amazed curiosity as to Spencer, Darwin, Huxley, following his first trip abroad (*Innocents Abroad* [1869]), led naturally, if interruptedly—that is by way of fame—to introduction to the literary pundits of the East, marriage into a conservative and well-to-do family, the Langdons of Elmira, New York, the undying friendship and guidance of the conservative and even moralistic William Dean Howells, Charles Dudley Warner, Thomas Bailey Aldrich, and, naturally, Harper and Brothers, to name but a few. Also to such modified social protests (with brakes) as *The Prince and the Pauper*, *A Connecticut Yankee in King Arthur's Court*, etc. But not to the *Personal Recollections of Joan of Arc* or at long last to *The Man Who Corrupted Hadleyberg*, *The Mysterious Stranger*, or *What Is Man?* As I have said, these last two, though written in 1898, were not published in his lifetime. And his old-time contemporaries never lived to see them.

But of what was Twain so terrified? For contemporary with him was Zola—of equal fame—and D'Annunzio, and Chekhov, and Dostoevski, and De Maupassant, and Strindberg, and Ibsen. And he must have heard of Whitman and Herman Melville, ostracized for so wild a thing as *Typee*. He most certainly did hear of Maxim Gorky, for when, in 1905, he and his Russian actress sweetheart arrived in America, neither he nor Howells—their reputations as well as their social connections prohibiting—would attend a reception in his honor. And yet Twain could write not only *1601* but the stories that his publishers think should never be published! And his daughter Jean, writing of him that, "at home, he talked largely of serious things, with only an occasional humorous remark thrown in."

His letters to his Eastern friends, the pundits and powers, were different.

My suspicion is that it was the secondary social and conventional forces enveloping him after his early success and marriage, and playing on this sympathetic, and, at times, seemingly weak humanist, that succeeded for a time in diverting him almost completely from a serious, realistic, and I might say Dostoevskian, presentation of the anachronisms, the cruelties, as well as the sufferings, of the individual and the world which, at bottom, seem most genuinely to have concerned him. For, to a study of these he would have turned, had it not been, I think, for the noisy and quite vacuous applause accorded him as Genius Jester to the American booboisie. And by that I mean almost the entire American world of his time. He was too warm-hearted— among the tenderest of the humanists—and, as such, almost refuting his own worst charges. More, he was born (1835) into a scene that included slavery in the South, and wage slavery in New England, plus the struggling pioneers of the West. To be sure—and this must have proved a factor in his mental orientation—the American scene was still softened, and even quite gaily colored in spots, by its fabulous resources, as well as the economic optimism generated by said resources and the then still slowly receding frontier. Yet, even so, he could not have been unaware of the degradations, the deprivations, the inequalities, and the sufferings of the majority of the men and women about him or in the world.

You are not to forget that slavery was a part of the daily life of his boyhood town of Florida, Missouri, and of Hannibal; and that, in his teens, he was eyewitness, as he himself reports, to negro slaves, men slaves, women slaves, children slaves, chained together and left on some levee walk of the Missouri, while they waited for the steamboat that was to convey them south where they were to be resold. Yes, and there were men and women and children among them, as he himself says, separated from wives, husbands, and parents. Yet never once in all of his American annals, apart from the foregoing note, did he ever write bitterly of that, not even in his note or in his *Autobiography*. Yet later he could write movingly of the Prince and the Pauper, and what it meant or could have meant to a prince to learn of poverty through the accident of circumstance! More, he could write movingly and beautifully, even tragically, of the temperament and sufferings of Joan of Arc—even of the tortured peasants of the Romanoff Czar! But not, for instance, of any phase of the War of the Rebellion in which, except for one attempt at organizing a confederate guerilla band whose activities appear to have come to nothing, he did not take any part. The best he did for the Negro at any time was to set over against Harriet Beecher Stowe's Uncle Tom, the more or less Sambo portrait of the Negro Jim who, with Huckleberry Finn, occupied the raft that was the stage of that masterly record of youthful life, *Huckleberry Finn*.

But why? For most certainly in addition to, and in spite of, his humorous bent, he was a realist at heart, and a most extraordinary one. One need only thumb through the *Innocents Abroad*, or *Roughing It*, or *Tom Sawyer*, or *Huckleberry Finn*, or *The Gilded Age*, to find page after page, character after character, scene after scene, drawn movingly as well as brilliantly enough, and this, in spite of his Brobdignagian humor, from the life about him. I hardly need remind you of the fortunes and misfortunes of the Colonel Mulberry Seller's family where, despite the colossally comic aspects of the colonel's ambitions and his methods (*There Are Millions in It*), the pathos of his career, and that of his wife and children, rings sonorously and sadly.

Again, in *Roughing It* consider its virility and its importance as a reconstruction of a fantastic and yet absolutely real phase of American history—an unforgettable and most important section of our national life. True, belly-shaking caricature plays over a cold sense of fact, yet the tragedy of the silver-boom town is as apparent as its comedy and takes permanent and accurate shape for the benefit, I hope, of an inquisitive posterity. In *Huckleberry Finn* consider the Granger-Sheperdson feud. And, in spite of the wholly humorous report of it, the tragic implications of it all. A single turn of the pen at any point in this narrative, and you would have a story which would startle, terrify, as well as thrill and entertain, the most avid seekers of realistic truth. The same is true of Colonel Sherburn's reception of and speech to the crowd that came to lynch him. No humor there, as you will note: only the hard, cold reality of a courageous man's confrontation of a reasonless, meaningless mob. It could as well have come out of Balzac, of Tolstoi, of Saltykoff. Here is no yielding to the necessity for humor, nor the exaggeration of jest, for Twain in his soberer moods was always the realist—and a great one. Yet, for reason of that bent of his toward caricature and towering exaggeration, almost wholly uppermost in his youth and early manhood, he was slow in coming to the more balanced aspects of his later work. One wishes at times that, like Shakespeare, he could have balanced the fantastically ridiculous with the truly tragic, and in some lovely American picture have dealt with what he knew to be the true features and factors of the period in which he lived.

Inquiry and reflection have caused me to assume as follows: To begin with, he was as a child, and in so far as a liberal—yes, even a conventional—education was concerned, but poorly dealt with. No public schooling after his eleventh year. Next, swirling about him were those western and middle-western Americans of his day, semi-lunatic with bonanza religious as well as financial and "moral" dreams, Ah, the twisted sociologic, as well as psychologic, forces playing upon a nature at once sensitive, kindly, and at the same time exaggeratedly humorous! The jest! The jest! And about him—in the American newspaper and upon the American platform—those reigning American models of his day: Artemus Ward, Josh Billings, Bill Nye, Petroleum V. Nasby. And all so stupendously successful. America could afford to laugh. As yet it was sufficiently free and happy to permit it so to do. And not only these, but consider the crudities and nonsensicalities of his own Missouri small-town world, Florida, Missouri! Hannibal, Missouri! Read of them in *Huckleberry Finn*. And related to him, even nondescript farmers, some of them owners of ill-kept and ill-trained slaves with whom, and with the children of whom, he, as a schoolboy and small-town loafer, played. And after that, the youthful life of a Mississippi pilot's apprentice, with all the crude midwestern river life that registered on the quivering, if jest-loving, sensibilities of a world genius of twenty—a stripling Falstaff as well as Dickens combined.

Yet, never a novelist—never. He could not write a novel. Consider only *The Gilded Age*! Rather, your humanist annalist, but without the complete and tragic life of any single defeated mortal burned deep in his heart. Why? He who could write of the Mysterious Stranger? And the sorrows of Joan of Arc? Why?

But after these early days, swift success, stupendous, worldwide fame! The laughter of England, America, Germany, France. Our simple and almost boobish genius thrust willy-nilly into the company of wealth, reputation, title, conventional and mental assumption and punditry, in its most aggravated forms. And with handclapping and backslapping everywhere. Oh, our darling Mark—the great American World Genius!

Consider his first journey abroad. And then, *Innocents Abroad*. And then all of the foregoing. And more: his meeting up with, and on the boat that carried him abroad—first the photo of the girl who was to be his wife, and then the girl herself, Miss Olivia Langdon, of Elmira, whom, on February 2, 1870, and in the full flare of his sudden and most unexpected acclaim, he married. And receiving at once, and along with fame and love, a completely furnished house, and even an interest in a Buffalo newspaper, as a wedding present! So you see fame, love, money tumbling in upon a hobbledehoy genius; and more and more fame and money, plus, and quite as swiftly, the companionship and applause of the acknowledged cognoscenti and literati of the ultra-snobbish literary East: Warner, Aldrich, Howells, Cable, Hay! And the cautious guidance of in-laws who were proud of, if slightly condescending toward, the upstart Genius who needed, of course—and of all things—polishing. Indeed, Charles Dudley Warner, critical poohbah of his hour, and so early as 1873 (!) already collaborating with Twain in the writing of that amazingly bad novel, *The Gilded Age*. And Howells hailing him as "Dear Mark!" in his book. Yet, with one deathless character at that, Twain's own maternal uncle—James Lampton—disguised as Colonel Mulberry Sellers.

And then after that, other successful books, of course: *Tom Sawyer*, *Life on the Mississippi*, *Huckleberry Finn*, *The Prince and the Pauper*, etc. And because of these, the this and the that of the European and American world of that day, doing all that they could to formalize and perpetuate this genius, as he was to them—not as he was to himself—in his deepest self. And so, letters and conversations indicating as much. His wife editing his books and cutting out the danger spots. Howells acclaiming him for his morality—he of *1601*. Yet, in spite of all the glamour, here was the other Twain thinking betimes of *What Is Man?* and *The Mysterious Stranger*, and, in his heart, hating his limitations. Do I need to ask you to re-read the quotation in the earlier part of this study?

But because it was so glamorous and so grand, and he hated to hurt people, and there was his publisher's investment in his books, and what his good friends thought of him, he did not dare to revolt! He feared what they would say. That ostracism awaited him, as it awaits every man who will not march with the crowd. And so, eventually—pain and morbidity. He could not do this, and he could not do that—write, for instance, a towering indictment of anything American. Ah no! For that, to those about him, would have been corrupting his art, falling from his high place as a moral, laughing genius! Hence, all that was really going on in America—its corrupt and shameless politics (only laughingly indicated in *The Gilded Age*); its robber finance such as ended in the monopoly of the railroads, the telegraph, the oil, the coal, the silver and gold of the nation; its lunatic snobbery in the form of the "Four Hundred," with its Fifth Avenues, Newports, Southamptons, and its yachts and gold harnesses and pet-dog dinners, and its most fantastic heirs and assigns of the second and third generation, all going untouched. At that time they were sacred. Too sacred for him, or his art.

Not that I am calling on Twain to be anything that he was not. It is he, himself, who has indicated in all that he feared to publish in life that he was really calling on himself to do differently and to be different. But convention—convention, the dross of a worthless and meaningless current opinion—this was the thing that restrained him. Because of Howells and Rogers and Hay, and the Aldriches and Warners and Langdons, he did not, even though he could have. And he, himself, has proved it. Why, from his grave he fairly yells: "I was restrained. I was defeated. I hate the lying, cowardly world that circumvented me. Man is not good. He is not honest. Life is a lie! Life is a lie!"

Read *What Is Man?*

Read *The Mysterious Stranger*.

The truth is, as you see, that Twain was *not* two people, but one—a gifted but partially dissuaded Genius who, in time, and by degrees changed into his natural self. This second Twain was observing the world as it truly is; but alas! as I have shown, he had already been inducted into the social world of which, temperamentally, he was not truly a part, and which, at bottom, he resented. In short, the raw genius of the river raft and the mining camp, and the western newspaper of that day, was confused and, for a time, hypnotized by this audacious and insistent authoritarian world of convention, into which, thoughtlessly, he had drifted. And it led him astray. For at the time, not later, it seemed to represent and verify to this raw, gay youth all the accepted claims and distinctions of a world that he did not clearly grasp— fame, love, marriage. But later, of course, came the warning finger of convention. Naughty, naughty! Must behave! Must be good! Otherwise Grandma Grundy will slap. And how!

I often think of this: In Twain's day lived Whitman. Did he ever hear of him? Herman Melville was his contemporary. Did he ever hear or speak of him? There is no evidence. Poe had gone but a little while before. Was Poe taboo? To Howells—yes. To Aldrich—yes. To Twain—???

Yet below all this, and that on which his feet were resting, was the solid rock of his own temperament and understanding. And with this as his point of vantage and departure, and despite the impact of the meretricious life that was spinning about him, came the final conviction that most of what he saw and was so busy with was mere sound and fury, signifying nothing—tinsel and tawdry make-believe which could only detract from his true stature. The truth of it is apparent, and not only that, but confessed, in his *Autobiography*, and in those really deathless works which his tinsel contemporaries never knew. I refer again to *The Mysterious Stranger* still sold, if you will believe it, as a Christmas book for children, and *What Is Man?* read by a corporal's guard of the initiated, in the course of, let us say, a year, if so often.

Sterling Brown

Sterling Brown (1901–1989) was a poet and critic who published his first book of poetry, *Southern Road*, in 1932. The poems focused on poor blacks in the rural South. He made free use of dialect and treated his subjects' lives with dignity and respect. Five years later Brown published *The Negro in American Fiction*, the first book to examine from a black perspective black stereotypes and their broader significance. It also presents the first acknowledgment by a black writer of the care with which Mark Twain portrayed Jim in *Huckleberry Finn*, and of the respect that Twain had for his character. (Booker T. Washington had attempted to say something similar in a tribute to Twain in the *North American Review* in 1910, but his misremembering of the novel's plot made his comments well-meaning but garbled.) Brown's characterization of Jim as "the best example in nineteenth century fiction of the average Negro slave (not the tragic mulatto or the noble savage), illiterate, superstitious, yet clinging to his hope for freedom, to his love for his own," a figure who is "completely believable, whether arguing that Frenchman should talk like people, or doing most of the work on the raft, or forgiving Huck whose trick caused him to be bitten by a snake" prefigures analogous readings of the novel by a younger generation of black writers that includes Ralph Wiley and David Bradley. *The Negro in American Fiction* also paved the way for later examinations of black stereotypes in American fiction and their cultural import by black writers such as Ralph Ellison and Toni Morrison. In 1984 the District of Columbia named Sterling Brown its first poet laureate.

FROM
The Negro in American Fiction

Mark Twain insisted that he was almost completely without race prejudice and that the color brown was "the most beautiful and satisfying of all the complexions vouchsafed to man." He loved the spirituals best among music. In his youth he grew up with slave boys as playmates; in his manhood he paid a Negro student's way through Yale, as "part of the reparation due from every white to every black man."

Twain's first treatment of Negroes in *The Gilded Age* (1873), however, is largely traditional, unlike "A True Story (Repeated Word For Word As I Heard It)" which is a bitter memory of cruelty and separation, contradicting Thomas Nelson Page's formula stories.

In *Huckleberry Finn* (1884) the callousness of the South to the Negro is indicated briefly, without preaching, but impellingly. Huck informs Aunt Sally that a steamboat blew out a cylinder head:

> "Good gracious! anybody hurt?"
> "No'm. Killed a nigger."
> "Well, it's lucky because sometimes people do get hurt . . ."

In this book Twain deepens the characterization of Jim, who, like Tom and Huck and the rest of that fine company, was drawn from life. He is no longer the simple-minded, mysterious guide in the ways of dead cats, doodle-bugs and signs of *The Adventures of Tom Sawyer*. Running away from old Miss Watson, who, though religious, "pecks on" him all the time, treats him "pooty rough" and wants a trader's eight hundred dollars for him, Jim joins Huck on the immortal journey down the Mississippi. His talks enlivens the voyage. He is at his comic best in detailing his experience with high finance—he once owned fourteen dollars. But the fun is brought up sharp by Jim's

> Yes, en I's rich now, come to look at it. I owns myself en I's wuth eight hund'd dollars. I wisht I had de money, I wouldn't want no mo'.

But he did want more. He wanted to get to a free state and work and save money so he could buy his wife, and then they would both work to buy their children, or get an abolitionist to go steal them. Huck is "frozen at such thoughts;" torn between what he had been taught was moral and his friendliness for an underdog. Jim is the best example in nineteenth century fiction of the average Negro slave (not the tragic mulatto or the noble savage), illiterate, superstitious, yet clinging to his hope for freedom, to his love for his own. And he is completely believable, whether arguing that Frenchman should talk like people, or doing most of the work on the raft, or forgiving Huck whose trick caused him to be bitten by a snake, or sympathizing with the poor little Dauphin, who, since America has no kings, "cain't git no situation." He tells of his little daughter, whom he had struck, not knowing she disobeyed because she had become deaf from scarlet fever:

> . . . En all uv a sudden I says pow! jis' as loud as I could yell. She never budge! Oh, Huck, I bust out a-cryin' en grab her up in my arms, en say, "Oh, de po' little thing! De Lord God Almighty forgive po' ole Jim, kaze he never gwyne to forgive hisself as long's he live!" Oh, she was plumb deef en dumb, Huck, plum deef en dumb—en I'd been a-treatin' her so!

From the great tenderness and truth of this portrait *Pudd'n-head Wilson* (1894), Twain's last novel concerning Negroes, falls a great way. In violent, ugly Dawson's Landing a fantastic tale is set. Roxana, only one-sixteenth Negro, a handsome earthy Amazon, is the mother of a son, Valet de Chambre, fathered by a gentleman of the F. F. V's. This baby was born on the same day as her master's son, Thomas a Becket Driscoll, and looks exactly like him. In order to save the baby from slavery, Roxy exchanges the two. The boys grow up with their positions reversed; the false Valet is ruined by slavery, and Tom, ruined by pampering, becomes a liar, coward, gambler, thief and murderer. In desperate straits, he tricks his mother and sells her down the river. Although Tom's character could be attributed to a rigid caste system that granted excessive power to petty people, Twain leaves many readers believing that he agrees with Roxy who, astounded by her son's worthlessness, muttered: "Ain't nigger enough in him to show in his finger-nails, en dat takes mighty little, yit dey's enough to paint his soul." Twain has little good to say for slavery in this book. Roxy's terror of being sold "down the river," and her experiences there under a vicious Yankee overseer are grimly realistic. Roxy is a first-rate preliminary sketch. By no means faultless, a petty thief and a liar, she is capable of sacrifice, and has intelligence, pride, and courage. If Twain had spent more time in developing her portrait, *Pudd'nhead Wilson* would have been a better novel.

1937

Ink drawing by Jean Cocteau, 1958.
Text: "Mark Twain n'est pas un humoriste c'est un poète et je l'aime Jean Cocteau" (Mark Twain is not a humorist he is a poet and I love him)
From *Mark Twain Journal* (cover), Spring/Summer, 1958

Grant Wood

Grant Wood (1891–1942) was an American regionalist painter best known for his scenes of the rural Midwest, notably the iconic *American Gothic* (1930). In this essay Wood credits his encounter with *Huckleberry Finn* for the "revelation" that allowed him to break from the limited and outdated tastes that had surrounded him during his Iowa childhood: "Having been born into a world of Victorian standards, I had accepted and admired the ornate, the lugubrious and the excessively sentimental naturally and without question." He tells us that reading *Huckleberry Finn*—and in particular meditating on Mark Twain's description of Emmeline Grangerford's art work—"was my first intimation that there was something ridiculous about sentimentality."

My Debt to Mark Twain

My father was a Quaker farmer who sternly disapproved of graven and pictorial representation and fiction. When I was a boy, he once returned an unread copy of Grimm's Fairy Tales to a neighbor, thanking him, but explaining "We Quakers read only true things." His own reading was for the most part confined to Macaulay's History of England and a biography of Abraham Lincoln.

Yet, this narrowness which made him forbid my reading a book as harmless as Grimm's Fairy Tales must have been offset by a rich and tolerant wisdom. For he did not object to my having the two volumes which meant more to me than all the others—*Tom Sawyer* and *Huckleberry Finn*. Works of fiction he surely realized they were, but some intuition must have informed him that in a broad sense, they were "true things."

There were Tom and Huck and Nigger Jim and the rest; buried treasure and deliciously exciting adventures in the night; series upon series of breathless exploits, one after the other, yet none of them seeming too extravagant; and through it all the Mississippi with its tangled shores, thicketed islands, and broad, mysterious flow.

This was the world that grew out of the two red-covered books I read and re-read until the pages were dingy and dog-eared and the covers tattered. Pity the boy who had to grow up without them! There were evenings in the kitchen, flat on my stomach on the scrubbed white softwood floor—at first by oil lamp, later by flickering gas jet—that I forgot what was around me and was whisked away to help Tom as he fought the new boy in town, to hurry Huck in his escape from his Pap, to shrink with them both in the tree during those blood-curdling moments of the grave-robbing and murder. Then almost before I had become started in the adventure, it seemed, my Mother's voice would float in with sweet but cruel insistence that it was time to go to bed.

The world those books created was almost as real to me as that of my mother, Aunt Minnie, the brown-and-white collie Dewey and the acres of patterned prairie land which I knew so well. As I recall it, there is no detailed physical description of either of the heroes in the books. That helped. In my imagination I was sometimes Tom, sometimes Huck. Like most farm-boys, I was interested in the common things I saw out of doors—spiders, snakes, dead animals, tree stumps. But in the world of Tom Sawyer and Huckleberry Finn, everything had a special meaning. If a spider crawled up Huck's shoulder and he flipped it into a candle-flame, it was a sign of bad luck. Or if a little green worm climbed over Tom, it meant that the worm was measuring him for a suit of clothes he was to have.

Of the two books, my favorite was *Huckleberry Finn*; probably, I realize now, because of its richness in sense impressions of the type that made my own boyhood so vivid. How abundant are those descriptive passages that are palpable and exciting even to a small boy! "Jackson's island about two mile and a half down stream, heavy-timbered, and standing up out of the middle of the river, big and dark and solid, like a steamboat without any lights." Or Huck's eerie description of the night including that memorable, shivery sentence—"Then away out in the woods I heard the kind of sound that a ghost makes when it wants to tell about something that's on its mind and can't make itself understood, and so can't rest easy in its grave, and has to go about that way every night grieving." Or the intense drama of a thunderstorm over Jackson's Island.

I have found that at every stage of life one can discover new enjoyments in *Tom Sawyer* and *Huckleberry Finn*. When I was a youngster, it was the narrative that absorbed me. My excitement in the story never waned—even after I came to know every turn in the book by memory. Incidents were not overdone; they retained their freshness. I never failed to respond to the intense suspense of such episodes as Jim and Huck stranded on the wreck in the middle of the river; Becky and Tom trapped in the cave; or Huck trailing Injun Joe. I used to have nightmares about the bag of money that Huck secreted in the casket to hide from the Duke and the Dauphin. And, at the end of the chapter telling of Jim's and Huck's visit to the house of death, what a profound relief it was to come to that sentence: "We got home all safe!"

In common with most grown folks, I suppose, when I read the books now I revel in their boy-magic, in those priceless, authentic bits which recreate so vividly my own boyhood: Tom and Becky swapping the chewing gum, Huck's interpretation of history for Jim, the episode of the dog and the beetle in church. Remember Tom's elaborate self-pity when Aunt Polly cuffed him for breaking the sugar bowl which Sid actually upset? "He pictured himself lying sick unto death and his aunt bending over him beseeching one forgiving word, but he would turn his face to the wall, and die with that word unsaid."

Of course, there was no moral in the books and I should be the last to want to be banished for suggesting that there was. Yet, in general, children can be depended upon to have a keen, penetrating sense of fairness, and if the books had contained anything that went against this, they could never have retained their popularity the way they have. Sometimes Tom seemed pretty much the hard-hearted juvenile adventurer, but from time to time he could be depended upon to redeem himself to Aunt Polly or Huck with brief, sunny flashes. Remember this one? "Only if you get married I'll be lonesomer than ever," said Huck wistfully when Tom was telling him about his plans to marry Becky. And Tom replied: "No you won't. You'll come and live with us."

As I have suggested, much of the humor of the books escaped me when I read them as a boy. Yet, this was not always the case and I recall distinctly that one of my earliest realizations of the humorous grew out of reading *Huckleberry Finn*. It was the part wherein Huck, staying with Grangerfords describes the sentimental pictures a daughter in the family had painted before her premature death. "They was different from any pictures I ever see before—" Huck said, "Blacker, mostly, than is common." And of all the pictures, you will remember, the masterpiece was the unfinished study of a grief-stricken young woman ready to leap off a bridge, tears, gown and hair flowing and with three pairs of arms—all in different positions. The idea had been to see which pair of arms would look the best and then to scratch out the other two, but the young artist had died before she had made up her mind. "The young woman in the picture," Huck remarked, "had a kind of nice, sweet face but there was so many arms it made her look too spidery, it seemed to me."

As I look back on it now, I realize that my response to this passage was a revelation. Having been born into a world of Victorian standards, I had accepted and admired the ornate, the lugubrious and the excessively sentimental naturally and without question. And this was my first intimation that there was something ridiculous about sentimentality.

Had *Tom Sawyer* and *Huckleberry Finn* never been written, we should have loved and honored Sam Clemens for his rich humor, for the vigor which he could breathe into written words, for his fine clear pictures of our West, for the brave way in which—in an age of submission—he lashed out against the artificialities and false standards of his time. We should have thought of him as one who in his life and work embodied the restless spirit of new America—building, pressing westward, and ruggedly coming of age.

But, by virtue of Tom Sawyer and Huck Finn, our debt to Mark Twain is too deep and too intimate for tribute.

The only river I knew as a boy was the Wapsipinicon, a small stream compared with the Ohio or Missouri, but carrying immeasurable dignity and mystery in my eyes because it likewise, I heard, flowed into the Mississippi. It was one of the intense ambitions of my boyhood to follow the Wapsie down to the "monstrous big river" of Tom Sawyer and Huckleberry Finn. And even now, I can never cross the Mississippi without unconsciously straining my eyes toward where Saint Petersburgh and Jackson's Island should be, half-expecting to see, emerging from the shelter of the cottonwoods along the banks of the river, a raft bearing Huck and Jim and perhaps the Duke and the Dauphin.

Mark Twain Quarterly, 1937

George Orwell

In 1934 George Orwell (the pen name of British writer Eric Blair) (1903–1950), approached an editor at Harper and Brothers with a request that he be commissioned to write a biography of Mark Twain. The publisher turned him down. But if Orwell shelved the idea, he retained an interest in Twain, and he published this essay about him in the London *Tribune* the same month that he was named the newspaper's literary editor. Orwell was by now the acclaimed author of *Down and Out in Paris and London* (1933), *The Road to Wigan Pier* (1937), and *Homage to Catalonia* (1938). He was intrigued by Twain, but he was also frustrated by him. Orwell was fascinated by the vision of the American West he glimpsed in Twain's work—but described it in terms that only an Englishman would use: the central themes of *Roughing It* (also called *The Innocents at Home*) and *Life on the Mississippi* expressed, "how human beings behave when they are not frightened of the sack." Orwell was entranced by the freedom of a land in which "If you disliked your job you simply hit the boss in the eye and moved further west." But he believed that Twain, who "had in him an iconoclastic, even revolutionary vein," had failed to be the "destroyer of humbugs and a prophet of democracy" that he might have been; he thought he settled instead for being his society's "licensed jester," a man who "never attacks established beliefs in a way that is likely to get him into trouble." Orwell seems to have been unaware of the writings Twain published that *did* get him into trouble—such as "To the Person Sitting in Darkness" and other anti-imperialist essays. This is not surprising: Harper and Brothers, Twain's publisher—the same publisher that wouldn't commission Orwell's biography—did what it could during this period (along with Twain's biographer Albert Bigelow Paine and daughter Clara) to downplay the subversive side of Mark Twain.

Mark Twain—the Licensed Jester

Mark Twain has crashed the lofty gates of the Everyman Library, but only with *Tom Sawyer* and *Huckleberry Finn*, already fairly well known under the guise of 'children's books' (which they are not). His best and most characteristic books,

Roughing It, The Innocents at Home [*Abroad*], and even *Life on the Mississippi* are little remembered in this country, though no doubt in America the patriotism which is everywhere mixed up with literary judgement keeps them alive.

Although Mark Twain produced a surprising variety of books, ranging from a namby-pamby 'life' of Joan of Arc to a pamphlet so obscene that it has never been publicly printed, all that is best in his work centres about the Mississippi river and the wild mining towns of the West. Born in 1835 (he came of a Southern family, a family just rich enough to own one or perhaps two slaves), he had had his youth and early manhood in the golden age of America, the period when the great plains were opened up, when wealth and opportunity seemed limitless, and human beings felt free, indeed *were* free, as they had never been before and may not be again for centuries. *Life on the Mississippi* and the two other books that I have mentioned are a ragbag of anecdotes, scenic descriptions and social history both serious and burlesque, but they have a central theme which could perhaps be put into these words: 'This is how human beings behave when they are not frightened of the sack.' In writing these books Mark Twain is not consciously writing a hymn to liberty. Primarily he is interested in 'character', in the fantastic, almost lunatic variations which human nature is capable of when economic pressure and tradition are both removed from it. The raftsmen, Mississippi pilots, miners and bandits whom he describes are probably not much exaggerated, but they are as different from modern men, and from one another, as the gargoyles of a medieval cathedral. They could develop their strange and sometimes sinister individuality because of the lack of any outside pressure. The State hardly existed, the churches were weak and spoke with many voices, and land was to be had for the taking. If you disliked your job you simply hit the boss in the eye and moved further west; and moreover, money was so plentiful that the smallest coin in circulation was worth a shilling. The American pioneers were not supermen, and they were not especially courageous. Whole towns of hardy gold miners let themselves be terrorized by bandits whom they lacked the public spirit to put down. They were not even free from class distinctions. The desperado who stalked through the streets of the mining settlement, with a Derringer pistol in his waistcoat pocket and twenty corpses to his credit, was dressed in a frock coat and shiny top-hat, described himself firmly as a 'gentleman' and was meticulous about table manners. But at least it was not the case that a man's destiny was settled from his birth. The 'log cabin to White House' myth was true while the free land lasted. In a way, it was for this that the Paris mob had stormed the Bastille, and when one reads Mark Twain, Bret Harte and Whitman it is hard to feel that their effort was wasted.

However, Mark Twain aimed at being something more than a chronicler of the Mississippi and the Gold Rush. In his own day he was famous all over the world as a humorist and comic lecturer. In New York, London, Berlin, Vienna, Melbourne and Calcutta vast audiences rocked with laughter over jokes which have now, almost without exception, ceased to be funny. (It is worth noticing that Mark Twain's lectures were only a success with Anglo-Saxon and German audiences. The relatively grown-up Latin races—whose own humour, he complained, always centred round sex and politics—never cared for them.) But in addition, Mark Twain had some pretensions to being a social critic, even a species of philosopher. He had in him an iconoclastic, even revolutionary vein which he obviously wanted to follow up and yet somehow never did follow up. He might have been a destroyer of humbugs and a prophet of democracy more valuable than Whitman, because healthier and more humorous. Instead he became that dubious thing a 'public figure', flattered by passport officials and entertained by royalty, and his career reflects the deterioration in American life that set in after the Civil War.

Mark Twain has sometimes been compared with his contemporary, Anatole France. This comparison is not so pointless as it may sound. Both men were the spiritual children of Voltaire, both had an ironical, sceptical view of life, and a native pessimism overlaid by gaiety; both knew that the existing social order is a swindle and its cherished beliefs mostly delusions. Both were bigoted atheists and convinced (in Mark Twain's case this was Darwin's doing) of the unbearable cruelty of the universe. But there the resemblance ends. Not only is the Frenchman

enormously more learned, more civilized, more alive aestheti-
cally, but he is also more courageous. He does attack the things
he disbelieves in; he does not, like Mark Twain, always take refuge behind the amiable mask of the 'public figure' and the licensed jester. He is ready to risk the anger of the Church and to
take the unpopular side in a controversy—in the Dreyfus case,
for example. Mark Twain, except perhaps in one short essay
'What is Man?', never attacks established beliefs in a way that is
likely to get him into trouble. Nor could he ever wean himself
from the notion, which is perhaps especially an American notion, that success and virtue are the same thing.

In *Life on the Mississippi* there is a queer little illustration of
the central weakness of Mark Twain's character. In the earlier
part of this mainly autobiographical book the dates have been
altered. Mark Twain describes his adventures as a Mississippi
pilot as though he had been a boy of about seventeen at the
time, whereas in fact he was a young man of nearly thirty. There
is a reason for this. The same part of the book describes his exploits in the Civil War, which were distinctly inglorious. Moreover, Mark Twain started by fighting, if he can be said to have
fought, on the Southern side, and then changed his allegiance
before the war was over. This kind of behaviour is more excus-
able in a boy than in a man, whence the adjustment of the dates.
It is also clear enough, however, that he changed sides because
he saw that the North was going to win; and this tendency to
side with the stronger whenever possible, to believe that might
must be right, is apparent throughout his career. In *Roughing It*
there is an interesting account of a bandit named Slade, who,
among countless other outrages, had committed twenty-eight
murders. It is perfectly clear that Mark Twain admires this disgusting scoundrel. Slade was successful; therefore he was admirable. This outlook, no less common today, is summed up in the
significant American expression 'to *make good*'.

In the money-grubbing period that followed the Civil War it
was hard for anyone of Mark Twain's temperament to refuse to
be a success. The old, simple, stump-whittling, tobacco-chewing
democracy which Abraham Lincoln typified was perishing: it
was now the age of cheap immigrant labour and the growth of

Big Business. Mark Twain mildly satirized his contemporaries in *The Gilded Age*, but he also gave himself up to the prevailing fever, and made and lost vast sums of money. He even for a period of years deserted writing for business; and he squandered his time on buffooneries, not merely lecture tours and public banquets, but, for instance, the writing of a book like *A Connecticut Yankee in King Arthur's Court*, which is a deliberate flattery of all that is worst and most vulgar in American life. The man who might have been a kind of rustic Voltaire became the world's leading after-dinner speaker, charming alike for his anecdotes and his power to make businessmen feel themselves public benefactors.

It is usual to blame Mark Twain's wife for his failure to write the books he ought to have written, and it is evident that she did tyrannize over him pretty thoroughly. Each morning, Mark Twain would show her what he had written the day before, and Mrs Clemens (Mark Twain's real name was Samuel Clemens) would go over it with the blue pencil, cutting out everything that she thought unsuitable. She seems to have been a drastic blue-penciller even by nineteenth-century standards. There is an account in W. D. Howells's book *My Mark Twain* of the fuss that occurred over a terrible expletive that had crept into *Huckleberry Finn*. Mark Twain appealed to Howells, who admitted that it was 'just what Huck would have said', but agreed with Mrs Clemens that the word could not possibly be printed. The word was 'hell'. Nevertheless, no writer is really the intellectual slave of his wife. Mrs Clemens could not have stopped Mark Twain writing any book he really wanted to write. She may have made his surrender to society easier, but the surrender happened because of that flaw in his own nature, his inability to despise success.

Several of Mark Twain's books are bound to survive, because they contain invaluable social history. His life covered the great period of American expansion. When he was a child it was a normal day's outing to go with a picnic lunch and watch the hanging of an Abolitionist, and when he died the aeroplane was ceasing to be a novelty. This period in America produced relatively little literature, and but for Mark Twain our picture of a

Mississippi paddle-steamer, or a stage-coach crossing the plains, would be much dimmer than it is. But most people who have studied his work have come away with a feeling that he might have done something more. He gives all the while a strange impression of being about to say something and then funking it, so that *Life on the Mississippi* and the rest of them seem to be haunted by the ghost of a greater and much more coherent book. Significantly, he starts his autobiography by remarking that a man's inner life is indescribable. We do not know what he would have said—it is just possible that the unprocurable pamphlet, *1601*, would supply a clue but we may guess that it would have wrecked his reputation and reduced his income to reasonable proportions.

Tribune (London), 1943

Bernard DeVoto

Utah-born and Harvard-educated Bernard DeVoto (1897–1955) was a novelist and journalist becoming known as good at explaining the West to the rest of the nation when he contracted to write a book about Mark Twain in 1926. Six years earlier, Van Wyck Brooks had published *The Ordeal of Mark Twain*, a book that, in Frederick Anderson's words, "attempted to prove that the limitations of crude frontier origins compounded by frustrating social and emotional pressures exerted by his wife and his friends had restrained Mark Twain from realizing his genius"; it was an emblem of "the genteel view that underlay critical distaste for Mark Twain's 'vulgarity' in his lifetime." DeVoto's biographer, Wallace Stegner, described, *Mark Twain's America*, which DeVoto published in 1932, as a book that "set out to demolish *The Ordeal of Mark Twain* as a theory based on false facts, inadequate facts, misunderstood facts, and sometimes no facts at all." The West, in DeVoto's view, far from constraining Twain's genius, was its wellspring. Although the book did much to rescue Twain from the charges Brooks had leveled against him, DeVoto raised some important new criticism of his own: most notably he was the first critic to condemn the ending of *Huckleberry Finn*, claiming that "in the whole reach of the English novel there is no more abrupt or chilling descent." He was also probably the first to recognize Jim as the hero of the novel. Six years after *Mark Twain's America* appeared, DeVoto was chosen to oversee the Mark Twain Papers. In that capacity, he edited a selection of as yet unpublished writings in volumes that included *Mark Twain in Eruption* (1942) and *Letters from the Earth* (1962). Both books made public material that Twain's biographer and executor, Albert Bigelow Paine, had withheld from print out of fear that it would damage Twain's reputation. DeVoto also produced a study of the author's craft, *Mark Twain at Work* (1946), as well as two cultural studies of the West: *Across the Wide Missouri* (1947) and *The Course of Empire* (1953).

Introduction to
The Portable Mark Twain

Mark Twain was a man of moods, of the extreme of moods. He had a buoyancy which, twinned as it was with gentleness and intuition and wit, gave him a personal magnetism which his friends did not hesitate to call enchantment. Yet it alternated with an anger that readily became fury and was rooted in a revulsion between disgust and despair. The alternation suggests a basic split; it is clearly marked in his personality and equally evident in his books. The splendor his friends felt, his kindness to the unfortunate and the lowly and the oppressed, his generosity, his sensitiveness unite in a singular luminosity of spirit. Yet he was capable of savage vindictiveness, he exaggerated small or imaginary grievances out of all reason, and on little or no provocation he repeatedly believed himself misrepresented or betrayed. One doubts if any other American writer was ever so publicly beloved or privately adored; one is certain that no other was involved in so many lawsuits. "I am full of malice, saturated with malignity," he wrote eight months before his death. His malice and malignity of that moment were for the damned human race, but he could feel them in his private life whenever he thought he had been wronged. When *A Connecticut Yankee* was finished he wrote Howells that if he could write it over again "there wouldn't be so many things left out. They burn in me and they keep multiplying and multiplying, but now they can't even be said. And besides they would require a library—and a pen warmed up in hell." With a pen warmed up in hell he did fill a library and an extraordinary bulk of letters too. If it was sometimes avenging personal, usually imaginary wrongs, that private activity was only a reflex of the public function. For what burned in him was hatred of cruelty and injustice, a deep sense of human evil, and a recurrent accusation of himself. Like Swift he found himself despising man while loving Tom, Dick, and Harry so warmly that he had no proper defense against the anguish of human relationships. The trouble was that in terms of either earth or heaven he was never sure what to make of Samuel L. Clemens and so is recorded on both sides.

He is usually to be found on both sides of any question he argues. His intelligence was intuitive, not analytical. He reasoned fluently, with an avidity that touched most of the surface flow of his time, but superficially and with habitual contradictions. He had little capacity for sustained thought and to get to the heart of a question had to abandon analysis and rely on feeling. The philosophy which he spent years refining and supposed he had perfected is a sophomoric determinism, Even so, it is less a philosophy than a symbol or a rationalization; the perceptions it stood for are expressed at the level of genius in his fiction—not as idea but in terms of human life. Most of the nineteenth century's optimisms were his also. He fiercely championed the democratic axioms; they are the ether of his fiction and the fulcrum of his satire. He thought too that the nineteenth century, especially as Progress, and more especially as Progress in the United States, was the happiest estate of man; he believed that it was bringing on a future of greater freedom and greater happiness. This was basic and spontaneous in his mind, but at the same time he felt something profoundly wrong. There seemed to be some limitation to freedom, some frustration of happiness. He never really came to grips with the conflict. Only in the last fifteen years of his life did he ascribe any part of what might be wrong to any but superficial injustices in American life or any but slight dislocations in our system. By the time he became aware of serious threats to freedom they did not seem to matter much: he was so absorbed in the natural depravity of man that the collapse or frustration of democracy, which he was by then taking for granted, seemed only an unimportant detail. Ideally, his last years would have been spent in more rigorous analysis—if not of the objective data, then of his intuitive awareness of them. They were not and so his judgments remained confused—and his principal importance in our literature belongs to his middle years, the period when his mind and feelings are in healthy equilibrium. It is an importance of his perceptions, not his thinking, and it exists primarily in his fiction, most purely in *Huckleberry Finn*. The best of Mark Twain's fiction is, historically, the first mature realization in our literature of a conflict between the assumptions of democracy and the limitations on democracy. Between the ideal of freedom and the nature of man.

Not less important is the fact that there is a reconciliation, even an affirmation. Detachment could be no greater but it is still somehow compassionate; condemnation could be no more complete, but it is somehow magnanimous. The damned human race is displayed with derision and abhorrence, yet this is on the ground that it has fallen short of its own decencies. Moreover at least *Huckleberry Finn* has a hero, the only heroic character (apart from Joan of Arc, a debauch of gyneolatry) he ever drew, and it is the essence of what Mark Twain had to say that the hero is a Negro slave. It has also a vindication not only of freedom, but of loyalty and decency, kindness and courage; and it is the essence of Mark Twain that this vindication is made by means of a boy who is a spokesman of the folk mind and whom experience has taught wariness and skepticism. Like all great novels *Huckleberry Finn* moves on many levels of significance, but it describes a flight and a struggle for freedom, and the question it turns on is a moral question.

Mark found zest and gusto—nouns that do not describe very much American literature of the first rank—in whatsoever was alive. He liked few novels except those of his intimate friends. What he praised in the ones he did like was reality of behavior, speech, or motive; his notebooks are sulphurous with comments on merely literary, that is false, characters. His taste was for biography, autobiography, history—life direct, men revealing themselves. No doubt the race was damned but it was fascinating. And that was proper for if his fiction is the best of his work, his most salient talent as a novelist is the life giving power. It is a careless and prodigal fecundity, but nevertheless remarkably concentrated. Old Man Finn, for instance, is greatly imagined and he seems to fill the first half of the book, yet he appears in only a few pages. Mrs. Judith Loftus lives completely in a single chapter. A mere passer-by, a casual of the river or a thug heard talking in a frowzy town, may reveal a whole personality in a few paragraphs. Nor is this fecundity confined to Mark's fiction, for the framework of all his books is anecdotal and all the people in them are dramatized. The whole population of his principal books, nine-tenths of the population of all his books, has the same vividness. Boys, villagers, the rivermen, the Negroes, Colonel Sellers, the two great vagabonds—there is nothing quite like the Mark Twain gallery elsewhere in American literature.

But there is a striking limitation: nowhere in that gallery are there women of marriageable age. No white women, that is, for the slave Roxana in *Pudd'nhead Wilson* lives as vividly as Old Man Finn himself. It must be significant that the only credible woman of an age that might sanction desire is withdrawn from desire behind the barrier of race. None of Mark Twain's nubile girls, young women, or young matrons are believable; they are all bisque, saccharine, or tears. He will do girl children in the romantic convention of boys' books and he is magnificent with the sisterhood of worn frontier wives whom Aunt Polly climaxes, but something like a taboo drains reality from any woman who might trouble the heart or the flesh. There is no love story in Mark Twain, there is no love at all beyond an occasional admission, for purposes of plot only, that someone is married or is going to be. Women seldom have husbands and men seldom have wives unless they are beyond middle age. Mark's endless absorption in human motives did not, for literary purposes at least, extend to sexual motives. Sex seems to be forbidden unless it can be treated mawkishly, and this writer of great prose who habitually flouted the genteel proprieties of language was more prudish than the most tremulous of his friends in regard to language that might suggest either desire or its gratification. So there is a sizable gap in the world he created. That gap has never been accounted for. Certainly there was nothing bloodless about Mark Twain; and his marriage, one of the happiest of literary marriages, was clearly passionate. Yet he did not marry till he was thirty-five (1870), and there may have been something permissive—to a man whose characters have usually lost a father if not both parents—in the fact that he married an invalid.

Few Americans have written as much as Mark Twain. His published works are not much greater in bulk than his unpublished manuscripts, the books he finished fewer than the ones he broke off and abandoned. He wrote on impulse and enthusiasm and while they lasted he wrote easily, but he wrote as needs must, for he had little faculty of self-criticism and but small ability to sustain or elaborate an idea. He was best at the short haul. Not only his fiction but the personalized narrative that is the vehicle of *Innocents Abroad, A Tramp Abroad, Life on the Mississippi*, and much else is episodic. When what he was writing was in circuit with his deepest perceptions he was superb. The breaking of the circuit always threw him into extemporization, which meant that fiction fell away into extravaganza and satire into burlesque. At such times he did not know that he was flatting; the serious artist could become a vaudeville monologuist in a single page without being aware that the tone had changed. That such a well-imagined novel as *Pudd'nhead Wilson* was written round the grotesque joke called "Those Extraordinary Twins" would be incredible if the same tone-deafness were not plentifully evident elsewhere. He thought the mawkish *Joan of Arc* and the second-rate *The Prince and the Pauper* his best work. He interrupted his masterpiece before it was half-finished, liking it so little that he threatened to burn it, and ignored it for six years during which, though he wrote constantly, he wrote nothing of importance. Then he finished it almost as casually as he had begun it. There is no greater book in American literature, but critics agree that the last quarter of it is impaired by the extravaganza that begins when Huck gets to Uncle Silas's farm. It is typical of Mark Twain that he felt no difference in kind or key between this admittedly superb extravaganza and the searching of American society and human experience that precedes it. In fact, the delivery of Jim from the dungeon was one of Mark's favorite platform readings.

Furthermore, he lacked the attribute of the artist—whatever it may be—that enables him to think a novel through till its content has found its own inherent form. Of his novels only *Joan of Arc, The Prince and the Pauper*, and *Tom Sawyer* have structures that have developed from within; significantly, all are simple and only one is first-rate. Mark lived with his material for a long time, sometimes for many years, but not consciously, not with critical or searching dissatisfaction. A book must come of its own momentum from the unconscious impulse, be it as a whole, as a fragment, or as something that hardly got started before it broke off. This is to say that he had no conscious esthetic. He stood at the opposite pole from Henry James, with the other great contemporary of both, Howells, in between but nearer to James. Yet he had as large a share as either of them in creating the modern American novel.

The explanation for his lack of self-criticism and for his innocence of esthetics is not to be found in the supposed naïveté of the society that bore him. In the first place, that society was far from naïve; in the second place, not only did the fine artist Howells come from it, but Mark himself raised its native tale-telling to a fine art, which surely establishes a discipline. He had, besides, two other disciplines: that of the daily job, which he observed as faithfully as any writer who ever lived, and the taskmastership of a great style. Nor can Mark's own explanation, which he pleads so earnestly in the letter to Andrew Lang, be supported: that he wrote for the belly and members only. *Huckleberry Finn* is no more written for the belly and members only than *War and Peace* is or *Recherche du Temps Perdu*. But it is written at the behest of an instinctive drive, and explanation need go no farther if it could, for this time at least Mark's whole personality was behind it. In short, he wrote trivially or splendidly or magnificently as what appears to have been little more than chance might determine: he was not a fully self-conscious artist. But when he wrote greatly he was writing from an inner harmony of desire and will. Or call it a harmony of his deepest self and his inheritance from the Great Valley.

Only that harmony, seen in relation to time and history, can explain him. For no man ever became a great writer more inadvertently than Mark Twain. He first became famous as a superior Artemus Ward, and that corresponded to his idea of himself. A long time passed before he had any desire to be more. He exploited a joke-maker's talent as systematically as a production manager could have done it for him, delighted by the discovery that he could raise his status, prestige, and income beyond Tom Sawyer's dreams. Nevertheless there is the paradox that almost from the beginning the attack of the funny man had been supported by that of a serious artist. Already in "The Jumping

Frog" mastery of fictional character is clearly presaged, and the prophecy is fulfilled as early as *The Gilded Age* (1874). By *The Gilded Age* also a satirist is dealing maturely with a wide expanse of American life. From this composite the funny man cannot be separated out for a long time, and during that time there are only sporadic indications that Mark saw either the novelist or the satirist as more than instrumentalities of the humorist. The paradox resists criticism. One can only repeat that Mark Twain's greatness developed because the time and the continent had shaped him at their core.

This representative centrality goes on undiminished after the establishment of his fame. Following his marriage he was briefly a newspaper owner in Buffalo but abandoned that career to move to a provincial New England city, Hartford, and set up as a professional writer. His periodic restlessness continued; he never spent the full year in Hartford, he made at least twelve trips abroad, and he once expatriated himself for nine years. The Hartford period, 1874–1891, covered his greatest happiness and the beginning of his catastrophe. His was an unusually happy family life, and he was the center of an always widening circle. Howells and the Rev. Joseph Twichell were his closest friends; Cable, Aldrich, most of the leading writers of his generation were of the circle, and it widened to include the rich, the famous, the powerful, and the great. Mark ruled it by divine right: there have always been conflicting opinions about his books, but only one has ever been possible about his dominion over men's affections. He seemed alien to mortality. A fantasy of his childhood is frequently set down in notes and fragments of manuscript: the child had identified himself with a romantic stranger in Hannibal, a mysterious, perhaps supernatural visitor from Elsewhere. As the one-gallus village boy came to be a world figure, that fantasy seemed on the way to being confirmed. There was further confirmation as the author of *The Gilded Age* entered with a blithe and innocent heart on another career as a speculator, and the stamp-mill operator and tramp printer, who sincerely believed all his life that he was a member of the laboring class, undertook with the same innocence to be an industrial promoter.

Always convinced that his publishers were defrauding him, Mark had established his own firm to publish his books. The expansion it underwent in order to handle the bestseller of the generation, *Personal Memoirs of U. S. Grant*, could not be sustained. The firm sank into insolvency and finally went bankrupt. It could probably have been saved except that the most fantastic of Mark's promotions failed at the same time and left him bankrupt. For years he had been pouring his earnings and his wife's fortune into a mechanical typesetter which would indeed have made him a multimillionaire if it had succeeded. Its failure and that of the publishing firm were only the beginning of a series of disasters on the same scale as his fantastic rise. He paid off his indebtedness by a heroic lecture tour that took him round the world but his health broke. The oldest of his three daughters, the one who seemed most like him in temperament and talent, died during his absence. An agonizing personality change in his youngest daughter was finally diagnosed as epilepsy. Mrs. Clemens declined into permanent invalidism and in 1904 died.

This prolonged catastrophe brought Mark's misanthropy out of equilibrium; it dominated the rest of his life. The disasters were, of course, personal and yet it is hardly straining the facts to find him here also representative of the nineteenth-century America that had already found so much expression in him. As the century neared its end there was a good deal of pessimism and disenchantment in the United States. A wave of doubt and questioning swept many minds. The people who began an imperialistic adventure in the Pacific with the same naïve enthusiasm that had taken Mark Twain into the industrial life were widely, at the very time they stepped out on the world stage, beginning to be troubled about themselves. The nineteenth century, looking back on its course, found cause to be dismayed. Was the democratic dream being served as well as the nation had assumed? Had the United States gone wrong somewhere during the avalanche of expansion? Were there, then, limits to what democracy could do, or flaws or contradictions in its theses, or impassable barriers in its path? Was the good time ending, were the vigorous years running out under a gathering shadow?

However deep or shallow this *fin de siècle* weariness may have been in the United States at large, Mark Twain's last fifteen years must be seen as related to it, if only distantly. During this period he wrote as much as in any similar length of time in his life, perhaps more, but most of it is fragmentary, unfinished. Almost all of it deals with the nature of man, man's fate, and man's conceptions of honor and morality. There are fables, dialogues, diatribes—sometimes cold, sometimes passionate, derisive, withering, savage. Mark sees the American republic perishing, like republics before it, through the ineradicable cowardice, corruption, and mere baseness of mankind. He elaborates theories, which he embodies in imaginary histories of the world (and sometimes of extra-mundane societies) to support his prophecy, and yet he cannot be much troubled by the going-down of this western land, for year by year he is writing a general apocalypse. The Old Testament fables had always served him for humorous derision of man's gullibility, but now he uses them as missiles in a ferocious attack on human stupidity and cruelty. Man is compact of malignity, cowardice, weakness, and absurdity, a diseased organism, a parasite on nature, a foolish but murderous animal much lower than the swine.

Yet *What Is Man?* (published anonymously in 1906 but written before the turn of the century), the fullest of many developments of these themes, cannot be seen solely as a document in anthropophobia. It is also in complex ways a justification, even a self-justification. Its fixed universe, with an endless chain of cause and effect from the beginning of time, permits Mark to compose many variations on the theme of human pettiness, but also it serves to free man of blame—and thus satisfies a need deeply buried in Mark's personal remorse. To this period also belongs *Mark Twain's Autobiography*, which serves him as an escape into the security of the boyhood idyl he had made immortal in *Tom Sawyer*. The need to escape is significant, but the release is even more so, for it breaks the obsession signified by *What Is Man?* But a much truer release and a fulfillment as well came, as always, when Mark turned from reasoning to the instinctual portions of his mind. The highest reach of his last period is *The Mysterious Stranger*. It is an almost perfect book—

perfect in expression of his final drive, in imaginative projection of himself, in tone and tune, in final judgment on the nature of man and the experience of Mark Twain. It is on a humbler level than his great books. More than any of them it is Mark Twain somewhat in disregard of America. It is not, finally, a major work; but in its small way it is a masterpiece. Those who know and love Mark Twain will always find it as revealing as *Huckleberry Finn*.

Mark Twain died in 1910 with, as he had foretold, the return of the mysterious visitor from beyond the solar system under whose sign he had been born, Halley's comet. His last years had been as full of honors as his middle years had been of fame. Even so, in 1910 it was hardly possible to define his importance in American literature as clearly as we can after another generation.

No doubt his first importance in that literature is the democratizing effect of his work. It is a concretely liberating effect, and therefore different in kind from Whitman's vision of democracy, which can hardly be said to have been understood by or to have found a response among any considerable number of Americans. Mark Twain was the first great American writer who was also a popular writer, and that in itself is important. Much more important is the implicit and explicit democracy of his books. They are the first American literature of the highest rank which portrays the ordinary bulk of Americans, expresses them, accepts their values, and delineates their hopes, fears, decencies, and indecencies as from within. The area proper to serious literature in the United States was enormously widened by them, in fact widened to the boundaries it still observes today. There have been no acknowledged priorities of caste in American writing since Mark Twain. Moreover, in his native equalitarian point of view, in his assertion of the basic democratic axioms, in his onslaught on privilege, injustice, vested power, political pretense, and economic exploitation (much of it admittedly superficial or confused, though much else is the most vigorous satire we have), in his transmutation of the town-meeting or country-store sharpness of judgment into a fine art—he is midnineteenth-century

American democracy finding its first major voice in literature, ultimately its strongest voice. In him the literature of democracy becomes more robust than it had been before, such part of that literature, at least, as may be said to contain multitudes and speak to them. And this, to return to our starting point, embodies the transforming experience of the American people as they occupied the Great Valley and pushed beyond it, on the way forging the continental mind.

The nature of his writing is hardly less important. Mark Twain wrote one of the great styles of American literature, he helped develop the modern American style, he was the first writer who ever used the American vernacular at the level of art. There has been some failure to understand this achievement. Shortly before this Introduction was written, the most pontifical American critic guessed that Mark must have turned to the vernacular of *Huckleberry Finn* because he lacked education, was unacquainted with literary traditions, and therefore wrote thin or awkward prose. That absurdity disregards Mark's life and his books as well. The reader may determine herein whether the style of *The Mysterious Stranger* lacks strength or subtlety, lacks any quality whatever for the effects required of it, or if that represents too late a period, may turn to "Old Times on the Mississippi," which was written before *Huckleberry Finn*, or "The Private History of a Campaign That Failed," which was written while *Huck* was still half finished. Mark Twain wrote English of a remarkable simplicity and clarity, and of singular sensitiveness, flexibility, and beauty as well. Its simplicity might deceive a patronizing reader for the sentence structure is not involved, usually consisting of short elements in natural sequence, and in order to understand without analysis how much art has gone into it one must have an ear for the tones and accents of speech as well as some feeling for the vigor of words. It is so lucid that it seems effortless—but just what is style?

Now, it is important that Mark made the American vernacular the medium of a great novel. Even before that he had used local, class, and racial dialects with immeasurably greater skill than anyone before him in our literature. "The Jumping Frog" raised such dialects above the merely humorous use which was the only one they had previously had and gave them a function in the writing of fiction. And the first two chapters of *The Gilded Age* bring to American literature genuine Negro speech and a rural dialect that are both genuine and an instrument of art— literally for the first time. In the rendition of Negro speech he may have had one equal, though there are those who will not grant that Harris is an equal; but it is doubtful if anyone has used the dialects of the middle South, or for that matter any other American dialect, as well as he. This on the basis of *The Gilded Age* and its immediate successors: the achievement of *Huckleberry Finn* is greater still. Huck's style, which is the spoken language of the untutored American of his place and time, differentiates the most subtle meanings and emphases and proves capable of the most difficult psychological effects. In a single step it made a literary medium of the American language; the liberating effect on American writing could hardly be overstated. Since *Huckleberry Finn* the well of American undefiled has flowed confidently.

Nevertheless, Mark's principal service to the American language was not Huck's vernacular: it lay within the recognized limits of literary prose. Within those limits he was a radical innovator, a prime mover who changed the medium by incorporating in it the syntax, the idioms, and especially the vocabulary of the common life. The vigor of his prose comes directly from the speech of the Great Valley and the Far West. A superlative may be ventured: that Mark Twain had a greater effect than any other writer on the evolution of American prose.

His place in that evolution cannot be analyzed or even illustrated here. He is in the direct succession and he powerfully accelerates the movement. The evolution is of course older than our independence, even older than our nationality—which it helped to produce. Only an American could have said, "We must all hang together, or assuredly we shall all hang separately" in the traditional context. Only an American could have written, "It is not necessary that a man should earn his living by the sweat of his brow unless he sweats easier than I do." Only an American could have written, "the calm confidence of a Christian with four aces." The sequence is Franklin, Thoreau, Mark

Twain; and the point here made lightly can be made with as profound a search into the fusion of thought, expression, and nationality as anyone may care to undertake. But before Mark Twain no
American, no one writing in English, could have launched a novel
into the movement of fiction with such a passage as:

> At the end of an hour we saw a far-away town sleeping in
> a valley by a winding river, and beyond it on a hill, a vast
> gray fortress with towers and turrets, the first I had ever
> seen out of a picture.
> "Bridgeport?" said I, pointing.
> "Camelot," said he.

Such questions as these, however, interest the historian of
literature more than the general reader. The general reader
who, it may be worth reminding you, continues to read Mark
Twain, here and in Europe, more often by far than any other of
our great dead. It is not difficult to say why.

The Americanism just mentioned is part of it. Any unidenti-
fied quotation from Mark Twain will be recognized at sight as
American. It is, furthermore, a national Americanism; his great
books are set along the Mississippi, but no one can think of
them as local or regional. But there is also a kind of centripetal
Americanism, so that he seems frequently to speak for the nation. The character of national spokesman is in his work as early
as *Innocents Abroad*; by *Huckleberry Finn* it is self-evident. Fifteen
years before he died it was generally acknowledged—so that if
the nation's mood changed or its honor came in peril, the newspapers could hardly be put to bed till Mark Twain had spoken.

1946

Leslie Fiedler

For much of his career, writer and critic Leslie Fiedler (1917–2003) was known—as he once put it—as a "disturber of the peace, an *enfant terrible*, the 'wild man of American Letters.'" The occasion on which he characterized himself in these words was his being honored with the Hubbell Medal in 1994, the most prestigious award given by the American Section of the Modern Language Association; Fiedler was somewhat amazed and amused by the fact that he had come to be thought of as "perfectly respectable." His bold and controversial 1948 essay "Come Back to the Raft Ag'in, Huck Honey!" was Fiedler's first publication as a critic (its title does not reflect any line Mark Twain wrote in the book). It drew (and continues to draw) hostility from many quarters, often from people who have not read it. As Christopher Lehmann-Haupt observed, "far from suggesting some hanky-panky going on between Huck and Jim on the raft, as many accused him of doing," what the essay actually does is highlight "the important roles of race and male bonding in American literature." Issues of race and gender had not generally been a part of discussions about American literature before Fiedler contentiously placed them there, but they would become increasingly central over the next decades. Fiedler's criticism was a pioneering declaration of independence from the New Criticism's determination to divorce works of literature from the broader social, cultural, and psychological contexts that inform them. In 1955 he published another seminal essay on Twain, focused on *Pudd'nhead Wilson*. In "As Free as Any Cretur . . . ," which ran in *The New Republic*, Fiedler argued that the novel, which critics had mainly ignored, "is, after all, a fantastically good book, better than Mark Twain knew or his critics have deserved. Morally, it is one of the most honest books in our literature, superior in this one respect to *Huckleberry Finn*; for here Twain permits himself no sentimental relenting, but accepts for once the logic of his own premises." Fiedler saw the book as "a dark mirror image of the world evoked in the earlier work," in which the "lyricism and euphoria" of *Huckleberry Finn* has given way to "a world of prose, and there are no triumphs of Twain's rhetoric to preserve us from the revealed failures of our own humanity." The best-known of Fiedler's many provocative books, *Love and Death in the American Novel*, came out in 1960. Fiedler's writing—in more than 40 volumes of nonfiction and fiction—helped transform the ways in which Americans understood themselves for much of the 20th century.

Come Back to the Raft Ag'in, Huck Honey!

It is perhaps to be expected that the Negro and the homosexual should become stock literary themes, compulsive, almost mythic in their insistence, in a period when the reassertion of responsibility and of the inward meaning of failure has become again a concern of our literature. Their locus is, of course, discrepancy—in a culture which has no resources (no tradition of courtesy, no honored mode of cynicism) for dealing with a contradiction between principle and practice. It used once to be fashionable to think of puritanism as a force in our life encouraging hypocrisy; quite the contrary, its rigid emphasis upon the singleness of belief and action, its turning of the most prosaic areas of common life into arenas where one's state of grace is symbolically tested, confuse the outer and the inner and make among us, perhaps more strikingly than ever elsewhere, hypocrisy *visible*, visibly detestable, a cardinal sin. It is not without significance that the shrug of the shoulders (the acceptance of circumstance as a sufficient excuse, the vulgar sign of self-pardon before the inevitable lapse) seems in America an unfamiliar, an alien gesture.

And yet before the underground existence of crude homosexual love (the ultimate American epithets of contempt notoriously exploit the mechanics of such affairs), before the blatant ghettos in which the cast-off Negro conspicuously creates the gaudiness and stench that offend him, the white American must over and over make a choice between coming to uneasy terms with an institutionalized discrepancy, or formulating radically new ideologies. There are, to be sure, stop-gap devices, evasions of that final choice; not the least interesting is the special night club: the fag café, the black-and-tan joint, in which fairy or Negro exhibit their fairyness, their Negro-ness as if they were mere divertissements, gags thought up for the laughs and having no reality once the lights go out and the chairs are piled on the tables for the cleaning-women. In the earlier minstrel show, a negro performer was required to put on with grease paint and burnt cork the formalized mask of blackness.

The situations of the Negro and the homosexual in our society pose precisely opposite problems, or at least problems suggesting precisely opposite solutions: Our laws on homosexuality and the context of prejudice and feeling they objectify must apparently be changed to accord with a stubborn social fact, whereas it is the social fact, our overt behavior toward the Negro, that must be modified to accord with our laws and the, at least official, morality they objectify.

It is not, of course, quite so simple. There is another sense in which the fact of homosexual passion contradicts a national myth of masculine love, just as our real relationship with the Negro contradicts a myth of that relationship, and those two myths with their betrayals are, as we shall see, one.

The existence of overt homosexuality threatens to compromise an essential aspect of American sentimental life: the camaraderie of the locker-room and ball park, the good fellowship of the poker game and fishing trip, a kind of passionless passion, at once gross and delicate, homoerotic in the boy's sense, possessing an innocence above suspicion. To doubt for a moment this innocence, which can survive only as *assumed*, would destroy our stubborn belief in a relationship simple, utterly satisfying, yet immune to lust; physical as the handshake is physical, this side of copulation. The nineteenth-century myth of the Immaculate Young Girl has failed to survive in any *felt* way into our time; rather in the dirty jokes shared among men in the smoking-car, the barracks, or the dormitory there is a common male revenge against women for having flagrantly betrayed that myth, and under the revenge, there is the rather smug assumption of the chastity of the group as a masculine society. From what other source could that unexpected air of good clean fun which overhangs such sessions arise? It is this self-congratulatory buddy-buddiness, its astonishing naiveté, that breeds at once endless opportunities for inversion and the terrible reluctance to admit its existence, to surrender the last believed-in stronghold of love without passion.

It is, after all, what we know from a hundred other sources that is here verified: the regressiveness, in a technical sense, of American life, its implacable nostalgia for the infantile, at once wrongheaded and somehow admirable. The mythic America is boyhood—and who would dare be startled to realize that two (and

the two most popular, the two most *absorbed*, I think) of the handful of great books in our native heritage are customarily to be
found, illustrated, on the shelves of the Children's Library. I am
referring of course to *Moby Dick* and *Huckleberry Finn*, splendidly
counterpoised in their oceanic complexity and fluminal simplicity, but alike children's books, or more precisely, *boys'* books.

Among the most distinguished novelists of the American
past, only Henry James escapes completely classification as a
writer of juvenile classics; even Hawthorne, who did write
sometimes for children, must in his most adult novels endure,
though not as Mark Twain and Melville submit to, the child's
perusal; a child's version of *The Scarlet Letter* would seem a
rather far-fetched joke if it were not a part of our common experience. On a lower level of excellence, there are the Leatherstocking Tales of Cooper and Dana's *Two Years Before the Mast*,
books read still, though almost unaccountably in Cooper's case,
by boys. What do all these novels have in common?

As boys' books we would expect them shyly, guilelessly as it
were, to proffer a chaste male love as the ultimate emotional experience—and this is spectacularly the case. In Dana, it is the
narrator's melancholy love for the *kanaka*, Hope; in Cooper, the
lifelong affection of Natty Bumppo and Chingachgook; in Melville, Ishmael's love for Queequeg; in Twain, Huck's feeling for
Nigger Jim. At the focus of emotion, where we are accustomed to
find in the world's great novels some heterosexual passion, be it
Platonic love or adultery, seduction, rape or long-drawn-out
flirtation, we come instead upon the fugitive slave and the no-
account boy lying side by side on a raft borne by the endless
river towards an impossible escape, or the pariah sailor waking
in the tattooed arms of the brown harpooner on the verge of
their impossible quest. "Aloha, aikane, aloha nui," Hope cries to
the lover who prefers him above his fellow-whites; and Ishmael,
in utter frankness, tells us: "Thus, then, in our heart's honey-
moon, lay I and Queequeg—a cosy, loving pair." Physical it all
is, certainly, yet of an ultimate innocence; there is between the
lovers no sword but a child-like ignorance, as if the possibility of
a fall to the carnal had not yet been discovered. Even in the *Vita
Nuova* of Dante there is no vision of love less offensively, more

unremittingly chaste; that it is not adult seems sometimes beside the point.

The tenderness of Huck's repeated loss and refinding of Jim, Ishmael's sensations as he wakes under the pressure of Queequeg's arm, the role of almost Edenic helpmate played for Bumppo by the Indian—these shape us from childhood: we have no sense of first discovering them, of having been once without them.

Of the infantile, the homoerotic aspects of these stories we are, though vaguely, aware, but it is only with an effort that we can wake to a consciousness of how, among us who at the level of adulthood find a difference in color sufficient provocation for distrust and hatred, they celebrate, all of them, the mutual love of *a white man and a colored*.

So buried at a level of acceptance which does not touch reason, so desperately repressed from overt recognition, so contrary to what is usually thought of as our ultimate level of taboo—the sense of that love can survive only in the obliquity of a symbol, persistent, archtypical, in short, as a myth: the boy's homoerotic crush, the love of the black fused at this level into a single thing.

I hope I have been using here a hopelessly abused word with some precision; by myth I mean a coherent pattern of beliefs and feelings, so widely shared at a level beneath consciousness that there exists no abstract vocabulary for representing it, and (this is perhaps another aspect of the same thing) so "sacred" that unexamined, irrational restraints inhibit any explicit analysis. Such a complex achieves a formula or pattern story, which serves both to embody it, and, at first at least, to conceal its full implications. Later the secret may be revealed, the myth (I use a single word for the formula and what is formulized) "analyzed" or "allegorically interpreted" according to the language of the day.

I find the situation we have been explicating genuinely mythic; certainly it has the concealed character of the true myth, eluding the wary pounce of Howells or of Mrs. Twain who excised from *Huckleberry Finn* the cussin' as unfit for children, but left, unperceived, a conventionally abhorrent doctrine of ideal love. Even the writers in whom we find it, attained it, in a sense, dreaming. The felt difference between *Huckleberry Finn* and Twain's other books must lie surely in the release from conscious restraint inherent in the author's assumption of the character of Huck; the passage in and out of darkness and river mist, the constant confusion of identities (Huck's ten or twelve names—the questions of who is the real uncle, who the true Tom), the sudden intrusions into alien violences without past or future, give the whole work for all its carefully observed detail, the texture of a dream. For *Moby Dick*, such a point need scarcely be made. Even Cooper, despite his insufferable gentlemanliness, his civilized tedium, cannot conceal from the kids who continue to read him the secret behind the overconscious, stilted prose: the childish impossible dream. D. H. Lawrence saw in him clearly the kid's Utopia: the absolute wilderness in which the stuffiness of home yields to the wigwam and "My Wife" to Chingachgook.

I do not recall ever having seen in the commentaries of the social anthropologist or psychologist an awareness of the role of this profound child's dream of love in our relation to the Negro. (I say Negro, though the beloved in the books we have mentioned is variously Indian and Hawaiian, because the Negro has become more and more exclusively for us *the* colored man, the colored man par excellence.) Trapped in what has by now become a shackling cliché: the concept of the white man's sexual envy of the Negro male, they do not sufficiently note the complementary factor of physical attraction, the mythic love of white male and black. I am deliberately ignoring here an underlying Indo-European myth of great antiquity, the Manichaean notion of an absolute Black and White, hostile yet needing each other for completion, as I ignore more recent ideologies that have nourished the view that concerns us: the Shakespearian myth of good homosexual love opposed to an evil heterosexual attachment, the Rousseauistic concept of the Noble Savage; I have tried to stay within the limits of a single unified myth, re-enforced by disparate materials.

Ishmael and Queequeg, arm in arm, about to ship out, Huck and Jim swimming beside the raft in the peaceful flux of the Mississippi,—it is the motion of water which completes the syndrome, the American dream of isolation afloat. The Negro as homoerotic lover blends with the myth of running off to sea, of running the great river down to the sea. The immensity of water defines a loneliness that demands love, its strangeness symbolizes the disavowal of the conventional that makes possible all versions of love.

In *Two Years Before the Mast*, in *Moby Dick*, in *Huckleberry Finn* the water is there, is the very texture of the novel; the Leatherstocking Tales propose another symbol for the same meaning: the virgin forest. Notice the adjective—the virgin forest and the forever inviolable sea. It is well to remember, too, what surely must be more than a coincidence, that Cooper who could dream this myth invented the novel of the sea, wrote for the first time in history the sea-story proper. The rude pederasty of the forecastle and the Captain's cabin, celebrated in a thousand jokes, is the profanation of a dream. In a recent book of Gore Vidal's an incipient homosexual, not yet aware of the implications of his feelings, indulges in the apt reverie of running off to sea with his dearest friend. The buggery of sailors is taken for granted among us, yet it is thought of usually as an inversion forced on men by their isolation from women, though the opposite case may well be true, the isolation sought more or less consciously as an occasion for male encounters. There is a context in which the legend of the sea as escape and solace, the fixated sexuality of boys, the dark beloved are one.

In Melville and Twain at the center of our tradition, in the lesser writers at the periphery, the myth is at once formalized and perpetuated; Nigger Jim and Queequeg make concrete for us what was without them a vague pressure upon the threshold of our consciousness; the proper existence of the myth is in the realized character, who waits, as it were, only to be asked his secret. Think of Oedipus biding in silence from Sophocles to Freud.

Unwittingly we are possessed in childhood by the characters and their undiscriminated meaning, and it is difficult for us to dissociate them without a sense of disbelief. What! these household figures clues to our subtlest passions! The foreigner finds it easier to perceive the remoter significance; D. H. Lawrence saw in our classics a linked mythos of escape and immaculate

male love; Lorca in *The Poet in New York* grasped instinctively
the kinship of Harlem and Walt Whitman, the fairy as bard. Yet
in every generation of our own writers the myth appears; in the
Gothic reverie of Capote's *Other Voices, Other Rooms*, both elements of the syndrome are presented, though disjunctively: the
boy moving between the love of a Negro maid-servant and his
inverted cousin.

In the myth, one notes finally, it is always in the role of outcast, ragged woodsman, or despised sailor (Call me Ishmael!), or
unregenerate boy (Huck before the prospect of being 'sivilized'
cries, "I been here before!") that we turn to the love of a colored
man. But how, we must surely ask, does the vision of the white
American as pariah correspond with our long-held public status: the world's beloved, the success? It is perhaps only the artist's portrayal of *himself*, the notoriously alienated writer in
America, at home with such images, child of the town drunk,
the survivor. But no, Ishmael is all of us, our unconfessed universal fear objectified in the writer's status as in the sailor's: that
compelling anxiety, which every foreigner notes, that we may
not be loved, that we are loved for our possessions and not ourselves, that we are really—*alone!* It is that underlying terror
which explains our almost furtive incredulity in the face of adu-
lation or favor, what is called (once more the happy adjective)
our "boyish modesty."

Our dark-skinned beloved will take us, we assure ourselves,
when we have been cut off, or have cut ourselves off from all
others, without rancor or the insult of forgiveness; he will fold us
in his arms saying "Honey" or "Aikane!", he will comfort us, as
if our offense against him were long ago remitted, were never
truly *real*. And yet we cannot really forget our guilt ever; the
stories that embody the myth dramatize almost compulsively the
role of the colored man as victim: Dana's Hope is shown dying of
the white man's syphilis; Queequeg is portrayed as racked by fever, a pointless episode except in the light of this necessity; Cooper's Indian smolders to a hopeless old age conscious of the imminent disappearance of his race; Jim is shown loaded down with
chains, weakened by the hundred torments of Tom's notion of
bullyness. The immense gulf of guilt must be underlined, just as

is the disparity of color (Queequeg is not merely brown but monstrously tatooed, Chingachgook is horrid with paint, Jim is shown as the Sick A-rab dyed blue), so that the final reconciliation will seem more unbelievable, more tender. The myth makes no attempt to whitewash our outrage as a fact; it portrays it as meaningless in the face of love.

There would be something insufferable, I think, in that final vision of remission if it were not for the apparent presence of a motivating anxiety, the sense always of a last chance; behind the white American's nightmare that someday, no longer tourist, inheritor, or liberator, he will be rejected, refused—he dreams of his acceptance at the breast he has most utterly offended. It is a dream so sentimental, so outrageous, so desperate that it redeems our concept of boyhood from nostalgia to tragedy.

In each generation we *play* out the impossible mythos, and we live to see our children play it, the white boy and the black we can discover wrestling affectionately on any American street, along which they will walk in adulthood, eyes averted from each other, unwilling to touch. The dream recedes; the immaculate passion and the astonishing reconciliation become a memory, and less, a regret, at last the unrecognized motifs of a child's book. "It's too good to be true, Honey," Jim says to Huck. "It's too good to be true."

Partisan Review, 1948

T. S. Eliot

Although his urban St. Louis childhood as the son of a successful businessman could not have been more different from the rural Hannibal childhood that Sam Clemens experienced half a century earlier as the son of a failed shopkeeper, Thomas Stearns Eliot (1888–1965) shared with Mark Twain an appreciation for the power of the river that ran through both of their hometowns. Eliot increasingly turned his back on Missouri as he developed as a writer, eventually becoming a British subject, while Mark Twain returned to Missouri again and again in his fiction as well as in person. Eliot had little interest in any work by Mark Twain other than *Huckleberry Finn*. But he had no hesitation about asserting that the novel was "a masterpiece," as he notes in this 1950 introduction to the book. Many writers and critics have been less satisfied than Eliot was with the ending of the novel; few, however, would take issue with his statement that in *Huckleberry Finn*, "Mark Twain wrote a much greater book than he could have known he was writing." Fifteen years after he wrote this essay, Eliot argued again for the novel's greatness. In "American Literature and the American Language" he wrote that "Twain, at least in *Huckleberry Finn*, reveals himself to be one of those writers, of whom there are not a great many in literature, who have discovered a new way of writing, valid not only for themselves but for others. I should place him in this respect, even with Dryden and Swift, as one of those rare writers who have brought their language up to date, and in doing so, 'purified the dialect of the tribe.'"

Introduction to
Huckleberry Finn

*T*he *Adventures of Huckleberry Finn* is the only one of Mark Twain's various books which can be called a masterpiece. I do not suggest that it is his only book of permanent interest; but it is the only one in which his genius is completely realized, and the only one which creates its own category. There are pages in *Tom Sawyer* and in *Life on the Mississippi* which are, within their limits, as good as anything with which one can compare them in *Huckleberry Finn*; and in other books there are drolleries just as good of their kind. But when we find one book by a prolific author which is very much superior to all the rest, we look for the peculiar accident or concourse of accidents which made that book possible. In the writing of *Huckleberry Finn* Mark Twain had two elements which, when treated with his sensibility and his experience, formed a great book: these two are the Boy and the River.

Huckleberry Finn is, no doubt, a book which boys enjoy. I cannot speak from memory: I suspect that a fear on the part of my parents lest I should acquire a premature taste for tobacco, and perhaps other habits of the hero of the story, kept the book out of my way. But *Huckleberry Finn* does not fall into the category of juvenile fiction. The opinion of my parents that it was a book unsuitable for boys left me, for most of my life, under the impression that it was a book suitable only for boys. Therefore it was only a few years ago that I read for the first time, and in that order, *Tom Sawyer* and *Huckleberry Finn*.

Tom Sawyer did not prepare me for what I was to find its sequel to be. *Tom Sawyer* seems to me to be a boys' book, and a very good one. The River and *the* Boy make their appearance in it; the narrative is good; and there is also a very good picture of society in a small mid-Western river town (for St Petersburg is more Western than Southern) a hundred years ago. But the point of view of the narrator is that of an adult observing a boy. And Tom is the ordinary boy, though of quicker wits, and livelier imagination, than most. Tom is, I suppose, very much the boy that Mark Twain had been: he is remembered and described as he seemed to his elders, rather than created. Huck Finn, on the other hand, is the boy that Mark Twain still was, at the time of writing his adventures. We look at Tom as the smiling adult does: Huck we do not look at—we see the world through his eyes. The two boys are not merely different types; they were brought into existence by different processes. Hence in the second book their roles are altered. In the first book Huck is merely the humble friend—almost a variant of the traditional valet of comedy; and we see him as he is seen by the conventional respectable society to which Tom belongs, and of which, we feel sure, Tom will one day become an eminently respectable and conventional member. In the second book their nominal relationship remains the same; but here it is Tom who has the secondary role. The author was probably not conscious of this, when he wrote the first two chapters: *Huckleberry Finn* is not the kind of story in which the author knows, from the beginning, what is going to happen. Tom then disappears from our view; and when he returns, he has only two functions. The first is to provide a foil for Huck. Huck's persisting admiration for Tom only exhibits more clearly to our eyes the unique qualities of the former and the commonplaceness of the latter. Tom has the imagination of a lively boy who has read a good deal of romantic fiction: he might, of course, become a writer—he might become Mark Twain. Or rather, he might become the more commonplace aspect of Mark Twain. Huck has not imagination, in the sense in which Tom has it: he has, instead, vision. He sees the real world; and he does not judge it—he allows it to judge itself.

Tom Sawyer is an orphan. But he has his aunt; he has, as we learn later, other relatives; and he has the environment into which he fits. He is wholly a social being. When there is a secret band to be formed, it is Tom who organizes it and prescribes the rules. Huck Finn is alone: there is no more solitary character in fiction. The fact that he has a father only emphasizes his loneliness; and he views his father with a terrifying detachment. So we come to see Huck himself in the end as one of the permanent symbolic figures of fiction; not unworthy to take a place with Ulysses, Faust, Don Quixote, Don Juan, Hamlet and other great discoveries that man has made about himself.

It would seem that Mark Twain was a man who—perhaps like most of us—never became in all respects mature. We might even say that the adult side of him was boyish, and that only the boy in him, that was Huck Finn, was adult. As Tom Sawyer grown up, he wanted success and applause (Tom himself always needs an audience). He wanted prosperity, a happy domestic life of a conventional kind, universal approval, and fame. All of these things he obtained. As Huck Finn he was indifferent to all these things; and being composite of the two, Mark Twain both strove for them, and resented their violation of his integrity. Hence he became the humorist and even clown: with his gifts, a certain way to success, for everyone could enjoy his writings without the slightest feeling of discomfort, self-consciousness or self-criticism. And hence, on the other hand, his pessimism and misanthropy. To be a misanthrope is to be in some way divided; or it is a sign of an uneasy conscience. The pessimism which Mark Twain discharged into *The Man That Corrupted Hadleyburg* and *What is Man?* springs less from observation of society, than from his hatred of himself for allowing society to tempt and corrupt him and give him what he wanted. There is no wisdom in it. But all this personal problem has been diligently examined by Mr Van Wyck Brooks; and it is not Mark Twain, but *Huckleberry Finn*, that is the subject of this introduction.

You cannot say that Huck himself is either a humorist or a misanthrope. He is the impassive observer: he does not interfere, and, as I have said, he does not judge. Many of the episodes that occur on the voyage down the river, after he is joined by the Duke and the King (whose fancies about themselves are akin to the kind of fancy that Tom Sawyer enjoys) are in themselves farcical; and if it were not for the presence of Huck as the reporter of them, they would be no more than farce. But, seen through the eyes of Huck, there is a deep human pathos in these scoundrels. On the other hand, the story of the feud between the Grangerfords and the Shepherdsons is a masterpiece in itself: yet Mark Twain could not have written it so, with that economy and restraint, with just the right details and no more, and leaving to the reader to make his own moral reflections, unless he had been writing in the person of Huck. And the *style* of the book, which is the style of Huck, is what makes it a far more convincing indictment of slavery than the sensationalist propaganda of *Uncle Tom's Cabin*. Huck is passive and impassive, apparently always the victim of events; and yet, in his acceptance of his world and of what it does to him and others, he is more powerful than his world, because he is more *aware* than any other person in it.

Repeated readings of the book only confirm and deepen one's admiration of the consistency and perfect adaptation of the writing. This is a style which at the period, whether in

America or in England, was an innovation, a new discovery in the English language. Other authors had achieved natural speech in relation to particular characters—Scott with characters talking Lowland Scots, Dickens with cockneys: but no one else had kept it up through the whole of a book. Thackeray's Yellowplush, impressive as he is, is an obvious artifice in comparison. In *Huckleberry Finn* there is no exaggeration of grammar or spelling or speech, there is no sentence or phrase to destroy the illusion that these are Huck's own words. It is not only in the way in which he tells his story, but in the details he remembers, that Huck is true to himself. There is, for instance, the description of the Grangerford interior as Huck sees it on his arrival; there is the list of the objects which Huck and Jim salvaged from the derelict house:

> We got an old tin lantern, and a butcher-knife without any handle, and a bran-new Barlow knife worth two bits in any store, and a lot of tallow candles, and a tin candlestick, and a gourd, and a tin cup, and a ratty old bedquilt off the bed, and a reticule with needles and pins and beeswax and buttons and thread and all such truck in it, and a hatchet and some nails, and a fish-line as thick as my little finger, with some monstrous hooks on it, and a roll of buckskin, and a leather dog-collar, and a horseshoe, and some vials of medicine that didn't have no label on them; and just as we was leaving I found a tolerable good curry-comb, and Jim he found a ratty old fiddle-bow, and a wooden leg. The straps was broke off of it, but barring that, it was a good enough leg, though it was too long for me and not long enough for Jim, and we couldn't find the other one, though we hunted all round.
>
> And so, take it all round, we made a good haul.

This is the sort of list that a boy reader should pore over with delight; but the paragraph performs other functions of which the boy reader would be unaware. It provides the right counterpoise to the horror of the wrecked house and the corpse; it has a grim precision which tells the reader all he needs to know about the way of life of the human derelicts who had used the house; and (especially the wooden leg, and the fruitless search for its mate) reminds us at the right moment of the kinship of mind and the sympathy between the boy outcast from society and the negro fugitive from the injustice of society.

Huck in fact would be incomplete without Jim, who is almost as notable a creation as Huck himself. Huck is the passive observer of men and events, Jim the submissive sufferer from them; and they are equal in dignity. There is no passage in which their relationship is brought out more clearly than the conclusion of the chapter in which, after the two have become separated in the fog, Huck in the canoe and Jim on the raft, Huck, in his impulse of boyish mischief, persuades Jim for a time that the latter had dreamt the whole episode.

> '. . . my heart wuz mos' broke bekase you wuz los', en I didn' k'yer no mo' what become er me en de raf'. En when I wake up en fine you back agin', all safe en soun', de tears come en I could a got down on my knees en kiss' yo' foot, I's so thankful. En all you wuz thinkin' 'bout wuz how you could make a fool uv ole Jim wid a lie. Dat truck dah is *trash*; en trash is what people is dat puts dirt on de head er dey fren's en makes 'em ashamed.' . . .
>
> It was fifteen minutes before I could work myself up to go and humble myself to a nigger—but I done it, and I warn't ever sorry for it afterwards, neither.

This passage has been quoted before; and if I quote it again, it is because I wish to elicit from it one meaning that is, I think, usually overlooked. What is obvious in it is the pathos and dignity of Jim, and this is moving enough; but what I find still more disturbing, and still more unusual in literature, is the pathos and dignity of the boy, when reminded so humbly and humiliatingly, that his position in the world is not that of other boys, entitled from time to time to a practical joke; but that he must bear, and bear alone, the responsibility of a man.

It is Huck who gives the book style. The River gives the book its form. But for the River, the book might be only a sequence of adventures with a happy ending. A river, a very big and powerful river, is the only natural force that can wholly determine the course of human peregrination. At sea, the wanderer may sail or be carried by winds and currents in one direction or another; a change of wind or tide may determine fortune. In the prairie, the direction of movement is more or less at the choice of the caravan; among mountains there will often be an alternative, a guess at the most likely pass. But the river with its strong, swift current is the dictator to the raft or to the steamboat. It is a treacherous and capricious dictator. At one season, it may move sluggishly in a channel so narrow that, encountering it for the first time at that point, one can hardly believe that it has travelled already for hundreds of miles, and has yet many hundreds of miles to go; at another season, it may obliterate the low Illinois shore to a horizon of water, while in its bed it runs with a speed such that no man or beast can survive in it. At such times, it carries down human bodies, cattle and houses. At least twice, at St Louis, the western and the eastern shores have been separated by the fall of bridges, until the designer of the great Eads Bridge devised a structure which could resist the floods. In my own childhood, it was not unusual for the spring freshet to interrupt railway travel; and then the traveller to the East had to take steamboat from the levee up to Alton, at a higher level on the Illinois shore, before he could begin his rail journey. The river is never wholly chartable; it changes its pace, it shifts its channel, unaccountably; it may suddenly efface a sandbar, and throw up another bar where before was navigable water.

It is the River that controls the voyage of Huck and Jim; that will not let them land at Cairo, where Jim could have reached freedom; it is the River that separates them and deposits Huck for a time in the Grangerford household; the River that re-unites them, and then compels upon them the unwelcome company of the King and the Duke. Recurrently we are reminded of its presence and its power.

> When I woke up, I didn't know where I was for a minute. I set up and looked around, a little scared. Then I remembered. The river looked miles and miles across. The moon was so bright I could a counted the drift-logs that went a-slipping along, black and still, hundreds of yards out

from shore. Everything was dead quiet, and it looked late, and *smelt* late. You know what I mean—I don't know the words to put it in.

It was kind of solemn, drifting down the big still river, laying on our backs looking up at the stars, and we didn't ever feel like talking loud, and it warn't often that we laughed, only a little kind of a low chuckle. We had mighty good weather as a general thing, and nothing ever happened to us at all, that night, nor the next, nor the next.

Every night we passed towns, some of them away up on black hillsides, nothing but just a shiny bed of lights, not a house could you see. The fifth night we passed St Louis, and it was like the whole world lit up. In St Petersburg they used to say there was twenty or thirty thousand people in St Louis, but I never believed it till I see that wonderful spread of lights at two o'clock that still night. There wasn't a sound there; everybody was asleep.

We come to understand the River by seeing it through the eyes of the Boy; but the Boy is also the spirit of the River. *Huckleberry Finn*, like other great works of imagination, can give to every reader whatever he is capable of taking from it. On the most superficial level of observation, Huck is convincing as a boy. On the same level, the picture of social life on the shores of the Mississippi a hundred years ago is, I feel sure, accurate. On any level, Mark Twain makes you see the River, as it is and was and always will be, more clearly than the author of any other description of a river known to me. But you do not merely see the River, you do not merely become acquainted with it through the senses: you experience the River. Mark Twain, in his later years of success and fame, referred to his early life as a steamboat pilot as the happiest he had known. With all allowance for the illusions of age, we can agree that those years were the years in which he was most fully alive. Certainly, but for his having practised that calling, earned his living by that profession, he would never have gained the understanding which his genius for expression communicates in this book. In the pilot's daily struggle with the River, in the satisfaction of activity, in the constant attention to the River's unpredictable vagaries, his consciousness was fully occupied, and he absorbed knowledge of which, as an artist, he later made use. There are, perhaps, only two ways in which a writer can acquire the understanding of environment which he can later turn to account: by having spent his childhood in that environment—that is, living in it at a period of life in which one experiences much more than one is aware of; and by having had to struggle for a livelihood in that environment—a livelihood bearing no direct relation to any intention of writing about it, of *using* it as literary material. Most of Joseph Conrad's understanding came to him in the latter way. Mark Twain knew the Mississippi in both ways: he had spent his childhood on its banks, and he had earned his living matching his wits against its currents.

Thus the River makes the book a great book. As with Conrad, we are continually reminded of the power and terror of Nature, and the isolation and feebleness of Man. Conrad remains always the European observer of the tropics, the white man's eye contemplating the Congo and its black gods. But Mark Twain is a native, and the River God is his God. It is as a native that he accepts the River God, and it is the subjection of Man that gives to Man his dignity. For without some kind of God, Man is not even very interesting.

Readers sometimes deplore the fact that the story descends to the level of *Tom Sawyer* from the moment that Tom himself re-appears. Such readers protest that the escapades invented by Tom, in the attempted 'rescue' of Jim, are only a tedious development of themes with which we were already too familiar—even while admitting that the escapades themselves are very amusing, and some of the incidental observations memorable. But it is right that the mood of the end of the book should bring us back to that of the beginning. Or, if this was not the right ending for the book, what ending would have been right?

In *Huckleberry Finn* Mark Twain wrote a much greater book than he could have known he was writing. Perhaps all great works of art mean much more than the author could have been aware of meaning: certainly, *Huckleberry Finn* is the one book of Mark Twain's which, as a whole, has this unconsciousness. So what seems to be the rightness, of reverting at the end of the book to the mood of *Tom Sawyer*, was perhaps unconscious art. For Huckleberry Finn, neither a tragic nor a happy ending would be suitable. No worldly success or social satisfaction, no domestic consummation would be worthy of him; a tragic end also would reduce him to the level of those whom we pity. Huck Finn must come from nowhere and be bound for nowhere. His is not the independence of the typical or symbolic American Pioneer, but the independence of the vagabond. His existence questions the values of America as much as the values of Europe; he is as much an affront to the 'pioneer spirit' as he is to 'business enterprise'; he is in a state of nature as detached as the state of the saint. In a busy world, he represents the loafer; in an acquisitive and competitive world, he insists on living from hand to mouth. He could not be exhibited in any amorous encounters or engagements, in any of the juvenile affections which are appropriate to Tom Sawyer. He belongs neither to the Sunday School nor to the Reformatory. He has no beginning and no end. Hence, he can only disappear; and his disappearance can only be accomplished by bringing forward another performer to obscure the disappearance in a cloud of whimsicalities.

Like Huckleberry Finn, the River itself has no beginning or end. In its beginning, it is not yet the River; in its end, it is no longer the River. What we call its headwaters is only a selection from among the innumerable sources which flow together to compose it. At what point in its course does the Mississippi become what the Mississippi *means*? It is both one and many; it is the Mississippi of this book only after its union with the Big Muddy—the Missouri; it derives some of its character from the Ohio, the Tennessee and other confluents. And at the end it merely disappears among its deltas: it is no longer there, but it is still where it was, hundreds of miles to the North. The River cannot tolerate any design, to a story which is its story, that might interfere with its dominance. Things must merely happen, here and there, to the people who live along its shores or who commit themselves to its current. And it is as impossible for Huck as for the River to have a beginning or end—a *career*. So the book has the right, the only possible concluding sentence. I do not think that any book ever written ends more certainly with the right words:

> But I reckon I got to light out for the Territory ahead of the rest, because Aunt Sally she's going to adopt me and civilize me, and I can't stand it. I been there before.

1950

W. H. Auden

The poet W. H. Auden (1907–1973) was born in York, England, the year that Mark Twain traveled to Oxford to be awarded an honorary degree. Twain was thrilled to have his achievements as a writer in English honored at this august seat of learning and delighted by the affection the illustrious assemblage showered upon him. (For the rest of his life, Twain, a democrat famous for skewering the pretensions of royalty in his books, would raise eyebrows by showing up at special events in America proudly wearing his regal Oxford robe—no matter how inappropriate for the occasion.) Some three decades later Auden traveled from England to America, where (particularly after he gave up his British citizenship) he was embraced by many as an Anglo-American poet. Auden had an enormous impact on poetry in the United States, through his writing and his role as editor of the Yale Younger Poets series from 1948 to 1959. While the journeys that Twain and Auden made across the ocean reminded Britain and America of the language and literature that were a common patrimony, each writer also felt compelled to probe the ways in which the two nations differed. That topic is central to "Huck and Oliver," which Auden published in 1953, some nine years after he had become an American citizen. Auden explores the differing attitudes toward nature and toward the fixity and stability of natural law (which also figured in the poetry he was writing at the time). Referring to Huck's decision not to return Jim to his owner, Auden writes, "What Huck does is a pure act of moral improvisation," a peculiarly American act based on assumptions about the world an Englishman would be unlikely to share. His comment echoes something Twain wrote in a notebook: "What is an Englishman? A person who does things because they have been done before. What is an American? A person who does things because they *haven't* been done before." "We live in a time," Auden wrote in the essay that follows, "when it has never been so important that America and Great Britain should understand each other." Britain and America may be, as George Bernard Shaw claimed, "two countries divided by a common language," but Twain and Auden helped build bridges across that transatlantic divide.

Huck and Oliver

About six months ago I re-read *Huckleberry Finn*, by Mark Twain, for the first time since I was a boy, and I was trying when I read it to put myself back in the position of what it would seem like to re-read the book without knowing the United States very well. Because *Huckleberry Finn* is one of those books which is a key book for understanding the United States; just as I think one could take other books, English books—shall I say *Oliver Twist*?—as corresponding pictures of a British attitude.

When you read *Huckleberry Finn*, the first thing maybe that strikes somebody who comes from England about it is the difference in nature and in the attitude towards nature. You will find the Mississippi, and nature generally, very big, very formidable, very inhuman. When Oliver goes to stay in the country with Mrs Maylie, Dickens writes:

> Who can describe the pleasure and delight and peace of mind and tranquility the sickly boy felt in the balmy air, and among the green hills and rich woods of an inland village.

All very human, very comforting. Huck describes how he gets lost in a fog on the Mississippi, and he writes as follows:

> I was floating along, of course, four or five miles an hour; but you don't ever think of that. No, you *feel* like you are laying dead still on the water; and if a little glimpse of a snag slips by, you don't think to yourself how fast *you're* going, but you catch your breath and think, my! how that snag's tearing along. If you think it ain't dismal and lonesome out in a fog that way, by yourself, in the night, you try it once—you'll see.

One of the great differences between Europe in general and America is in the attitude towards nature. To us over here, perhaps, nature is always, in a sense, the mother or the wife: something with which you enter into a semi-personal relation. In the United States, nature is something much more savage; it is much more like—shall we say?—St George and the dragon.

Nature is the dragon, against which St George proves his manhood. The trouble about that, of course, is that if you succeed in conquering the dragon, there is nothing you can do with the dragon except enslave it, so that there is always the danger with a wild and difficult climate of alternating, if you like, between respecting it as an enemy and exploiting it as a slave.

The second thing that will strike any European reader in reading *Huckleberry Finn* is the amazing stoicism of this little boy. Here he is, with a father who is a greater and more horrible monster than almost any I can think of in fiction, who very properly gets murdered later. He runs into every kind of danger; he observes a blood feud in which there is a terrible massacre, and he cannot even bear, as he writes afterwards, to think exactly what happened. Yet, in spite of all these things, which one would expect to reduce a small child either into becoming a criminal or a trembling nervous wreck, Huck takes them as Acts of God which pass away, and yet one side of this stoicism is an attitude towards time in which the immediate present is accepted as the immediate present; there is no reason to suppose that the future will be the same, and therefore it does not, perhaps, have to affect the future in the same kind of way as it does here.

Then, more interestingly, the European reader is puzzled by the nature of the moral decision that Huck takes. Here Huck is with his runaway slave, Jim, and he decides that he is not going to give Jim up, he is going to try to get him into safety. When I first read *Huckleberry Finn* as a boy, I took Huck's decision as being a sudden realization, although he had grown up in a slave-owning community, that slavery was wrong. Therefore I completely failed to understand one of the most wonderful passages in the book, where Huck wrestles with his conscience. Here are two phrases. He says:

> I was trying to make my mouth *say* I would do the right thing and the clean thing, and go and write to that nigger's owner and tell where he was; but deep down inside I knowed it was a lie, and He knowed it. You can't pray a lie—I found that out.

He decides that he will save Jim. He says:

> I will go to work and steal Jim out of slavery again; and
> if I could think up anything worse, I would do that, too;
> because as long as I was in, and in for good, I might as well
> go the whole hog.

When I first read the book I took this to be abolitionist satire
on Mark Twain's part. It is not that at all. What Huck does is a
pure act of moral improvisation. What he decides tells him
nothing about what he should do on other occasions, or what
other people should do on other occasions; and here we come to
a very profound difference between American and European
culture. I believe that all Europeans, whatever their political
opinions, whatever their religious creed, do believe in a doctrine
of natural law of some kind. That is to say there are certain things
about human nature, and about man as a historical creature, not
only as a natural creature, which are eternally true. If a man is a
conservative, he thinks that law has already been discovered. If
he is a revolutionary he thinks he has just discovered it; nobody
knew anything in the past, but now it is known. If he is a liberal,
he thinks we know something about it and we shall gradually
know more. But neither the conservative, nor the revolutionary,
nor the liberal has really any doubt that a natural law exists.

It is very hard for an American to believe that there is anything in human nature that will not change. Americans are often
called, and sometimes even believe themselves to be, liberal op-
timists who think that the world is gradually getting better and
better. I do not really believe that is true, and I think the evidence of their literature is against it. One should say, rather, that
deep down inside they think that all things pass: the evils we
know will disappear, but so will the goods.

For that very reason you might say that America is a country
of amateurs. Here is Huck who makes an essentially amateur
moral decision. The distinction between an amateur and a professional, of course is not necessarily a matter of learning; an
amateur might be a very learned person, but his knowledge would
be, so to speak, the result of his own choice of reading and chance.
Vice versa, a professional is not necessarily unoriginal, but he will

always tend to check his results against the past and with his colleagues. The word 'intellectual' in Europe has always meant, basically, the person who knew what the law was, in whatever sphere, whether it was religion, medicine, or what have you. There has always been a distrust in the States of the person who claimed in advance to know what the law was. Naturally, in any country where people are faced with situations which are really new, the amateur often is right where the professional is wrong; we sometimes use the phrase 'professional caution,' and that sometimes applies when situations are quite different. On the other hand, the amateur tends, necessarily, to think in terms of immediate problems and to demand immediate solutions, because if you believe that everything is going to be completely different the day after tomorrow, it is no good trying to think about that.

A third thing, coupled with that, is that on reading *Huckleberry Finn* most Europeans will find the book emotionally very sad. Oliver Twist has been through all kinds of adventures; he has met people who have become his friends, and you feel they are going to be his friends for life. Huck has had a relationship with Jim much more intense than any that Oliver has known, and yet, at the end of the book, you know that they are going to part and never see each other again. There hangs over the book a kind of sadness, as if freedom and love were incompatible. At the end of the book Oliver the orphan is adopted by Mr Brownlow, and that is really the summit of his daydream—to be accepted into a loving home. Almost the last paragraph of *Oliver Twist* runs:

> Mr Brownlow went on, from day to day, filling the mind of his adopted child with stores of knowledge . . . becoming attached to him, more and more, as his nature developed itself, and showed the thriving seeds of all he wished him to become . . .

How does Huck end:

> I reckon I got to light out for the Territory ahead of the rest, because Aunt Sally she's going to adopt me and sivilise me, and I can't stand it. I been there before.

In that way, of course, he is like a character in *Oliver Twist*—the Artful Dodger. But in the case of the Artful Dodger, Dickens shows us this charming young man as nevertheless corrupt, and over him hangs always the shadow of the gallows; he is not the natural hero, as Huck is in *Huckleberry Finn*.

In addition to the attitude towards nature, the attitude towards natural law, there are two more things one might take up briefly; the attitude towards time, and the attitude towards money. Imagine two events in history, (*a*) followed by (*b*), which in some way are analogous. The danger to the European will be to think of them as identical, so that if I know what to do over (*a*), I shall know exactly what to do with (*b*). The danger in America will be to see no relation between these things at all, so that any knowledge I have about (*a*) will not help me to understand (*b*). The European fails to see the element of novelty; the American fails to see the element of repetition. You may remember that both Oliver and Huck come into some money. In Oliver's case it is money that is his by right of legal inheritance. In Huck's case, it is pure luck. He and Tom Sawyer found a robber's cache. The money came to them only because it could not be restored to its rightful owners. The money, therefore, is not something that you ever think of inheriting by right.

One might put it this way: in Europe, money represents power—that is to say, freedom from having to do what other people want you to do, and freedom to do what you yourself want to do; so that in a sense all Europeans feel they would like to have as much money themselves as possible, and other people to have as little as possible.

In the States, money, which is thought of as something you extract in your battle with the dragon of nature, represents a proof of your manhood. The important thing is not to have money, but to have made it. Once you have made it you can perfectly well give it all away. There are advantages and disadvantages on both sides. The disadvantage in Europe is a tendency towards avarice and meanness; the danger in America is anxiety because, since this quantitative thing of money is regarded as a proof of your manhood, and to make a little more of it would make you even more manly, it becomes difficult to know where to stop. This ties up with something that always annoys me: when I see Europeans accusing Americans of being materialists. The real truth about Americans is they do not care about matter enough. What is shocking is waste; just as what shocks Americans in Europe is avarice.

I have mentioned a few of these things because we live in a time when it has never been so important that America and Great Britain should understand each other. Many misunderstandings arise, not over concrete points, but over a failure to recognize certain presuppositions or attitudes which we all make, according to our upbringing, in such a way that we cannot imagine anybody taking any other one. When those are understood, it is much more possible to help each other's strong points and weaknesses by exchanging them to our mutual profit.

In so far as that can be done, and I am sufficiently much of a liberal optimist to believe it can, the alliance between the States and Great Britain can become a real and genuine and mutually self-critical thing, instead of the rather precarious relationship forced by circumstances which it seems to be at present.

The Listener (London), 1954

Ralph Ellison

A photograph of Mark Twain in his Oxford robes hung over the desk of Ralph Ellison (1913–1994), the American writer best known as the author of the magisterial novel *Invisible Man*. Ellison first encountered Mark Twain when he was around eight and promptly nicknamed his brother Herbert "Huck." He returned to *Huckleberry Finn* when he began to hone his skills as a writer. Twain was "exhibit A" in Ellison's argument for why a segregated American literary history (in which white writers come from other white writers) was a false one. As Ellison observed in 1970, "the black man [was] a co-creator of the language that Mark Twain raised to the level of literary eloquence." According to Ellison, "The spoken idiom of Negro Americans, its flexibility, its musicality, its rhythms, free-wheeling diction, and metaphors, as projected in Negro American folklore, were absorbed by the creators of our great nineteenth-century literature even when the majority of blacks were still enslaved. Mark Twain celebrated it in the prose of *Huckleberry Finn*." Ellison found Twain's "free-wheeling appropriation of the vernacular, his transforming it into an agency of literature," exhilarating. Twain's influence on Ellison's own work and on the work of other African-American writers was profound; as Ellison put it in a 1991 interview, "He made it possible for many of us to find our own voices." Ellison criticized readers who paid attention to only half of the famous comment he made about *Huckleberry Finn* in 1958 in his essay "Change the Joke and Slip the Yoke": "Writing at a time when the blackfaced minstrel was still popular, and shortly after a war which left even the abolitionists weary of those problems associated with the Negro, Twain fitted Jim into the outlines of the minstrel tradition, and it was from behind this stereotype mask that we see Jim's dignity and human capacity—and Twain's complexity—emerge." In 1991 Ellison emphasized that readers who saw the "stereotype mask" but not Jim's "dignity and human capacity—and Twain's complexity" were failing to pay attention to "the teller of the tale," failing to remember that it was Huck, not Twain, who was telling the story. Throughout his career as a writer, Ellison continued to find inspiration in the "transcendent truth and possibilities" (as he put it in his preface to the 1982 edition of *Invisible Man*) of Mark Twain's imaginative vision in *Huckleberry Finn*.

Twentieth-Century Fiction
and the Black Mask of Humanity

When this essay was published in 1953, it was prefaced with the following note:

When I started rewriting this essay it occurred to me that its value might be somewhat increased if it remained very much as I wrote it during 1946. For in that form it is what a young member of a minority felt about much of our writing. Thus I've left in much of the bias and shortsightedness, for it says perhaps as much about me as a member of a minority as it does about literature. I hope you still find the essay useful, and I'd like to see an editorial note stating that this is an unpublished piece written not long after the Second World War.

Perhaps the most insidious and least understood form of segregation is that of the word. And by this I mean the word in all its complex formulations, from the proverb to the novel and stage play, the word with all its subtle power to suggest and foreshadow overt action while magically disguising the moral consequences of that action and providing it with symbolic and psychological justification. For if the word has the potency to revive and make us free, it has also the power to blind, imprison and destroy.

The essence of the word is its ambivalence, and in fiction it is never so effective and revealing as when both potentials are operating simultaneously, as when it mirrors both good and bad, as when it blows both hot and cold in the same breath. Thus it is unfortunate for the Negro that the most powerful formulations of modern American fictional words have been so slanted against him that when he approaches for a glimpse of himself he discovers an image drained of humanity.

Obviously the experiences of Negroes—slavery, the grueling and continuing fight for full citizenship since Emancipation, the stigma of color, the enforced alienation which constantly knifes into our natural identification with our country—have not been those of white Americans. And though as passionate believers in democracy Negroes identify themselves with the broader American ideals, their sense of reality springs, in part, from an American experience which most white men not only have not had, but one with which they are reluctant to identify themselves even when presented in forms of the imagination. Thus, when the white American, holding up most twentieth-century fiction, says, "This is American reality," the Negro tends to answer (not at all concerned that Americans tend generally to fight against any but the most flattering imaginative depictions of their lives), "Perhaps, but you've left out this, and this, and this. And most of all, what you'd have the world accept as *me* isn't even human."

Nor does he refer only to second-rate works but to those of our most representative authors. Either like Hemingway and Steinbeck (in whose joint works I recall not more than five American Negroes), they tend to ignore them, or like the early Faulkner, who distorted Negro humanity to fit his personal versions of Southern myth, they seldom conceive Negro characters possessing the full, complex ambiguity of the human. Too often what is presented as the American Negro (a most complex example of Western man) emerges an oversimplified clown, a beast or an angel. Seldom is he drawn as that sensitively focused process of opposites, of good and evil, of instinct and intellect, of passion and spirituality, which great literary art has projected as the image of man. Naturally the attitude of Negroes toward this writing is one of great reservation. Which, indeed, bears out Richard Wright's remark that there is in progress between black and white Americans a struggle over the nature of reality.

Historically this is but a part of that larger conflict between older, dominant groups of white Americans, especially the Anglo-Saxons, on the one hand, and the newer white and non-white groups on the other, over the major group's attempt to impose its ideals upon the rest, insisting that its exclusive image be accepted as *the* image of the American. This conflict should not, however, be misunderstood. For despite the impact of the American idea upon the world, the "American" himself has not (fortunately for the United States, its minorities, and perhaps for the world) been finally defined. So that far from being socially undesirable this struggle between Americans as to what the American is to be is part of that democratic process through which the nation works to achieve itself. Out of this conflict the ideal American character—a type truly great enough to possess the greatness of the land, a delicately poised unity of divergencies—is slowly being born.

But we are concerned here with fiction, not history. How is it then that our naturalistic prose—one of the most vital bodies of twentieth-century fiction, perhaps the brightest instrument for recording sociological fact, physical action, the nuance of speech, yet achieved—becomes suddenly dull when confronting the Negro?

Obviously there is more in this than the mere verbal counterpart of lynching or segregation. Indeed, it represents a projection of processes lying at the very root of American culture, and certainly at the central core of its twentieth-century literary forms, a matter having less to do with the mere "reflection" of white racial theories than with processes molding the attitudes, the habits of mind, the cultural atmosphere and the artistic and intellectual traditions that condition men dedicated to democracy to practice, accept and, most crucial of all, often blind themselves to the essentially undemocratic treatment of their fellow citizens.

It should be noted here that the moment criticism approaches Negro-white relationships it is plunged into problems of psychology and symbolic ritual. Psychology, because the distance between Americans, Negroes and whites, is not so much spatial as psychological; while they might dress and often look alike, seldom on deeper levels do they think alike. Ritual, because the Negroes of fiction are so consistently false to human life that we must question just what they truly represent, both in the literary work and in the inner world of the white American.*

---

*Perhaps the ideal approach to the work of literature would be one allowing for insight into the deepest psychological motives of the writer at the same time that it examined all external sociological factors operating

Despite their billings as images of reality, these Negroes of fiction are counterfeits. They are projected aspects of an internal symbolic process through which, like a primitive tribesman dancing himself into the group frenzy necessary for battle, the white American prepares himself emotionally to perform a social role. These fictive Negroes are not, as sometimes interpreted, simple racial clichés introduced into society by a ruling class to control political and economic realities. For although they are manipulated to that end, such an externally one-sided interpretation relieves the individual of personal responsibility for the health of democracy. Not only does it forget that a democracy is a collectivity of *individuals*, but it never suspects that the tenacity of the stereotype springs exactly from the fact that its function is no less personal than political. Color prejudice springs not from the stereotype alone, but from an internal psychological state; not from misinformation alone, but from an inner need to believe. It thrives not only on the obscene witch-doctoring of men like Jimmy Byrnes and Malan, but upon an inner craving for symbolic magic. The prejudiced individual creates his own stereotypes, very often unconsciously, by reading into situations involving Negroes those stock meanings which justify his emotional and economic needs.

Hence whatever else the Negro stereotype might be as a social instrumentality, it is also a key figure in a magic rite by which the white American seeks to resolve the dilemma arising between his democratic beliefs and certain antidemocratic prac-

---

within a given milieu. For while objectively a social reality, the work of art is, in its genesis, a projection of a deeply personal process, and any approach that ignores the personal at the expense of the social is necessarily incomplete. Thus, when we approach contemporary writing from the perspective of segregation, as is commonly done by sociologically minded thinkers, we automatically limit ourselves to one external aspect of a complex whole, which leaves us little to say concerning its personal, internal elements. On the other hand, American writing has been one of the most important twentieth-century literatures, and though negative as a social force it is technically brilliant and emotionally powerful. Hence were we to examine it for its embodiment of these positive values, there would be other more admiring things to be said.

tices, between his acceptance of the sacred democratic belief that all men are created equal and his treatment of every tenth man as though he were not.

Thus on the moral level I propose that we view the whole of American life as a drama acted out upon the body of a Negro giant, who, lying trussed up like Gulliver, forms the stage and the scene upon which and within which the action unfolds. If we examine the beginning of the Colonies, the application of this view is not, in its economic connotations at least, too far-fetched or too difficult to see. For then the Negro's body was exploited as amorally as the soil and climate. It was later, when white men drew up a plan for a democratic way of life, that the Negro began slowly to exert an influence upon America's moral consciousness. Gradually he was recognized as the human factor placed outside the democratic master plan, a human "natural" resource who, so that white men could become more human, was elected to undergo a process of institutionalized dehumanization.

Until the Korean War this moral role had become obscured within the staggering growth of contemporary science and industry, but during the nineteenth century it flared nakedly in the American consciousness, only to be repressed after the Reconstruction. During periods of national crises, when the United States rounds a sudden curve on the pitch-black road of history, this moral awareness surges in the white American's conscience like a raging river revealed at his feet by a lightning flash. Only then is the veil of anti-Negro myths, symbols, stereotypes and taboos drawn somewhat aside. And when we look closely at our literature it is to be seen operating even when the Negro seems most patently the little man who isn't there.

I see no value either in presenting a catalogue of Negro characters appearing in twentieth-century fiction or in charting the racial attitudes of white writers. We are interested not in quantities but in qualities. And since it is impossible here to discuss the entire body of this writing, the next best thing is to select a framework in which the relationships with which we are concerned may be clearly seen. For brevity let us take three representative writers: Mark Twain, Hemingway and Faulkner. Twain for historical perspective and as an example of how a great nineteenth-century writer handled the Negro; Hemingway as the prime example of the artist who ignored the dramatic and symbolic possibilities presented by this theme; and Faulkner as an example of a writer who has confronted Negroes with such mixed motives that he has presented them in terms of both the "good nigger" and the "bad nigger" stereotypes, and who yet has explored perhaps more successfully than anyone else, either white or black, certain forms of Negro humanity.

For perspective let us begin with Mark Twain's great classic, *Huckleberry Finn*. Recall that Huckleberry has run away from his father, Miss Watson and the Widow Douglas (indeed the whole community, in relation to which he is a young outcast), and has with him as companion on the raft upon which they are sailing down the Mississippi Miss Watson's runaway Negro slave, Jim. Recall, too, that Jim, during the critical moment of the novel, is stolen by two scoundrels and sold to another master, presenting Huck with the problem of freeing Jim once more. Two ways are open: he can rely upon his own ingenuity and "steal" Jim into freedom, or he might write Miss Watson and request reward money to have Jim returned to her. But there is a danger in this course, remember, since the angry woman might sell the slave down the river into a harsher slavery. It is this course which Huck starts to take, but as he composes the letter he wavers.

> It was a close place. I took it up, and held it in my hand. I was a trembling, because I'd got to decide, forever, betwixt two things, and I knowed it. I studied a minute, sort of holding my breath, and then says to myself:
>
> "All right, then, I'll *go* to hell"—and tore it up.
>
> It was awful thoughts, and awful words, but they was said. And I let them stay said; and never thought no more about reforming. I shoved the whole thing out of my head; and said I would take up wickedness again, which was in my line, being brung up to it, and the other warn't. And for a starter I would go to work and steal Jim out of slavery again. . . .

And a little later, in defending his decision to Tom Sawyer,

Huck comments, "I know you'll say it's dirty, low-down business but *I'm* low-down. And I'm going to steal him . . ."

We have arrived at a key point of the novel and, by an ironic reversal, of American fiction, a pivotal moment announcing a change of direction in the plot, a reversal as well as a recognition scene (like that in which Oedipus discovers his true identity), wherein a new definition of necessity is being formulated. Huck Finn has struggled with the problem posed by the clash between property rights and human rights, between what the community considered to be the proper attitude toward an escaped slave and his knowledge of Jim's humanity, gained through their adventures as fugitives together. He has made his decision on the side of humanity. In this passage Twain has stated the basic moral issue centering around Negroes and the white American's democratic ethics. It dramatizes as well the highest point of tension generated by the clash between the direct, human relationships of the frontier and the abstract, inhuman, market-dominated relationships fostered by the rising middle class—which in Twain's day was already compromising dangerously with the most inhuman aspects of the defeated slave system. And just as politically these forces reached their sharpest tension in the outbreak of the Civil War, in *Huckleberry Finn* (both the boy and the novel) their human implications come to sharpest focus around the figure of the Negro.

Huckleberry Finn knew, as did Mark Twain, that Jim was not only a slave but a human being, a man who in some ways was to be envied, and who expressed his essential humanity in his desire for freedom, his will to possess his own labor, in his loyalty and capacity for friendship, and in his love for his wife and child. Yet Twain, though guilty of the sentimentality common to humorists, does not idealize the slave. Jim is drawn in all his ignorance and superstition, with his good traits and his bad. He, like all men, is ambiguous, limited in circumstance but not in possibility. And it will be noted that when Huck makes his decision he identifies himself with Jim and accepts the judgment of his superego—that internalized representative of the community—that his action is evil. Like Prometheus, who for mankind stole fire from the gods, he embraces the evil implicit in his act in order to affirm his belief in humanity. Jim, therefore, is not simply a slave, he is a symbol of humanity, and in freeing Jim, Huck makes a bid to free himself of the conventionalized evil taken for civilization by the town.

This conception of the Negro as a symbol of Man—the reversal of what he represents in most contemporary thought—was organic to nineteenth-century literature. It occurs not only in Twain but in Emerson, Thoreau, Whitman and Melville (whose symbol of evil, incidentally, was white), all of whom were men publicly involved in various forms of deeply personal rebellion. And while the Negro and the color black were associated with the concept of evil and ugliness far back in the Christian era, the Negro's emergence as a symbol of value came, I believe, with Rationalism and the rise of the romantic individual of the eighteenth century. This, perhaps because the romantic was in revolt against the old moral authority, and if he suffered a sense of guilt, his passion for personal freedom was such that he was willing to accept evil (a tragic attitude), even to identifying himself with the "noble slave"—who symbolized the darker, unknown potential side of his personality, that underground side, turgid with possibility, which might, if given a chance, toss a fistful of mud into the sky and create a "shining star."

Even that prototype of the bourgeois, Robinson Crusoe, stopped to speculate as to his slave's humanity. And the rising American industrialists of the late nineteenth century were to rediscover what their European counterparts had learned a century before: that the good man Friday was as sound an investment for Crusoe morally as he was economically, for not only did Friday allow Crusoe to achieve himself by working for him, but by functioning as a living scapegoat to contain Crusoe's guilt over breaking with the institutions and authority of the past, he made it possible to exploit even his guilt economically. The man was one of the first missionaries.

Mark Twain was alive to this irony and refused such an easy (and dangerous) way out. Huck Finn's acceptance of the evil implicit in his "emancipation" of Jim represents Twain's acceptance of his personal responsibility for the condition of society. This was the tragic face behind his comic mask.

But by the twentieth century this attitude of tragic responsibility had disappeared from our literature along with that broad conception of democracy which vitalized the work of our greatest writers. After Twain's compelling image of black and white fraternity the Negro generally disappears from fiction as a rounded human being. And if already in Twain's time a novel which was optimistic concerning a democracy which would include all men could not escape being banned from public libraries, by our day his great drama of interracial fraternity had become, for most Americans at least, an amusing boy's story and nothing more. But while a boy, Huck Finn has become by the somersault motion of what William Empson terms "pastoral," an embodiment of the heroic, and an exponent of humanism. Indeed, the historical justification for his adolescence lies in the fact that Twain was depicting a transitional period of American life; its artistic justification is that adolescence is the time of the "great confusion," during which both individuals and nations flounder between accepting and rejecting the responsibilities of adulthood. Accordingly, Huck's relationship to Jim, the river and all they symbolize, is that of a humanist; in his relation to the community he is an individualist. He embodies the two major conflicting drives operating in nineteenth-century America. And if humanism is man's basic attitude toward a social order which he accepts, and individualism his basic attitude toward one he rejects, one might say that Twain, by allowing these two attitudes to argue dialectically in his work of art, was as highly moral an artist as he was a believer in democracy, and vice versa.

History, however, was to bring an ironic reversal to the direction which Huckleberry Finn chose, and by our day the divided ethic of the community had won out. In contrast with Twain's humanism, individualism was thought to be the only tenable attitude for the artist.

Thus we come to Ernest Hemingway, one of the two writers whose art is based most solidly upon Mark Twain's language, and one who perhaps has done most to extend Twain's technical influence upon our fiction. It was Hemingway who pointed out that all modern American writing springs from *Huckleberry Finn*. (One might add here that equally as much of it derives from Hemingway himself.) But by the twenties the element of rejection implicit in Twain had become so dominant an attitude of the American writer that Hemingway goes on to warn us to "stop where the Nigger Jim is stolen from the boys. That is the real end. The rest is just cheating."

So thoroughly had the Negro, both as man and as a symbol of man, been pushed into the underground of the American conscience that Hemingway missed completely the structural, symbolic and moral necessity for that part of the plot in which the boys rescue Jim. Yet it is precisely this part which gives the novel its significance. Without it, except as a boy's tale, the novel is meaningless. Yet Hemingway, a great artist in his own right, speaks as a victim of that culture of which he is himself so critical, for by his time that growing rift in the ethical fabric pointed out by Twain had become completely sundered—snagged upon the irrepressible moral reality of the Negro. Instead of the single democratic ethic for every man, there now existed two: one, the idealized ethic of the Constitution and the Declaration of Independence, reserved for white men, and the other, the pragmatic ethic designed for Negroes and other minorities, which took the form of discrimination. Twain had dramatized the conflict leading to this division in its earlier historical form, but what was new here was that such a moral division, always a threat to the sensitive man, was ignored by the artist in the most general terms, as when Hemingway rails against the rhetoric of the First World War.

Hemingway's blindness to the moral values of *Huckleberry Finn* despite his sensitivity to its technical aspects duplicated the one-sided vision of the twenties. Where Twain, seeking for what Melville called "the common continent of man," drew upon the rich folklore of the frontier (not omitting the Negro's) in order to "Americanize" his idiom, thus broadening his stylistic appeal, Hemingway was alert only to Twain's technical discoveries—the flexible colloquial language, the sharp naturalism, the thematic potentialities of adolescence. Thus what for Twain was a means to a moral end became for Hemingway an end in itself. And just as the trend toward technique for the sake of technique and production for the sake of the market lead to the neglect of the human need out of which they spring, so do they lead in literature to a marvelous technical virtuosity won at the expense of a gross insensitivity to fraternal values.

It is not accidental that the disappearance of the human Negro from our fiction coincides with the disappearance of deep-probing doubt and a sense of evil. Not that doubt in some form was not always present, as the works of the lost generation, the muckrakers and the proletarian writers make very clear. But it is a shallow doubt, which seldom turns inward upon the writer's own values; almost always it focuses outward, upon some scapegoat with which he is seldom able to identify himself as Huck Finn identified himself with the scoundrels who stole Jim, and with Jim himself. This particular naturalism explored everything except the nature of man.

And when the artist would no longer conjure with the major moral problem in American life, he was defeated as a manipulator of profound social passions. In the United States, as in Europe, the triumph of industrialism had repelled the artist with the blatant hypocrisy between its ideals and its acts. But while in Europe the writer became the most profound critic of these matters, in our country he either turned away or was at best half-hearted in his opposition—perhaps because any profound probing of human values, both within himself and within society, would have brought him face to face with the rigidly tabooed subject of the Negro. And now the tradition of avoiding the moral struggle had led not only to the artistic segregation of the Negro but to the segregation of real fraternal, i.e., democratic, values.

The hard-boiled school represented by Hemingway, for instance, is usually spoken of as a product of World War I disillusionment; yet it was as much the product of a tradition which arose even before the Civil War—that tradition of intellectual evasion for which Thoreau criticized Emerson in regard to the Fugitive Slave Law, and which had been growing swiftly since the failure of the ideals in whose name the Civil War was fought.

The failure to resolve the problem symbolized by the Negro has contributed indirectly to the dispossession of the artist in several ways. By excluding our largest minority from the democratic process, the United States weakened all national symbols and rendered sweeping public rituals which would dramatize the American dream impossible; it robbed the artist of a body of unassailable public beliefs upon which he could base his art; it deprived him of a personal faith in the ideals upon which society supposedly rested; and it provided him with no tragic mood indigenous to his society upon which he could erect a tragic art. The result was that he responded with an attitude of rejection, which he expressed as artistic individualism. But too often both his rejection and individualism were narrow; seldom was he able to transcend the limitations of pragmatic reality, and the quality of moral imagination—the fountainhead of great art—was atrophied within him.

Malraux has observed that contemporary American writing is the only important literature not created by intellectuals, and that the creators possess "neither the relative historical culture, nor the love of ideas (a prerogative of professors in the United States)" of comparable Europeans. And is there not a connection between the nonintellectual aspects of this writing (though many of the writers are far more intellectual than they admit or than Malraux would suspect) and its creators' rejection of broad social responsibility, between its non-concern with ideas and its failure to project characters who grasp the broad sweep of American life, or who even attempt to state its fundamental problems? And has not this affected the types of heroes of this fiction? Is it not a partial explanation of why it has created no characters possessing broad insight into their situations or the emotional, psychological and intellectual complexity which would allow them to possess and articulate a truly democratic world view?

It is instructive that Hemingway, born into a civilization characterized by violence, should seize upon the ritualized violence of the culturally distant Spanish bullfight as a laboratory for developing his style. For it was, for Americans (though not for the

Spaniards), an amoral violence which he was seeking. Otherwise he might have studied that ritual of violence closer to home, that ritual in which the sacrifice is that of a human scapegoat, the lynching bee. Certainly this rite is not confined to the rope as agency, nor to the South as scene, nor even to the Negro as victim.

But let us not confuse the conscious goals of twentieth-century fiction with those of the nineteenth century; let us take it on its own terms. Artists such as Hemingway were seeking a technical perfection rather than moral insight. (Or should we say that theirs was a morality of technique?) They desired a style stripped of unessentials, one that would appeal without resorting to what was considered worn-out rhetoric, or best of all without any rhetoric whatsoever. It was felt that through the default of the powers that ruled society the artist had as his major task the "pictorial presentation of the evolution of a personal problem." Instead of re-creating and extending the national myth as he did this, the writer now restricted himself to elaborating his personal myth. And although naturalist in his general style, he was not interested, like Balzac, in depicting a society, or even, like Mark Twain, in portraying the moral situation of a nation. Rather he was engaged in working out a personal problem through the evocative, emotion-charged images and ritual therapy available through the manipulation of art forms. And while art was still an instrument of freedom, it was now mainly the instrument of a questionable personal freedom for the artist, which too often served to enforce the "unfreedom" of the reader.

This because it is not within the province of the artist to determine whether his work is social or not. Art by its nature *is* social. And while the artist can determine within a certain narrow scope the type of social effect he wishes his art to create, here his will is definitely limited. Once introduced into society, the work of art begins to pulsate with those meanings, emotions, ideas brought to it by its audience, and over which the artist has but limited control. The irony of the "lost generation" writers is that while disavowing a social role it was the fate of their works to perform a social function which reenforced those very social values which they most violently opposed. How could this be? Because in its genesis the work of art, like the stereotype, is personal; psychologically it represents the socialization of some profoundly personal problem involving guilt (often symbolic murder—parricide, fratricide, incest, homosexuality—all problems at the base of personality) from which by expressing them along with other elements (images, memories, emotions, ideas) he seeks transcendence. To be effective as personal fulfillment, if it is to be more than dream, the work of art must simultaneously evoke images of reality and give them formal organization. And it must, since the individual's emotions are formed in society, shape them into socially meaningful patterns (even Surrealism and Dadaism depended upon their initiates). Nor, as we can see by comparing literature with reportage, is this all. The work of literature differs basically from reportage not merely in its presentation of a pattern of events, nor in its concern with emotion (for a report might well be an account of highly emotional events), but in the deep personal necessity which cries full-throated in the work of art and which seeks transcendence in the form of ritual.

Malcolm Cowley, on the basis of the rites which he believes to be the secret dynamic of Hemingway's work, has identified him with Poe, Hawthorne and Melville, "the haunted and nocturnal writers," he calls them, "the men who dealt with images that were symbols of an inner world." In Hemingway's work, he writes, "we can recognize rites of animal sacrifice . . . of sexual union . . . of conversion . . . and of symbolic death and rebirth." I do not believe, however, that the presence of these rites in writers like Hemingway is as important as the fact that here, beneath the deadpan prose, the cadences of understatement, the anti-intellectualism, the concern with every "fundamental" of man except that which distinguishes him from the animal— that here is the twentieth-century form of that magical rite which during periods of great art has been to a large extent public and explicit. Here is the literary form by which the personal guilt of the pulverized individual of our rugged era is expatiated: not through his identification with the guilty acts of an Oedipus, a Macbeth or a Medea, by suffering their agony and loading his sins upon their "strong and passionate shoulders," but by being gored with a bull, hooked with a fish, impaled with a grasshopper on a fishhook; not by identifying himself with human heroes, but with those who are indeed defeated.

On the social level this writing performs a function similar to that of the stereotype: it conditions the reader to accept the less worthy values of society, and it serves to justify and absolve our sins of social irresponsibility. With unconscious irony it advises stoic acceptance of those conditions of life which it so accurately describes and which it pretends to reject. And when I read the early Hemingway I seem to be in the presence of a Huckleberry Finn who, instead of identifying himself with humanity and attempting to steal Jim free, chose to write the letter which sent him back into slavery. So that now he is a Huck full of regret and nostalgia, suffering a sense of guilt that fills even his noondays with nightmares, and against which, like a terrified child avoiding the cracks in the sidewalk, he seeks protection through the compulsive minor rituals of his prose.

The major difference between nineteenth- and twentieth-century writers is not in the latter's lack of personal rituals—a property of all fiction worthy of being termed literature—but in the social effect aroused within their respective readers. Melville's ritual (and his rhetoric) was based upon materials that were more easily available, say, than Hemingway's. They represented a blending of his personal myth with universal myths as traditional as any used by Shakespeare or the Bible, while until *For Whom the Bell Tolls* Hemingway's myth was weighted on the personal side. The difference in perspective is that Melville's belief could still find a public object. Whatever else his works were "about," they also managed to be about democracy. But by our day the democratic dream had become too shaky a structure to support the furious pressures of the artist's doubt. And as always when the belief which nurtures a great social myth declines, large sections of society become prey to superstition. For man without myth is Othello with Desdemona gone: chaos descends, faith vanishes and superstitions prowl in the mind.

Hard-boiled writing is said to appeal through its presentation of sheer fact, rather than through rhetoric. The writer puts nothing down but what he pragmatically "knows." But actually

one "fact" itself—which in literature must be presented simultaneously as image and as event—became a rhetorical unit. And
the symbolic ritual which has set off the "fact"—that is, the fact
unorganized by vital social myths (which might incorporate the
findings of science and still contain elements of mystery)—is
the rite of superstition. The superstitious individual responds
to the capricious event, the fact that seems to explode in his
face through blind fatality. For it is the creative function of
myth to protect the individual from the irrational, and since it
is here in the realm of the irrational that, impervious to science,
the stereotype grows, we see that the Negro stereotype is really
an image of the unorganized, irrational forces of American life,
forces through which, by projecting them in forms of images of
an easily dominated minority, the white individual seeks to be at
home in the vast unknown world of America. Perhaps the object
of the stereotype is not so much to crush the Negro as to console the white man.

Certainly there is justification for this view when we consider
the work of William Faulkner. In Faulkner most of the relationships which we have pointed out between the Negro and contemporary writing come to focus: the social and the personal,
the moral and the technical, the nineteenth-century emphasis
upon morality and the modern accent upon personal myth. And
on the strictly literary level Faulkner is prolific and complex
enough to speak for those Southern writers who are aggressively anti-Negro and for those younger writers who appear
most sincerely interested in depicting the Negro as a rounded
human being. What is more, he is the greatest artist the South
has produced. While too complex to be given more than a
glance in these notes, even a glance is more revealing of what
lies back of the distortion of the Negro in modern writing than
any attempt at a group survey might be.

Faulkner's attitude is mixed. Taking his cue from the Southern mentality in which the Negro is often dissociated into a
malignant stereotype (the bad nigger) on the one hand and a
benign stereotype (the good nigger) on the other, most often
Faulkner presents characters embodying both. The dual func-

tion of this dissociation seems to be that of avoiding moral pain and thus to justify the South's racial code. But since such a social order harms whites no less than blacks, the sensitive Southerner, the artist, is apt to feel its effects acutely—and within the deepest levels of his personality. For not only is the social division forced upon the Negro by the ritualized ethic of discrimination, but upon the white man by the strictly enforced set of anti-Negro taboos. The conflict is always with him. Indeed, so rigidly has the recognition of Negro humanity been tabooed that the white Southerner is apt to associate any form of personal rebellion with the Negro. So that for the Southern artist the Negro becomes a symbol of his personal rebellion, his guilt and his repression of it. The Negro is thus a compelling object of fascination, and this we see very clearly in Faulkner.

Sometimes in Faulkner the Negro is simply a villain, but by an unconsciously ironic transvaluation his villainy consists, as with Loosh in *The Unvanquished*, of desiring his freedom. Or again the Negro appears benign, as with Ringo, of the same novel, who uses his talent not to seek personal freedom but to remain the loyal and resourceful retainer. Not that I criticize loyalty in itself, but that loyalty given where one's humanity is unrecognized seems a bit obscene. And yet in Faulkner's story "The Bear," he brings us as close to the moral implication of the Negro as Twain or Melville. In the famous "difficult" fourth section, which Malcolm Cowley advises us to skip very much as Hemingway would have us skip the end of *Huckleberry Finn*, we find an argument in progress in which one voice (that of a Southern abolitionist) seeks to define Negro humanity against the other's enumeration of those stereotypes which many Southerners believe to be the Negro's basic traits. Significantly, the mentor of the young hero of this story, a man of great moral stature, is socially a Negro.

Indeed, through his many novels and short stories Faulkner fights out the moral problem which was repressed after the nineteenth century, and it was shocking for some to discover that for all his concern with the South, Faulkner was actually seeking out the nature of man. Thus we must turn to him for that continuity of moral purpose which made for the greatness of our classics. As for the Negro minority, he has been more willing perhaps than any other artist to start with the stereotype, accept it as true, and then seek out the human truth which it hides. Perhaps his is the example for our writers to follow, for in his work technique has been put once more to the task of creating value.

Which leaves these final things to be said. First, that this is meant as no plea for white writers to define Negro humanity, but to recognize the broader aspects of their own. Secondly, Negro writers and those of the other minorities have their own task of contributing to the total image of the American by depicting the experience of their own groups. Certainly theirs is the task of defining Negro humanity, as this can no more be accomplished by others than freedom, which must be won again and again each day, can be conferred upon another. A people must define itself, and minorities have the responsibility of having their ideals and images recognized as part of the composite image which is that of the still-forming American people.

The other thing to be said is that while it is unlikely that American writing will ever retrace the way to the nineteenth century, it might be worthwhile to point out that for all its technical experimentation it is nevertheless an ethical instrument, and as such might well exercise some choice in the kind of ethic it prefers to support. The artist is no freer than the society in which he lives, and in the United States the writers who stereotype or ignore the Negro and other minorities in the final analysis stereotype and distort their own humanity. Mark Twain knew that in *his* America humanity masked its face with blackness.

Shadow and Act, 1964
Originally published in *Confluence*, 1953

Wallace Stegner

Wallace Stegner (1909–1993), American fiction writer and historian, wrote these comments on the occasion of the publication of *The Complete Stories of Mark Twain*, edited by Charles Neider in 1957. It is not surprising that Stegner chose to write about the "deceptive shape" of *Roughing It* and *Life on the Mississippi*, of their "faithfulness to both the fact and the spirit of the raw societies they mirrored," for writing about the West and the shape that writing took were topics Stegner cared deeply about. When he wrote this review he was still a decade away from writing his own novels set partly in the West: *Angle of Repose* (1972) and *The Spectator Bird* (1977). Stegner, who has been referred to as "the dean of Western writers," was very active in the conservation movement. He also founded the creative writing program at Stanford University.

Yarn-Spinner in the American Vein

On first glance it seems curious that the most natural and fecund story-teller in our literature—and a story-teller moreover who was best at the short haul—should not until now have had his short stories collected. But it is not so curious as it seems; he had few short stories to be collected. Charles Neider in his introduction makes an eloquent apologia for the entertaining volume he has produced, and for the things he has put in it, but the fact is that he has had to make it largely of sketches, parodies, jokes, anecdotes, yarns, fables, episodes from longer works and occasionally the longer works themselves.

Only by stretching definition past its elastic limits can one call both "A Day at Niagara" and "The Mysterious Stranger"— or either of them—short stories. The one is a piece of frivolous journalism and the other is a novel. And some of the things that may legitimately be called short stories in this collection look alarmingly like old-fashioned pieces of contrivance, more reminiscent of Fitz-James O'Brien and Frank R. Stockton than suggestive of the modern short story with its organic structure, its fetish of compression and its concern with psychological states.

Mr. Neider's anthology offers a convenient basis for reappraisal; the sixty pieces which are here hospitably called short stories illustrate both the weaknesses and the strengths of Mark Twain as a writer of fiction. They teach us all over again that Mark was not a fully conscious artist, that he was a fiction writer more by accident than by design, that he fell much too frequently into triviality and improvisation, and that at their best both his materials and his forms are an inheritance from the forming culture of the Mississippi Valley and the experiences of his boyhood and youth. In almost nothing was he an innovator: his genius was essentially nostalgic, his forms and techniques most naturally those he adapted from the journalism, the lecture platforms and the law-circuit yarning of his time and place. His achievement was to elevate these shapes of folklore and journalism, and along with them the vernacular in which they were expressed, into literature.

When he followed the lead of books and other writers he often went wrong. His bookish vein is represented in this collection by such respectable fabrications as "The £1,000,000 Bank Note" and "The $30,000 Bequest," by some sentimentalized and Harteian items such as "The Californian's Tale," and by the pure saccharinity of "A Horse's Tale." His non-bookish vein is more than sufficiently demonstrated by a dozen or two humorous sketches that would probably not be preserved if they had been written by a lesser writer. But his pure native vein, his Mother Lode, is also represented by some pieces completely inimitable; and though I should say the proportion of good Twain to bad is actually rather low in these collected sketches and stories, even one or two of Mark at his best and truest is enough to redeem the rest.

Mr. Neider is quite right in saying that Mark Twain had no formal interest in the short story, and quite justified in extracting from "Roughing It," "A Tramp Abroad," the "Autobiography," or anywhere else the yarns and fables that Mark scattered through them. But it would be a mistake to assume that because Mark gave the formal short story only token attention, he was utterly indifferent to form in anything. His novels, it is true, are episodic and his attempts at the literary short story seem contrived. But the yarns that he scattered through his books, the stories that fall as naturally from the lips of his characters as they did from his own, the beast-fables which conceal behind their apparent innocence an irony as alert as a black-snake—these are not formless. They have their own esthetic, they are built to a traditional pattern, which Mark Twain had not so much learned as caught, like chickenpox, from the air of his youth.

"The Notorious Jumping Frog," the blue jay yarn from "A Tramp Abroad," the old ram story from "Roughing It," are of the kind that illustrates Mark's talents best. Their lingo even yet falls upon the ear with the magical rhythms of spoken speech. Their narrators—those garrulous, innocent, wandering, tedious old yarners whose very point is their pointlessness—represent Mark's improvement upon a stock character of the frontier humorists, particularly of Artemus Ward. The stories utilize the devices of the humorous story, described by Mark himself in "How to Tell a Story," one of his few ventures into formal esthetics. And if they are baited for laughter, they catch other and bigger game: Jim Baker's blue jay yarn is a fable in every way worthy of Aesop or La Fontaine, and in some ways perhaps beyond them.

So Mark Twain is less a short-story writer than a fabulist, satirist, parodist. If he did not write such neatly shaped and picturesquely colored narratives as those of Bret Harte and the other local colorists, he did better: he embedded in "Roughing It" and "Life on the Mississippi" stories with their own deceptive shape and their casual and incomparable faithfulness to both the fact and the spirit of the raw societies they mirrored. Modern students of the short story will be going to Henry James, with his impeccable and self-conscious craftsmanship and his subtle modulations, or to Stephen Crane with his precocious impressionism, when they want ancestral models for their own stories. But Mark Twain's fables and yarns, looked at closely, reveal themselves to be just as truly "rendered," just as completely "written," just as fully under the control of an artistic intelligence and an extraordinary artistic sensibility, as their more formal stories.

The writers who seem to derive from Mark Twain are not the advocates of that formal short story that Mr. Neider rather irritably blames on the French. The writers who derive from Mark Twain are the Will Rogerses, the Thurbers, the Whites, the Disneys, the yarners and parodists and satirists and fabulists, workers in another tradition. They need go no farther than Mark in their search for a father; Hemingway was probably right in declaring that in Mark all American writing begins.

He was maimed, a little, like many American artists; his sensibility was more delicate than the instruments his society gave him. He never fully mastered the most sophisticated (and borrowed) elements of his culture. But he brought triumphantly to full usefulness some of the half-developed and sub-literary and Beowulfian elements of a stage of American life. He made silk purses from sows' ears, and if—as in the present collection—there are some untransformed ears among the purses, we should not complain. For the virtues and the weaknesses of a writer like Mark Twain are inseparable, sometimes almost interchangeable.

The New York Times, 1957

Mike Gold

Mike Gold was the pseudonym of Itzok Isaac Granich (1893–1967), editor, poet, novelist, and critic who was a founder of the radical magazine *New Masses* and who championed leftist literature in the United States in the 1930s. *Jews Without Money* (1930), Gold's fictionalized autobiography about his childhood in the tenements of New York City's Lower East Side, was translated into 14 languages and became the most famous proletarian narrative of the era. Jews often saw parallels, like those that Gold's father draws here, between Mark Twain and the Yiddish writer Sholem Aleichem. In addition to frequenting the Lower East Side's "old-world cafés where the writers, actors, doctors, and other Jewish intellectuals all day drank tea and philosophized" (as Gold puts it), Twain was an avid supporter of a children's theater organized by a neighborhood settlement house, where children who spoke Yiddish at home performed stage adaptations of works like Twain's *The Prince and the Pauper* in flawless English. Gold published "Twain in the Slums" in *People's World*, a San Francisco newspaper published by the Communist Party, U.S.A.

Twain in the Slums

Though surrounded by it for decades, my father never dared to speak English. He was subjective. But English wasn't really needed on the old East Side, that Jewish metropolis where one could work and love, live and die only with Yiddish.

At home our parents talked to us in Yiddish, and we answered in English. It is a custom among all immigrant families in America. A young Mohawk bridge worker once told me it is just as common among Indians, where the older generation is often un-American and can't speak English.

Language is important. You can get to feel lost and inferior not to understand the speech of the people around you. But I think my father envied me only for the story books in English I brought from the public library. Above everything, he loved a good, flowing yarn. He himself used to hold groups of his friends with wonderful tales from the Arabian Nights that he'd learned in youth from the Rumanian peasants.

Now it was the epoch of Mark Twain in America. That great story-teller was almost as famous as Jim Jeffries, the heavyweight champion. He was perhaps the last of our national writers, loved by the whole people. The East Side kids knew him and loved him as well as did other Americans. My father watched my fascination, heard my chuckles, as I devoured *Huckleberry Finn* under the gaslight.

He offered me a nickel an hour if I'd read it to him. A nickel was big money then, but he was a lusty young house painter, free with his nickels.

So I read him the history of free-hearted Huck Finn and the noble slave, Jim, and their escape from injustice on the broad Mississippi, with its starlight, rafts and mystery. "It's like when I was a boy on our own Danube," said my father, fondly.

How he laughed when I read about those brassy swindlers, the self-styled "Dauphin" and the crummy old "Duke." He compared them to a certain Count in Rumania who tried to swindle his father, the potter, but was exposed as a forger and the bigamous husband of fifteen wives. "Your Mark Twain, he understands the aristocrats!" my father chuckled. "He spits on them, he has a heart of gold! Like our own Sholem Aleichem he wants to help people to laugh. Laughter is healthy, all the doctors prescribe it, says Sholem Aleichem. But I think he also feels the tears of the people. Mark Twain has no tears."

"I love Mark Twain better. And I wish I could live on a raft like *Huckleberry Finn*."

"We would all like to live on a raft," smiled my father. "But God wants us to live in these tenements. And cats and dogs do their business in the halls."

Mark Twain often visited the East Side. He liked to talk in the old-world cafés where the writers, actors, doctors and other Jewish intellectuals all day drank tea and philosophized. Mark Twain showed a deep concern for the Jews, would issue frequent protests against their slaughter by the ugly Russian tsardom. The East Side loved him the more deeply for such passionate friendship.

San Francisco People's World, 1959

Yan Bereznitsky

In 1959 Yan Bereznitsky (1922–2005), a respected Soviet writer and critic, charged in the *Literaturnaya Gazeta* (the official organ of the Union of Soviet Writers) that Charles Neider, the American editor who had just published his version of *The Autobiography of Mark Twain*, had presented a sanitized and censored Mark Twain to the public—that he had portrayed Twain as a harmless, benevolent, simpleminded "scoffer," burying and ignoring Twain's searing criticisms of his country. Bereznitsky's quarrel was not just with Neider but with American critics' habit (during an era when New Criticism was gaining sway) of viewing the social content and historical context of works of art as relatively unimportant. While readers in the Soviet Union would study a writer in part because of the radical social and political critiques they found implicit or explicit in his or her work, readers in the United States would focus on the inherent artistry of a poem—on its formal aspects rather than on the cultural context. In Bereznitsky's opinion Neider was feeding the public trivial anecdotes about Twain when readers hungered for insight into his social and political criticisms of American society. Neider wrote to Premier Nikita Khrushchev requesting the right to reply in the pages of *Literaturnaya Gazeta*. The exchange of views, which was published in both the Soviet Union and the United States, revealed that the Russians disagreed sharply with Neider's view that Twain "is of course primarily a humorist"; for the Russians he would always be the "great critic of democratic morals." The Cold War inevitably played into the debate. Neider wrote, "If one were exposed only to the official Soviet view one might think that Mark Twain spent most of his time in attacking aspects of his own country. . . ." Ten years after this exchange, at least one American critic staked out a position similar to that of Bereznitsky. In 1970 Maxwell Geismar wrote in *Scanlan's Monthly*, "During the Cold War era of our culture, mainly in the 1950's although extending back into the '40s and forward far into the '60s, Mark Twain was both revived and castrated. The entire arena of Twain's radical social criticism of the United States—its racism, imperialism, and finance capitalism—has been repressed or conveniently avoided by the so-called Twain scholars precisely because it is so bold, so brilliant, so satirical. And so prophetic."

Mark Twain on the Bed of Procrustes

S hortly before the opening of the American exhibit in Moscow, the correspondents of the *Literary Gazette* who were getting acquainted with its proposed exposition were amazed to notice that among the books selected for display at the exhibit there were neither any new editions of the works of Mark Twain nor any interesting new publications about his works. Obviously the organizers of the exhibit caught themselves in time, and recently on one of the bookshelves in the Sokolniki [Park] there stood *The Autobiography of Mark Twain*, newly edited in New York.

Still, that initial forgetfulness expresses fairly accurately the relationship of official America to its greatest writer. They try to forget him. And if they have to take notice of him anyway, then in that case everything possible is done to crop the great writer's hair, to deflower the blazing and furious colors of his satire, to eat away the socially unmasking resonance of Twain's work and, in the last analysis, to make him up as a benevolent and simple-minded scoffer. The new edition of the *Autobiography* is the logical fruit of these efforts at literary hairdressing.

*   *   *

Who does not know Twain's famous pronouncements about American "democracy," his indignant notes about the predatory wars which the United States carried on half a century ago, his satirical sketches, cutting as a slap in the face, of the oil king, Rockefeller, Senator Clark, General Wood, President Theodore Roosevelt, and other knights and henchmen of American expansionism. All these materials (except for an insignificant part which came out in the 1924 edition) came out in the 1940 edition. True, even then an effort was made to soften Twain's more than unambiguous remarks about the bosses of political life in the America of his time. Bernard DeVoto, the editor of that edition, expressed, in part, a naïve amazement that Mark Twain, who had once called himself "an unwashed son of labor," could not accept in Rockefeller and T. Roosevelt fellow "sons of labor." But the debunking voice of Mark Twain cuts through the most stifling editorial comments. In 1959 Charles Neider found the precautions of his predecessors insufficient, and he decided without superfluous ceremony to "shut Twain's trap," blotting out from his edition all the notes mentioned above. This is a supreme example of scholarly ill faith and of that very political tendentiousness whose pretended absence certain American men of letters so love to boast on occasion.

As to previously unpublished materials, Neider resolved to introduce into his edition Twain's meditations on baldness, on the value of hair-washing, on beginning writers, on phrenology, on honorary degrees, etc. It is naturally hard to say anything against the inclusion of these notes in *The Autobiography of Mark Twain*. But it is no less hard to come to terms with the idea that these few, inoffensive trifles are called upon to replace the brilliant, angry pages of the original, unprocessed Twain, which are many times superior to them in scope and significance. It is plain that the bitter prophecy which Twain made in the midst of work on his Autobiography in a letter to William Dean Howells is coming true:

"Tomorrow I mean to dictate a chapter which will get my heirs and assigns burned alive if they venture to print it this side of A.D. 2006—which I judge they won't. There'll be lots of such chapters if I live 3 or 4 years longer. The edition of A.D. 2006 will make a stir when it comes out. I shall be hovering around taking notice, along with other dead pals. You are invited."

Not very happy lines. And although there remains almost a half century till the time Twain mentioned, it would hardly have pleased him to watch how the editor of an eviscerated and washed-out edition of his Autobiography tries to put forth his crime as a virtue and does not burn alive for shame at that. Literally, "virtue." This is how he expresses it: "My volume," writes Neider in his Introduction, "is to a high degree anecdotic, but I believe this to be a virtue rather than a defect, in that it correctly represents the creative slant of Mark Twain's mind."

An anecdote. Fine and dandy. And though this anecdote is far from young, it grows none the less sad for that, none the less exacerbating to the memory of the greatest American writer.

Translated by Robert L. Belknap
Literaturnaya Gazeta (Moscow), 1959

The Question Is Significantly More Profound:
A Letter to Charles Neider

Twain's political writings (it is hard for me to understand why you put the word "political" in quotation marks in your letter) are interesting not only because in them he "preaches," "proclaims," but also because they express his "feelings and his interests." Remember the words with which he begins his story of the annihilation by General Wood in the Philippines of six hundred men, women, and children of the Moro tribe (of course this passage is omitted from your edition):

"We will stop talking about my schoolmates of sixty years ago, for the present, and return to them later. They strongly interest me, and I am not going to leave them alone permanently. Strong as that interest is, it is for the moment pushed out of the way by an incident of to-day, which is still stronger."

That is what *interests* Twain.

*   *   *

In your edition Twain actually appears as you are trying to present him. And you are trying to present him as a "great fabulist" (from your letter) or a master of "anecdote" (from your Introduction). But is the real Twain like that? Let us try to remember what he himself said about this. This citation is doubtless well known to you. I am taking it from your edition of his Autobiography:

". . . within the compass of these forty years wherein I have been playing professional humorist before the public, I have had for company seventy-eight other American humorists. . . . Why have they perished? Because they were *merely humorists*. [Here and in the later quotations the italics are mine. Y. B.] Humorists of the 'mere' sort cannot survive. . . . I have always preached. That is the reason that I have lasted thirty years. If the humor came of its own accord and uninvited I have allowed it a place in my sermon, but I was not writing the sermon for the sake of the humor."

The sermons about which Twain writes are just what constitute the social content of his work. This content is inseparable from the humor, just as the humor is inseparable from it. And you cut Twain's work in two and call the part which you don't like "dated, dull, and trivial." Yes, in your Introduction you listed just what you left out. "From the published parts I have omitted such matter as the . . . Morris incident . . . elongated remarks on Theodore Roosevelt, Andrew Carnegie, the plutocracy, and so on." If it were only a matter of remarks (or "attacks" as you call them in your letter) it might really not be worth while building up a case. But in these "remarks" or "attacks" are expressed Twain's feelings, thoughts, interests; and this all helps re-establish the writer's countenance, a goal, which from my point of view, should also be sought by the autobiography of a great writer.

*　　*　　*

I would be sorry if you took all the above as only my comments, or even attacks, on your book, or your method of editorial work. No, the question is significantly more profound, and the dispute is going on actually not between you and me, but between two opposed tendencies in literary scholarship. One of them, which you represent, and which appears to be if not official, then at least the governing one in American literary scholarship, tries to show the social content of the work of this or that writer as something petty, secondary, incidental, and sometimes simply nonexistent. The representatives of this tendency try to present the great democrat and lover of life, Walt Whitman, as "a poet of death" and a "conservative" (the collection of essays, *Leaves of Grass One Hundred Years Later*). The representatives of this tendency try to reduce the meaning of the plays of the greatest contemporary American playwright, Arthur Miller, to "the history of a personal disorder and not to social disorganization" (Joseph T. Shipley). Every representative of this tendency has ignored the work of Dreiser in the thirties, and *An American Tragedy* appears in their interpretation like a private occurrence in the life of a certain Clyde Griffiths. Understandably, no one will begin to assert that there are no representatives of other tendencies in literary criticism in America, tendencies trying to clarify the phenomenon of literature in all its integrity and complexity. In our press, for example, there has already been given a detailed evaluation of P. Foner's interesting book, *Mark Twain: Social Critic*.

In conclusion, I would like to make it known to you that of those thirty or forty thousand words which you first included in your edition, and toward which in your words I "behaved scornfully" (on what basis you reached that conclusion is a riddle to me), a significant part was published in our press (in the magazine *Crocodile*, with an edition of 1,200,000 copies, and in the Estonian newspaper, *Hammer and Sickle*) even before the appearance of your book, on the basis of the preliminary publication in *Harper's Magazine*. I mention this to show you how great is our interest in the work of Mark Twain, what joy every new publication of his text furnishes us, how dear to us are all the manifestations of his genius, and what incomprehension and protest is called from us by any attempt to narrow and present in an impoverished light his wonderful and many-faceted countenance.

Translated by Robert L. Belknap
Literaturnaya Gazeta (Moscow), 1959

Lao She

Lao She (the pen name used by Shu She Yu, 1899–1966) was one of the leading Chinese authors of the 20th century. In 1960 Lao She, then president of the National Association of Writers, delivered this speech in Beijing to commemorate the 50th anniversary of Mark Twain's death. For decades scholars had assumed it had been lost, but determined searching over many years by J. R. Le Master, a literature professor at Baylor University, and Chinese scholar Zhao Huazhi managed to locate a copy. Lao was in the United States between 1946 and 1949 and returned home soon after Mao Zedong announced the establishment of the People's Republic of China. An influential novelist and dramatist, he was named "People's Artist" and "Grand Master of Language," and played a prominent role in the Chinese literary establishment—before he was purged from the Communist Party and became a victim of the Cultural Revolution. As the scholar Xilao Li has noted, after the founding of the People's Republic, Mark Twain was one of the very few foreign writers whose works were allowed to be translated and published; particularly during the Korean War, the anti-imperialist, anti-war aspects of his work were emphasized. Although Lao's speech fits this mold and served China's ruling interests at the time, it also contains some insightful readings of pieces by Twain with which American readers were then largely unfamiliar. With the exception of Philip Foner's 1958 book *Mark Twain: Social Critic*, Twain's trenchant critiques of the country he loved tended to be as ignored in the United States at mid-century as they were celebrated in China. Only in the 1990s would American scholars decide that this aspect of Twain deserved their attention.

FROM
Mark Twain: Exposer of the "Dollar Empire"

Mark Twain, an outstanding writer of critical realism in the United States as well as an exposer of imperialist aggression and the hypocritical civilization of U.S. capitalism, passed away fifty years ago. However, his criticism of the "dollar empire" has retained profound and immediate significance throughout the past half century.

*   *   *

Mark Twain's reprimand of the imperialist aggressive powers and sympathy for the anti-colonialist Asian and African people are especially significant to us. This is the part of his literary heritage we should value most. From the nineties of the last century, when the United States fell into imperialism, Mark Twain began to condemn his country severely. In his *The American Claimant* (1892) he ridiculed those wicked American careerists who attempt to conquer the world. Sellers' dream of conquering the world, derided by Twain in his novel, has quickly become the goal pursued by those politicians who represent the power of American financial capital. Sellers is the prototype of Acheson, Dulles and their like in our time. Although *Following the Equator* (1897) seems to be merely a series of travel notes, it is of great significance in terms of opposing world imperialism. In his round-the-world trip, Twain observed the lives of the people in some of the colonial countries. He exposed wrathfully the "civilization" brought to them by the white invaders. He cited various examples to show that the white invaders had treated the native Australians as scum by slaughtering them or even poisoning them with arsenic trioxide. Meanwhile the imperialists boasted that they had propagated among the natives the "Gospel of Civilization," which was upbraided by Twain as a "chronic slaughter with hunger and alcohol." He reproached the British invasion of South Africa as "murder committing."

In the fall of 1900, Mark Twain returned to the United States after being absent nine years. He told the press, "And so I am an anti-imperialist. I am opposed to having the eagle put its talons on any land."

He also gave strong support to the Chinese people's fierce struggle against imperialist aggression. As early as 1868, in his essay entitled "Treaty with China," he berated the shameless invaders for their forceful setting up of concessions. On August 12, 1900, just one day before the invasion of Peking by the eight-powers Allied Forces, he wrote to one of his friends, "It is all China now and my sympathies are with the Chinese. . . . I hope they will drive all the foreigners out and keep them out for good." In November of the same year he made a speech at an annual meeting of the Public Education Association, proclaiming, "The Boxer is a patriot. . . . I wish him success. I am a Boxer myself."

During the 20 years following the nineties, Twain courageously continued attacking the imperialist aggressive powers with excellent political comments and essays. In 1900, in his "Salutation Speech from the Nineteenth Century to the Twentieth," he remarked sarcastically, "I bring you the stately matron named Christendom, returning bedraggled, besmirched and dishonored from pirate raids in Kiao-chew, Manchuria, South Africa and the Philippines, with her soul full of meanness, her pocket full of boodle and her mouth full of pious hypocrisies. Give her soap and a towel, but hide the looking glass." He thought the American invasion of the Philippines had stained the American flag, on which the only thing fit to be drawn were "the white stripes painted black and the stars replaced by the skull and cross bones." Written in the winter of 1901, "To the Person Sitting in Darkness" is an excellent essay that exposes the invaders' so-called "civilization," an essay in which the author uncovered the essence of the "Blessings of Civilization" brought to colonial people (i.e. the person sitting in darkness) by imperialists. These blessings include chains, "Maxim Guns and Hymn Books, and Trade Gin," and also such lies as justice, liberty, equality and so on. He writes, "It is merely an outside cover, gay and pretty and attractive. . . . while inside the bale is the Actual Thing that the Customer Sitting in Darkness buys with his blood and tears and land and liberty." All the people in bondage to the imperialists can demonstrate that this is an accurate assessment of colonial policies. Twain derided bitterly the "peace loving" invader with his "banner of the Prince of Peace in one hand" and his "loot basket and . . . butcher knife in the other." The vivid figurative depiction reminds us of Eisenhower's eleven-nation trip not long ago.

In 1905 Mark Twain wrote a satirical short story, "The War Prayer," which suggests that the essence of the invaders' prayer for victory is to grant death to the fallen aliens. "O Lord our God, help us to tear their soldiers to bloody shreds with our shells . . . for our sakes who adore Thee, Lord, blast their hopes . . . stain the white snow with the blood of their wounded feet." To the Asian and African people who have been suffering from American imperialist invasion, his exposure is really to the point and very significant.

Mark Twain's work in this respect are powerful weapons for progressive human beings in opposing aggressive wars, imperialism, colonialism, and in safeguarding world peace.

*   *   *

"My idea of our civilization is that it is a shabby poor thing and full of cruelties, vanities, arrogancies, meanesses and hypocrisies. As for the word, I hate the sound of it, for it conveys a lie." Such is Mark Twain's estimate of American capitalist civilization.

There is a striking but brutal phenomenon in American bourgeois "civilized" society, that is, discrimination against and enslavement of the black race. Twain did not have clear ideas about this in his early years and at one time supported the system of slavery in the south. He did not recognize the evils of racial discrimination until the end of the Civil War. He then shifted his attitude in favor of black people. At that time, like many other kind and naive Americans, he thought the black people would really be free. However, the practices of the American bourgeoisie shattered this illusion. Even to this day black people in America are being enslaved and oppressed. Resentfully, Twain called his country the United States of Lyncherdom. His novel, *The Adventures of Huckleberry Finn*, published in 1884, with the theme of opposing the enslavement of black people, has become one of the most significant works of 19th century American literature. In it he described the sincere friendship that takes place between the white boy Huck and the black man Jim. Jim is a fine man with noble sentiments, which disconcerts Huck, who has not yet questioned his own prejudice. This theme was enough to cause this novel to be placed on the list of books banned by the reactionaries. The image of Jim in American literature contains great significance because at the time it was a bold challenge to the hired novels of the bourgeoisie, novels which maliciously distorted the image of the blacks. At that time, when the Ku Klux Klan was running amuck with lynching, Twain strongly advocated the protection of the blacks' freedom, existence and rights.

Referred to by George Bernard Shaw as the Voltaire of the United States, Twain, in many of his works, threw light on the important events of American society. Even in his fantasy novels, he clearly demonstrated his attitude toward real life. Written in the eighties, *A Connecticut Yankee in King Arthur's Court* is a satirical political novel with great significance for our time. The weal and woe of the masses, the horrible conditions of slavery, as well as the ruthlessness of the tyrannical ruling class, witnessed by the author in 19th century America, all find indirect expression in comments on the medieval British political and social system by the protagonist in the novel. Twain demonstrated his ideas on democracy by presenting a sharp contrast between the dissipated and unashamed ruling class on one hand and the creative working class on the other. He said, "The master minds of all nations, in all ages, have sprung in multitude from the mass of the nation, and from the mass of the nation only—not from its privileged classes." What is more important is that he believed that in order to overthrow the dictatorial system, the people had the right to resort to armed struggle.

Peace loving, democracy loving, anti-imperialist and anti-colonialist, Twain was sure to be feared by American reactionary forces. Both before and after his death he suffered persecution from these forces. They banned many of his books and threw them out of public libraries. Publishers hired by the bourgeoisie abridged and even disallowed publication of autobiographical essays Twain wrote in his last years. Considering the emphasis in America on freedom of the press, this is gross irony. Some critics, bribed by Wall Street, even labeled Twain as just a humorist, trying to wipe out the bitter sarcasm behind his humor.

Twain by no means was a mere humorist. He was a profound and excellent satirist. He said, "Against the shock of laughter nothing can stand." He exposed the despicable and ridiculous aspects of life in American capitalist society so as to make his readers feel indignant and disgusted when they laugh. He was born in the Western part of the United States, and in his early years worked as a typesetter, miner and pilot. Keeping in frequent touch with the working people, he gained a lot from the heritage of humorous literature of the Western folk. By means of extreme exaggeration, sharp contrasts, crosscurrents of tragedy and comedy, etc., which are characteristic of humorous folk tales, he effectively castigated the ugly capitalist civilization of the United States.

*   *   *

Mark Twain has been away from us for half a century, in which time the U.S. imperialism that he has berated strongly turned out to be more and more rotten and brutal. It has become the most fiendish enemy of people around the world and is jeopardizing the peace of mankind. The world's people will never forgive it. Today, in Japan, the Congo, Cuba, South Korea, Turkey and many other countries in Asia, Africa and Latin America, courageous people are waging dynamic struggles against U.S. imperialists, their partners and their followers. Twain always stood on the side of the American people and the people of the world as well. As we are commemorating him today, we feel as if he were still standing among us, struggling side by side with us against the imperialists headed by the United States.

Translated by Zhao Yuming and Sui Gang
Speech delivered in 1960
Published in *US-China Review*, 1995

Edward Field

The mixture of playfulness and accessibility that characterizes "Mark Twain and Sholem Aleichem" has been a hallmark of the poetry of Edward Field from the start. Field (born in 1924), who has lived in New York City's Greenwich Village for most of the last half century, is the author of 16 books of poetry, including *After the Fall* (2007), *Magic Words* (1997), *Counting Myself Lucky* (1992), *New and Selected Poems from the Book of My Life* (1987), *A Full Heart* (1977), and *Stand Up, Friend, with Me* (1963), in which this poem first appeared, and which was the 1962 Lamont Poetry Selection of the Academy of American Poets. He is also the co-author of several novels with Neil Derrick and has written a memoir, *The Man Who Would Marry Susan Sontag and Other Intimate Literary Portraits of the Bohemian Era* (2005). Field is well known for public readings of his honest, quirky, impassioned, and often political poems (which have been likened to works by Allen Ginsberg and Walt Whitman). He has been a gay activist for many years and has made urban, gay life central to much of his work. Field has also brought his Jewish heritage into a number of his poems. The cadences of the imaginary conversation that takes place in this poem between Twain and Aleichem reflect the cadences of Yiddish that floated through Field's Brooklyn childhood.

Mark Twain and Sholem Aleichem

Mark Twain and Sholem Aleichem went one day to Coney
    Island—
Mark wearing a prison-striped bathing costume and straw
    hat,
Sholem in greenish-black suit, starched collar, beard,
Steelrimmed schoolmaster glasses, the whole works,
And an umbrella that he flourished like an actor
Using it sometimes to hurry along the cows
As he described scenes of childhood in the village in Poland,
Or to spear a Jew on a sword like a cossack.

Sitting together on the sand among food wrappers and lost
    coins,
They went through that famous dialogue
Like the vaudeville routine, After-you-Gaston:
"They tell me you are called the Yiddish Mark Twain."
"Nu? The way I heard it you are the American Sholem
    Aleichem."
And in this way passed a pleasant day admiring each other,
The voice of the old world and the voice of the new.

"Shall we risk the parachute jump, Sholem?"
"Well, Markele, am I properly dressed for it?
Better we should go in the water a little maybe?"
So Sholem Aleichem took off shoes and socks (with holes—
    a shame),
Rolled up stiff-serge pants showing his varicose veins;
And Mark Twain, his bathing suit moth-eaten and gaping
In important places, lit up a big cigar,
And put on a pair of waterwings like an angel.

The two great writers went down where the poor
Were playing at the water's edge
Like a sewer full of garbage, warm as piss.
Around them shapeless mothers and brutal fathers
Were giving yellow, brown, white, and black children
Lessons in life that the ignorant are specially qualified to
    give:
Slaps and scoldings, mixed with food and kisses.

Mark Twain, impetuous goy, dived right in,
And who could resist splashing a little the good-natured
    Jew?
Pretty soon they were both floundering in the sea
The serge suit ruined that a loving daughter darned and
    pressed,
The straw hat floating off on the proletarian waters.

They had both spent their lives trying to make the world a
    better place
And both had gently faced their failure.
If humor and love had failed, what next?
They were both drowning and enjoying it now,
Two old men of the two worlds, the old and the new,
Splashing about in the sea like crazy monks.

Stand Up, Friend, with Me, 1963

"The American Lion of St. Mark's" by William H. Walker, 1901.
From *Life*, February 28, 1901

Abel Startsev

Abel Startsev (1909–2005) was a Russian literary critic, translator, and editor of many significant and (for his time) controversial anthologies and commentaries on American literature and culture. Despite the fact that much of what Startsev translated and published from the American literary canon was critical of U.S. imperialism, Startsev's Jewish background and expertise in American literature made him an easy target for Stalin's campaign of "anti-cosmopolitanism." Startsev, who was a professor at the Institute of World Literature of the Russian Academy of Sciences, was dismissed from his position as editor-in-chief of the anthology *History of American Literature* (1947) because he admired American literature too much and was too sympathetic to Western culture. Mark Twain was hugely popular in the Soviet Union throughout the 20th century: by 1959 about 11 million copies of Twain's works—some translated by Startsev—had been distributed there. Startsev's *Mark Twain and America* (1963, revised 1985), from which the following selections are taken, was apparently influenced by Philip Foner's groundbreaking *Mark Twain: Social Critic*, which was published in New York in 1958 and in Russia shortly after. Foner's book was the first major study of Twain that gave his social criticism center stage. Maxwell Geismar's *Mark Twain: An American Prophet* followed suit in 1970. But it would not be until much later—the 1980s and 1990s—that American scholars would pay comparable attention to Twain's anti-racism and anti-imperialism.

FROM

Марк Твен и Америка
(Mark Twain in America)

T oday, on the basis of recently published materials and their analysis, we can firmly establish that the legacy of Twain was shaped by serious contradictions, that the great American humorist laughed not always because he wanted to laugh, that in the latest period of his work he became a passionate critic of American capitalist civilization and avoided an open rift with the American bourgeoisie only by suffering a torturous split of his writer's identity.

*   *   *

The evaluation of the relationship between Twain and American capitalism has become a litmus test of sorts of American literature. It is used to establish the position of any American author on the main social and political questions of American life, both in the past and in the present. It's not an exaggeration to say that the literary legacy of Twain became an arena of a struggle of "two cultures"—the bourgeois, which defends the main capitalist establishment, and, in opposition to it, those American democratic tendencies which together throughout American history define American national culture.

*   *   *

Although the mood of Twain's later works is one of darkness and yields bitter views of human life and human nature, everything that he writes in this period, characterized by a deep and sharp criticism of the exploitive side of civilization, by protest against social injustice, grew into a passionate call to humanity to defend a purity of human relationships without corruption and false morality. These years were signified by the crush of the last "American taboo" in his consciousness.

*   *   *

Twain already saw that South Africa, China, and the Philippines were all links in the chain of the imperialist politics of the American government and the imperialist robbery by European countries. He was an anti-imperialist and stated his position openly. . . . [In his article] "A Salutation Speech from the Nineteenth Century to the Twentieth," he says, "I give you the respectable matron that is called Christian Civilization which returned from her pirate attacks on Kiao Chau, Manchuria, South America and the Philippines, covered with blood, her honor lost, her soul depraved, her pockets filled with stolen goods, and her hypocritical speech—lies. Give her a towel and soap, but hide the mirror."*

---

*Startsev's translation differs from Twain's original which reads, "I bring you the stately matron named Christendom, returning bedraggled, besmirched, and dishonored, from pirate raids in Kiaochow, Manchuria, South Africa, and the Philippines, with her soul full of meanness, her pocket full of boodle, and her mouth full of pious hypocrisies. Give her soap and towel, but hide the looking glass."

*   *   *

It was said about Twain . . . that his love for his motherland is mixed with bitterness; indeed, one has to love one's motherland infinitely, and also suffer similarly, without end, for the shame which is brought forth by the fundamentalists and racists and lynchers, to love it so much to call it the United States of Lyncherdom for all the world to see.

Translated by Katya Vladimirov
and Nina Yermakov Morgan
1963

Kenzaburō Ōe

Kenzaburō Ōe (born in 1935) first read *Huckleberry Finn* as a boy in a remote mountain village on the island of Shikoku. In the essay that follows he notes that he cannot recall who gave him the Japanese translation of the novel, but likes to think that it was his father. (He has sometimes said that his mother got the copy that he read, but when he does, he credits his father with having told her that it was the best novel for a child or an adult to read.) The United States and Japan were at war at the time, and his mother told him that if his teacher caught him with the book, he should tell her that "Mark Twain" was the pseudonym of a German author. As Ōe recalled in his Nobel Prize acceptance speech, "The whole world was then engulfed by waves of horror. By reading *Huckleberry Finn* I felt I was able to justify my act of going into the mountain forest at night and sleeping among the trees with a sense of security which I could never find indoors." Ōe's first novella, *Prize Stock* (published in Japan in 1957), is set during World War II; in it two boys are assigned to guard an African-American prisoner of war whose plane has crashed on a remote Japanese island. When asked about the striking resonances between *Prize Stock* and *Huckleberry Finn* and if Twain's novel had been on his mind as he wrote his own first novel, Ōe responded: "Yes, I agree with you about *Huck*, the narrative of my first novel is under the shadow of *Huck*." Twain's novel would make its presence felt in other work by Ōe—books which often center on marginal people and outcasts, on existential heroes sickened by civilization who choose to "light out for the territory." Ōe is also the author of nonfiction including *Hiroshima Notes*, a series of pieces that include extended interviews with survivors of the atomic bomb in World War II, and *Okinawa Notes*, an essay about the Japanese military's coercion of masses of civilians into committing suicide during the Allied invasion of Okinawa in 1945. *Okinawa Notes* was a thorn in the side of those who wanted to whitewash this chapter of the past, and Ōe had to defend himself in a drawn-out libel trial from 2006 to 2008. The court ended up dismissing all the charges. The 1994 Nobel Prize citation noted that "with poetic force" Ōe "creates an imagined world, where life and myth condense to form a disconcerting picture of the human predicament today." Mark Twain played a seminal role in sparking Ōe's initial interest in literature, and in sustaining his interest in the ways in which he could engage moral, political, social, and psychological challenges as a writer.

アメリカ旅行者の夢—

地獄にゆくハックルベリィ・フィン

(An American Traveler's Dreams—
Huckleberry Finn Who Goes to Hell)

T he summer of 1965, one morning, about the hour when the already sharp sunshine was further heating the air that was dry and not hard to bear, I was in America—Cambridge, Massachusetts—facing the subway entrance at the center of Harvard Square, the plaza in front of the university, and the newsstand surrounding it selling foreign magazines and newspapers, not to mention America's domestic magazines and newspapers, waiting for the moment for the traffic signals to change so I might cross the paved crosswalk. I was holding to my chest a large paper bag with salami sandwiches and bread to take to the sea that afternoon and eat with friends, along with orange juice and a bottle of bourbon whiskey. In my trouser pocket I had a small edition of *Adventures of Huckleberry Finn*. It felt bulky against my thigh through the lightweight summer trousers. Sweat, heat. But with that inciting mood of a summer morning that invigorates human beings, and at the same time, with a sense of exhaustion and dullness, I was enjoying the whole morning, as I chatted with a French woman writer who was already beginning not to be young, who stood alongside me also staring at the traffic signals.

Like me she was a member of Harvard University's international summer seminar, and in accordance with the unwritten rule of the seminar I was speaking with her in English. I should have been able to talk with this French writer in French, too, but the fact that we were, quite naturally, speaking in English seems quite important in recreating my mood of that morning. I had arrived in America just about fifty days earlier. That first evening, as I mixed with the crowd of the same plaza, I had gotten a tumultuous, sloppy impression from the racial diversity of the people who were around me. And I had felt as though excluded from that tumultuous momentum. For all that, just about fifty days later, I, like my French comrade, had blended into what I had once felt was tumultuous, was using the same language as that of my surroundings, and was existing there, without any particular sense of strangeness. Furthermore, we two outsiders were sharing a conversation critical of the political trends of that country, in the language of that country. The atmosphere that allowed us to do such things naturally had widely and deeply pervaded that university town.

I had just talked about America's bombing of North Vietnam, had said that Gen. LeMay had been identified as a leading force pushing the hard-line policy at the Joint Chiefs of Staff, that the said Gen. LeMay was the person who had actually, locally, made the plan to drop atomic bombs in Hiroshima and Nagasaki, and was also the person who had received the First Order of Merit with the Grand Cordon of the Rising Sun from the Japanese government on account of his contribution to the expansion of the Japanese Self-Defense Forces. About this Gen. LeMay, several months later I read America's veteran radical and independent journalist I. F. Stone writing in detail, touching on the heart of the matter: LeMay had said solemnly in a recent AP interview that Americans could accomplish "our mission" better by the use of the Air Force than by the use of the ground forces. By "our mission," he means: North Vietnam, you better surrender; otherwise, we'll burn your country up. "[LeMay] reminds us that in the Korean war his 'immediate suggestion' was to 'go up north and burn the principal cities.'" He believed that that would end the war extremely fast, with minimum damage. It was also his prescription for winning in Vietnam.

"He reveals that for three years—that is since 1962—he had been urging in the Joint Chiefs of Staff that the way to end the war in Vietnam was to let them know that 'we're going to bomb them back into the Stone Age.' This is one of his favorite phrases; in World War II he boasted that the Japanese air raids 'were driving them back to the Stone Age.' The Stone Age is a metaphor for the days when brute force reigned supreme; instinctively LeMay harks back to it."

Gen. LeMay's obsession with the term the Stone Age demonstrates not so much psychologically as directly, behind his tactical imagery, the weight of his experience of Hiroshima and Nagasaki and the slowly ballooning stockpile of nuclear weapons. Our government had decorated a man like that. Concerning Hiroshima's protests, someone responsible in government said thus: "My house was burnt during an air raid, too, but that was twenty years ago. To go beyond love and hate and award a medal to a soldier who bombed various Japanese cities during the war, that's just fitting for the people of a large, relaxed, good nation, isn't it?" I once wrote about this dull-wittedness, saying this was moral wasteland, that it was a betrayal of human beings in Hiroshima. Yet I, too, did not go so far as to realize that these words and the decoration would have the effect of encouraging Gen. LeMay psychologically, yes, and giving him confidence in the bombing of North Vietnam. When we think that, in thinking of dropping napalm bombs on North Vietnam to burn human beings, Gen. LeMay, instead of keeping in the back of his head the images of the ghastly corpses and those alive and suffering, had nothing but the memories of the First Order of Merit with the Grand Cordon of the Rising Sun and the easygoing people of the victim nation, should not we Japanese have before our eyes the reality of a conspiratorial relationship actually in progress at present toward a certain, most terrible thing?

When I talked about Gen. LeMay's roles of today and yesterday, such as these, the French woman writer told me that several days ago, on the 20th anniversary of the dropping of an atomic bomb on Hiroshima, a disk jockey at a local station of this Commonwealth of Massachusetts sang "Happy Birthday, Hiroshima Day! Happy Birthday, Hiroshima Day!" and was fired on the spot.

And so I was asking her, "Did you hear the broadcast yourself or did you read about it in a newspaper?" when four American youths in a Volkswagen with the top down (like a deep boot that can carry human beings) swept by just inches away from us, each shouting words of derision at us. The words I was able to understand were something like,

—Hey, did you learn your lesson? and a phrase that I had thought had become extinct, *yellow peril*. Also my woman friend was ridiculed, though of course it was not the fact, for having sexual relations with the yellow race.

And so I suddenly remembered that morning was the morning of August 15 and, realizing that I had been utterly unconscious of it till then, I felt deeply disturbed on both counts. Then, the bundle of *elastic* threads of various, mutually contradictory remembrances and emotions concerning America, and the enormous sense of humiliation, sense of liberation, and the sense of freedom on that day twenty years earlier and since, filled me overwhelmingly, with almost blinding force. At the same time, *caught* between the expression of the woman friend who, standing next to me as she was, pretended not to have noticed the ridicule from the Volkswagen and the voice of nakedly sexual derision, I felt my face turning totally red. The phrase *yellow peril*, just as it was, reminded me of the picture of a bespectacled buck-toothed ugly midget figure that was an exact caricaturization of the word *Jap* that cheerful American college students had shown us on Castle Hill in a regional city. I was looking at myself through the eyes of that American comic artist. I who until then, lost in the crowd of Harvard Square, had not felt the slightest discomfort, now found myself alone, standing there as a bespectacled buck-toothed midget, an ugly Japanese, like a comic strip come to life. And I, with no evidence whatsoever, felt as if this comical version of myself was trying to seduce a white woman standing next to me, and was most upset, involved as I was with sexual feelings as it were. I felt truly, deeply, isolated and helpless, in a sort of terror. I thought I wanted to run into the entrance of a dark, tumultuous bar just behind us and hide among the alcoholics who inhabited it from morning on. But at present, now that the signals changed to the green light shaped like a pedestrian, and the French woman writer, having taken one step into the paved street, was looking back at me in puzzlement, it was obvious that I had to cross; and so I felt even more intimidated and, looking out at the newsstand for magazines and newspapers at the center of the plaza as if it were something dazzling, my legs feeble, body clumsily bent, comically yes, I was about to step forward . . . when, as if utterly unrelated to our conversation up to then, my friend (her language had switched, defiantly from English to French) said furiously:

—I can't understand why you see a film like *Dr. Strangelove* and don't get put off by the way wars and nuclear weapons are treated in it.

Concerning this experience on that summer morning in Cambridge that lasted only a few seconds, I am led in two directions. Toward two books, I can also say, but about the latter book in particular, I must try not so much to simply think about a single book as to link it to my broader, more essential sense of America.

The first book is what *The Saturday Review* called "a novella of a hair-raising racial protest like a scream in the dark" that the black writer Chester Himes published in the year the war ended: *If He Hollers Let Him Go*. It was in particular the impression of one passage that was evoked for me. There is a black youth. The war begins, and he is working at a shipyard; he is in love with a daughter of the prosperous black elite, and he is a youth with potential who plans to go to college once the war is over. But from a certain moment on, he ends up becoming a completely *scared* human being. Or he ends up noticing that he is a human being who has been completely scared throughout his life. And so the black youth comes to repeat obviously desperate behavior, comes to be hunted as the perpetrator of an attempted rape through the *trickery* of a white female worker, to be sent into the military in the end: it's that kind of story. Why did the youth end up becoming so scared, how did he realize he was a human being who had been scared all his life?

When the war started, the youth saw Japanese Nisei in Los Angeles being sent to the camps. "Maybe it had started then, I'm not sure, or maybe it wasn't until I'd seen them send the Japanese away that I'd noticed it. Little Riki Oyana singing 'God Bless America' and going to Santa Anita with his parents next day. It was taking a man up by the roots and locking him up without a chance. Without a trial. Without a charge. Without even giving him a chance to say one word. It was thinking about if they ever did that to me, Robert Jones, Mrs. Jones's dark son, that started me getting scared."

That is, that morning in Cambridge, I was identifying myself with the two of them, the Japanese Nisei being sent to a concentration camp and the black youth who began to be scared by having premonitions about his own identical fate. Of course, no one came to take me up by the roots. But for nearly fifty days until that morning, since my arrival in America, I had not been scared for a single moment, I had not looked at myself through the caricaturing eyes of an American, that is, through the most sharply objectifying eyes that the Japanese in America could suffer. When I was looking at TV with seminar colleagues in the *common room* of the dormitory, even when more or less caricaturized Japanese appeared on the screen, no one paid attention to me, and I couldn't care less, either. In other words, for nearly fifty days, I had had the illusion of blending into American society like a colorless solvent. But my experience that morning (to be fair, it was the only experience of that kind that occurred during my four-month stay in America) gave me, at least in the world of my consciousness, an opportunity to imagine the presence of the eyes of Americans looking at me with the most sharply caricaturizing intent, an opportunity to reflect on it.

Now, the other book that I, guided by the experience of that morning, began to think about anew, is *Adventures of Huckleberry Finn*, which happened to make my summer trouser pocket bulky at that moment. That moment, *Adventures of Huckleberry Finn* in my trouser pocket, truly like a weight, stabbed vertically into the depths of my consciousness. To me *Adventures of Huckleberry Finn* was the only book by an American that I had loved to read *through the time before and after* the summer experience, going back twenty years from that moment, but until then I had not thought that it had any special meaning, nor had I thought about why I had cut it off from my extremely complicated complex toward America *through the time before and after* the summer twenty years earlier. I came to think, I must examine anew what on earth had been the kind of image of a human being *Adventures of Huckleberry Finn* had continued to give me. Why was it that, for me, Huckleberry Finn was for some reason a different *type* from an ordinary American? Isn't Huckleberry Finn probably the most *popular hero* for boys, in today's America as well?

And also, have I not found, so often, among the heroes of the writers of postwar American literature who must have grown up reading *Huckleberry Finn*, the heirs of Huckleberry Finn? In *The Adventures of Augie March*, in *The Deer Park*, in *From Here to Eternity*, in *Catcher in the Rye*, in *Rabbit, Run*. The twentieth-century Huckleberry Finn who adopted a car dashing through the highways that cover the whole American land, instead of a raft floating down the Mississippi River, is the hero of *On the Road*. Every time I traveled by car in America, had I not understood that today's car gives you a spiritual and physical experience similar to that of a raft one hundred years ago. About this, I must write in greater detail on another occasion.

In the midst of the war, ducking the network of enmity, loathing, contempt, and terror of everything American, *Adventures of Huckleberry Finn* had reached me. And in no time Huckleberry became the first *hero* I acquired through literature. I cannot remember who my benefactor was who gave me the Iwanami paperback edition of *Adventures of Huckleberry Finn*, translated by Nakamura Tameji, but by thinking that it was my late father, I was able to create the best memory of my father.

To the story of Huckleberry, by order of the author, the chief of ordnance, 1st Infantry Regiment, Royal Guard, England, added a caution: "Persons attempting to find a motive in this narrative will be prosecuted; persons attempting to find a moral in it will be banished; persons attempting to find a plot in it will be shot." So I became passionate about neither the motive, nor the moral, nor the plot, but about one image. It was a terrifyingly fascinating image of Huckleberry Finn going to hell. It is natural for a wartime child to think more often about death than a peacetime child. The teacher of my national school often tested us thus:

—Come, tell me, if His Majesty the Emperor tells you to die, what will you do?

And the expected answer was, I will die, sir, I will disembowel myself and die. Of course, I was sure in some way that His Majesty the Emperor was unlikely to come all the way to a village in a valley like this looking for me, a dirty little thing, but in repeating this solemn lie about death so many times, it seemed that I ceased feeling unrelated to the word hell.

After his cavern exploration with Tom Sawyer (he is also a unique *hero*, but I was never attracted to him in any way), Huckleberry was adopted by a strict and mannerly widow, and removed from his drifter's life. But Huckleberry is terribly tormented by that life. "The widow's sister tried to educate him. Then she told me all about the bad place, and I said I wished I was there. She got mad, then, but I didn't mean no harm. All I wanted was to go somewheres; all I wanted was a change, I warn't particular."

In the end Huckleberry set out on a journey with the black slave Jim floating down the Mississippi River on a raft. The same Jim presents him with a profound dilemma, and Huckleberry ends up facing his own hell.

"Jim said it made him all over trembly and feverish to be so close to freedom. Well, I can tell you it made me all over trembly and feverish, too, to hear him, because I begun to get it through my head that he *was* most *free*—and who was to blame for it? Why, *me*. I couldn't get that out of my conscience, no how nor no way. It got to troubling me so I couldn't rest; I couldn't stay still in one place. It hadn't ever come home to me before, what this thing was that I was doing. But now it did; and it staid with me, and scorched me more and more. I tried to make out to myself that *I* warn't to blame, because *I* didn't run him off from his rightful owner, but it warn't no use."

"It would get all around, that Huck Finn helped a nigger to get his freedom; and if I was to ever see anybody from that town again, I'd be ready to get down and lick his boots for shame. That's just the way: a person does a low-down thing, and then he don't want to take no consequences of it. Thinks as long as he can hide it, it ain't no disgrace. That was my fix exactly. The more I studied about this, the more my conscience went to grinding me, and the more wicked and low-down and ornery I got to feeling. And at last, when it hit me all of a sudden that here was the plain hand of Providence slapping me in the face and letting me know my wickedness was being watched all the time from up there in heaven, whilst I was stealing a poor old woman's nigger that hadn't ever done me no harm, and now was showing me there's One that's always on the lookout, and ain't agoing to allow no such miserable doings to go only just so fur and no further, I most dropped in my tracks I was so scared."

After such troubling thoughts, Huckleberry, who writes a letter secretly telling the rightful owner that a white man has happened to capture Jim, must make the final decision on whether to send it or not. "It was a close place. I took it up, and held it in my hand. I was a trembling, because I'd got to decide, forever, betwixt two things, and I knowed it. I studied a minute, sort of holding my breath, and then says to myself:

" 'All right, then, I'll *go* to hell'—and tore it up.

"It was awful thoughts, and awful words, but they was said. And I let them stay said; and never thought no more about reforming. I shoved the whole thing out of my head; and said I would take up wickedness again, which was in my line, being brung up to it, and the other warn't. And for a starter, I would go to work and steal Jim out of slavery again; and if I could think up anything worse, I would do that, too; because as long as I was in, and in for good, I might as well go the whole hog."

Compared with Tom Sawyer who is inside the social order, Huckleberry, who is outside society, freely chooses hell for his own sake. In doing so, Huckleberry must have enabled our side, Japanese children, to observe him as a free *hero* who is not glued to America, in any of the eras influenced by fear or hatred of America, or of the total dependence on America. Furthermore, now, I thought I often discovered in the culture of today's America something resembling an attitude toward nature deeply chiseled with superstitions, following the antisocial *jump* of Huckleberry of the age of great forests and rivers. Needless to say, I do not say this in the schematic conception of human beings as *hip* and *square*, according to the fad of the Beat Generation. That is, this does not concern the superficial amusement of finding the heirs of Huckleberry in hippies and calling all the other average Americans, all together, squares, along with Tom Sawyer. Rather, in my clear and extensive impression I might even call classical, I felt, in today's America, for example on Fifth Avenue, in New York, the existence of Americans with their destitute hearts listening to the calls of nighthawks and the barks of dogs in the depths of forests. I think I will think about it anew as one way the Americans who are the descendents of Oscar Handlin's so-called "uprooted" (*The Uprooted*) can exist in the great forest of ultra-modern civilization.

Translator's note:

This is a translation of the second half of Ōe Kenzaburō's article *America ryokōsha no yume—jigoku ni yuku Huckleberry Finn*, which was first published in the September 1966 issue of the monthly *Sekai (The World)*, the most liberal magazine of what was then the liberal publisher Iwanami Shoten. The untranslated first half begins, "America. I shall never become entirely free from the oppressing, demonic power of the word America," and describes how the writer has lived since boyhood "within the conflicting, extremely complicated [inferiority] complex that the word America touches off."

Ōe, born in 1935, is known for his singularly awkward Japanese. Of his style, Mishima Yukio, no less, said as early as 1959, "Who would be puzzled if someone said Mr. Ōe Kenzaburō's prose, as is, is a translation of Sartre?" Ōe, who won the prestigious Akutagawa Prize when a 23-year-old student, in 1958, and thereby became the youngest writer to do so, was a French major at the University of Tokyo. At the time, existentialism was the rage, and Jean-Paul Sartre was a demigod for many Japanese intellectuals, including university students. Ōe wrote, at least in those days, in what may be called "deliberate translationese"—an exercise in projecting foreignness by writing syntactically tortured sentences. His prose includes the use of long modifying clauses in a way unnatural to Japanese and the repetition of common and proper nouns, such as personal names and titles of books.

Translated by Hiroaki Sato
Sekai (Tokyo), 1966

John Seelye

In 1970 John Seelye (born in 1931), then a literature professor at the University of Connecticut, published *The True Adventures of Huckleberry Finn*, a book that *Time* called "a puckish attempt to satisfy those critics who have found Mark Twain's masterpiece either artless, craftless, sexless, a gutless accommodation with commercialism or an overstuffed moral copout." The magazine dubbed it "a unique work of what can best be described as picaresque criticism." In the selection presented here of "Huck's" introduction to this new version of "his book," Seelye takes on critics such as Van Wyck Brooks, T. S. Eliot, Lionel Trilling, Henry Seidel Canby, Leo Marx, Richard Poirier, and William Van O'Connor—a project not in and of itself particularly different from ones that other scholars have embarked on before. But what makes Seelye's venture unusual is that he does all this in *huck-speak*—the language Huck Finn himself would use if he were doing the arguing. The result is a deliciously amusing *tour de force* which has the effect of making the reader want to return to Twain's original.

FROM
The True Adventures of Huckleberry Finn

"De ole true Huck"

Some years ago, it don't matter how many, Mr Mark Twain took down some adventures of mine and put them in a book called *Huckleberry Finn*—which is my name. When the book come out I read through it and I seen right away that he didn't tell it the way it was. Most of the time he told the truth, but he told a number of stretchers too, and some of them was really whoppers. Well, that ain't nothing. I never seen anybody but lied one time or another. But I was curious why he done it that way, and I asked him. He told me it was a book for children, and some of the things I done and said warn't fit for boys and girls my age to read about. Well, I couldn't argue with that, so I didn't say nothing more about it. He made a pile of money with that book, so I guess he knowed his business, which was children. They liked it fine.

But the grownups give him trouble from the start. When the book first come out the liberrians didn't like it because it was trashy, and they hadn't but just got used to it being trash when somebody found out there was considerable "niggers" in it, which was organized by then. Well, the liberrians didn't want no trouble, so they took it off the shelves again. And the crickits was bothered by the book too. At first they agreed with the liberrians that the book was trash, but about the time the liberrians had got used to the trashiness, the crickits decided the book warn't trashy enough, and then when the liberrians got in a sweat about the word "nigger," the crickits come out and said there warn't anything wrong with that word, that it was just the sort of word a stupid, no-account, white-trash lunkhead would use—meaning me, I suppose, not Mr Mark Twain. They said it suited the book's style. Well, the liberrians and the crickits ain't spoke to each other since.

There was a crickit named Mr Van Wyck Brooks who was particular hard on Mark Twain. He said that Mark Twain was the victim of women, mostly his mother and his wife, and his friend, Mr William Dean Howells, who had crossed out all the rough words in his books—including mine. He thought it was too bad that Mark Twain was brung up where he was, in Hannibal, Missouri, which was just a ramshackly river town, and he thought it was even worse that he had got married and went to Hartford, Connecticut, where he got mixed up with the quality, mostly preachers and such. He said if it warn't for Christianity, women, and Hartford, Connecticut, Mr Mark Twain might a come to something.

Well, Mr Bernard DeVoto put Mr Brooks straight on that score. He showed where Hannibal warn't at fault at all, nor religion, nor women, nor even Hartford. He said that Mark Twain *asked* to have all them rough words cut out, and that it was his own doing, and nobody else's. He said it was because he wanted to sell his books.

Mr Van Wyck Brooks, now, even though he said some ornery things about Mark Twain, he kinder liked my book. He said it was the only *honest* thing Mark Twain ever wrote. But Mr DeVoto come down pretty damn hard on it. It warn't that he didn't enjoy it, because he did—some parts of it, anyway—but he couldn't help pointing out where Mark Twain went wrong. He could see all the little lies and the short cuts and the foolishness that was in it, and he wrote considerable about them in two books of his own. He was especially hard on the ending Mark Twain had thought up, and said it actually give him a *chill*.

It warn't that Mr DeVoto didn't like Mark Twain, because he did. He even called him "Mark" most of the time. But he could see where he had his faults, and he didn't hang back none in telling about them. Like *sex*, which Mark Twain couldn't ever bring himself to write about. Mr DeVoto said it was silly having a fourteen-year-old boy like me not thinking about sex *some* of the time. He didn't say what kind of sex. He left that up to Mr Leslie Fiedler.

Mr DeVoto was tolerable lengthy, but he didn't settle the matter. The next thing you know Mr T. S. Eliot and Mr Lionel Trilling come right out and said they *admired* the book. Well, that was foolish enough, but then they went on to say that the ending seemed all right to them, and that was suicide. Mr Eliot let on that Tom Sawyer's pranks and foolishness was on the tiresome side, and Mr Trilling admitted that the ending warn't exactly up to the rest of the story, but they didn't stop there, and that's how the trouble started. Mr Eliot allowed that *he* didn't know of any ending that was better than Mark Twain's ending, and Mr Trilling said it was fit that I should finish up where I started out, only a thousand miles south. Which was interesting, but a trifle tough.

Well, there was this crickit named Mr Henry Seidel Canby, and he got hopping mad. He said that there warn't no ending *worse* than that ending, and that Mark Twain ought to be shot for writing it, but he had died anyway, so nobody took him up on it. Then along comes Mr Leo Marx, and give both Mr Eliot and Mr Trilling hell. 'Cording to him, that ending warn't *moral*, and it was all because Mark Twain couldn't face up to his own story—by which he meant mine. He said that Mark Twain couldn't measure up to the nat'ral ending his book deserved, that he just plain lost his nerve and had to cheat by tacking on a faint-hearted, immoral ending.

Mr Marx said that Mr Eliot and Mr Trilling warn't no better than Mark Twain. He said they was immoral too, and done nobody any favors by making out that ending was worth more than shucks. He said maybe Mr Eliot couldn't think of a better ending, but *he* knowed of one, and though he warn't up to messing around with Mark Twain's ending, because that warn't very moral either, he didn't think there would be any harm in *suggesting* how the story *should* a come out, which he done. He said the book ought to end so as to make something out of our escape down the Mississippi. He knowed that Jim couldn't ever a found his freedom down river in no moral way, so that was out, and whatever other ending you chose would just disappoint everybody. But he said that was the *point*, and the only honest way to end the book was to leave me and Jim no better off than we ever was, but still more or less trying to get clear. He claimed this ending was more moral than Mark Twain's, and it certainly would a been disappointing.

Well, Mr Eliot and Mr Trilling was squshed flat, and never did answer up to Mr Marx, but Mr James Cox did. He said that maybe the ending warn't as good as Mr Eliot and Mr Trilling claimed it was, but nuther was it as bad as Mr Marx had let on. He said it warn't perfect, but it was *explainable*, and that was the important thing. He explained all about death and reborning and nitiation, and how it was fit that Jim and I should a come back from the river, because the free and easy life on the raft was a lie. He said what was wrong with the ending was Tom Sawyer, because Tom's *style* was all wrong. That made Tom biling mad, but before he had a chance to say anything about Mr Cox's explanation, a whole passel of crickits jumped in with theirs, and there was a power of explaining and arguments and reasons the like of which I never heard before unless it was at the coroner's jury where the remainders had been pisoned, stabbed, shot, and hung, and they was trying to figure out what had killed him.

Right in the middle of all this powwow the door opened up, so to speak, and in walked Mr William Van O'Connor. He give all those other crickits a sad kind of smile, like he felt sorry for them poor ingoramuses, and then he let rip with a damn stunner. He didn't mess around with the ending. He said he was only interested in that ending because everybody seemed to think it was the only thing wrong with the book. He said he reckoned they was modest in their estimate, and then he got right to work, down in the innards of the book, and showed how sloppy it was put together. He would tear a part out and show how loose it had been wired in, and then he would reach down and tear out another part. It was bloody, but grand. The floor was simply covered with poor transitors, and claptrappy episodes, and melerdramas, and minstrel shows, and sentimentering. Mr Van O'Connor said they warn't nothing, though. He said the worse thing about the book was its *innerscents*, which was wickeder than the sloppy work by far. He said if you took out the innerscents, you'd have something, by which he meant the book's skin I reckon, because that's all there was left.

Nobody said a word for quite a spell, and it did seem there warn't nothing left *to* say, like at the end of a six-hour funeral, where the dear departed has begun to stink a bit and the windows is stuck shut because of the rain. But if there's one thing a crickit can't stand, it's stillness, and after a time they begun to creep around in the wreck, seeing if there warn't anything worth salvage. Mr Henry Nash Smith, f'rinstance, give it a try. He said the important thing was the way Mark Twain *told* my story, that's what saved it and made it great, never mind how it was hung together. And he said you couldn't take out the innerscents without making the rest go bust, that it was needle and thread for the whole pair of britches. He wouldn't a had it no other way, because it was the innerscents that made the wickedness all the worse. If quality and style counted, he said, it was just about the best damned innerscents on the market. Mr Smith allowed the ending was slack on innerscents, but he seemed to figure the book had stocked up a whole wood-yard of it by then, and could go the rest of the way on credit. Chapter XXXI all by itself had enough innerscents to keep a saint in good supply for a year, with enough left over for a hard-shell Baptist or two.

Well, that seemed to keep the other crickits satisfied for a while, but then along came Mr Richard Poirier, and after he got through, what Mr Van O'Connor done seemed like a Sunday-school picnic.

Mr Poirier said the trouble with the book was it warn't in-nerscent *enough*, and not just the ending nuther. He said if you chopped off the end you still had too much snake, that you had to keep chopping back and chopping back till you got to Chapter XV or thereabouts, which warn't much farther south than the neck. All that come after it just ain't the true Huck, he said, and some parts above it ain't all that long on innerscents either, having too much society or Tom Sawyer or something else bothersome and contrary in them. He let on that finding the bits worth saving was harder than getting a meal off an owl, and he give it up for a bad job all round. He said it was all because of Miss Jane Austin, a tolerable slim old maid which Mark Twain didn't much cotton to on account of she was always harping on marriage.

After that, it did look like the kindest thing you could do for the book was scrape it up and bury it. People still read *Huckle-berry Finn*, but the ones that see what Mr O'Connor and Mr Poirier done to it say it just ain't the same afterwards. They can't forget the sight of all them damn parts laying around, and it makes them uneasy.

Well, it was kinder sad, in a way, with everything scattered about and people saying it was a good book they guessed, but it had terrible weaknesses, and nobody really able to enjoy it any more except childen. So I thought to myself, if the book which Mr Mark Twain wrote warn't up to what these men wanted from a book, why not pick up the parts—the good ones—and put together one they *would* like? So I done it, the best I could anyways, only this time I told the story like it really happened, leaving in all the cuss words and the sex and the sadness.

Everything went just dandy till I got to the end. I nailed her down easy enough, but then it hit me that maybe the crickits wouldn't like this one any better than they liked Mr Mark Twain's. Well, after I had sweat over that thought considerable, it come to me that there ain't nothing a body can do except what is in him *to* do, and since there just warn't no other ending besides that one in me, I said what the hell, and let her ride. All the same, I didn't want no trouble from the crickits if I could help it, so I left in a spare page, where anybody that wants to can write in his own ending if he don't care for mine. I suppose the liberrians ain't a-going to like this book much either, but maybe now the crickits will be a little less ornery.

And I want you to understand that this is a different book from the one Mr Mark Twain wrote. It may look like *The Adventures of Huckleberry Finn* at first sight, but that don't mean a thing. Most of the parts was good ones, and I could use them. But Mark Twain's book is for children and such, whilst this one here is for crickits. And now that they've got *their* book, maybe they'll leave the other one alone.

1970

Robert Penn Warren

Kentucky-born Robert Penn Warren (1905–1989), one of the most versatile writers of the 20th century, is the only author to have been awarded a Pulitzer Prize for both poetry and fiction. He was also the first poet laureate of the United States. Warren became associated during his college years at Vanderbilt with the Southern Agrarian poets who would create the literary magazine *Fugitive*, and he later edited the *Southern Review* with Cleanth Brooks. The textbook that he edited with Brooks, *Understanding Poetry* (1938), is widely credited with having established New Criticism, with its focus on close reading and its emphasis on a poem's formal elements, as the dominant method of teaching poetry for the next several decades. The author of ten novels, 16 collections of poetry, more than a dozen works of nonfiction, and a play, Warren is best known for his novel *All the King's Men*. The conversational tone of "Last Laugh" aids in the fusion of the personal past and present that Warren saw at the core of Mark Twain's art. Warren juxtaposed two chapters from Twain's life in the poem: his possibly having witnessed his father's autopsy as a child and the despair he felt at the death of his wife—"grief compounded by his sense of guilt for having robbed her of the Christian faith" (as Warren described it in *American Literature: The Makers and the Making*). Twain, though generally hostile to organized religion, was a seeker open to the possibility of faith but frustrated by his inability to find it—and increasingly skeptical about a God who failed to intervene to stop human suffering. Warren, like Twain, viewed himself as a nonbeliever: "I tried to talk myself into some religion in my freshman year at college," he once wrote, "but no dice."

Last Laugh

The little Sam Clemens, one night back in Hannibal,
Peeped through the dining-room keyhole, to see, outspread
And naked, the father split open, lights, liver, and all
Spilling out from that sack of mysterious pain, and the head

Sawed through, where his Word, like God's, held its deepest
          den,
And candlelight glimmered on blood-slick, post-mortem steel,
And the two dead fish eyes stared steadily ceilingward—well,
          then,
If you yourself were, say, eleven, just how would you feel?

Oh, not that you'd loved him—that ramrod son of Virginia,
Though born for success, failing westward bitterly on.
"Armed truce," was all, years later, you could find to say in you.
But still, when a father's dead, an umbrella's gone

From between the son and the direful elements.
No, Sam couldn't turn from the keyhole. It's not every night
You can see God butchered in such learned dismemberments,
And when the chance comes you should make the most of the
          sight.

Though making the most, Sam couldn't make terms with the
          fact
Of the strangely prismatic glitter that grew in his eye,
Or, climbing the stairs, why his will felt detached from the act,
Or why, stripping for bed, he stared so nakedly

At the pore little body and thought of the slick things therein.
Then he wept on the pillow, surprised at what he thought
          grief,
Then fixed eyes at darkness while, slow, on his face grew a grin,
Till suddenly something inside him burst with relief,

Like a hog bladder blown up to bust when the hog-killing frost
Makes the brat's holiday. Then he just began laughing and
          could not
Stop, and so laughed himself crying to sleep. At last,
Far off in Nevada, by campfire or sluice or gulch-hut,

Or in roaring S.F., in an acre of mirror and gilt,
Where the boys with the dust bellied-up, he'd find words
    come,
His own face as stiff as a shingle, and him little-built.
Then whammo—the backslapping riot! He'd stand, looking
    dumb.

God was dead, for a fact. He knew, in short, the best joke.
He had learned its thousand forms, and, since the dark stair
    hall,
Had learned what was worth more than bullion or gold-
    dust-plump poke,
And married rich, too, with an extra spin to the ball,

For Livy loved God, and he'd show her the joke, how they
    lied.
Quite a tussle it was but, hot deck or cold, he was sly
And won every hand but the last. Then, at her bedside,
He watched dying eyes look up at a comfortless sky,

And was left alone with his joke, God dead, till he died.

The New Yorker, 1978

Norman Mailer

Perhaps only a writer as bold as Norman Mailer (1923–2007) could have dared to "review" *Huckleberry Finn* a hundred years after its original publication as if it were a new "first novel"—which is what he did in 1984. On this occasion Mailer slyly accused the novel's author of being unduly influenced by a range of 20th-century writers to whom his prose was obviously indebted. Clearly, Mailer wrote, Mark Twain had learned a lot from Dos Passos, Lewis, Steinbeck, Faulkner, Vonnegut, Heller, Bellow, and others. Indeed, Mailer went so far as to accuse Twain of having plagiarized from Hemingway. Of course readers of *The New York Times Book Review* got the point: every writer Mailer mentioned had learned key things *from* Twain and 20th-century American literature looked the way it did largely because of lessons that Twain had taught them. One could make a strong case for the idea that a major strain of Mailer's success as a writer—beginning with the dazzling, raucous *Armies of the Night*—was shaped by Twain's experiments in nonfiction a century before. Certainly *The Innocents Abroad* and *Roughing It* were precursors to the brand of "new journalism" that Mailer helped make famous—a style of autobiographical nonfiction narrative melding history, fiction, and social commentary in which the writer himself figured centrally. Like Twain, Mailer was prolific, publishing well over 30 books and scores of shorter pieces; and, like Twain, he often wrote because he needed the money. Mailer was not proud of everything he wrote and didn't make unwarranted claims for its worth. But as his "review" of *Huckleberry Finn* makes clear, he was confident about his standards for good writing even though he knew he sometimes failed to meet them himself. He appreciated Twain's achievement as a writer because he knew how hard it was to get words to work the way Twain made them work in that book. He spoke of *Huckleberry Finn* "as kin to a first novel because it is so young and fresh and so all-out silly in some of the chances it takes and even wins." One only wishes that Mailer had refrained from calling Jim "Nigger Jim." Twain's first biographer, Albert Bigelow Paine, referred to "Nigger Jim" and so did Hemingway, Ellison, and others. Mark Twain never did.

Huck Finn, Alive at 100

Is there a sweeter tonic for the doldrums than old reviews of great novels? In 19th-century Russia, "Anna Karenina" was received with the following: "Vronsky's passion for his horse runs parallel to his passion for Anna" . . . "Sentimental rubbish" . . . "Show me one page," says The Odessa Courier, "that contains an idea." "Moby-Dick" was incinerated: "Graphic descriptions of a dreariness such as we do not remember to have met with before in marine literature" . . . "Sheer moonstruck lunacy" . . . "Sad stuff. Mr. Melville's Quakers are wretched dolts and drivellers and his mad captain is a monstrous bore."

By this measure, "Huckleberry Finn" (published 100 years ago this week in London and two months later in America) gets off lightly. The Springfield Republican judged it to be no worse than "a gross trifling with every fine feeling. . . . Mr. Clemens has no reliable sense of propriety," and the public library in Concord, Mass., was confident enough to ban it: "the veriest trash." The Boston Transcript reported that "other members of the Library Committee characterize the work as rough, coarse, and inelegant, the whole book being more suited to the slums than to intelligent, respectable people."

All the same, the novel was not too unpleasantly regarded. There were no large critical hurrahs but the reviews were, on the whole, friendly. A good tale, went the consensus. There was no sense that a great American novel had landed on the literary world of 1885. The critical climate could hardly anticipate T. S. Eliot and Ernest Hemingway's encomiums 50 years later. In the preface to an English edition, Eliot would speak of "a masterpiece. . . . Twain's genius is completely realized," and Ernest went further. In "Green Hills of Africa," after disposing of Emerson, Hawthorne and Thoreau, and paying off Henry James and Stephen Crane with a friendly nod, he proceeded to declare, "All modern American literature comes from one book by Mark Twain called 'Huckleberry Finn.' . . . It's the best book we've had. All American writing comes from that. There was nothing before. There has been nothing as good since."

Hemingway, with his nonpareil gift for nosing out the perfect *vin du pays* for an ineluctable afternoon, was nonetheless more like other novelists in one dire respect: he was never at a loss to advance himself with his literary judgments. Assessing the writing of others, he used the working author's rule of thumb: if I give this book a good mark, does it help appreciation of my work? Obviously, "Huckleberry Finn" has passed the test.

A suspicion immediately arises. Mark Twain is doing the kind of writing only Hemingway can do better. Evidently, we must take a look. May I say it helps to have read "Huckleberry Finn" so long ago that it feels brand-new on picking it up again. Perhaps I was 11 when I saw it last, maybe 13, but now I only remember that I came to it after "Tom Sawyer" and was disappointed. I couldn't really follow "The Adventures of Huckleberry Finn." The character of Tom Sawyer whom I had liked so much in the first book was altered, and did not seem nice any more. Huckleberry Finn was altogether beyond me. Later, I recollect being surprised by the high regard nearly everyone who taught American Lit. lavished upon the text, but that didn't bring me back to it. Obviously, I was waiting for an assignment from The New York Times.

Let me offer assurances. It may have been worth the wait. I suppose I am the 10-millionth reader to say that "Huckleberry Finn" is an extraordinary work. Indeed, for all I know, it is a great novel. Flawed, quirky, uneven, not above taking cheap shots and cashing far too many checks (it is rarely above milking its humor)—all the same, what a book we have here! I had the most curious sense of excitement. After a while, I understood my peculiar frame of attention. The book was so up-to-date! I was not reading a classic author so much as looking at a new work sent to me in galleys by a publisher. It was as if it had arrived with one of those rare letters which says, "We won't make this claim often but do think we have an extraordinary first novel to send out." So it was like reading "From Here to Eternity" in galleys, back in 1950, or "Lie Down in Darkness," "Catch-22," or "The World According to Garp" (which reads like a fabulous first novel). You kept being alternately delighted, surprised, annoyed, competitive, critical and finally excited. A new writer had moved onto the block. He could be a potential friend or enemy but he most certainly was talented.

That was how it felt to read "Huckleberry Finn" a second time. I kept resisting the context until I finally surrendered. One always does surrender sooner or later to a book with a strong magnetic field. I felt as if I held the work of a young writer about 30 or 35, a prodigiously talented fellow from the Midwest, from Missouri probably, who had had the audacity to write a historical novel about the Mississippi as it might have been a century and a half ago, and this young writer had managed to give us a circus of fictional virtuosities. In nearly every chapter new and remarkable characters bounded out from the printed page as if it were a tarmac on which they could perform their leaps. The author's confidence seemed so complete that he could deal with every kind of man or woman God ever gave to the middle of America. Jail-house drunks like Huck Finn's father take their bow, full of the raunchy violence that even gets into the smell of clothing. Gentlemen and river rats, young, attractive girls full of grit and "sand," and strong old ladies with aphorisms clicking like knitting needles, fools and confidence men—what a cornucopia of rabble and gentry inhabit the author's river banks.

It would be superb stuff if only the writer did not keep giving away the fact that he was a modern young American working in 1984. His anachronisms were not so much in the historical facts—those seemed accurate enough—but the point of view was too contemporary. The scenes might succeed—say it again, this young writer was talented!—but he kept betraying his literary influences. The author of "The Adventures of Huckleberry Finn" had obviously been taught a lot by such major writers as Sinclair Lewis, John Dos Passos and John Steinbeck; he had certainly lifted from Faulkner and the mad tone Faulkner could achieve when writing about maniacal men feuding in deep swamps; he had also absorbed much of what Vonnegut and Heller could teach about the resilience of irony. If he had a surer feel for the picaresque than Saul Bellow in "Augie March," still he felt derivative of that work. In places one could swear he had memorized "The Catcher in the Rye," and he probably dipped into "Deliverance" and "Why Are We in Vietnam?" He might even have studied the mannerisms of movie stars. You could feel traces of John Wayne, Victor McLaglen and Burt Reynolds in his pages. The author had doubtless digested many a Hollywood comedy on small-town life. His instinct for life in hamlets on the Mississippi before the Civil War was as sharp as it was farcical, and couldn't be more commercial.

No matter. With talent as large as this, one could forgive the obvious eye for success. Many a large talent has to go through large borrowings in order to find his own style, and a lust for popular success while dangerous to serious writing is not necessarily fatal. Yes, one could accept the pilferings from other writers, given the scope of this work, the brilliance of the concept—to catch rural America by a trip on a raft down a great river! One could even marvel uneasily at the depth of the instinct for fiction in the author. With the boy Huckleberry Finn, this new novelist had managed to give us a character of no comfortable, measurable dimension. It is easy for characters in modern novels to seem more vivid than figures in the classics but, even so, Huckleberry Finn appeared to be more alive than Don Quixote and Julian Sorel, as naturally near to his own mind as we are to ours. But how often does a hero who is so absolutely natural on the page also succeed in acquiring convincing moral stature as his adventures develop?

It is to be repeated. In the attractive grip of this talent, one is ready to forgive the author of "Huckleberry Finn" for every influence he has so promiscuously absorbed. He has made such fertile use of his borrowings. One could even cheer his appearance on our jaded literary scene if not for the single transgression that goes too far. These are passages that do more than borrow an author's style—they copy it! Influence is mental, but theft is physical. Who can declare to a certainty that a large part of the prose in "Huckleberry Finn" is not lifted directly from Hemingway? We know that we are not reading Ernest only because the author, obviously fearful that his tone is getting too near, is careful to sprinkle his text with "a-clutterings" and "warn'ts" and "anywheres" and "t'others." But we have read Hemingway—and so we see through it—we know we are reading pure Hemingway disguised:

"We cut young cottonwoods and willows, and hid the raft with them. Then we set out the lines. Next we slid into the river and had a swim . . . then we set down on the sandy bottom where the water was about knee-deep and watched the daylight come. Not a sound anywheres . . . the first thing to see, looking away over the water, was a kind of dull line—that was the woods on t'other side; you couldn't make nothing else out; then a pale place in the sky; then more paleness spreading around; then the river softened up away off, and warn't black anymore . . . by and by you could see a streak on the water which you know by the look of the streak that there's a snag there in a swift current which breaks on it and makes that streak look that way; and you see the mist curl up off of the water and the east reddens up and the river."

Up to now I have conveyed, I expect, the pleasure of reading this book today. It is the finest compliment I can offer. We use an unspoken standard of relative judgment on picking up a classic. Secretly, we expect less reward from it than from a good contemporary novel. The average intelligent modern reader would probably, under torture, admit that "Heartburn" was more fun to read, minute for minute, than "Madame Bovary," and maybe one even learned more. That is not to say that the first will be superior to the second a hundred years from now but that a classic novel is like a fine horse carrying an exorbitant impost. Classics suffer by their distance from our day-to-day gossip. The mark of how good "Huckleberry Finn" has to be is that one can compare it to a number of our best modern American novels and it stands up page for page, awkward here, sensational there—absolutely the equal of one of those rare incredible first novels that come along once or twice in a decade. So I have spoken of it as kin to a first novel because it is so young and so fresh and so all-out silly in some of the chances it takes and even wins. A wiser older novelist would never play that far out when the work was already well along and so neatly in hand. But Twain does.

For the sake of literary propriety, let me not, however, lose sight of the actual context. "The Adventures of Huckleberry Finn" is a novel of the 19th century and its grand claims to literary magnitude are also to be remarked upon. So I will say that the first measure of a great novel may be that it presents—like a human of palpable charisma—an all-but-visible aura. Few works of literature can be so luminous without the presence of some majestic symbol. In "Huckleberry Finn" we are presented (given the possible exception of Anna Livia Plurabelle) with the best river ever to flow through a novel, our own Mississippi, and in the voyage down those waters of Huck Finn and a runaway slave on their raft, we are held in the thrall of the river. Larger than a character, the river is a manifest presence, a demiurge to support the man and the boy, a deity to betray them, feed them, all but drown them, fling them apart, float them back together. The river winds like a fugue through the marrow of the true narrative which is nothing less than the ongoing relation between Huck and the runaway slave, this Nigger Jim whose name embodies the very stuff of the slave system itself—his name is not Jim but Nigger Jim. The growth of love and knowledge between the runaway white and the runaway black is a relation equal to the relation of the men to the river for it is also full of betrayal and nourishment, separation and return. So it manages to touch that last fine nerve of the heart where compassion and irony speak to one another and thereby give a good turn to our most protected emotions.

Reading "Huckleberry Finn" one comes to realize all over again that the near-burned-out, throttled, hate-filled dying affair between whites and blacks is still our great national love affair, and woe to us if it ends in detestation and mutual misery. Riding the current of this novel, we are back in that happy time when the love affair was new and all seemed possible. How rich is the recollection of that emotion! What else is greatness but the indestructible wealth it leaves in the mind's recollection after hope has soured and passions are spent? It is always the hope of democracy that our wealth will be there to spend again, and the ongoing treasure of "Huckleberry Finn" is that it frees us to think of democracy and its sublime, terrifying premise: let the passions and cupidities and dreams and kinks and ideals and greed and hopes and foul corruptions of all men and women have their day and the world will still be better off, for there is more good than bad in the sum of us and our workings. Mark Twain, whole embodiment of that democratic human, understood the premise in every turn of his pen, and how he tested it, how he twisted and tantalized and tested it until we are weak all over again with our love for the idea.

The New York Times Book Review, 1984

David Carkeet

David Carkeet (born in 1946), from Sonora, California, was trained as a linguist before he turned to writing fiction—a fact that helps explain the attention paid to the nuances of language in his novels. In *I Been There Before* (1985), which came out the year of the 150th anniversary of Mark Twain's birth and the 75th anniversary of his death, Twain catches a ride back to earth on Halley's Comet—the comet that appeared in both the year of his birth and the year of his death, and which came back into view in 1985. The novel is at once science fiction time travel and a parody of academic scholarship and archival research. Carkeet somehow manages to create a character who talks and acts enough like Mark Twain for the reader to believe that Twain *would* have sounded like he sounds in the book if he actually *had* come back to earth on Halley's Comet. In addition to works of fiction including a mystery featuring a linguist-detective, *Double Negative* (1980), and a novel about a baseball team, *The Greatest Slump of All Time* (1984), Carkeet has also written two scholarly articles about dialect and language use in *Huckleberry Finn*.

FROM

I Been There Before

San Francisco

Feb. 5/86

L ivy darling, what a fool I am! I am a much bigger fool than ever you imagined. I have been duped—completely sold. I cannot tell you how—it would break your heart to hear of it. If only I could set it right! The world has *good* people in it, Livy, not just bad; but what an ugly & distrusting nature I have.

You see, Livy, to-day I visited the Mark Twain Papers. Quite a busy little beehive across the Bay, & *I'm* the honey that all the buzzing is about. I heard of the place from a librarian here. He said if I was as interested in Mark Twain as I appeared to be, I *must* go visit the Mark Twain Papers. He wouldn't tell me what was there. He just said *go*. So I went.

I bought a subway ticket *from a machine*, & then rode in a

tunnel *under the water* to Berkeley—unlikely beginnings for a journey into the past. I found my way to the University library & took an elevator to the 4th floor. As I stepped out I saw the sign: "Mark Twain Papers," along with an arrow pointing the way. I made a right turn & came to a large room full of news-papers. Was this it—piles & piles of the dozens of different newspapers I wrote for? No—farther down the hall I saw another sign about my papers. I walked on, past one blue-painted office door after another, & I saw yet *another* sign & arrow, & made *another* right turn. Was *this* the Mark Twain Pa-pers—a devilishly endless circle without beginning or end?

But the hall was not infinite after all. It ended at a closed door & a strangely out-of-place doorbell, which I pressed. After a time, the door swung open; a head peeked out; a rather nice head, with long black hair. She was a young woman, & very tall. When she looked down to me she made me feel very . . . well, short. She didn't mean to, though.

"Can I help you?" she asked.

"So far, so good," I say to myself; then, to her, "I want to see these Mark Twain Papers."

"Which ones in particular?"

"Whatever you have."

"What are you interested in?"

"Anything that has to do with Mark Twain."

She smiled. "*Everything* here has to do with Mark Twain. Do you know anything about the Papers?"

"No."

"Come on in. We don't like to leave this door open." I joined her inside, in a hall so narrow we were thrown together some-what. The door clicked behind us, making it even cozier. "We have manuscripts, letters, notebooks . . . Are you a Mark Twain scholar?"

"Hmmm," I thought. "No," I said.

"A buff?"

"Hmmm" again. My thoughts drifted to buffalo skin, to light yellow. I warned myself not to be a ninny. I hung fire.

"A fan?"

I wasn't at all warm, so *this* offer puzzled me.

"Hello?" she said, to see if my spirit was still present, I suppose.

"Hi!" says I, hoping this would put us on a modern & friendly footing.

She frowned. It didn't suit her soft face. She asked, as a last resort, "Do you have any favorites among his works?"

"*Joan of Arc*?" Livy, I don't know why I *asked* it like that, but at least I got that frown off her face—now she was grinning. I was mighty pleased with myself.

"That's refreshing," says she. "Did you want to see the original manuscript? Is that what you want?"

"Yes."

"Come with me." She led me to a narrow room with a long empty table facing the windows, & invited me to sit down. "Do you plan to work with it for very long? We normally ask patrons to work downstairs in the reading room. You can request the material down there, & a page will bring it to you."

"I just want to see it. Just for a moment."

"All right." She left. I looked around. Along the wall behind my chair were rows & rows of books, all by me, though some had been given titles that I didn't use, like *Early Tales & Sketches*. I didn't know they were "early" when I wrote them . . .

* * *

I took down a book called *The Mysterious Stranger Manuscripts*. It was a wonder. The very first sentence in it read, "Mark Twain's *The Mysterious Stranger, A Romance*, as published in 1916 & reprinted since that date, is an editorial fraud perpetrated by Twain's official biographer & literary executor, Albert Bigelow Paine, & Frederick A. Duneka of Harper & Brothers publishing company." When I read it I burst out laughing.

The young woman caught me. She had returned, & I could see that my outburst had reinstated her frown, but she just said, with a glance to the book, "It's about time we set the record straight, don't you think? Here—I've got the MS." She set a bright orange box down on the table, opened it, & took out the manuscript.

I turned a few leaves. "This is it," I said, because I didn't know what else to say. "It hurts to look at it. All that labor."

She heaved a sigh. "And such an awful waste."

I looked at her. I meant to indicate that she had my full attention, because she did.

"That's what most people feel, anyway," she said.

"Oh?"

She nodded—slowly, & with an indefinable sadness. "I don't want to hurt your feelings, or anything like that—you said it was your favorite, & to each his own, of course. But I think Clemens tried to be something he wasn't when he wrote *Joan*. He was tired of being the buffoon, so he tried to be high-toned & serious. The result was a very boring book. I think he was his best when he was being funny." She paused. "It's a shame he didn't understand himself better. You study him, & his works"—she waved an arm around the room, taking in the bookshelf, maybe even the entire building—"& you can feel the pain of a man who doesn't understand himself. This whole collection just aches with his pain."

It was strange, Livy. I felt the pain—felt it being transmitted from the surroundings through this young woman to me. My nerves felt exposed, as if I had just been completely stripped—of my clothing, & of my skin as well.

"He loved this work," I said, feebly.

"Even Howells panned it."

I sighed. "I know," I said. I felt as if one of my children had been slandered. I also wondered if the child hadn't deserved it! Still, one must defend one's children. "After *Joan* was published," I said, "Clemens met the Archbishop of Orleans, & the Archbishop assured him that anyone who had written so lovingly about Joan was bound to join her in heaven; she knew the right people & would see to it, without fail."

The woman gave me a tired smile. "I know that story. Clemens used to brag about it all the time. But it's just one more sign of his divided nature. I can imagine half of him wanting to rejoice at the Archbishop's comment, & the other half howling at it & scorning it. He's an endless contradiction."

I sat in silence & contemplated my two halves. Having peeled me, now she had sliced me in two.

Chuck Jones

Chuck Jones (1912–2002) was one of the pioneers of American cartoon art, playing a key role in developing such icons of American popular culture as Road Runner, Wile E. Coyote, Pepé Le Pew, Bugs Bunny, and Daffy Duck for Warner Brothers Cartoon Studio, where he directed the Looney Tunes and Merrie Melodies series. He subsequently developed cartoons (including a Tom & Jerry series) for Metro-Goldwyn-Mayer. Jones himself was an animator, artist, screenwriter, director, and producer. He collaborated with Theodor Geisel (Dr. Seuss) on animated versions of several of Geisel's books (including *How the Grinch Stole Christmas*). Jones, whose work was acknowledged by three Oscars, was given an Honorary Academy Award in 1996 for "the creation of classic cartoons and cartoon characters whose animated lives have brought joy to our real ones for more than half a century." As Jones notes in his autobiography, *Chuck Amuck*, as a child he had a memorable cat named Johnson who had an uncontrollable passion for grapefruit. Johnson would "leave a Bismarck herring, a stick of catnip, or a decayed seagull for a single wedge of grapefruit. For a whole grapefruit he would have committed fraud or practiced usury." Looking back on his career, Jones remarked: "What grapefruit was to Johnson the cat, Mark Twain became to me." Jones came to understand that "Mark Twain used words the way the graphic artist used line control." Through his influence on Jones and others (including Walt Disney), Mark Twain helped shape the Saturday mornings of American children for generations to come.

FROM

Chuck Amuck: The Life and Times
of an Animated Cartoonist

One fateful day our family moved into a rented house, furnished with a complete set of Mark Twain, and my life changed forever. What grapefruit was to Johnson the cat, Mark Twain became to me.

For instance:

Mark Twain used words the way the graphic artist uses line

control. He was terribly afraid of what he called his "darlings."
That is: phrases of such delicious mushy grandeur and melliflu-
ous cadence that they protruded from the clean line of his prose
like a puce Christmas tree. He "murdered his darlings" without
mercy, but admitting to the same agony that we all feel when we
sense that what we see in our drawing is more than is there.
Dorothy Parker said it more clearly after seeing a brilliantly
pageanted, dull musical comedy called *Jumbo*. "There is less
here than meets the eye," she said. Tattoo that across your reluctant retina and you will never confuse superficial technique
with the subject matter at hand.

Mark my words, this is my dearest friend

I first became interested in the Coyote while devouring Mark
Twain's *Roughing It* at the age of seven. I had heard of the coyote
only in passing references from passing adults and thought of
it—if I thought of it at all—as a sort of dissolute collie. As it turned
out, that's just about what a coyote is, and no one saw it more
clearly than Mark Twain.

"The coyote is a long, slim, sick and sorry-looking skeleton, with a gray wolf-skin stretched over it, a tolerably bushy tail that forever sags down with a despairing expression of forsakenness and misery, a furtive and evil eye, and a long, sharp face, with slightly lifted lip and exposed teeth. He has a general slinking expression all over. The coyote is a living, breathing allegory of Want. He is *always* hungry. He is always poor, out of luck and friendless . . . even the fleas would desert him for a veloci-pede . . . He does not mind going a hundred miles to break-fast, and a hundred and fifty to dinner, because he is sure to have three or four days between meals, and he can just as well be traveling and looking at the scenery as lying around doing nothing and adding to the burdens of his parents."

The Coyote—Mark Twain discovered him first

Who could resist such an enchanting creature? He and I had so much in common! Rushing to the encyclopedia, I found our mea-surements to be about the same, too: four feet long in our stocking feet; weight about fifty pounds stripped (fur long and coarse, griz-zled buff below and sun-bleached whitish above—a minor detail). But the clincher was this: "Noted for its nightly serenades of short yaps and mournful yowls." That was me all right, I had been as-sured too often by parents and siblings alike that my nocturnal serenades consisted of short yaps and mournful yowls.

Boy meets protagonist

I cannot begin to express the relief I felt at finding a companion to my own unique ineptness. It was so reassuring to find someone else of my own age (another characteristic we shared was our age: between seven and eight) who also could be a burden to his parents. I was beginning to believe that I was a failure in life, and to find a colorfully inept companion was a happy and stunning surprise.

I wish I had known then what I found to be true many years later: that comedy is nearly always the stuff of the ordinary, concerning itself with simple matters and simple ambitions, with ordinary pursuits and ordinary ambitions.

1989

David Bradley

In a 1985 address delivered in Hartford, Connecticut, David Bradley (born in 1950) noted the common definition of "black" literature as literature written by black authors. He then startled the audience by announcing, "*Huckleberry Finn* is a black novel." He paused and then went on: "Yes, you've seen pictures of Samuel Clemens, and he's white. Super white. White hair. White suit. White skin. But nobody's ever seen Mark Twain, who was a figment—and a pigment—of Samuel Clemens' imagination. And Mark Twain was black." Mark Twain, he suggested, was a black alter ego for Samuel Clemens, a vehicle through which Clemens was able to connect with ideas that he, as Clemens, could not have expressed. Bradley proceeded to make a case for Twain as a key figure in the development of African-American writing in the 20th century—including his own. He titled his talk, "*Huckleberry Finn*, The First 'Nigger' Novel." Three years earlier his second novel, *The Chaneysville Incident*, had appeared, a work that engaged history and memory with a sharpness that Twain himself would have relished. The book was hailed by one critic as "perhaps the most significant work by a new male black author since James Baldwin dazzled the early '60s with his fine fury," and by another critic as a work that "may be placed on the honor shelf, right next to Ellison's." The essay that follows describes how Mark Twain inspired and guided Bradley as he honed his skill as a writer. A trenchant and provocative commentator on race, literature, and the craft of fiction, Bradley has also published widely in anthologies and in periodicals. He has been an eloquent voice in debates about the racial politics of Mark Twain's greatest novel and the challenges of teaching it, speaking at universities and in documentaries such as Ken Burns' *Mark Twain*. In a 1995 speech he observed, "A lot of snotty academics have spent a lot of time and wasted a lot of journal ink criticizing the ending of *Huckleberry Finn*. But I notice none of them has been able to suggest, much less write, a better ending. Two actually tried—and failed. They all failed for the same reason that Twain wrote the ending as he did. America has never been able to write a better ending. America has never been able to write any ending at all."

Introduction to
How to Tell a Story and Other Essays

I was one month shy of ten years old when I first saw Mark Twain. He was a spade.

It was early August of 1960, a hot, humid, dusty Sunday afternoon. I was sitting on the screened-in side porch, reading the Old Testament, when my mother came out and suggested that she and I play a game.

This may seem quite ordinary, but it shocked me right down to the soles of my Red Ball Jets, for mine was a religious family, by both faith and profession. My father was a minister of the African Methodist Episcopal Zion Church, as was his father, and his father before him. That first father had been a slave, and one of my more eccentric cousins claimed that before him had come several plantation jacklegs and before them a long line of West African conjurers. Though my clan's Elders—Grandmother, Eldest Uncle, Father—doubted the shamanic speculation (in their opinion 'twas mercy brought us from our pagan land and taught our souls to understand salvation), they didn't mind the idea that we had preached the Word even when we were in chains, for they took great pride in saying that at least one male in each of our generations had been Called by Jehovah. And as I was the only male in my generation, and more, a son born to my father's second wife after much prayer and many years of barrenness, they made sure I ciphered the syllogism, saw my destiny as manifest, and worked to keep my heart open to and my soul worthy of the Call.

My grandmother was principal in this instruction. She believed a Call could only come from God, and so never expressed an expectation, but when I was very young she would put aside her knitting, take me onto her ancient lap—she was in her eighties when I was born—and spin me yarns of my namesake king, and of Samuel and John the Baptist, other late-born sons who became servants of Jehovah. When I grew older, she told tales of my clan's history, which by her account so closely paralleled Genesis and Exodus that we might have been Children of

Israel. The old lady knew how to tell a story; later, when I read the Scripture for myself, I would realize she was not above altering the timing of even a biblical tale to add suspense and surprise. In her revised standard version, David knocked out Goliath with his fifth stone, not his first, and the Philistine staggered around for half an hour before finally falling to the ground.

In addition to action, Grandmother's stories had authority, for though my clan was partrilineal, patrilocal, and prima facie male-dominated, it was in fact a matriarchy. My father may have been High Priest, my Uncle John Chieftain, but Grandmother was Judge, as in Israelite tradition. When I was born she had held office for over half a century, and her influence extended into every aspect of my life, even to my play.

Grandmother did not hold with play. While recreation *might* enable one to work with renewed vigor, play was linked with acts unholy, for it was written in Exodus, chapter 32, that after defiling their spirits by worshiping the golden calf, the Children of Israel "rose up to play." She accepted that children needed play, and that I, entirely deprived of it, might become the proverbial dull boy. But she paid more heed to Proverbs, wherein was written, "Even a child is known by his doings, whether his work be pure, and whether it be right," and she taught me, quoting First Corinthians, that if I wanted to be a Christian, a man, and a minister, I had to put away such childish needs.

Verily, I would have despised her, had she not known that work and play are the same thing under differing conditions, and mastered the knack of making the former seem like the latter. As it was, I spent many a contented day at her place, my clan's Homestead, a clapboard-faced log farmhouse equipped with neither central heat nor running water, helping her stack wood, split kindling, or fetch water from the spring that welled up cold and pure in a shady glen a hundred yards away. Such tasks were becoming outmoded, even in the rural mountain country where we lived; Grandmother used this increasing obsolescence to make them seem like frontier adventures.

When work was unmistakably that—even a dull boy cannot confuse liming the outhouse with having a good time—she'd enliven drudgery with more of her tales, these from the old days, when the workday stretched from can to can't and life was so routine that repainting the privy was almost a privilege.

Finally, when enough work had been done—you could never *finish* work, any more than you could finish the Bible—or in the evenings, after she, leaving the Homestead, came to my father's modern house, where she condescended to spend the night, she *might* find it permissible to play a game, but only because completely idle hands were Satan's workshop.

Still, Satan was the source of games—see Job, chapter 1. So Grandmother had a hierarchy of which games were less corrupting. She actually approved of checkers, and was herself adept at several varieties, especially Chinese. Of field games she was grudgingly accepting; young people had excessive energies, which, if not expended in work, were better exhausted outdoors in daylight than left undissipated indoors after dark. Of board games like Parcheesi, however, she entirely disapproved, for these games called for throwing at least one die, and sometimes dice. This led to more perditive pastimes; after all, the Romans had cast lots for Jesus' robes. As for card games—don't even mention them. In fact, don't mention cards, for they in themselves were evil. What could you do with cards but gamble? And what were the depictions of kings, queens, and jacks but violations of the Second Commandment, at least in spirit? No deck of cards had ever crossed the threshold of the Homestead, nor were such allowed in my father's house; when my mother once introduced an Old Maids deck, Grandmother threw it in the stove, lest I learn to shuffle.

This made sense to me, not only because I revered Grandmother (though sometimes I didn't like her much) but also because, when I had seen cards played in television Westerns, they were associated with smoking and drinking and led inevitably to fights. Though I was sometimes tempted by other sins, I did not find card games intriguing; I had sampled both tobacco and Demon Rum when the chance was offered by some of my less holy cousins (on my mother's side, of course), but when they'd offered to teach me pinochle I hotly refused. Now, at almost ten, though I sometimes touched myself, I had never touched a card. But here was my mother, suggesting a card game—and on the Sabbath! She would never have done such a thing had Grandmother been there. But Grandmother wasn't there. She was dead. I had killed her.

I hadn't meant to kill her. I had just wanted to reconcile the Gospel of Matthew—wherein Jesus commanded, among other things, "Love your enemies, bless them that curse you, do good to them that hate you, and pray for them which despitefully use you, and persecute you"—with the fact that I was being bullied and beaten up on the school playground with appalling regularity and sometimes dangerous severity. This was hard spiritual teaching, but my pastoral destiny demanded that I try to follow it, and I was doing fairly well. But I was doing less well with other parts of the Gospel. Like "resist not evil: but whosoever shall smite thee on thy right cheek, turn to him the other also," and the required attitudes in the Beatitudes. I didn't see, for example, how I could be a peacemaker when I was not making the war, or how I could feel blessed for being meek when by the time I inherited the earth, I'd be six feet under it, or how I could rejoice and be exceedingly glad about being reviled and persecuted when my reward would be in Heaven. I wanted to go to Heaven, of course, but not quite yet.

My training had not equipped me to grapple with such questions. My training had not equipped me to grapple with *any* questions of a spiritual nature. Certainly I had not been taught to ask questions; if questions somehow arose, I was supposed to search for answers in Scripture. Right was following the Commandments—see Exodus—or the teachings of Jesus—see the Gospels, or the Epistles, or Acts. Wrong was forgetting of the Covenant or of the Lord—see Deuteronomy. Pain was testing—see Job. Though I had been allowed, even encouraged, to explore the physical world without restraint, when it came to the metaphysical world I had been given a road map and instructions from Isaiah: "This is the Way, walk ye in it." My clan's tradition was exegetical, not charismatic; I'd been taught to heed not ranting exhortations or parroted precepts, but well-worded meditations and clear positions supported by citations from the Bible. But I had not been taught to test meditation against observation, nor to extrapolate static position into dynamic action, nor even to compare one Scripture with another; rather, I had been taught to overlook inconsistencies, rationalize apparent contradictions. And I had learned well; I could cite passages, behave kindly and gently, just as I could do simple calculations: add, subtract, multiply, divide, even use a slide rule. But there were branches of human mathematics I did not even know existed—the geometry of history, the algebra of hate and fear and prejudice, the calculus of irony.

And so, predictably, when I tried to plot a human vector on a religious graph I failed, and committed serious sins. First, an act of violence—a clear violation of the Beatitudes, and but for the grace of God, the Sixth Commandment. Then, a failure to repent; what I well knew was wrong felt justified, necessary and *right*. Then, a thought; that what felt right *was* right—that Faith, the Gospel, the Teaching of Jesus, was really what was wrong.

As soon as that thought came to me, I knew my life was over. For though I did not know the word "heresy," I knew for a true Christian such a thought would have been unthinkable. I knew God would forgive me for thinking it, if I could truly and earnestly repent, but I could not imagine He would ever after Call me to His ministry. I was certain I had lost my destiny, and worse, my family's destiny—single-handedly, I had blown a century-and-a-quarter-long tradition. Nor was I going to be able to keep it secret; although it was not absolutely necessary that I receive my Call soon, it had been known to happen to some as young as I. I had always been precocious. Surely I had never been slow. So sooner or later, I was going to have to explain why I, unlike my fathers before me, was not acceptable to God, and the later it got the more explaining I would have to do. Either that, or I was going to have to fake the Call—which notion only proved how far I'd fallen and pushed me further from Grace.

For months I wrestled with the problem. Finally I decided my only course was to preempt Jehovah: to publicly exchange what was no longer my sacred destiny for something that might get me back into the Grace of God—and off the hook with Man. I would, I decided, become a scientist—a doctor or a physicist.

Instead of battling Satan directly, I would wrestle with pestilence or famine or war. I'd find a cure for something, like Jonas Salk, or a zillion uses for something humble, like George Washington Carver, or a way to keep the Russian H-bomb from exploding.

So through the spring and summer of 1959 I practiced diligently with my Acu-math slide rule, spent hours doing experiments with my Gilbert microscope and chemistry sets. To the disconcertion of the county librarian, I abandoned fictional "storybooks" in favor of factual texts; by the time school resumed, I had fought my way through *Kon-Tiki* and *Deliver Us from Evil*, and had so thoroughly absorbed the Real Book series that I could discourse *extempore* and *ad nauseam* on such topics as "The Submarine from David Bushnell's *Turtle* to the USS *Nautilus*" or "The Indian Tribes of North America." Then, toward the end of September, a few weeks after my ninth birthday, I happened on what seemed a way to mitigate my failure. One chill October afternoon I informed Grandmother that when I grew up I wanted to be a medical missionary, like Albert Schweitzer or Tom Dooley. I did not have the courage to make it explicit, but the implication was clear: I did not intend to preach.

Grandmother said nothing, then or ever. For weeks I wondered if she accepted my new vocation or was just waiting on the Lord to change my mind. But when, in early December, she went into physical decline, I could not help but think that she was sick with disappointment. When she died, just after Christmas, I believed I'd killed her, never mind that she was ninety-one. Following her funeral, I dedicated myself to regaining my lost destiny. I cleaved unto Grandmother's teachings more faithfully than when she was alive, and sought more rules to follow; I parsed the Pentateuch like some pedomorphic Essenian, and forced myself to accept as necessary whatever I read there.

Though my behavior was motivated mostly by guilt, terror was also a factor. My mother, seeing that I shied away from Grandmother's body laid out in the funeral home, had told me Grandmother was not really there, but in Heaven, watching over me. My mother meant well but failed to realize how literal were my notions of the Afterlife. Hell—a cave of horror where

there was fire and brimstone always and forever, ruled by red
devils and a snaky, scaly monster—was *real* to me. No less real
was Heaven, where All God's (Departed) Children were issued
white robes and shoes, haloes, and wings, and given power to
look down upon the earth. The idea that Grandmother was
there did not make me feel watched over; it made me feel
watched. Alive, the old lady had been able to suspect, sometimes
anticipate, my mischiefs; now she didn't have to think, all she
had to do was look. There had to be some limit on what she
could see, for the penalty for what I sometimes did beneath my
sheets was to be struck dead—see Genesis 38:9–10. Of course,
it was the Lord who slew Onan, but I did not fear God half so
much as I feared Grandmother. Which was why I quaked in my
hightops when my mother asked me to leave Leviticus and play
cards on Sunday.

Since, I have sometimes wondered at my mother's motivation. Perhaps she hoped to shock me out of what was obviously
an unhealthy state of mind. Perhaps she had merely tired of my
being a pietistic pain in the posterior. Or perhaps she had a vision of the Afterlife as literal as I, pictured Grandmother looking
down from Paradise, and wanted to blow the fuses in the old
lady's halo; though of course I didn't realize it, Grandmother
and my mother had cordially despised each other for decades.

I have also sometimes wondered if my mother knew she was
at risk. For in my aberrant state of mind I might have been capable of rejecting her as an Agent of Satan, tempting me with
pasteboard iniquity. Fortunately I had been steeped in the Principle of Obedience. Though I had not been trained to be a "good
Nazi"—indeed, I was told that even though I was a child, I was
solely responsible for my acts—I had been taught that personal
understanding was not requisite for right action and that it was
more important that I follow instructions than that I know the
reason for them. In fact, I believed I had no right to reasons, or
to think that any offered would seem reasonable to me. Though
I did not love Obedience, I did not question it, for examples of it
were all around me. Daily I saw my Elders striving to obey the
Word of God, despite the illogic and injustice of His world. I saw
them praying prayers that were not answered clearly, if at all, and

persevering in the face of pain, insult, indignity. I believed I too had to learn to act on faith, and if I did not have faith, to act as if I did. In the meantime there was the Commandment to obey, which put it simply: Honor thy father and mother.

So when my mother asked me not just to touch a playing card but to take an *entire deck* into my hand, I did so—but only because the cards were still in the box. Then she told me to open the box, and I found myself between the Scylla of immorality and the Charybdis of disobedience. But in that strait I found insight, and opportunity; this, I decided, was one of those moments when I had to act on faith. I whispered a prayer, closed my eyes, and removed the first card from the box.

Nothing happened.

After a minute I opened my eyes and saw why there had been neither earthquake nor lightning bolt: this card was different from any of the cards over which men died in Dodge City or Tombstone Territory. Although it displayed the black, satanic symbol that denoted the ace of spades, it also bore a human face.

It was not a good face. Nor was it a bad one. It was too . . . complicated for such words. The hair was an unruly white mane, echoed by a fulsome, unabashed mustache; this suggested the rebellious, or worse, the libertine. But the brow was furrowed, as if in disapproval; the nose, presented in left half-profile, was aquiline, authoritative; the jaw was unyielding, the chin severe. And the eyes—there was something *sinister* about the eyes; the left one seemed fixed on some object in the middle distance, the right one peered out accusingly from behind the high nasal bridge.

Few children would have found this portrait prepossessing. But I found it eased my soul. For I recognized it as the visage of an Elder—craggy, experienced, and stern. This, I realized, not the countenance cosmetologically imposed upon her by a saccharine mortician, was the true expression of Grandmother's life and teaching. Seeing it on this playing card, I understood that I loved the old lady far more than I feared her, and missed her more than I could ever say.

And so I came to play cards on Sunday. The game was called Authors, a literary variation on that venerable children's pastime

Go Fish. I'd never played Go Fish and never would—but I did play Authors, in which the usual denominations were assigned to some famous writer, with each card in that denomination representing one of that writer's works and each of the four aces was a novel by Mark Twain. In the coming weeks and months I continued to play Authors, and with a conscience that was almost clear, for I rationalized that these were not really *cards* but *books*, something of which Grandmother had heartily approved.

And if ascent to heaven had gifted her with an enlarged perspective, Grandmother approved my playing, because Authors was for me a vital canon, introducing me by name to some of the great writers and texts. I lost my innocence of cards, but I also lost my ignorance of literature. In the next few years the game would guide me to read works that even my most encouraging mentors might have said were inappropriate to my age. I took a run at *Julius Caesar* and delighted in the language, which reminded me of the King James Bible, though I had no real understanding of what was ultimately at issue. I was less delighted with *The Deer-slayer*—I hated Cooper's prose, found his woodcraft ludicrous and his Indians lacking in the spiritual life other reading had taught me to expect—but I liked Longfellow and was excited by the rhythm of "Song of Hiawatha." Though I did not know a trochee from an anapest, I identified with the characters and situation of Whittier's "Snow-Bound." By the time I started junior high I had at least attempted many of the works everybody wants to have read and nobody wants to read. But none would mean as much to me as the works from the Authors canon that I first took up: two novels by Mark Twain.

I was a few days shy of six years old when I first saw the face of bigotry. It was September of 1956. I was on the playground, during the first recess of my first day of school, looking to make friends, as my mother said I should. I approached a little boy of Irish ancestry. Shyly, I introduced myself. The little Irish boy took one look at me and called me a nigger.

This was more or less predictable, for though I did not grow up in a locale renowned for racial outrage, in the outback of Arkansas or Alabama, say, or of Mississippi or Missouri, I did grow up in the mountains of western Pennsylvania, an area with some history of hostility—in the 1920s the Klan had been a major political party—and the kind of rural isolation some find picturesque, idyllic, even virtuous.

In 1956, the poor little one-horse town outside of which I lived, though it was the largest for forty miles and the county seat, had three traffic lights, one thousand-watt sunup-to-sundown AM radio station, and a telephone system entirely dependent on human operators. Locals thought of the place as God's Country, in part because there were a hundred and seventy-three churches there, by actual count. But if it was God's Country, He had no love of blacks. In 1910, when my clan immigrated, there was a Negro community of perhaps four score and ten, but by 1960 there were only a third as many blacks as churches, and in terms of racial brotherhood it was a valley in the shadow of nowhere.

Not that the whites were bigots, exactly. But many lived in secluded coves and hollows, in a rustic style about which only an opiated romantic would rhapsodize; a sober realist would have termed their lives depressing, delimiting, and deprived. Many of these whites had never left the county; some had seldom been to town. To them, Negroes were *rarae aves*, as unusual as such miracles of rare device as radio, telephone, and indoor plumbing; their feelings may have been hostile but were as much xenophobic as racist.

Some of their more cosmopolitan cousins were real racists, classic ones, who justified white political supremacy on a theory of white superiority taken from Scripture: Negroes wore the mark of Cain or were the accursed sons of Ham. But most whites, if asked, would have paid at least lip service to brotherhood; more than a few preached it, and some practiced what they preached. Still, even most of these were segregationists who believed that "folks should stick to their own kind."

And so God's Country had a number of quaint customs reminiscent of points south of Mason and Dixon's Line. No law, and few formal customs, mandated segregation, but basically blacks lived, loved, worshiped God, died, and were buried among themselves; and in all things purely social they were separate as the thumb.

This made God's Country seem a placid place, for that which was not *de jure*, or even uniformly *de facto*, could be kept *sub rosa*. Blacks who did not like it left it; those who stayed stayed quiet, in part because their heads were in the lion's mouth, in part because they *liked* quiet. Though there were incidents from time to time, confrontations were short-lived and physical assaults virtually unknown.

Verbal disparagements were, if not unheard of, then unheard. Some blacks spoke resentfully of whites, but never said a mumbling word when any whites were present. Whites were equally circumspect. Though few used the term "Negro," which my family preferred, most blacks were not insulted by the term most whites did use: "colored." Even bigots did not say "nigger" to a black person's face; in God's Country, all but the worst bigots were polite.

But "nigger" did come trippingly off some white tongues when no blacks were present. Somehow children learned the word. Even if they had been bred in some hillbilly hollow where a black child was a vague abstraction, they knew one when they saw one, and what to call him when they did. So it was with the little boy of Irish ancestry, whose dress and accent suggested that the school bus had transported him to what must have seemed to him an alien place. No doubt he felt lost, and terrified—terrified, perhaps, of me. But before he boarded that bus he'd learned the word "nigger," and that someone who looked like me should be hurt by it.

I had learned no such thing. Though my Elders had wanted to warn me about "nigger" and the iceberg of bigotry of which it was the tip, my mother had insisted I not be led to expect an evil I might not experience. Until the little boy of Irish ancestry hurled his epithet, I had never heard the word. I had never even heard *of* it. I did not know what a nigger was, or that I was supposed to be one, or that hearing the word was supposed to hurt me. So I stood there, unintimidated, uncomprehending, certainly uninjured, albeit a bit confused. Which confused him. He grew impatient, then frustrated—his face turned pink, then red. "Nigger!" he repeated, shouting, as if he thought I might be deaf. Then he punched me in the nose.

Such things did not happen every day, but they were fairly frequent—more frequent as I acquired a reputation for being good at schoolwork. They did not always escalate from insult to assault, but it happened often enough to make insults alone terrifying. I still did not know what "nigger" meant, but I began to cringe before the word, as if I had been struck. I made no mention of this persecution; the bruises did not show much on my brown skin; the stains I explained away as residue of spontaneous nosebleeds.

But eventually my Elders discovered what was going on. My mother, who at the time had lived in God's Country for less than a decade, swore to put a stop to it, and telephoned some of the other mothers. She learned a lesson about God's Country when one of them called *her* a nigger. Grandmother, who had resided in God's Country for almost half a century, said I might as well learn now how to deal with "poor white trash," and taught me to keep my expression impassive and move past my tormentors sedately, or turn and walk away "with dignity"—all in order to deny the poor white trash the satisfaction of knowing they had hurt my feelings. My father, who had grown up in God's Country, said I should learn to *have* no feelings; then sticks and stones might break my bones, but names would never hurt me.

It seemed my father missed the fact that these little bigots were *using* sticks and stones, but I accepted his instruction, and Grandmother's, and worked to master my new lessons. Meanwhile, I happened on a technique of my own: to retaliate with nastier names. Grandmother had unknowingly supplied one basic formulation, and by attending to the vernacular of some of the less pious blacks in town, I compiled a lexicon of racial insults. I understood the connotation of "trash," "redneck," "peckerwood," or "ofay" no better than I understood that of "nigger," but I wielded those words with force and flair, and soon I learned to modify the nouns with vulgar adjectives. Usually this language set the little bigots back on their heels long enough for me to walk away with what looked like dignity—though in my heart I knew I was running scared.

In September of 1958, when I was almost eight, verbal retaliation began to fail. Frank exchanges of epithets led to violent attacks with greater frequency. From these I could not defend myself, for I lacked both the training and the will to fight. I had been taught that physical resistance was morally wrong. So I did what I had been trained to do: I took it to the Lord in prayer. I thought I'd found a surefire formula in the language of Psalm 144, and while winter kept us much indoors, it did seem God had promised to "rid me, and deliver me from the hand of strange children."

But that spring, on Good Friday, as it happened, God failed to protect me. In protecting myself I committed the violent act that led to heresy and the loss of my destiny, and my clan's. Though I longed for redemption, I clung to the fruit of heresy: a clear decision to defend myself by any means necessary. Even after Grandmother's death and my rededication to the faith, I continued to do battle, for the way of meekness seemed a sure road to suicide. But though I fought, I understood I could not win. Violence was *wrong*; therefore victory was no reason for rejoicing; indeed, every triumph took me further from salvation, and made it less likely I could regain my destiny. Yet it seemed that the only way to preserve my body was to put my soul in peril.

In fact, my mind was in greater peril. For though I still did not know many of the connotations of the word "nigger," I had come to a fuller understanding of the phrase "poor white trash." At first I had assumed white trash identified themselves as such by the way they treated me, but eventually I noticed that the children most prone to insult and assault me did tend to be poor. They also tended to come from families which were less educated, less sober, less hardworking, less devout than mine. Though I had thought little about "poor white trash" while Grandmother was alive, after her death, like all her recollected utterances, it assumed biblical proportions. I began to see whites who were poor as both enemies and social and intellectual inferiors. And so, despite my suffering at the hands of bigots, by August of 1960, I was well on the way to becoming a bigot myself.

Enter, to the rescue, the Authors ace of spades, *The Adventures of Tom Sawyer*, which I borrowed from the county library, much to the relief of the librarian, who found my penchant for nonfiction abnormal. But in fact I checked the novel out because "the author" assured me that it *wasn't* fiction, but rather a recording of "adventures" that had "really occurred," and that the people who appeared in it were real—Tom Sawyer was a combination of three boys, but somebody else named Huck Finn was "drawn from life."

And indeed, when I read in the opening lines how Aunt Polly "pulled her spectacles down and looked over them" and then "put them up and looked out under them," I felt a warm surge of recognition and affection, for I had seen Grandmother do those very things at least a thousand times. I also liked Sid, the "quiet boy" with "no adventurous, troublesome ways," who attended school regularly, and liked it, and always did his chores; he reminded me of me. And I was thoroughly intrigued by "the small colored boy," the hard-working Jim, who was the first Negro I had ever seen in a storybook. I did not realize Jim was a slave and had no choice other than to be industrious; I just noted that even when Tom supposedly helped Jim split kindling, "Jim did three-fourths of the work," and I liked Jim the more because of it.

I did not like Tom. He was a lazy, lying hooky-player, and not so much clever as slick. My dislike crystallized at the end of the first chapter, where Tom picks a fight with a boy who is better dressed and a stranger. Though the insults that lead to combat are nonracial, I read my experience and myself into the situation. While I did not see this strange boy as black, I did see him as *me*, assaulted for no reason other than difference. Tom, I decided, had he lived in God's Country, would have been among the worst of my tormentors.

So disgusted was I with Tom that I almost put the book down at the end of chapter 1. But I had learned from hours of Bible reading to peruse with patience and persistence, and so pushed on to chapter 2. Then things grew complicated. Jim made his second appearance, and I saw that he was a slave, and worse, that he had to kowtow to "Marse Tom," and worst, that Aunt Polly, who seemed so much like Grandmother, owned him.

Again I almost put the book down. Once more I persisted, and was rewarded with rich recountings of the familiar rituals of Sunday services, and with a scene of poetic punishment for

Tom, who not only broke Commandments, but failed to take learning Scriptures seriously, and even perverted Sunday school to accomplish selfish ends.

At that point I thought I understood what the story was about: sin and salvation. Obviously, these characters were going to see the error of their ways. Aunt Polly was already crying over a minor wrong done to Tom; she would soon see she was doing a major wrong to Jim. And Tom would either repent or come to a gruesome end. I read on, at least half hoping for the latter resolution. But then another character entered, and upset my simplistic morality play.

I hated Huck as soon as I saw him, for he seemed to epitomize the poor white trash that was making my life miserable. But then I began to pity him. Unlike Tom, I did not envy Huck the "freedom" to sleep "on doorsteps in fine weather and in empty hogsheads in wet." I didn't know what a hogshead was, but it sounded like it had something to do with pigs. I knew pigs, and so I saw nothing romantic in Huck's sleeping arrangements, or in any other aspect of his poverty, illiteracy, and religious sciolism. Indeed, Huck seemed lonely and sad. I fixed on his status as "the juvenile pariah of the village," whose society was forbidden to other boys, whose condition was outcast. Not that I saw myself in him, but I did know how he must have felt. Sympathy became empathy, and a subconscious decision to give Huck a chance. After all, he hadn't done anything bad . . . and then he did, in one bit of dialogue, concerning the use of "spunk-water" to cure warts: "Jeff told Johnny Baker, and Johnny told Jim Hollis, and Jim told Ben Rogers, and Ben told a nigger, and the nigger told me."

That did it for Huckleberry Finn, that ignorant redneck white trash peckerwood. That did it for Tom Sawyer, too, because he replied, "They'll all lie. Leastways all but the nigger. I don't know *him*. But I never see a nigger that *wouldn't* lie." In fact that did it for the book; that book was *closed*. Had it not been property of the county library, that book would have suffered serious damage.

But what was so easily put out of sight was not so easily put out of mind, for when my fury faded it came to me that what went on in the book was actually quite similar to what happened in God's Country. The author, this Mark Twain, was like the white people who were not bigots. He called Negroes "negroes," or "colored," which was acceptable. He did use the word "nigger," but only to report what the people in the book said—people he'd grown up with, "schoolmates of mine," he'd written. In that sense, I used "nigger" too—how else would I describe what the little bigots called me? And even Huck and Tom, although they used the word, did not use it in front of Jim. Nor did they beat him up. So I went back to the book.

Then I realized something more complicated: both Huck and Tom used the word, but with a crucial difference. When Huck said "nigger" he meant somebody who was a Negro but as truthful as a person who was white. Tom rejected the Negro's knowledge, and not because he'd known this Negro to lie; Tom knew nothing about the Negro, not even his name. When Tom said "nigger" he meant somebody who was a liar because he was a Negro, and for no other reason. Tom Sawyer was a bigot. But Huck accepted the knowledge of this Negro—this *nigger*. He set the nigger equal with the white boys, and apparently thought nothing of it.

Once again I found myself sympathizing with Huck, making excuses for him. Tom was supposedly a respectable boy, with the advantages of education and religion; for him to use the word "nigger" was obviously wrong. But Huck was ignorant, innocent of both public and Sunday school. Perhaps he knew no better than to say "nigger." I found myself actually liking him, and when I went back to the book it was not to follow the adventures of Tom Sawyer but to discover the fate of Huckleberry Finn. I was overjoyed that in the end he was rescued from poverty, homelessness, illiteracy, and apostasy —that he slept on clean sheets, went to school, was taught the Bible; that he had a future on earth and a chance at Heaven. Since I knew from the Authors cards that there was a book by the name of *Adventures of Huckleberry Finn*, that was the next thing I borrowed from the library.

I did not know that *Huckleberry Finn* was a trickier text than *Tom Sawyer*. I did not know that dramatic irony and first-person narration created serious critical problems, or that subtleties of grammar and diction—like the difference between connotation and denotation—were beyond my intellectual grasp. I did not even realize I was reading fiction—how could I, when in the conclusion of *Tom Sawyer*, Twain claimed not only that the characters were real, but that most of them still lived? And so Huck lived for me, though I felt a bit superior to him, since I already knew how to read and had long understood that Moses had been dead a considerable time. And I understood that the word "nigger" appeared often because Huck was doing the writing, as well as much of the talking. I was a bit surprised to find that Jim used it—I had never imagined a Negro would use that word, much less heard one do so—but I was so happy to see him again that I let it slide; such was my unsophistication that I thought this was Jim from *Tom Sawyer* miraculously grown to manhood.

Eventually I forgave Huck's use of the word, for I noticed that while he occasionally referred to Jim as a nigger, he never *called* him nigger. The difference was clear when Huck's father used the word, railing about "a prowling, thieving, infernal, white-shirted free nigger" who was also a college professor. Pap Finn's use of "nigger" was not only insulting but indiscriminate; he hated Negroes, even if they were as clean and respectable as any Negro could be; Huck, for all his crudeness, was obviously better than his upbringing. This impressed me.

What impressed me more, as I read on, was not what Huck called Jim but the way he treated him. Tom wanted to tie Jim up, but Huck refused and wouldn't even go with Tom when he crawled off to play a trick on Jim. Huck would not tell Judge Thatcher that he feared his father had returned, but he did tell Jim. And though in *Tom Sawyer*, Huck says eating with a Negro is something "a body's got to do . . . when he's awful hungry" that "he wouldn't want to do as a steady thing," in his own book Huck just says to Jim, "Pass me along another hunk of fish and some hot corn-bread."

I was still more impressed by what happens on the one occasion when Huck is unkind to Jim. After being lost in thick fog, he plays a Sawyerish trick on Jim and calls him "a tangle-headed old fool." Jim fights back with word I recognized: "Dat truck dah is *trash*; en trash is what people is dat puts dirt on de head er dey fren's en makes 'em ashamed." Though I could not then appreciate the risk Jim ran by showing such spirit to a white, I recognized the virtue in Huck's response.

> It was fifteen minutes before I could work myself up to go and humble myself to a nigger—but I done it, and I warn't ever sorry for it afterward, neither.

But what most impressed me—what almost had to, given my upbringing—was the moment in chapter 31 when Huck resolves that rather than turn Jim in he'll go to Hell. Not that I thought that Huck was really wrong. But I understood that Huck thought he was wrong, and thought he would go to a Hell as literal as the one in which I myself believed. I was awed by Huck's defiance. I *admired* it. I wondered if I would have the courage to do such a thing. I wondered if St. John might not have quoted Jesus incorrectly, for it was clear to me that to lay down your soul for a friend required greater love than to lay down your life.

I did not think much more about Mark Twain for almost a decade. During that time I did not become a literary sophisticate; though I read a number of the classics, I also devoured a lot of so-called trash, and often got the categories mixed. (I thought *A Connecticut Yankee* had much in common with *Glory Road*, a science fantasy penned by Twain's fellow Missourian Robert A. Heinlein.) But at least I learned what fiction *was*, and how to deal with symbolism and several types of irony.

I did become what some might call a religious sophisticate— or a secular humanist. Not that I became an atheist, but I stopped believing in a literal Hell or a factual Bible, or that the solution to every earthly problem could be found in Scripture. Rather, I decided the solution to every earthly problem could be found in a library, provided it had books enough.

Certainly that seemed true for me. It was not hyperbole to say that books borrowed from the county library had kept me almost sane during my adolescence in God's Country. And when, in the fall of 1968, I matriculated at the University of Pennsylvania in Philadelphia, I quickly found refuge from the cultural contradictions thrust upon me by the City of Brotherly

Love and the Ivy League in the Van Pelt Library. Partly to escape the dormitory and my ultra-preppy roommate, I studied
there almost every night, and when I wasn't doing assignments,
I went roaming through the stacks, picking books at random. I
had been admitted to the university's General Honors Program, and one of the perks was access to a private study lounge,
where I could stretch out on a couch, drink a smuggled-in cup
of coffee, and think in peace. It was there that I learned to
read—not just to absorb a text, but to trace origins, parse meanings. It was there that I discovered the power of plain language.
And it was there, at long last, that I received my Call—not to
minister, but to write.

This was not the usual undergraduate "career decision"; that,
I'd already made. I was as serious about writing as a student
could be. I took creative writing workshops, invented my own
major so I could take more writing courses, submitted stories to
campus magazines, even collected rejection slips from all the
best national magazines and journals. But though I hoped I'd
make a living as a writer, I had never seen that as a replacement
for the ministry. Then one night I underwent a classic conversion experience, with symptoms right out of William James—
heart palpitations, euphoria, a sensation of mental clarity. I felt
that some internal void had suddenly been filled, that I knew,
now, not what I wanted to do in life, but what I was *supposed* to
do. I felt free and happy and ineffably light.

It was a glorious moment, but it fell somewhat short of
Pentecost—the Spirit filled me but somehow failed to give me
the gift of utterance; no multitudes gathered suddenly to marvel at my words. My fellow students still had trouble
understanding my characters' motivations. My teachers were
neither more encouraging nor less critical—those who heard
me bear witness to my experience suspected I was full of new
wine. Meanwhile, editors who weighed my work in the balance still found it wanting.

Had I been trained in a more demonstrative tradition I might
have been discouraged. But I knew that even in matters of faith,
spirit alone was insufficient; you might have been licked by
tongues as of fire, but you still had to go to seminary. I was

already at a university—a secular seminary—and I thought all I had to do was follow the formula of the curriculum: read the work of great writers, and write constantly, sometimes in imitation of those writers, until I "found my own voice," as they say. It might even have been that simple had I not been black and had it not been the fag end of the sixties. But I was and it was, and so I was forced to deal with a host of complications arising out of something called "The Black Aesthetic."

The assumption behind the Black Aesthetic was that there was or ought to be some *difference* between works of art produced by persons of African ancestry, black Americans in particular, and those produced by persons of European ancestry, white Americans in particular. The idea had its origins in the eighteenth-century European belief that there were inherent physical, intellectual, and even moral differences between the races (with the Europeans being superior, of course), which could be measured by the standard of literary production—by the fact, as one Frenchman put it, that "Negroes . . . have never written a philosophical treatise, and never will." This notion was promoted in America by Thomas Jefferson, who reported in his *Notes on the State of Virginia*,

> . . . never yet could I find that a black had uttered a thought above the level of a plain narration. . . . Misery is often the parent of the most affecting touches in poetry.—Among the blacks is misery enough, God knows, but no poetry. Love is the peculiar cestrum of the poet. Their love is ardent, but it kindles the senses only, not the imagination.

Jefferson used this literary "evidence" to argue that blacks "are inferior to the whites in the endowments both of body and mind," and that this "unfortunate difference . . . of faculty, is a powerful obstacle to the emancipation of these people."

For the next hundred and fifty years or so, Negro intellectuals wasted their time trying to argue the reverse. As late as 1931, for example, James Weldon Johnson declared:

> The world does not know that a people is great until that people produces great literature and art. No people that has

produced great literature and art has ever been looked on by the world as distinctly inferior. The status of the Negro in the United States is more a question of national attitude toward the race than of actual conditions. And nothing will do more to change that mental attitude and raise his status than a demonstration of intellectual parity by the Negro through the production of literature and art.

But a few years later, in his "Blueprint for Negro Writing," Richard Wright dismissed most "Negro writing in the past" as a collection of "prim and decorous ambassadors who went a-begging to white America . . . dressed in the knee-pants of servility, curtsying to show that the Negro was not inferior"; and by the fifties and sixties many black intellectuals had more or less agreed that consciously attempting to demonstrate anything to white people through literature was both counterproductive and counterrevolutionary. LeRoi Jones, even before he took the name Baraka, claimed there in fact *was* no legitimate Negro literature, nor had there ever been, because historically "Negroes who found themselves in a position to pursue some art, especially the art of literature, have been members of the Negro middle class."

Oddly, ironically, perhaps even embarrassingly, Jones sometimes agreed with Jefferson. Of pioneer black poet Phillis Wheatley—he called her "Phillis Whatley"—Jefferson said, "The compositions published under her name are below the dignity of criticism." Jones said that Wheatley's "pleasant imitations of eighteenth century English poetry are . . . ludicrous departures from the huge black voices that splintered southern nights with their *hollers, chants, arwhoolies, and ballits.*" If there was ever going to be a Negro literature, Jones went on to insist, "it must disengage itself from the weak, heinous elements of the culture that spawned it," and learn that "the most successful fiction of most Negro writing is in its emotional content."

Strong as Jones' opinion was, an even stronger one was in vogue in 1971, especially among black students at the University of Pennsylvania. It was that of James T. Stewart, a Philadelphia-based saxophonist whose essay "The Development of the Black

Revolutionary Artist" had been published in *Black Dialogue* in the winter of 1966.

> The dilemma of the "negro" artist is that he makes assumptions based on the wrong models. He makes assumptions based on white models. These assumptions are not only wrong, they are even antithetical to his existence. The black artist must construct models which correspond to his own reality. The models must be non-white. Our models must be consistent with a black style, our natural aesthetic styles, and our moral and spiritual styles.

My dilemma was that I wanted—more, needed—to be an artist. Perforce, I wanted to be a Negro artist, for it never occurred to me I *could* be any other kind. But what Stewart called "white" models were the only ones I had—the only ones I had ever had. From the point of view of the Black Aesthetic, I had spent my life reading all the wrong things—most recently, the texts required by the university's English department, before that, the Authors canon, and before that the hymns of Charles Wesley, Isaac Watts, and James Claire Taylor, and the King James Version of the Bible. In fact, these last were for me less models or assumptions than elements of my identity; I wasn't sure I could accept other models, even if I found them.

And finding them wasn't easy. Not that anthropological and archaeological descriptions of non-western art and culture, and even examples thereof, were entirely absent from the library's catalogue and stacks. But the essence of the argument was that nothing created by white people—which is to say, most of what was in the library, including the logic of the catalogue—could provide an accurate guide to the quality of the examples. As Stewart put it, "the point of the whole thing is that we must emancipate our minds from Western values and standards."

Which meant there was no reliable canon—not even the comfort of a card game. Nor did Jones or Stewart offer much help; they seemed to think the only American Negro art form worth talking about was music. Jones mentioned some writers—Jean Toomer, Richard Wright, Ralph Ellison, and James Baldwin—but only to damn them with faint praise.

Nor were there clear criteria by which a canon might be identified. It helped only somewhat to say that the texts should be "non-white"—which I assumed meant the author would be non-white. According to my own logic and the arguments of both Jones and Stewart, there had to be more to it. But what? Jones suggested that "Negro literature" should be "a legitimate product of the Negro experience in America," which suggested that the "more" might have something to do with another rubric then in vogue, the Black Experience. But that led to some nasty questions.

For example, though Phillis Wheatley's poetry was hardly "non-white" in form, Wheatley herself had been born in Africa and had lived there until she was seven or eight years old—long enough, surely, to have internalized some awareness of the cultural forms of her people. Then she had been captured, transported, auctioned, and enslaved; if there was a quintessential "Negro experience in America" Phillis Wheatley had it. So who was James T. Stewart, Philadelphia resident and player of an instrument invented in Paris, by a Frenchman, to suggest that her models were "antithetical?" Who was LeRoi Jones, born in Newark, educated at Howard, Columbia, and the New School for Social Research, to deride her as one who had failed to "tap" her "legitimate cultural tradition" and who "did not realize where the reality of [her] experience lay"? Maybe it was just that Wheatley, in her genius, discerned something Jones did not—a human, artistic, spiritual link between eighteenth-century English poetry and those "*hollers, chants, arwhoolies, and ballits.*"

Nor did it help to link "non-white" aesthetics to some political position. If, as Stewart said, "the point of the whole thing" was to "emancipate our minds," then surely one of my models had to be *Narrative of the Life of Frederick Douglass*, which was about mental and religious and spiritual liberation as much as physical liberation. True, Douglass had described how he derived the determination to resist whipping from a juju root provided by a "genuine African." But he'd also described how he derived artistic models from *The Columbian Orator*, how the documents it contained "gave tongue to interesting thoughts of my own soul, which had frequently flashed through my mind, and died away for want of utterance." Should Douglass have rejected Sheridan because he was not a Negro but an Irishman, and because the emancipation for which he called was not for Negroes but for Catholics? And should I reject the most powerful of the slave narratives because its formal antecedents were "white"?

And beyond the problem of the canon, there was the problem of aesthetic *principles*—the criteria by which something could be judged good or bad. Jones said, "A Negro literature, to be a legitimate product of the Negro experience in America, must get at that experience in exactly the terms America has proposed for it, in its most ruthless identity," but I couldn't make much sense of that, nor of "the most successful fiction of most Negro writing is in its emotional content"; maybe I was blind, or maybe it was the error of a white copyeditor, but it seemed to me that sentence didn't even track. And Stewart threw me for a total loop with this:

> In our movement toward the future, "ineptitude" and "unfitness" will be an aspect of what we do. These are the words of the established order—the middle-class value judgments. We must turn these values on themselves . . . ultimately, be estranged from the dominant culture. This estrangement must be nurtured in order to generate and energize our black artists. This means that he cannot be "successful" in any sense that has meaning in white critical evaluations. Nor can his work ever be called "good" in any context or meaning that could make sense to that traditional critique.

Like every aspiring writer, I badly wanted to believe that all those who criticized my work were ignoramuses who could be ignored with impunity, and while I tried to tell myself that my artistic failures were in fact brilliant successes that suffered from being judged by Philistines according to inappropriate, European-oriented standards, I just could not accept an aesthetic theory that transformed me from apprentice to master craftsman without benefit of labor, especially a theory expressed in such reactive terms.

But if I did not accept it, or something like it, my fate, according to Jones, was to produce work of "agonizing mediocrity," especially as I was surely an embodiment of the Negro middle-class artist Jones had damned. And yet what Jones said about such artists was not true of me. I emphatically did *not* want to write only to "exhibit" my "familiarity with social graces," or look "at literature as merely another way of gaining prestige in the white world for the Negro middle-class." I emphatically *did* want to investigate the human soul. But I wanted to do it for what in Jones' view were emphatically the wrong reasons: moral imperatives drawn from precisely the models I was supposed to reject. It seemed I had to come up with something *different*—if I didn't, my work would be not only mediocre but almost sinful; like a minister who preached falsely, I would damn myself to the Hell in which I no longer—supposedly—believed.

For weeks I roamed the library stacks, looking for answers, finding none. But finally I came upon a fat volume with a thin title—*Literary Geniuses on Literary Genius*, or something like that. It was one of those hodgepodge anthologies slammed together in haste by academics desperate to pad the curriculum vitae, and published by presses too cheap to pay for permission to reprint anything protected by copyright. This particular academic had ranged widely through the public domain, coming up with everything from long-winded Greek expositions to whole sections from John Locke to pithy aphorisms from Chinese mystics and American humorists. One of those short statements caught my eye: "the difference between the *almost right* word and the *right* word is really a large matter—'tis the difference between the lightning-bug and the lightning."

What attracted me was not that the attribution was to my old friend Mark Twain, but rather that there was nothing *cultural* about the statement. There was nothing political about it. There was nothing middle-class about it, nor anything black or white—except the meaning. There was nothing *linguistic* about it, either. Although in another language it might not be a bon mot, it would still make sense. It would make sense to an African; it would have to, because if it didn't, *Africans* couldn't make sense to other Africans. If you wanted to construct a literary aesthetic, it seemed like a pretty good place to start.

Of course, there was a problem: Mark Twain was a white guy. Worse, he was a middle- if not upper-class white guy. Worst, he was a Southerner. Stewart, Jones, et alia would have rejected him out of hand, and I almost did too. But fortunately that desperate academic had also included a longer piece called "How to Tell a Story," and fortunately I had not grown so narrowminded as not to read it. That essay made it clear to me that Mark Twain understood the aesthetics of literature a lot better than Stewart or even Jones.

"How to Tell a Story" was premised on a frankly nationalistic aesthetic.

> The humorous story is American, the comic story is English, the witty story is French . . .
>
> . . . The art of telling a humorous story . . . was created in America, and has remained at home.

But one was not able to tell an American story simply because one was an American—indeed, Twain began the essay with a careful disclaimer.

> I do not claim that I can tell a story as it ought to be told. I only claim to know how a story ought to be told, for I have been almost daily in the company of the most expert story-tellers for many years.

Nor was one endowed with the ability to tell a humorous story by experience alone.

> The humorous story is strictly a work of art—high and delicate art—and only an artist can tell it.

And then came the surprise: despite the opening disclaimer, at the end Twain talked about a story he himself told from the platform. He described it as a "negro ghost story," and proceeded to reproduce it in dialect. I knew that Jones and others would have called that cultural appropriation and derided it as an insult. But however Twain came by the tale, and however he told it, four things about his treatment of it could not be ignored.

First, Twain had respect for the source of the tale and was not ashamed to acknowledge it—he specifically called the tale a "negro ghost story." Second, he had respect for the original form; the story was told in dialect, which meant that Twain, in telling it, took on a black persona—something he didn't seem to mind. Third, he had respect for the artistry of the form; far from implying that to tell a "negro ghost story" was an easy thing, he spoke of practicing the technique and said that getting the pause at the end right was "the most troublesome and aggravating and uncertain thing you ever undertook." To me, confused as I was about aesthetics in general, and the racial dynamics of aesthetics in particular, all this was tremendously exciting, for it seemed so clear, so . . . *settling*. Accordingly, I searched the stacks for other of Twain's aesthetic pronouncements.

I had to do a bit of digging, because those pronouncements were scattered about and often seemed offhand. One piece I happened upon was written, apparently, when an editor invited Twain to discourse on his methods. Twain claimed not to have any methods, but went on to give a different spin on the business of aesthetic models.

> Let us guess that whenever we read a sentence and like it, we unconsciously store it away in our model-chamber; and it goes with the myriad of its fellows to the building, brick by brick, of the eventual edifice which we call our style. And let us guess that whenever we run across other forms—bricks—whose colour, or some other defect, offends us, we unconsciously reject these, and so one never finds them in our edifice. If I have subjected myself to any training processes, and no doubt I have, it must have been in this unconscious or half-conscious fashion. I think it unlikely that deliberate and consciously methodical training is usual in the craft. I think it likely that the training most in use is of this unconscious sort, and is guided and governed and made by-and-by unconsciously systematic, by an automatically-working taste—a taste which selects and rejects without asking you for any help, and patiently and steadily improves itself without troubling you to approve or applaud.

Of course I realized that Twain was begging the aesthetic question as much as answering it. From whence came the initial criteria by which bricks were accepted or rejected? And what of that line from the Gospel, "The stone which the builders rejected, the same is become the head of the corner"? And yet I was not so hung up on logic as to miss Twain's point: that whatever the aesthetic criteria were, and wherever they originated, the process of becoming a writer meant not applying them so much as internalizing them, and making them undeniably and idiosyncratically *yours*.

And unlike Jones and Stewart, Twain offered, in "Fenimore Cooper's Literary Offences," precise criteria. I was fascinated to discover that although his objections were not exactly what mine had been, he also rejected Cooper's Indians, and felt, as I had, that the book had been written by somebody who had never spent an hour in the woods. I did not at first realize that Twain was being his usual ironic self with all this business about the "nineteen rules governing literary art in the domain of romantic fiction," but by the time I figured out there was no such list outside Twain's own head, I had decided that the rules made *sense*. A tale *should* accomplish something and arrive somewhere; the episodes *should* be necessary parts of the tale; the characters *should* talk like normal people, and *should* be so clearly defined that the reader can predict their behavior. And even though I noticed that Twain only listed eighteen rules, it seemed to me they were a pretty good blueprint for writing—Negro writing included.

Of course Twain was still a white guy; his rules therefore constituted exactly the kind of "white model" that Stewart said a black artist had to eschew. Which left me with a problem until I found a little essay called "What Paul Bourget Thinks of Us," wherein was written:

Does the native novelist try to generalize the nation? No, he lays plainly before you the ways and speech and life of a few people grouped in a certain place—his own place—and that is one book. In time he and his brethren will report to you the life and the people of the whole nation—the life of a group in a New England village; in a New York village; in

a Texan village; in an Oregon village; in villages in fifty
States and Territories; then the farm-life in fifty States and
Territories; a hundred patches of life and groups of people in
a dozen widely separated cities. And the Indians will be attended to; and the cowboys; and the gold and silver miners;
and the negroes; and the Idiots and Congressmen; and the
Irish, the Germans, the Italians, the Swedes, the French,
the Chinamen, the Greasers; and the Catholics, the Methodists, the Presbyterians, the Congregationalists, the Bap-
tists, the Spiritualists, the Mormons, the Shakers, the
Quakers, the Jews, the Campbellites, the infidels, the Christian Scientists, the Mind-Curists, the Faith-Curists, the
train-robbers, the White Caps, the Moonshiners. And
when a thousand able novels have been written, *there* you
have the soul of the people, the life of the people, the speech
of the people: and not anywhere else can these be had. And
the shadings of character, manners, feelings, ambitions, will
be infinite.

I sat there in the private lounge of the General Honors Program of the Van Pelt Library of the University of Pennsylvania,
and I thought about that. I thought about being black and middle-class, and Christian—about all my antithetical models. I
thought about James T. Stewart and all the black artists in the
world, on the one hand, and Mark Twain on the other. I thought
about Grandmother. I thought about Aunt Polly. I thought about
Jim, the runaway slave, who called himself rich because he had
stolen himself, and about Huck, the piece of poor white trash,
who first humbled himself to a nigger and then abandoned all
hope of Heaven to free that nigger, and about the middle-class
white Southern man who had created both of them. I thought
not only about wanting and needing to write, but about what
kind of writer I wanted to be, what kind of stories I wanted to
tell. It seemed to me I had to decide, forever, between two things.
I studied a minute, sort of holding my breath, and then I said to
myself, "All right, then, I'll *go* to hell."

1996

E. L. Doctorow

American writer E. L. Doctorow (born in 1931), known for novels that deftly blend fiction and fact, is the author of several books set in 19th-century America. These include *Welcome to Hard Times* (1960), which reclaimed the genre of the Western; *The Waterworks* (1994), which is set in 1870s New York City; and *The March* (2005), which fictionalized General William Tecumseh Sherman's Civil War march through Georgia. He is also the author of a number of works set in the 20th century, including *The Book of Daniel* (1971), *Ragtime* (1975), *Loon Lake* (1980), *World's Fair* (1985), *Billy Bathgate* (1989), and *City of God* (2000). Doctorow worked as a book editor for nearly a decade before focusing on his own writing full time. One can almost hear the voice of the editor in him in the piece that follows, pointing out to Mark Twain the inconsistencies in his portrayal of Tom Sawyer, who sometimes seems to be an adolescent, sometimes a child, sometimes not any particular age at all.

Introduction to
The Adventures of Tom Sawyer

Sam Clemens was thirty-seven when he began writing *The Adventures of Tom Sawyer*. He wrote most of it in the space of two summers, 1874 and 1875, devoting the year in between to the business schemes, lectures, writing projects, and domestic and financial matters with which they filled his exuberant life. He spent the summer of 1874 at Quarry Farm, in the countryside above Elmira, New York, with his young wife, Livy Langdon, and their two children, Susy, age two and Clara, a newborn. Each morning he went off to write in a self-contained study built specially for him, an octagonal room with big windows and panoramic views of the hills and valleys of upstate New York.

Clemens had made himself at home in many parts of the country, any one of which would have contained and nourished another writer for life. A Missourian by birth, he spoke with a slow Southern drawl. But it was out west that he had found fame as a journalist and humorist. His attachment to the state of New York came of his love and courtship of Livy, the daughter of a wealthy Elmira coal mine operator. And now, with his income as a popular American author and lecturer, he was building the grandiose mansion on Farmington Avenue in Hartford, Connecticut, that would establish him as a literary New Englander, a friend of the famous Beecher family—Harriet, the author of *Uncle Tom's Cabin*, and her brothers and sisters—a close colleague of William Dean Howells, the editor of the *Atlantic Monthly*, and a dinner companion of the elderly Brahmins Emerson and Oliver Wendell Holmes. He was the most peripatetic of authors, unparalleled in restlessness among American writers until then. But the purposive direction of all his travels was up.

The upwardly mobile Clemens was quick to understand both the opportunities and the obligations of his success. Received into the well-to-do Langdon family, he'd muted his views of Christianity and joined their daily prayers. He'd been a bachelor and free-living Bohemian until his mid-thirties. As a young man he'd worked on the Mississippi and gone silver prospecting. He'd become a celebrated drinker and cigar smoker in San Francisco saloons. He was the major means of support of his elderly mother, a widowed sister, and a hapless improvident brother. He'd written himself out of genteel Southern poverty and Western frontier gaucherie, but his first fame was as a humorist, a lower-class literary identification that he was still struggling to surmount.

It is the thesis of the most insightful and astute of his biographers, Justin Kaplan, that Sam Clemens' discovery of his "usable past" constituted "the central drama of his mature literary life." *Tom Sawyer*, the first major act of the drama, would come not a moment too soon—the self-attenuation of a literary careerist was as dire in the America of 1874 as it is now. At his writing table in northern New York State, Clemens went back to his beginnings in Hannibal, Missouri, thirty or so years before, a time when "all the summer world was bright and fresh" and "the sun rose upon a tranquil world, and beamed down . . . like a benediction." It was of course the time when the internal conflicts, the stresses and strains, of an invented self complete with its ironic-nostalgic name could hardly have been imagined. In Hannibal, renamed St. Petersburgh in the book, a person needed no education, social position, money, or renown to feel the radiance of heaven. He didn't even need shoes.

Writing without plan from some hastily scribbled notes, Clemens invoked from his past the boy his genius would descry as the carrier of our national soul. He didn't know where Tom Sawyer's adventures would end, thinking at first that they would take him into adulthood. Improvising from one episode to the next, he ran out of inspiration by the end of summer and waited—confident of the empowering past—until it kicked back in a year later. In the months intervening, the book's dimensions managed to clarify themselves in his mind and he decided to leave Tom forever in his boyhood. He wrote to Howells when the book was finished, in July of 1875, "If I went on, now, & took him into manhood, he would just be like all the one-horse men in literature & the reader would conceive a hearty contempt for him." The decision was the right one. But it did not resolve the larger question in his mind of the book's true audience, and both Livy and Howells had to persuade him not to publish it as a work for adults.

The fact is that Clemens' vision of *Tom Sawyer* never quite came into focus. He seemed to want more from the book than it could give—a creative dissatisfaction that would only be resolved with the writing of *Huckleberry Finn*. "Although my book is intended mainly for the entertainment of boys and girls," he wrote in his preface, "I hope it will not be shunned by men and women on that account." The reader today, remembering his own responses to the book as a child, realizes its peculiar duality in adulthood. We can read with a child's eye or an adult's, and with a different focal resolution for each.

Ever since its publication in 1876, children have been able to read *Tom Sawyer* with a sense of recognition for the feelings of childhood truly rendered: how Tom finds solace for his unjust treatment at the hands of Aunt Polly by dreaming of running away; or how he loves Becky Thatcher, the sort of simpering little blond girl all boys love, and how he does the absolutely right thing in lying and taking her punishment in school to protect her; or how he and his friends pretend to be pirates or the Merry Men of Sherwood Forest, accurately interrupting their scenarios with arguments about who plays what part and what everyone must say and how they must fight and when they must die. In addition, child readers recognize as true and reasonable Tom's aversion to soap and water; they share his keen interest in the insect forms of life, and they relish the not always kind attention he pays to dogs and cats. They understand the value he and his friends place on such items as pulled teeth, marbles, tadpoles, pieces of colored glass. And because all children are given to myth and superstition, they take as seriously as he does the proper rituals and necessary incantations for ridding oneself of warts or reclaiming lost possessions by using the divining powers of doodlebugs, as well as the efficacy of various spells, charms, and oaths drawn in blood, although it is sadly possible that children today, divested of their atavistic impulses by television cartoons and computer games, are no longer the natural repositories of such folklore.

There is perhaps less explicit recognition by young readers of the taxonomic world Tom Sawyer lives in, though it accredits and confirms their own: it is the world of two distinct and, for the most part, irreconcilable life forms, the Child and the Adult. As separate species children and adults have separate cultures which continually clash and cause trouble between them. All of Tom's adventures, from the simply mischievious to the seriously dangerous, arise in the disparity of the two cultures. And because power and authority reside in the Adult, he is necessarily a rebel acting in the name of freedom. Thus he is understood not as a bad boy but as a good boy who is amiably, creatively, and as a matter of political principle bad—unlike his half-brother Sid, who is that all too recognizable archetype of everyone's childhood, the actually bad boy who appears in the perverse eyesight of adults to be good. (The brothers stand in relation to each other as Tom Jones does to the wretched Blifil in Fielding's great work.)

The moral failures of the adult culture of St. Petersburgh are apparent to the child reader. They range from the imperceptions of the dithering Aunt Polly to the pure evil of Injun Joe. When, with chapter 9, the plot of the book is finally engaged, that is, when Tom and Huckleberry Finn witness the murder at night in the graveyard, the young reader finds everything from then on seriously satisfying, as how could it not be, in that it involves the fear of a murderer, the terror of being lost in a cave, the gratification of a court trial that rights an injustice, and the apotheosis of Tom Sawyer as hero of the whole town and possessor of a vast fortune.

Even more satisfying, though not to be consciously admitted as such, is the uniting of the child and adult communities in times of crisis. The whole town turns out along the river when it appears that Tom and Joe Harper have drowned. There is universal mourning. Similarly, when Tom and Becky are feared lost in the cave, the bereavement is understood as the entire community's. The government of the adults is washed away in their tearful expressions of love. And the young reader confirms his own hope that no matter how troubled his relations with his elders may be, beneath all their disapproval is their underlying love for him, constant and steadfast. This is the ultimate subtextual assurance Mark Twain provides his young reader, and it is no small thing for the child who understands, at whatever degree of consciousness, that his own transgressions are never as dire as they seem, and that there is a bond that unites old and young in one moral world in which truth can be realized and forgiveness is always possible.

But what the adult eye reads—ah, that is quite another matter. We open the book now and see Tom as a mysterious fellow, possibly, something of an anthropological construct, more a pastiche of boyhood qualities than a boy. He is a collection of traits we recognize as applicable to boyhood, or to American boyhood, all of them brought together and animated by the author's voice. In their encyclopedic accuracy they confer upon Tom an unnatural vividness rather than a human character.

Tom Sawyer is ageless. I don't mean that he is a boy for the ages, although he may be—I mean that he is a boy of no determinable age. When he falls in love he exhibits the behavior of a six-year-old. When he is cunning and manipulative he might be nine or ten. His athleticism places him nearer the age of twelve. And in self-dramatization and insensitivity to all feelings but his own he is unquestionably a teenager. The variety of his moods, including his deep funks when he feels unloved, his manic exhibitionism, his retributive fantasies, sweeps him up and down the scale of juvenile thought. The boy doing handstands to impress Becky Thatcher is not the same boy who swims across the river at night from Jackson's Island and, after eavesdropping on his grief-stricken aunt, elects not to relieve the poor woman's misery by telling her he is alive. Unlike Lewis Carroll's Alice, Tom does not have to drink anything to grow taller or shorter. (I note that the illustrations to the first edition can't seem to decide on Tom's proper height or bulk or the lineaments of his face.) He's a morally plastic trickster in part derived from the Trickster myths of the Afro-American and Native American traditions. He may also be the flighty, whimsical, sometimes kind, sometimes cruel minor sort of deity of classical myth, a god of mischief, with the capacity to manipulate the actions of normal human beings, evoke and deflect human emotions, and in general to arrange the course of history to bring honor to himself.

We do not minimize Mark Twain's achievement by noticing, as adults, some of the means by which it was accomplished. Tom Sawyer's thought has generative powers. What he fantasizes often comes to pass. In chapter 3 he receives a cuffing from his aunt when it is the detestable Sid who has broken the sugar bowl; in the sulking aftermath, he pictures himself "brought home from the river, dead, with his curls all wet and his sore heart at rest. How she [Aunt Polly] would throw herself upon him, and how her tears would fall like rain, and her lips pray God to give her back her boy and she would never, never abuse him any more! But he would lie there . . . and make no sign." As indeed he doesn't in chapter 15 when he hides under Aunt Polly's bed, still wet from his night swim, and listens as she weeps and mourns just as he once imagined, and remonstrates with herself in the belief that he has drowned. Tom's fantasies of buried pirate treasure metamorphose into the real buried treasure of Injun Joe. And after Tom and Huck thrill themselves imagining the devilish goings-on in graveyards at midnight in chapter 6, real deviltry arises in front of their eyes in chapter 9, when the grave robbers appear and fight among themselves until one of them is murdered in cold blood. Possibly we are ourselves witness to the author's exploratory method of composition, in which he first conceives of likely things for a boy's mind to imagine, and then decides some of them are too good not to be developed and played out as elements of a plot. In any event a godlike power of realization is conferred upon Tom, as if authorship itself is transferred, and we see a causal connection in what he seriously and intensely imagines and what comes to pass afterwards.

Lacking Tom's magical power, the other children in the book tend to be pallidly drawn, with the possible exception of Huck Finn, though he is clearly a preliminary one-dimensional Huck. Becky, we are disappointed to see, is too careless a sketch to be the ideal girl we half fell in love with ourselves as children, and Sid, though showing promise as a villainous Model Boy at the beginning, gradually fades into the background. Mary goes still once Tom's bath is administered, and finds no further reason to be included at all in the life of the village. It is as if the god of mischief sucks up all their vitality into himself—or as if Mark Twain put so much into this free-range American boyhood that he hadn't anything left for the others.

It is the same with the adult parents and authorities in St. Petersburgh, who lack any dimension except the forbearing kindness with which they foolishly greet every outrage perpetrated by the wretched children they have raised. They, too, are desultory parts of the composition, more impressive really as a village collective or chorus led by Aunt Polly. In some cases the author forgets the names he gives them and supplies them with others. Sometimes he so scants their reactions—as when Tom, the putative Bible-winning scholar, reveals his biblical illiteracy in Sunday school—that he pulls the curtain down over the scene before they can respond at all. And in the climactic return of Tom in time for his own funeral, they fall all over him unbelievably with kisses, and are allowed to ask no questions, let alone to work up an anger, before the chapter comes to its abrupt end.

And yet we indulge the flaws in the composition, perhaps in the author's own spirit of indulgence as he looks down on his lost rural world. In the post-industrial America of today, as in the industrial America of Clemens' own time, *Tom Sawyer* is a work of longing, a version of pastoral, with a built-in entreaty to our critical disbelief. What elicits our tolerance is the voice of the book, which first of all gives candid recognition to the true feelings of its people, and second of all grants them universal amnesty: it is Mark Twain's reigning voice of amused tolerance. Not only are we charmed by its perfect pitch for the American vernacular, but we derive from it a serious self-satisfaction. Its comic rhetoric, its hyperbole, its tongue-in-cheek ennoblement of the actions of a provincial country boy, ask to be read as implicit declaration of a young nation's cultural independence.

There is some indication that the author's own view of his work was less resolute. In his attempt to define what he had done, he claimed *Tom Sawyer* was a kind of hymn. It is "simply a hymn" to boyhood, Sam Clemens wrote to William Dean Howells as he struggled with the judgment that his book was more suitable for children than for adults. The claim has a defensive ring to it. Hymns ennoble or idealize life, express its pieties, and are made to be totally proper and appropriate for all ears. In the painful evolution of his creative genius Clemens was finding it difficult to accept the value of what he had written. He was having to consider the possibility that the voice he had chosen for the book was insufficient to the truth of his usable past. In its celebratory comedy, *The Adventures of Tom Sawyer* might be too forgiving of the racist backwater that had nurtured him. In that sense it purveyed a false sentimentality. If he troubled to draw his boys on a chart, Tom would stand between the Model Boy, Sid, on his right, and the unwashed, unschooled son of a drunkard, Huck Finn, on his left. Tom was a centrist, like Clemens himself, a play rebel who had been welcomed into the bosom of a ruling society he had sallied against. He had been rewarded with every honor it could bestow. It may even have occurred to Clemens that by some perverse act of literary transmutation he had not anticipated, Tom had replaced Sid as the detestable Model Boy.

How could his reviewing eye not wander then to the other one, the skinny, ragged, unredeemable one, swearing to give up all the benefits of civilization if only they would let him alone? What a glorious moment it must have been when the squire of Quarry Farm, the master builder of Hartford's grandest Eastern literary mansion, realized he was in creative contact with a true outsider, the real unrepentant thing, a boy who would never conform, a boy who couldn't read or write but who could turn the tables and speak for the author—a boy who could speak for Sam Clemens from the free territory that had once been his own.

1996

Charcoal sketch of Mark Twain by James Montgomery Flagg. From *Mark Twain Journal* (cover), January 12, 1949

Hal Holbrook

When the celebrated American actor Hal Holbrook (born in 1925) started researching a one-man show on Mark Twain in the mid-1950s, he had no idea that the performance he would create would enthrall audiences around the world for the next half century. Remarkably, Holbrook has been "Mark Twain" longer than Samuel Clemens was "Mark Twain." (Clemens first used the pen name "Mark Twain" in 1863 and died in 1910, having inhabited that persona for 47 years, while Holbrook is well past the half-century mark.) To create his performance as Mark Twain, Holbrook spent years researching reviews of Twain's lecture tours and combing through little-known texts in the Mark Twain Papers at the University of California in Berkeley. The spectacularly innovative off-Broadway (and later on-Broadway) show that he developed—*Mark Twain Tonight!*—initially ran 22 weeks in New York City and then toured the country, receiving rave reviews from coast to coast. A television special, two recorded albums, and State Department–sponsored tours abroad followed. Holbrook's daunting command of 16 hours of Twain material has allowed him to draw on new combinations of texts in each performance, making Twain topical as well as timeless in often uncanny ways. His painstaking research, his respect for Twain's words, and his fresh, carefully-crafted delivery have earned him the gratitude of Twain scholars. Holbrook's deeply engaged and engaging interpretations of Twain's words before hundreds of thousands of people have given Twain the one thing he could not give himself: a vitality beyond the grave that no author could expect. *Mark Twain Tonight!* has done more than keep Twain alive as a cultural presence: the show gives voice to a side of Twain that the author himself could not show the public during his lifetime. By brilliantly melding Twain's well-known platform gifts with some of the most biting satiric pieces of his later years that he left unpublished at his death, Holbrook has allowed a very different Twain to take shape in the public's imagination. Whether he was reading "The War-Prayer" at West Point during the Vietnam War or skewering the state of American politics in Ford's Theatre during the Bush years, Holbrook in effect has allowed Mark Twain to come to life as a social critic in our time. That Twain's criticisms wear so well is testimony not only to his prescience and sagacity, but to Holbrook's stunning gift for making his words live and breathe and take on new relevance in every era.

Introduction to
Mark Twain's Speeches

What did he sound like? I had read newspaper reports of his lectures which described his voice as a "nasal twang" or "a little buzz saw inside a corpse" and the *Detroit Free Press* referred to his "Down East" accent. Others called it a Missouri drawl. I learned early on in my research for the solo performance of Mark Twain that I would have to deal with inconsistency as well as the creative flights of the people doing the reporting. Some of them were trying to be funnier than Twain. And there was always the possibility that the man on the *Detroit Free Press* did not know a Down East accent from a Paiute Indian's.

Along about 1956 Professor Norman Holmes Pearson of Yale University called me up one day and said that he had heard a recording of Twain's voice on a television documentary, that he was suspicious of its authenticity and had acquired a copy. Would I listen to it and give him my opinion? I had met this eminent scholar at the Mark Twain House in Hartford and his call was a compliment. This was before I had acquired any wide reputation as an interpreter of Mark Twain, and I valued Professor Pearson's tacit imprimatur.

The recording was a rendition of the jumping frog story. The first thing that struck me about it was the obvious New England accent; having been brought up in New England, I knew what that sounded like. Then I remembered that in a letter to his wife in 1885, while on tour, Twain had listed timings for a Chicago lecture. He said the timing for the jumping frog story was the "fastest on record."[1] I timed Pearson's recording against my own reading of Twain's lecture version. Mark Twain's was thirteen minutes and the Pearson recording was nine. So something was off.

I told Professor Pearson that I doubted this voice he'd heard on the television documentary was really Mark Twain. Some months went by and he called me again. He had discovered that the television recording was originally made on wire in 1933 or 1934 in the home of Professor Packard of Harvard University, by the actor William Gillette. Gillette was making his last tour in the play *Secret Service*. He had lived only a few blocks from Mark Twain in Hartford and Twain had loaned him money to go to New York and pursue an acting career. So they were friends. The clincher was a preamble on the original tape during which other men in the room were heard urging "Bill" to recite his impersonation of Mark Twain doing the jumping frog story. Gillette demurred but finally gave in and delivered it. This whole introductory passage had been eliminated by some questionable character and the tape circulated as authentic Mark Twain. Professor "Sherlock" Holmes Pearson's sleuthing dashed everyone's hopes of finding a recording of Mark Twain's voice, although there was a persistent rumor that such a recording was lurking somewhere.

Years later, when I was doing Mark Twain at the Longacre Theatre in New York in 1966, a gentleman from Brooklyn wrote that he was coming to a matinee and would like to talk to me. He explained that he knew of a recording of Twain's voice. After the performance a courtly 92-year-old man came backstage and told me that he and his employer from the Columbia Vitaphone Company had gone to Mark Twain's home on Fifth Avenue in 1904 to record his voice on a wax cylinder. "Do you know where it is?" I asked, holding my breath. "It was stored in an attic and melted down," he said. To his knowledge there existed no other recording of Mark Twain's voice. That ended it. It appears the pursuit of his sound is left to our imagination.

He had a tenor singing voice. There's a clue. And we have many newspaper accounts describing the sound of his voice as well as his mannerisms and general appearance on the lecture platform.

> He speaks in a sort of mechanical drawl and with a most bored expression of countenance. . . . He jerks out a sentence or two and follows it with a silence that is more suggestive than words. (*Washington Post*, November 25, 1884)

> His deep voice and his pronunciation of many words are of Missouri, where he was brought up, his nasal twang is of New England where he has spent a good many years, and his drawl is of Mark Twain. (*Toronto Globe*, December 9, 1884)

That last description could send you in three different directions.

> When Mark Twain walked on the stage [with] his unruly
> hair like a halo around his head, and his discouraged expression of countenance, he was welcomed with a prolonged
> clapping of hands. Without apparently recovering his spirits, he sauntered to the reading desk, felt for it with his right
> hand, and began. (*New York Sun*, November 19, 1884)[2]

I remember thinking of Jack Benny. The man they were describing was coming out deadpan and after a few lugubrious
moments he was dropping comic bombshells and working the
audience into a fit of startled laughter. He was obviously a performer and he was going for the funny bone. He had acquired
the art of the tall story, that prize of our Wild West culture. You
built the story up higher and higher, seeing how long you could
sustain the ridiculousness of it before it crashed to the ground.
A good example is "His Grandfather's Old Ram."

I studied pictures of Twain. A cartoon in a New York magazine showed him in his lecture platform garb: formal black suit
with tails, white starched shirt, white tie—apparently the customary regalia for such an event in those days. But as I read
more newspaper reviews of his lectures in various parts of the
country, I got a clear picture of a man who was breaking all the
rules. Instead of standing at the lectern and delivering his remarks in the normal elocutionary manner, he leaned against the
lectern or slouched around the stage, sometimes with his hands
in his pockets, speaking as if he were back home circling his dining table. Many of the sponsoring organizations of the time, like
the Chautauquas, had a religious base, and this kind of behavior
was considered frivolous and in poor taste. Mark Twain was severely criticized in some holy quarters. He didn't act right. I
realized that what I had to do was find some way to represent
this idiosyncratic behavior to a modern audience accustomed to
informality and even questionable taste.

I thought about the cigar. Smoking cigars may have been
Twain's favorite pastime, that and billiards. His friend William
Dean Howells said that he smoked incessantly while visiting in

Boston and even went to bed with a cigar clamped in his teeth. Howells was afraid he'd burn the house down, so he used to creep in and remove the cigar after Twain went to sleep. I figured smoking a cigar during a lecture would be considered eccentric, even in our day, so I adopted it.

Then I thought of the white suit. He liked to wear white in his later years—said it made him feel pure. Sometimes he paraded down Fifth Avenue in white on a Sunday morning while people were coming out of church, the men looking like "a flock of crows." If the white suit did not seem eccentric to a modern audience, at least it would capture their attention.

I was going to characterize him at the age of seventy because by then he had written practically everything I wanted him to say. In 1954, when I began the solo Twain, I was twenty-nine years old—forty-one years shy of the mark (sorry). My first makeup took one hour and fifteen minutes and I looked like a boy with white hair. By the time it grew into a four-hour job I was quite convincing.

I needed to have him move around. He was a restless talker at home and would get up from the dinner table and march around it while discharging his observations about God's pitiful invention, Man, into the clouds of cigar smoke curling around him. His first biographer, Albert Bigelow Paine, described his "ceaseless slippered shuffling walk . . . the white figure with its rocking, rolling movement . . . his deliberate speech— always deliberate save at rare intervals."[3] So I put a lectern on one side of the stage and on the other side a smallish library table and an armchair. The space in the middle was for wandering around or acting out scenes from his books. I would need an ashtray for the cigar, so that went on the table, along with a few books from which I would pretend to read when I got around to it. And a water pitcher and glass. These props would give me objects to fool with and would seem to distract me. I would have to drop cigar ashes, which would require me to cross the stage to the ashtray every once in a while, motivating my movements while he walked and talked. These devices were also chosen to help break the rules of the "lecture platform" and make audiences feel at home with him.

In 1956 I did Mark Twain in a nightclub in Greenwich Village with only the cigar as a prop. The club was called Upstairs at the Duplex and seated fifty-nine people, legally. I worked in the curve of a baby grand piano, very close to the audience, and did two or three shows a night. By then the makeup took two and a half hours. I stayed there for eight months and developed my first two hours of Twain material. I experimented with the pause. Twain loved fooling around with the pause, toying with it like a cat, taking chances with it, and there in the nightclub I was able to get familiar with the pause, especially in the late show when no one was in a hurry to go anywhere, the smoke drifting up through the spotlights and people simmered down from a nice load of whiskey or gin. I could take my time telling the stories, let the stuff sink in, play around with the easy nature of American humor. In the theater you go for laughs, but in that little club the laughs were chuckles and the audience was a friend in your lap. I learned to trust Twain's material.

I worked on new material constantly while doing a television and radio soap opera in the daytime, then memorized it on the IRT subway to Sheridan Square. I read patiently through all his books, very patiently, marking anything that might be useful for the stage and ticking off stories and anecdotes that had some dramatic life to them. Since a club show was only fifteen or twenty minutes long, many of these routines were not unlike his speeches. One of my earliest routines was carved out of his "Seventieth Birthday" speech, which I slimmed down and refined in front of audiences, keeping what got the best laughs. Another early selection was the "Italian Guide" sequence from *Innocents Abroad*. In this one I played Mark Twain impersonating two characters, an Italian guide and an American doctor. Tricky, but the audience seemed to enjoy it. Twain did the same thing in his lectures. He acted out scenes from his books. He was an actor at heart, a born one, according to Sir Henry Irving, the preeminent British actor of his day.

When I began getting engagements in colleges and theaters around the country I had to put together a longer show. My aim was to avoid formality, not to construct a program of "readings." That seemed deadly to me. Twain followed a formal structure in his lectures, but his speeches sounded improvised, and I wanted to merge both styles because I was working for a modern audience with a faster heartbeat. I started with the self-introduction he sometimes used on the platform, followed it with a joke about the lawyer who introduced him with his hands in his pockets ("a rare creature—a lawyer who kept his hands in his own pockets"), and that got the audience laughing. Then I would pull out the cigar and go into a routine on smoking and the dangers of abstinence. Finally, I'd get down to business with my program notes and start in on the lecture the audience expected to hear, but pretty soon I'd lose track of that and get reminded of something else, and that would lead me into a routine on politics. Along about this time I'd remember a book I wrote called *Innocents Abroad*, and we were into the "Italian Guide." Or something else.

It was a meandering structure, purposefully improvisational, to keep the audience off guard and wondering what was coming next. It seemed to me that the most effective way to program an evening of Mark Twain was to give the impression that I was making it up on my feet, that I was taking chances. That would be more dangerous and create suspense. That was the effect I think he tried to achieve himself, particularly in his speeches. He rehearsed them with intense zeal (so did I) until he drilled them into his head. Then he strove to make the performance look spontaneous. This speaking style seemed to suit his style of writing. He was, after all, the first American author to write the way Americans speak. Bernard DeVoto caught the spirit of Twain's genius when he said,

> It is a literature of oral anecdote, whose purpose is the embodiment of character and the revelation of a *point*, whose aim is the entertainment of listeners, and whose origin is the life immediately at hand.[4]

It was in 1957, in Little Rock, Arkansas, that I first became aware of the potential for social commentary in Mark Twain's work. Until then I had been trying to put together a funny show, born in a nightclub, one that I hoped would survive on a variety of stages. I had played some pretty strange ones, from the curve of that piano to the basketball floors of rural schools with kids sitting on windowsills, so I knew that keeping the audience entertained meant the difference between life and death. But when President Eisenhower called out the troops to put down the racial explosion at Central High School in Little Rock, Mark Twain's social conscience began to cast its shadow over me. By some strange twist of fate (later to be repeated in the 1960s) I was scheduled to perform Mark Twain near Little Rock not long after the riots there. I did not yet have material in my repertoire that specifically commented on racial injustice. All I had was the Sherburn-Boggs selection from *Huckleberry Finn*, which ends with Colonel Sherburn's blistering speech to the mob that has come to lynch him. Although a white man is speaking to a white mob, Mark Twain is making a thinly veiled statement about the Ku Klux Klan. The portrait of sudden violence in the shooting of Boggs, of ignorance and the mob mentality that sweeps people along, was eerily appropriate to this modern-day crisis in Little Rock, and Twain's setting did happen to be a town in Arkansas. So that was the selection I chose to deliver.

I don't know how much the audience got out of it. I do know that my mind was honed like a silver blade on the point I wanted to get across. I hope it came through. I think it did to some of them. When I got back to New York City I started reading with a different appetite. I began exploring the social commentary of Mark Twain and in time there opened before me a mine of gold that I had overlooked. I found nuggets lying all around in those great books and essays and speeches and suddenly the show took on a feeling of importance it had never had before. I didn't know it then, but the civil rights movement had begun.

I read "To the Person Sitting in Darkness" and "To My Missionary Critics," "The United States of Lyncherdom," the wonderful material about the damned human race in the last volume of Paine's biography of Twain, much of it later included in *Letters to the Earth*; I read *Pudd'nhead Wilson*. I began to put together in my mind another Huckleberry number which would express the message of the entire book. In 1958 Philip S. Foner's riveting *Mark Twain: Social Critic* was published. It was a nest of mercurial opinions by Twain which led me in the direction of the material I developed later, when the 1960s matured and the passions of the civil rights movement and the Vietnam War struck fire together. I was creating a show which almost seemed to be commenting on the news of the day.

The *Mark Twain Tonight!* which opened at the Longacre Theatre in 1966 was judged very topical. It talked about the Silent Lie, how you could lie by remaining quiet in the shadow of a great injustice, as people did during the movement to abolish slavery.[5] Then came the new Huckleberry number, in which Huck characterizes his father giving that sublimely racist speech about the "free nigger from Ohio" and then grapples with the awful decision to turn Jim in: yes or no. When the dust settled down on that scene, I had Twain deliver his personal observation on how racism can be trained into you.

The Vietnam War was heating up while I was at the Longacre Theatre, so in the second act I moved from racism to patriotism, the right to speak your mind in times of national stress. In *Letters from the Earth*, I found this about our Philippine war: "*Our Country, right or wrong!* . . . every man who failed to shout it . . . was proclaimed a traitor—none but those others were patriots." He could have been talking about the war we were being drawn into in Vietnam. "Who is 'the Country'? Is it the Government? . . . The Government is merely a servant, . . . a temporary one. . . . If you alone of all the nation shall decide one way, and that way be the right way according to your convictions of the right, you have done your duty by yourself and by your country—hold up your head!"[6] Edited together from bits and pieces of Twain, this had an electric effect upon the audience in 1966. It reminded us that dissent is a tradition of our democracy, something we forget about six and a half days of every week.

I've been working this material for over forty years now and I see no shrinkage in its timeliness. Twain was talking about the human race, which seems always to run after itself in circles. On May 31, 1985, I gave a performance at the Jiri Wolker Theatre in Prague, before the Communist walls came down. At the beginning of the second act I started with the Silent Lie routine. The audience became profoundly attentive. After the line "when whole nations of people conspire to propagate gigantic mute lies like that one, in the interest of tyrannies and shams," someone in the audience started to applaud. Then someone else joined in. Just two people clapping. I felt a sudden concern for their safety and quickly continued. But the air was charged. In all the shows I've done, there were only two other performances where an audience clapped at that particular moment. The first was in Hamburg, Germany, in 1961. The second was in Oxford, Mississippi, on October 9, 1962, during the riots over the admission of the first black student, James Meredith, to the University of Mississippi.

Sometimes one piece of material from the repertoire will burn with relevance for a few years and then cool down as other social issues flare up. But then a routine which has occupied a modest niche, useful but not triumphant, will catch fire and smile out its timely perception of our foolish world.

Such is the case with a forty-year-old routine lifted from the "Seventieth Birthday" speech. (Here, as in many other routines in my show, the text has been altered slightly to simplify it for the stage.) "I have never taken any exercise except sleeping and resting. . . . I could never see any benefit in being tired." Then I splice in a remark attributed to Twain: "When the urge to exercise comes over me I lie down until it passes away." This has always been fun to do, but ever since the symbol of America became a pair of sneakers and the passion for health superseded any lingering passion for intelligence, Twain's commentary has become more than just a joke. It has a slim barb in it which the audience enjoys.

Sometimes events inspire me to construct a new routine. A few years ago we were in another war, this one in the desert, against Iraq. Everyone could see it coming, and as it built to a declaration I worried that the country would once again fly into the conflicting passions which had polarized us during the Vietnam War. Everyone would start shouting back and forth and the losers would be our soldiers: the men and women who had to go over there and lay their lives on the line and then come home to a nation that never thanked them for the job they'd been told to do. Whether the Gulf War was politically right or wrong, it was too sad to think of these soldiers coming back to experience the same cruel emptiness the Vietnam veterans have lived with for years—never to be thanked except for that eloquent black wall in Washington. I could sense that most people felt the same way I did. So I put together a number called "Opinions," whose point is that we should stop shouting at each other and start listening to what the other person is trying to say.

"Opinions" is made up of material from seven different sources, edited and arranged for the stage. The idea for it popped out of a paragraph from *Christian Science*. "When I, a thoughtful and unbiased Presbyterian, examine the Koran, I know that beyond any question every Mohammedan is insane. . . . I cannot prove to him that he is insane, because you can never prove anything to a lunatic." There follows a line I added for transition ("But it is perfectly clear to me"), and then back to the same passage in *Christian Science* (edited from first-person plural to first-person singular): "I know exactly where to put my finger upon his insanity. It is where his opinion differs from mine."[7] The "Opinions" selection ends with a paragraph from chapter 53 of *Following the Equator* (my words are in brackets):

> Reverence for one's own sacred things . . . religion, flag, laws, and respect for one's own beliefs—these are feelings which we cannot even help. . . . They are involuntary, like breathing. There is no personal merit in breathing. But the reverence which is difficult, and which has personal merit in it, is the respect which you [we] pay, without compulsion, to the political or religious attitudes of a man whose beliefs are not yours [ours]. You [We] can't revere his gods or his politics, and no one expects you [us] to do that, but you [we] could respect his belief in them if you [we] tried hard enough. . . . But it is very, very difficult; it is next to impossible, and so we hardly ever try. If the man doesn't believe as we do, we say he is a crank, and that settles it. I mean it does nowadays, because now we can't burn him.[8]

What makes Mark Twain so palatable even when he's beating up on us? I think it's that he includes himself in the beating.

The human race is a race of cowards. And I am not only
marching in that procession, I am carrying the banner.[9]

He too is culpable; that, together with his honesty and his
passion, helps us swallow his harshest criticism of us. It also allows him to put a lemon twist of humor into it.

In the beginning I tried to put together a funny show. One
that would survive in a nightclub and on the humble stages of
America. Then our reasonably ordered world began to break
apart. The civil rights movement exploded and has become a
lasting warfare. In the 1960s debate over the war in Vietnam
joined the passions generated by racial inequality. Restraint and
respect for civility were thrown aside. The traditional rebellion
of youth became violent to the point of anarchy; Dylan put it to
music and Elvis made it sensual. Now, thirty years later, staring
at the troubled wake behind us, at the old harbors we've abandoned, we find ourselves at sea without a star to bring us home,
sails flapping lugubriously in every squall, and we cannot find
our way because the crew is undisciplined and there is no captain to guide us.

What would he say about all this? Our world is losing its
humaneness. Anger is loose among us, riding in the streets,
spilling over again and again after all these years of trying to
contain it. Everybody wants what they ain't got, and sweating
hard for it seems to take too much time. Our young wear the
smile of cynicism to mask their pain. And immorality is on the
prowl.

> That California get-rich-quick disease of my youth spread
> like wildfire. It produced a civilization which has destroyed
> the simplicity and repose of life, its poetry, its soft romantic
> dreams and visions, and replaced them with the money fever,
> sordid ideals, vulgar ambitions and the sleep which does not
> refresh. It has created a thousand useless luxuries and turned
> them into necessities and satisfied nothing. It has dethroned
> God and set up a shekel in his place.[10]

The great thing about Mark Twain is that he makes you
smile, because he speaks the truth so well even when it has a

bitter taste. And it goes to your heart. Sometimes it makes you cry. Perhaps this is why he survives and why people still want to listen to him.

NOTES

1. *The Love Letters of Mark Twain*, ed. Dixon Wecter (New York: Harper and Brothers, 1949), p. 230.

2. These newspaper accounts are reprinted in Guy A. Cardwell, *Twins of Genius* (Ann Arbor: Michigan State College Press, 1953), pp. 23, 28, 20.

3. Albert Bigelow Paine, *Mark Twain: A Biography* (New York: Harper and Brothers, 1912), 4:1323.

4. Bernard DeVoto, *Mark Twain's America* (Boston: Little, Brown, 1932), p. 92.

5. "My First Lie, and How I Got Out of It," *The Man That Corrupted Hadleyburg and Other Stories and Essays* (New York: Harper and Brothers, 1900), pp. 147–49.

6. See *Letters from the Earth*, ed. Bernard DeVoto (New York: Harper and Brothers, 1962), pp. 108–9.

7. See *Christian Science, with Notes Containing Corrections to Date* (New York: Harper and Brothers, 1907), bk. 1, ch. 5, pp. 40–41.

8. See *Following the Equator: A Journey Around the World* (Hartford: American Publishing Company, 1897), ch. 53, p. 514.

9. See prefatory note, *Mark Twain in Eruption*, ed. Bernard DeVoto (New York: Harper and Brothers, 1940).

10. See *Letters from the Earth*, p. 98.

1996

Erica Jong

Erica Jong (born in 1942) had published two award-winning collections of well-crafted poetry before her first novel, *Fear of Flying*, came out in 1973. The recognition that the young poet had received in the form of prizes and awards did little to prepare readers for the maelstrom of attention that her novel would generate. *Fear of Flying*, a book whose female protagonist was as candid about sex as male protagonists in novels had long been, provoked fierce controversy. Was it art? Was it pornography? And what was a woman doing writing this stuff, anyway? More than any other writer of her time, Jong has come to embody the impulse to break out of the stultifying conventions that have limited the roles women could play in American letters, becoming (as she once put it), an "Amanuensis to the Zeitgeist." Over 18 million copies of *Fear of Flying* are in print today, and the book has been translated into 27 languages. Jong is also the author of seven other novels, six books of poetry, and six volumes of nonfiction. In the essay that follows, She offers her insights into the role that *1601*, a relatively obscure piece by Mark Twain, may have played in his creative process. When it is mentioned at all, *1601* is most often dismissed as a curious and trivial excursion into pornography and scatology. But Jong argues convincingly that *1601*—written the same summer Twain began writing *Huckleberry Finn*—shows Twain "sneaking up on the muse so she would not be forewarned and escape." Jong makes a strong case for the idea that *1601* was a key part of the process by which Twain freed his imagination to write a book as boldly transgressive as *Huckleberry Finn*.

Introduction to
1601 and Is Shakespeare Dead?

"Deliberate Lewdness" and the Lure of Immortality

The form of government most suitable to the artist is no government at all.
—Oscar Wilde

We live in a time when the freedom to publish sexual oriented material is coming under attack, when large publishing conglomerates increasingly control all means of communication, and when the forces of cultural reaction are becoming extremely well organized. The brief cultural *glasnost* of the sixties is beginning to seem quaint. At such a juncture it is particularly important to reexamine what constitutes forbidden material in literature and to cut through the political grandstanding about its supposed evils in order to understand what *purpose* it actually serves in society. If nothing else, we should try to grasp what motivates the creators and consumers of it.

Pornographic material has been present in the art and literature of every society in every historical period. What has changed from epoch to epoch—or even from one decade to another—is the degree to which such material has flourished publicly and been distributed legally. In elitist societies there are, paradoxically, fewer calls for censorship than in democratic ones, since elitist societies function as de facto censors, keeping certain materials out of the purview of *hoi polloi*. As democracy increases, so does the demand for legal control over the erotic, the pornographic, the scatological. Our own century is a perfect example of the oscillations of taste regarding such material. We have gone from the banning and burning of D. H. Lawrence, James Joyce, Radclyffe Hall, Henry Miller and other avant-garde artists early in the century to a passionate struggle to free literature from censorship in mid-century to a new wave of reaction at century's end.

After many brave battles for the freedom to publish, we find that the enemies of freedom have multiplied rather than diminished. They include Christians, Muslims, oppressive totalitarian regimes, even well-meaning social libertarians who happen to be feminists, teachers, members of school boards, librarians. This should not surprise us, since the demand for state censorship is usually "a response to the presence within the society of heterogeneous groups of people with differing standards and aspirations," as Margaret Mead pointed out forty years ago. As our culture becomes more diverse, we can expect more calls for censorship rather than fewer. So we owe it to ourselves to understand the impulses toward pornography, eroticism, scatology, before resuming our contentious public debate about their uses and whether or not they should be restricted.

Our job is made tougher and more confusing by the fact that the spate of freedoms we briefly enjoyed in the late sixties, the seventies and the early eighties led to the proliferation of sexual materials so ugly, exploitative and misogynistic that it is difficult to defend them. The door was opened to *Lolita*, *Lady Chatterley's Lover*, *Tropic of Cancer*, *Couples*, *Portnoy's Complaint*, *Fear of Flying*, but it was also opened to *Debbie Does Dallas*, *Deep Throat* and an array of printed and filmed pornography that is deeply offensive to women and has understandably provoked the ire of feminists. Pornography also became hugely profitable once legal restraints were lifted, which in turn gave rise to another wave of reaction.

We stand at a crossroads now when many former libertarians and liberals suddenly want to ban sexual materials. The old dream of the avant-garde that eradicating sexual oppression would free human beings from their inhibitions and limitations has withered. We think we are sadder and wiser about what sexual freedom leads to, but in truth we never really *tried* sexual freedom. We only ballyhooed its simulacrum.

I want to bypass a reappraisal of the so-called sexual revolution for the moment and look instead at the impulse to create pornography and the role it plays in one artist's oeuvre. I should say that I use the terms "pornography" and "eroticism" interchangeably because I have come to the conclusion that only snobbery divides them. At one time I thought of pornography as purely an aid to masturbation, and of eroticism as something more high-toned and spiritual, like Molly Bloom's soliloquy in *Ulysses*. Now I doubt that division. Nearly every visual artist— from the anonymous sculptor of the bare-breasted Minoan snake goddess to Pompeii's brothel muralists to John Ruskin and Pablo Picasso—has been drawn to the erotic and the pornographic. So have literary artists throughout human history. Sometimes the urge has been to stimulate the genitals; sometimes the urge has been to stimulate the mind. Since the mind and the genitals are part of one organism, why distinguish between masturbatory dreams and aesthetic ones? Surely there is also an aesthetic of masturbation that our society is too sex-negative to explore. At any rate, it is time to go back to the origin of the pornographic impulse and explore the reasons it is so tenacious.

Mark Twain's *1601* is a perfect place to start. Although Twain lived in the Victorian age and knew he could never publish his pornographic fancies officially, they nevertheless occupied his energies from time to time, and he was so proud of them that he sought to disseminate them among his friends. I will argue that in Mark Twain's case, pornography was an *essential* part of his oeuvre because it primed the pump for other sorts of freedom of expression. It allowed him to fly free in fashioning a new sort of American vernacular in first-person narratives that drew on American speech patterns and revealed the soul of America as never before. Experiments with pornography, scatology and eroticism helped him to delve into the communal unconscious and create some of the most profound myths of American culture.

The notorious *1601*, or *Conversation, As It Was by the Social Fireside, in the time of the Tudors*, fascinates me because it demonstrates how closely Mark Twain's passion for linguistic experiment is allied with his compulsion toward "deliberate lewdness." The phrase is Vladimir Nabokov's. In a witty afterword to *Lolita* (1955), he links the urge to create pornography with "the verve of a fine poet in a wanton mood" and regrets that "in modern times the term 'pornography' connotes mediocrity, commercialism, and certain strict rules of narration." In contemporary porn, Nabokov says, "action has to be limited to the copulation of clichés." Poetry is always out of the question. "Style, structure, imagery should never distract the reader from his tepid lust." Motivated by such lackluster lust, the connoisseur of pornography is impatient with all attempts at verbal dexterity and linguistic wit. One is reminded that Henry Miller failed miserably as a paid pornographer because he could not leave the poetry out as his anonymous patron wished. Anaïs Nin fared better with *Delta of Venus* and *Little Birds*. For Henry Miller pornography mattered precisely *because* it aroused him to poetry. Miller and Nabokov shared the ancient pagan attitude toward pornography. For them, "deliberate lewdness" was an exuberant literary strategy.

Poetry and pornography went hand in hand in Roman, Renaissance and eighteenth-century literature. The pornographic flights of Catullus, Ovid, Petronius and Juvenal never sacrificed style. Boccaccio, Villon, Rabelais, Cervantes, Shakespeare, John Donne and Andrew Marvell all delighted in making porn poetic. Jonathan Swift, Alexander Pope and Laurence Sterne were equally drunk with lewdness and with language.

No creator should have to bother about "the exact demarcation between the sensuous and the sensual," says Nabokov. Let the censors worry about such hypocritical distinctions. The literary artist has another agenda: to free the imagination and let the wildness of the mind take flight. Nabokov is, of course, defending his own offspring *Lolita*, that light of his loins and pen which caused such consternation that it could not at first be published anywhere but in Paris by Maurice Girodias's Olympia Press. The pornographic verve of ancient literature was Nabokov's inspiration: in this he would have recognized Mark Twain as a brother.

In choosing to write *1601* from the point of view of "the Pepys of that day, the same being cup-bearer to Queen Elizabeth," Mark Twain was transporting himself to a world that existed before the invention of sexual hypocrisy. The Elizabethans were openly bawdy. They found bodily functions funny and sex arousing to the muse. Restoration wits and Augustan satirists had the same openness to the body and the same respect for eros. Only in the nineteenth century did prudery (and the threat of legal censure) begin to paralyze the author's hand. Shakespeare, Rochester and Pope were far more fettered *politically* than we are, but they were not required to put condoms on their pens when the matter of sex arose. They were *pleased* to remind their readers of the essential messiness of the body. They followed a classical tradition that often expressed moral indignation through scatology. "Oh Celia, Celia, Celia shits," writes Swift, as if she were the first woman in history to do so. In his so-called unprintable poems, Swift is debunking the conventions of courtly love (as well as expressing his own deep misogyny), but he is doing so in a spirit that Catullus and Juvenal would have recognized. The satirist lashes the world to bring the world to its senses. He does the dance of the satyrs around our follies.

Twain's scatology serves this purpose as well, but it is also a warm-up for his creative process. Stuck in the prudish nineteenth century, Mark Twain craved the freedom of the ancients. In championing "deliberate lewdness" in *1601*, he bestowed the gift of freedom on himself.

It is hardly coincidental that Mark Twain was writing *1601* during the same summer of 1876 when he was "tearing along on a new book"—the first sixteen chapters of a novel he then referred to as "Huck Finn's Autobiography." *1601* and *Adventures of Huckleberry Finn* have a great deal in common. According to Justin Kaplan, "Both were implicit rejections of the taboos and codes of polite society, and both were experiments in using the vernacular as a literary medium."

Is there a stronger connection between *Huckleberry Finn* and *1601*? As a professional writer whose process of composition often resembles Twain's (intermittent work on ambitious novels, writing blocks during which I put one project aside and devote myself to others, periods of lecturing and travel), I think I understand Twain's creative strategy. He was sneaking up on the muse so that she would not be forewarned and escape. Every author knows that a book only begins to live when the voice of its narrator comes alive. You may have plot ideas, characters may haunt you in the night, but the book does not fly until the sound of its voice is heard in the author's ear. And the sound of a book's voice is as individual as the sound of a child's voice. It may resemble that of other offspring, but it always has its own particular timbre, its own particular quirks.

In order to find the true voice of the book, the author must be free to play without fear of reprisal. All writing blocks come from excessive self-judgment, the internalized voice of the critical parent telling the author's imagination that it is a dirty little boy or girl. "Hah!" says the author. "I will flaunt the voice of parental propriety and break free!" This is why the pornographic spirit is *always* related to unhampered creativity. Artists are fascinated with filth because we know that in filth everything human is born. Human beings emerge between piss and shit, and so do novels and poems. Only by letting go of the inhibition that makes us bow to social propriety can we plumb the depths of the unconscious. We assert our freedom with pornographic play. If we are lucky, we *keep* that freedom long enough to create a masterpiece like *Huckleberry Finn*.

But the two compulsions are more than just related; they are *causally* intertwined. When *Huckleberry Finn* was published in 1885, Louisa May Alcott put her finger on exactly what mattered about the novel even as she condemned it: "If Mr. Clemens cannot think of something better to tell our pure-minded lads and lasses, he had best stop writing for them." What Alcott didn't know was that "our pure-minded lads and lasses" aren't. But Mark Twain knew. It is not at all surprising that during that summer of high scatological spirits Twain should also give birth to the irreverent voice of Huck. If *Little Women* fails to go as deep as Twain's masterpiece, it is precisely because of Alcott's concern with pure-mindedness. Niceness is ever the enemy of art. If you worry about what the neighbors, critics, parents and supposedly pure-minded censors think, you will never create a work that defies the restrictions of the conscious mind and delves into the world of dreams.

1601 is deliberately lewd. It delights in stinking up the air of propriety. It delights in describing great thunder-gusts of farts that make great stenches, and pricks that are stiff until cunts "take ye stiffness out of them." In the midst of all this ribaldry, the assembled company speaks of many things—poetry, theater, art, politics. Twain knew that the muse flies on the wings of flatus, and he was having such a good time writing this Elizabeth pastiche that the humor shines through a hundred years and twenty later. I dare you to read *1601* without giggling and guffawing.

In the last few years a great deal of pious politically correct garbage has been written about pornography. Pornography, the high-minded self-anointed feminist Catharine MacKinnon tells us, is tantamount to an assault on women and causes rape. Pornography, MacKinnon's comrade-in-arms Andrea Dworkin asserts, is a *form* of rape.

A chorus of younger feminists at last has come along to counter these dangerous unexamined contentions. Pornography, says Susie Bright, is necessary to liberation. Pornography, says Sallie Tisdale, is desired by women as well as men. Pornography, says Nadine Strossen, is guaranteed by the Bill of Rights.

But what about the Bill of Rights for artists? Could Robert Mapplethorpe's photographs of lilies have existed without his photographs of pricks? Could Henry Miller have grasped human transcendence in *The Colossus of Maroussi* without having wallowed in the sewers of Paris in *Tropic of Cancer*?

I say no. Without farts, there are no flowers. Without pricks, there are no poems.

This is not the first time in history we have seen an essentially libertarian movement like feminism devolve into a debate about pure-mindedness. The suffragists of the last century also turned into prudish prohibitionists who spent their force proscribing drink and policing morals. One might argue that a concern with pure-mindedness is fatal not only to art but also to political movements.

Why does this urge toward repression crop up in supposedly libertarian movements? And why does the puritanical drive to censor the artist keep recurring? The artist needs to be free to play in the id in order to bring back insights for the ego. But the id is scary. It yawns like a bottomless *vagina dentata*. It threatens to bite off heads, hands, cocks, and to swallow us up in our own darkest impulses. Society fears the id even as it yearns for the release to be found there. We retreat from dream and fantasy even as we long to submerge in them. Make no mistake about it: the primal ooze of creation *is* terrifying. It reminds us of how little control we have over our lives, over our deaths. It reminds us of our origins and inspires us to contemplate our inevitable annihilation.

Pornographic art is perceived as dangerous to political movements because, like the unconscious, it is not programmable. It is dangerous play whose outcome can never be predicted. Since dream is the speech of the unconscious, the artist who would create works of value must be fluent in the language of dream. The pornographic has a direct connection to the unconscious.

I suspect this was why Twain was having such fun with *1601* in the summer of 1876. The filth of *1601* fertilized the garden of Huck's adventures. Like any literary artist who is in touch with his id, Twain instinctively knew that sex and creativity were interrelated. He could not fill *Huckleberry Finn* with farts, pricks and cunts, but he could play in *1601* and prepare his imagination for the antisocial adventures he would give his antihero in the other book.

In his classic essay "Obscenity and the Law of Reflection," Henry Miller suggests that "when obscenity crops out in art, in literature more particularly, it usually functions as a technical device. . . . Its purpose is to awaken, to usher in a sense of reality. In a sense, its use by the artist may be compared to the use of the miraculous by the Masters." Here Miller means the *spiritual* masters. He believed that Christ and the Zen masters only resorted to miracles when such were absolutely necessary to awaken their disciples. The artist uses obscenity the same way. "The real nature of the obscene lies in its lust to convert," Miller says. Obscenity operates in literature as a sort of wake-up call to the unconscious. Obscenity transports us to "another dimension of reality."

Havelock Ellis once said that "adults need obscene literature, as much as children need fairy tales, as a relief from the obsessive force of convention." The urge toward obscenity is nothing more or less than the urge toward freedom. Those who condemn it are clearly afraid of the debauchery that freedom might unleash in them. They inevitably denounce what they are most attracted to. The censor is the one who slavers in private over books, films and visual artifacts that he or she then proscribes for the rest of society.

Throughout history, the urge to censor has always been strongest in those most attracted to the freedom of the obscene. In quashing freedom in others, the censor hopes to quash it within. "Liberation," says Henry Miller, "implies the sloughing off of chains, the bursting of the cocoon. What is obscene are the preliminary or anticipatory movements of birth, the preconscious writhing in the face of a life to be."

Miller goes on to say that the obscene "is an attempt to spy on the secret processes of the universe." The guilt of the creator when he or she knows that something extraordinary is being born comes from the knowledge of tampering with godlike powers, a Promethean guilt for impersonating the immortals. "The obscene has all the qualities of the hidden interval," Miller says. It is

> vast as the Unconscious itself and as amorphous and fluid as the very stuff of the Unconscious. It is what comes to the surface as strange, intoxicating and forbidden, and which therefore arrests and paralyzes, when in the form of Narcissus we bend over our own image in the mirror of our own iniquity. Acknowledged by all, it is nevertheless despised and rejected, wherefore it is constantly emerging in Protean guise at the most unexpected moments. When it is recognized and accepted . . . it inspires no more dread than . . . the flowering lotus which sends its roots down into the mud of the stream on which it is borne.

Sexuality and creativity were not always divorced as they are today and as they were in Mark Twain's day. All so-called primitive and pagan art exhibits the marriage of sexuality and creativity, whether in the form of giant phalluses, multitudinous breasts or pregnant bellies. But the divorce between body and mind that characterizes the Christian era has led the artist to curious strategies of creation and constant guilt for the possession of the creative gift.

We see this guilt as clearly in Mark Twain as in any artist who ever lived. His creative strategies of intermittent composition, his fear of working on a book once it became clear that the writing would inevitably lift the veil and take him into the sacred and forbidden precincts, betray his hypersensitivity to something we might call post-Christian creator guilt, if it weren't such a mouthful.

In "primitive" societies, the artist and the shaman are one. There *is* no discontinuity between artistic creation and the sacred. The shaman-artist creates in order to worship and worships in order to create. Not so the artist in our culture. Always wracked by guilt for the power of creativity itself, beset by censors within and without, our artists are shackled by a sense of transgression so deep it often destroys them. No wonder we use obscenity to break open the door, to lift the veil. No wonder we insist on our right to do so as if our lives depended on it.

They do.

1996

Ursula K. Le Guin

As a child growing up in Berkeley, California, Ursula K. Le Guin (born in 1929) devoured the family's Complete Works of Mark Twain "one red book after the other, snap, munch, gulp, snap, munch, gulp." That child grew up to become a writer of 22 novels, seven books of poetry, 11 collections of stories, four volumes of essays, 12 children's books, and four volumes of translations. Le Guin's work has been translated into 16 languages and has been honored with numerous prizes and awards. Although she has left her mark on the world of letters with projects as diverse as a new translation of the poems of Gabriela Mistral and a new version of Lao Tzu's *Tao Te Ching*, Le Guin is perhaps best known as a pioneer of feminist science fiction. Her groundbreaking exploration of gender in her novel *The Left Hand of Darkness* (1969) is widely credited with having had a transformative impact on the field of science fiction. Gender differences play a central role in Mark Twain's diaries of Adam and Eve. When she read them as a child, Le Guin tells us she "loved them instantly and permanently."

Introduction to
The Diaries of Adam and Eve

Reading Young, Reading Old

Every tribe has its myths, and the younger members of the tribe generally get them wrong. My tribal myth of the great Berkeley Fire of 1923 went this way: when my mother's mother-in-law, who lived near the top of Cedar Street, saw the flames sweeping over the hill straight towards the house, she put her Complete Works of Mark Twain in Twenty-five Volumes into her Model A and went away from that place.

Because I was going to put that story in print, I made the mistake of checking it first with my brother Ted. In a slow, mild sort of way, he took it all to pieces. He said, Well, Lena Brown never had a Model A. As a matter of fact, she didn't drive. The way I remember the story, he said, some fraternity boys came up the street and got her piano out just before the fire reached that hill. And a bearskin rug, and some other things. But I don't remember, he said, that anything was said about the Complete Works of Mark Twain.

He and I agreed, however, that fraternity boys who would choose to rescue a piano and a bear rug from a house about to be engulfed by a fiery inferno might well have also selected the works of Mark Twain. And the peculiarity of their selection may be illuminated by the fact that the piano ended up in the fraternity house. But after the fire or during it, Lena Brown somehow rescued the bear rug and the Complete Works from her rescuers; because Ted remembers the bear; and I certainly, vividly remember the Complete Works.

I also remain convinced that she was very fond of them, that she *would* have rescued them rather than her clothes and silver and checkbook. And maybe she really did. At any rate, when she died she left them to the family, and my brothers and I grew up with them, a full shelf of lightweight, middle-sized books in slightly pebbly and rather ratty red bindings. They are no longer, alas, in the family, but I have tracked down the edition in a library. As soon as I saw the row of red books I said Yes! with the startled joy one would feel at seeing an adult one had loved as a child, alive and looking just as he did fifty years ago. Our set was, to the best of my knowledge, the 1917 Authorized Uniform Edition, published by Harper and Brothers, copyright by the Mark Twain Company.

The only other Complete Works I recall around the house was my Great-Aunt Betsy's Dickens. I was proud of both sets. Complete Works and Uniform Editions are something you don't often see any more except in big libraries, but ordinary people used to own them and be proud of them. They have a majesty about them. Physically they are imposing, the uniform row of bindings, the gold-stamped titles; but the true majesty of a Complete Works is spiritual. It is a great mental edifice, a house of many mansions, into which a reader can enter at any of the doors, or a young reader can climb in the windows, and wander about, experiencing magnanimity.

My great-aunt was very firm about not letting us get into Dickens yet. She said nobody under eighteen had any business reading Dickens. We would merely misunderstand him and so spoil the pleasure we would otherwise take in him the rest of our lives. She was right, and I am grateful. At sixteen, I whined till she let me read *David Copperfield*, but she warned me about Steerforth, lest I fall in love with him as she had done, and break my heart. When Betsy died she left me her Dickens. We had him re-bound, for he had got a bit shabby traveling around the West with her for fifty or sixty years. When I take a book from that set, I think how she had this immense refuge and resource with her wherever she went, reliable as not much else in her life was.

Except for Dickens, nobody told us not to read anything, and I burrowed headlong into every book on the shelves. If it was a story, I read it. And there stood that whole row of red books, all full of stories.

Obviously I got to *Tom Sawyer* very soon, and *Huckleberry Finn*; and my next-older brother, Karl, showed me the sequels, which we judged pretty inferior, critical brats that we were. After *The Prince and the Pauper*, I got into *Life on the Mississippi* and *Roughing It*—my prime favorite for years—and the stories, and the whole Complete Works in fact, one red book after the other, snap, munch, gulp, snap, munch, gulp.

I didn't much like the Connecticut Yankee. The meaning of the book went right over my head. I just thought the hero was a pigheaded, loudmouthed show-off. But a little thing like not *liking* a book didn't keep me from *reading* it. Not then. It was like Brussels sprouts. Nobody could like them, but they existed, they were food, you ate them. Eating and reading were a central, essential part of life. Eating and reading can't all be Huck and corn on the cob; some of it has to be Brussels sprouts and the Yankee. And there were plenty of good bits in the Yankee. The only one of the row of red books I ever stuck at was *Joan of Arc*. I just couldn't swallow her. She wouldn't go down. And I believe our set was lacking the *Christian Science* volume, because I don't remember even having a go at that. If it had been there, I would have chewed at it, the way kids do, the way Eskimo housewives soften walrus hide, though I might not have been able to swallow it either.

My memory is that it was Karl who discovered Adam's and

Eve's diaries and told me to read them. I have always followed Karl's advice in reading, even after he became an English professor, because he never led me astray before he was a professor. I never would have got into *Tom Brown's School Days*, for instance, if he hadn't told me you can skip the first sixty pages, and it must have been Karl who told me to stick with *Candide* till I got to the person with one buttock, who would make it all worthwhile. So I found the right red book and read both the diaries. I loved them instantly and permanently.

And yet when I reread them not long ago, it was the first time for about fifty years. Not having the Complete Works with me throughout life, I have only reread my favorites of the books, picked up here and there, and the stories contained in various collections. And none of those collections contained the diaries.

This five-decade gap in time makes it irresistible to try and compare my reading of the diaries as a child with my reading of them now.

The first thing to be said is that when I reread them, there did not seem to have been any gap at all. What's fifty years? Well, when it comes to some of the books one read at five or at fifteen, it's an abyss. Many books I loved and learned from have fallen into it. I absolutely cannot read *The Swiss Family Robinson* and am amazed that I ever did—talk about chewing walrus hide! But the diaries give me a curious feeling of constancy, almost of immortality: because *they* haven't changed at all. They are just as fresh and surprising as when I read them first. Nor am I sure that my reading of them is very different from what it was back then.

I will try to follow that then-and-now response through three aspects of the diaries, humor, gender, and religion.

Though it seems that children and adults have different senses of humor, they overlap so much I wonder if people just don't use the same apparatus differently at different ages. At about the time I first came on the diaries, ten or eleven, I was reading the stories of James Thurber with sober, pious attention. I knew they were funny, that grown-ups laughed aloud reading them, but they didn't make me laugh. They were wonderful, mysterious tales of human behavior, like all the folktales and stories in which people did the amazing, terrifying, inexplicable things that grown-ups do. The various night wanderings of the Thurber family in "The Night the Bed Fell Down" were no more and no less strange to me than the behavior of the Reed family in the first chapter of *Jane Eyre*. Both were fascinating descriptions of life—eyewitness accounts, guidebooks to the world awaiting me. I was much too interested to laugh.

When I did laugh at Thurber was when he played with words. The man who came with the reeves and the cook who was alarmed by the dome-shaped thing on top of the refrigerator were a source of pure delight to me, then as now. The accessibility of Mark Twain's humor to a child surely has much to do with the way he plays with language, the deadpan absurdities, the marvelous choices of word. The first time I read the story about the bluejay trying to fill the cabin with acorns, I nearly died. I lay on the floor gasping and writhing with joy. Even now I feel a peaceful cheer come over me when I think of that bluejay. And it's all in the way he tells it, as they say. The story is the way the story is told.

Adam's diary is funny, when it is funny, because of the way Adam writes it.

> . . . This made her sorry for the creatures which live in there, which she calls fish, for she continues to fasten names on to things that don't need them and don't come when they are called by them, which is a matter of no consequence to her, as she is such a numskull anyway; so she got a lot of them out and brought them in last night and put them in my bed to keep warm, but I have noticed them now and then all day, and I don't see that they are any happier there than they were before, only quieter.

Now that is a pure Mark-Twain-tour-de-force sentence, covering an immense amount of territory in an effortless, aimless ramble that seems to be heading nowhere in particular and ends up with breathtaking accuracy at the gold mine. Any sensible child would find that funny, perhaps not following all its divagations but delighted by the swing of it, by the word "numskull," by the idea of putting fish in the bed; and as that child grew older and reread it, its reward would only grow; and if that grown-up child had to write an essay on the piece and therefore earnestly studied and pored over this sentence, she would end up in unmitigated admiration of its vocabulary, syntax, pacing, sense, and rhythm, above all the beautiful timing of the last two words; and she would, and she does, still find it funny.

Twain's humor is indestructible. Trying to make a study of the rhythms of prose last year, I analyzed a paragraph from the jumping frog story—laboring over it, dissecting it, counting beats, grouping phrases, reducing it to a mere drum score—and even after all that mauling, every time I read it, it was as fresh-flowing and lively and amusing as ever, or more so. The prose itself is indestructible. It is all of a piece. It is a living person speaking. Mark Twain put his voice on paper with a fidelity and vitality that makes electronic recordings seem crude and quaint.

I wonder if this is why we trust him, even though he lets us down so often. Lapses such as the silly stuff about Niagara in Adam's diary—evidently stuffed in to make it suit a publication about the Falls—would make me distrust most writers. But Mark Twain's purity is unmistakable and incorruptible, which is why the lapses stick out so, and yet are forgivable. I have heard a great pianist who made a great many mistakes in playing; the mistakes were of no account because the music was true. Though Mark Twain forces his humor sometimes, always his own voice comes back, comes through; and his own voice is one of hyperbole and absurdity and wild invention and absolute truth.

So all in all my response to the humor of the diaries is very much what it was fifty years ago. This is partly because a good deal of the humor is perfectly childish. I mean that as praise. There is no meanness in it, no nudging and winking, nothing snide. Now, as then, I find Adam very funny, but so obtuse I often want to kick him rather than laugh at him. Eve isn't quite as funny, but I don't get as cross with her, so it's easier to laugh.

A parenthesis. The illustrations which accompany the texts used for this edition pose a puzzle to me. The 1917 Authorized Edition in the library, "my" edition, does not contain any illustrations to Adam's diary at all; and yet Strothmann's "stone-carving" pictures were perfectly familiar. Where have I ever seen them before? I don't know. They certainly seem to belong. Yet—now—I am aware that they're not only amusing and inventive decorations, but also ironically interpret the text. For instance, on a Sunday when Adam's only diary entry is a sullen "Pulled through," the picture shows him in a Morris chair smoking a stogie and reading the papers in perfect Sunday luxury. Even as a child, I realized that Adam was what we now call an unreliable narrator. But it does appear that the illustrator went further than Mark Twain intended in betraying Adam's self-pity.

The 1917 edition contains only the first and the last of Lester Ralph's illustrations to Eve's diary, and no mention of the artist's name. I recognized those two with delight when I saw them again. I would have liked them all, as a child; their art nouveau style was familiar to me from picture books, and I felt at home with it. Though the whole set is rather repetitive, the pictures have charm and elegance; the line is sure and clean; and Eve is the robust and joyous young woman she ought to be. The text is, I think, genuinely enriched by them, though they bring out its sweetness rather than its humor.

I read the diaries before I had any personal interest, as you might say, in gender. I had noticed that there were males and females and had learned from a useful Germanic book how babies occurred, but the whole thing was entirely remote and theoretical, about as immediately interesting to me as the Keynesian theory of economics. "Latency," one of Freud's fine imaginative inventions, was more successful than most; children used to have years of freedom before they had to start working their hormones into the kind of lascivious lather that is now expected of ten-year-olds. Anyhow, in the 1940s gender was not a subject of discussion. Men were men (running things or in uniform, mostly), women were women (housekeeping or in factories, mostly), and that was that. Except for a few subversives like Virginia Woolf, nobody publicly questioned the institutions and assumptions of male primacy. It was the century's low point architecturally in the Construction of

Gender, reduced in those years to something about as spacious and comfortable as a broom closet.

But the diaries date from the turn of the century, a time of revolutionary inquiry into gender roles, the first age of feminism, the period of the woman suffrage movement and of the "New Woman"—who was precisely the robust and joyously competent Eve that Mark Twain gives us.

I see now in the diaries, along with a tenderness and a profound delicacy of feeling about women, a certain advocacy. Mark Twain is always on the side of the underdog; and though he believed it was and must be a man's world, he knew that women were the underdogs in it. This fine sense of justice is what gives both the diaries their moral complexity.

There was an element of discomfort in them for me as a child, and I think it lies just here, in that complexity and a certain degree of self-contradiction.

It is not Adam's superiority of brains or brawn, but his blockish stupidity, that gives him his absolute advantage over Eve. He does not notice, does not listen, is uninterested, indifferent, dumb. He will not relate to her; she must relate herself—in words and actions—to him, and relate him to the rest of Eden. He is entirely satisfied with himself as he is; she must adapt her ways to him. He is immovably fixed at the center of his own attention. To live with him she must agree to be peripheral to him, contingent, secondary.

The degree of social and psychological truth in this picture of life in Eden is pretty considerable. Milton thought it was a fine arrangement; it appears Mark Twain didn't, since he shows us at the end of both diaries that although Eve has not changed much, she has changed Adam profoundly. She always was awake. He slowly, finally wakes up, and does her, and therefore himself, justice. But isn't it too late, for her?

All this I think I followed pretty well, and was fascinated and somewhat troubled by, though I could not have discussed it, when I read the diaries as a child. Children have a seemingly innate passion for justice; they don't have to be taught it. They have to have it beaten out of them, in fact, to end up as properly prejudiced adults.

Mark Twain and I both grew up in a society that cherished a visionary ideal of gender by pairs: the breadwinning, self-reliant husband and the home-dwelling, dependent wife. He the oak, she the ivy; power his, grace hers. He works and earns; she "doesn't work," but she keeps his house, bears and brings up his children, and furnishes him the aesthetic and often the spiritual comforts of life. Now, at this latter end of the century, the religiopolitical conservative's vision of what men and women do and should do is still close to that picture, though even more remote from most people's experience than it was fifty or a hundred years ago. Do Twain's Adam and Eve essentially fit this powerful stereotype, or do they vary it significantly?

I think the variations are significant, even if the text fudges them in the end. Mark Twain is not supporting a gender ideal, but investigating what he sees as real differences between women and men, some of them fitting into that ideal, some in conflict with it.

Eve is the intellectual in Eden, Adam the redneck. She is wildly curious and wants to learn everything, to name everything. Adam has no curiosity about anything, certain that he knows all he needs to know. She wants to talk, he wants to grunt. She is sociable, he is solitary. She prides herself on being scientific, though she settles for her own pet theory without testing it; her method is purely intuitive and rational, without a shadow of empiricism. He thinks she ought to test her ideas, but is too lazy to do it himself. He goes over Niagara Falls in a barrel, he doesn't say why; apparently because a man does such things. Far more influenced by imagination than he, she does dangerous things only when she doesn't know they're dangerous. She rides tigers and talks to the serpent. She is rebellious, adventurous, and independent; he does not question authority. She is the innocent troublemaker. Her loving anarchism ruins his mindless, self-sufficient, authoritarian Eden—and saves him from it.

Does it save her?

This spirited, intelligent, anarchic Eve reminds me of H. G. Wells's Ann Veronica, an exemplary New Woman of 1909. Yet Ann Veronica's courage and curiosity finally lead her not to independence but to wifehood, seen as the proper and sufficient fulfillment of feminine being. We are ominously close to the Natasha Syndrome, the collapse of a vivid woman character into a brood sow as soon as she marries and has children. Once she has won Adam over, once the children come, does Eve stop asking and thinking and singing and naming and venturing? We don't know. Tolstoy gives us a horrible glimpse of Natasha married; Wells tries to convince us Ann Veronica is going to be just fine; but Mark Twain tells us nothing about what Eve becomes. She falls silent, which is not a good sign. After the Fall we have mostly Adam's voice, puzzling mightily over what kind of animal Cain is. Eve tells us only that she would love Adam even if he beat her—a very bad sign. And, forty years after, she says, "He is strong, I am weak, I am not so necessary to him as he is to me— life without him would not be life; how could I endure it?"

I don't know whether I am supposed to believe her, or can believe her. It doesn't sound like the woman I knew. Eve, weak? Rubbish! Adam's usefulness as a helpmeet is problematic: a man who, when she tells him they'll have to work for their living, decides, "She will be useful. I will superintend"—a man who thinks his son is a kangaroo? Eve did need him in order to have children, and since she loves him she would miss him; but where is the evidence that she couldn't survive without him? He would presumably have survived without her, in the brutish way he survived before her. But surely it is their *interdependence* that is the real point?

I want, now, to read the diaries as a subtle, sweet-natured send-up of the Strong Man/Weak Woman arrangement; but I'm not sure it's possible to do so, or not entirely. It may be both a send-up and a capitulation.

And Adam has the last word. But the poignancy of those six last words is utterly unexpected, a cry from the heart. It made me shiver as a child; it does now.

I was raised as irreligious as a jackrabbit, and probably this is one reason Mark Twain made so much sense to me as a child. Descriptions of churchgoing interested me as the exotic rites of a foreign tribe, and nobody described churchgoing better than Mark Twain did. But God, as I encountered him in my reading, seemed only to cause unnecessary complications, making people fall into strange postures and do depressing things; he treated Beth March abominably, and did his best to ruin Jane Eyre's life before she traded him in for Rochester. I didn't read any of the books in which God is the main character until a few years later. I was perfectly content with books in which he didn't figure at all.

Could anybody but Mark Twain have told the story of Adam and Eve without mentioning Jehovah?

As a heathen child I was entirely comfortable with his version. I took it for granted that it was the sensible one.

As an ancient heathen I still find it sensible, but can better appreciate its orginality and courage. The nerve of the man, the marvelous, stunning independence of that mind! In pious, prayerful, censorious, self-righteous Christian America of 1896, or 1996 for that matter, to show God as an unnecessary hypothesis, by letting Eve and Adam cast themselves out of Eden without any help at all from him, and really none from the serpent either—to put sin and salvation, love and death, in our own hands, as our own, strictly human business, our responsibility—now that's a free soul, and a brave one.

What luck for a child to meet such a soul when she is young. What luck for a country to have a Mark Twain in its heart.

1996

Toni Morrison

When Toni Morrison (born in 1931) was awarded the Nobel Prize in Literature in 1993, she was the first American woman to win it in 55 years and the first African-American author to win the prize. In "novels characterized by visionary force and poetic import," the citation read, she "gives life to an essential aspect of American reality." After an Ohio childhood Morrison studied literature at Howard University and Cornell, then went on to teach at Texas Southern, Yale, the State University of New York at Albany, and Princeton. She also worked as an editor at Random House in the 1960s. Her novels include *The Bluest Eye* (1970), *Sula* (1973), *Song of Solomon* (1977), *Tar Baby* (1981), *Beloved* (1987), *Jazz* (1992), *Paradise* (1999), *Love* (2003), and *A Mercy* (2008). Morrison's achievements have been recognized by many awards, including an honorary Doctor of Letters from Oxford in 2005—the same degree bestowed on Mark Twain 98 years earlier. Morrison's first readings of *Adventures of Huckleberry Finn* filled her with "fear and alarm," as she notes in the essay that follows. But when she returned to the work as she was honing her own skills as a novelist, she was impressed by the way the book managed to "transform its contradictions into fruitful complexities." Noting that "the 1880s saw the collapse of civil rights for blacks as well as the publication of *Huckleberry Finn*," a sign that the country wanted "to bury the combustible issues Twain raised in his novel," Morrison says, "the nation, as well as Tom Sawyer, was deferring Jim's freedom in agonizing play." Morrison has a succinctly eloquent response to efforts to take the book out of the curriculum in American high schools: "the cyclical attempts to remove the novel from classrooms extend Jim's captivity on into each generation of readers."

Introduction to
Adventures of Huckleberry Finn

Fear and alarm are what I remember most about my first encounter with Mark Twain's *Adventures of Huckleberry Finn*. Palpable alarm. Unlike the treasure-island excursion of *Tom Sawyer*, at no point along Huck's journey was a happy ending signaled or guaranteed. Reading *Huckleberry Finn*, chosen randomly without guidance or recommendation, was deeply disturbing. My second reading of it, under the supervision of an English teacher in junior high school, was no less uncomfortable—rather more. It provoked a feeling I can only describe now as muffled rage, as though appreciation of the work required my complicity in and sanction of something shaming. Yet the satisfactions were great: riveting episodes of flight, of cunning; the convincing commentary on adult behavior, watchful and insouciant; the authority of a child's voice in language cut for its renegade tongue and sharp intelligence. Liberating language—not baby talk for the young, nor the doggedly patronizing language of so many books on the "children's shelf." And there were interesting female characters: the clever woman undeceived by Huck's disguise; the young girl whose sorrow at the sale of slaves is grief for a family split rather than conveniences lost.

Nevertheless, for the second time, curling through the pleasure, clouding the narrative reward, was my original alarm, coupled now with a profoundly distasteful complicity.

Then, in the mid-fifties, I read it again—or sort of read it. Actually I read it through the lenses of Leslie Fiedler and Lionel Trilling. Exposed to Trilling's reverent intimacy and Fiedler's irreverent familiarity, I concluded that their criticisms served me better than the novel had, not only because they helped me see many things I had been unaware of, but precisely because they ignored or rendered trivial the things that caused my unease.

In the early eighties I read *Huckleberry Finn* again, provoked, I believe, by demands to remove the novel from the libraries and required reading lists of public schools. These efforts were based, it seemed to me, on a narrow notion of how to handle the offense Mark Twain's use of the term "nigger" would occasion for black students and the corrosive effect it would have on white ones. It struck me as a purist yet elementary kind of censorship designed to appease adults rather than educate children. Amputate the problem, band-aid the solution. A serious comprehensive discussion of the term by an intelligent teacher certainly would have benefited my eighth-grade class and would have spared all of us (a few blacks, many whites—mostly second-generation immigrant children) some grief. Name calling is a plague of childhood and a learned activity ripe for discussion as soon as it surfaces. Embarrassing as it had been to hear the dread word spoken, and therefore sanctioned, in class, my experience of Jim's epithet had little to do with my initial nervousness the book had caused. Reading "nigger" hundreds of times embarrassed, bored, annoyed—but did not faze me. In this latest reading I was curious about the source of my alarm—my sense that danger lingered after the story ended. I was powerfully attracted to the combination of delight and fearful agitation lying entwined like crossed fingers in the pages. And it was significant that this novel which had given so much pleasure to young readers was also complicated territory for sophisticated scholars.

Usually the divide is substantial: if a story that pleased us as novice readers does not disintegrate as we grow older, it maintains its value only in its retelling for other novices or to summon uncapturable pleasure as playback. Also, the books that academic critics find consistently rewarding are works only partially available to the minds of young readers. *Adventures of Huckleberry Finn* manages to close that divide, and one of the reasons it requires no leap is that in addition to the reverence the novel stimulates is its ability to transform its contradictions into fruitful complexities and to seem to be deliberately cooperating in the controversy it has excited. The brilliance of *Huckleberry Finn* is that it *is* the argument it raises.

My 1980s reading, therefore, was an effort to track the unease, nail it down, and learn in so doing the nature of my troubled relationship to this classic American work.

Although its language—sardonic, photographic, persuasively aural—and the structural use of the river as control and chaos seem to me quite the major feats of *Huckleberry Finn*, much of the novel's genius lies in its quiescence, the silences that pervade it and give it a porous quality that is by turns brooding and soothing. It lies in the approaches to and exits from action; the byways and inlets seen out of the corner of the eye; the subdued images in which the repetition of a simple word, such as "lonesome," tolls like an evening bell; the moments when nothing is said, when scenes and incidents swell the heart unbearably precisely because unarticulated, and force an act of imagination almost against the will. Some of the stillness, in the beautifully rendered eloquence of a child, is breathtaking. "The sky looks ever so deep when you lay down on your back in the moonshine." ". . . it was big trees all about, and gloomy in there amongst them. There was freckled places on the ground where the light sifted down through the leaves, and the freckled places swapped about a little." Other moments, however, are frightening meditations on estrangement and death. Huck records a conversation he overhears among happy men he cannot see but whose voices travel from the landing over the water to him. Although he details what the men say, it is how distant Huck is from them, how separated he is from their laughing male camaraderie, that makes the scene memorable. References to death, looking at it or contemplating it, are numerous. ". . . this drownded man was just his [Pap's] size, . . . but they couldn't make nothing out of the face . . . floating on his back in the waters . . . took him and buried him on the bank. . . . I knowed mighty well that a drownded man don't float on his back, but on his face." The emotional management of death seeds the novel: Huck yearns for death, runs from its certainty and feigns it. His deepest, uncomic feelings about his status as an outsider, someone "dead" to society, are murmuring interludes of despair, soleness, isolation and unlove. A plaintive note of melancholy and dread surfaces immediately in the first chapter, after Huck sums up the narrative of his life in a prior book.

> Then I set down in a chair by the window and tried to think of something cheerful, but it warn't no use. I felt so lonesome I most wished I was dead. The stars were shining, and the leaves rustled in the woods ever so mournful; and I heard an owl, away off, who-whooing about somebody that was dead, and a whippowill and a dog crying about somebody that was going to die; and the wind was trying to whisper something to me and I couldn't make out what it was, and so it made the cold shivers run over me. Then away out in the woods I heard that kind of a sound that a ghost makes. . . . I got so downhearted and scared I did wish I had some company.

Although Huck complains bitterly of rules and regulations, I see him to be running not from external control but from external chaos. Nothing in society makes sense; all is in peril. Upper-class, churchgoing, elegantly housed families annihilate themselves in a psychotic feud, and Huck has to drag two of their corpses from the water—one of whom is a just-made friend, the boy Buck; he sees the public slaughter of a drunk; he hears the vicious plans of murderers on a wrecked steamboat; he spends a large portion of the book in the company of "[Pap's] kind of people"—the fraudulent, thieving Duke and King who wield brutal power over him, just as his father did. No wonder that when he is alone, whether safe in the Widow's house or hiding from his father, he is so very frightened and frequently suicidal.

If the emotional environment into which Twain places his protagonist is dangerous, then the leading question the novel poses for me is, What does Huck need to live without terror, melancholy and suicidal thoughts? The answer, of course, is Jim. When Huck is among society—whether respectable or deviant, rich or poor—he is alert to and consumed by its deception, its illogic, its scariness. Yet he is depressed by himself and sees nature more often as fearful. But when he and Jim become the only "we," the anxiety is outside, not within. ". . . we would watch the lonesomeness of the river . . . for about an hour . . . just solid lonesomeness." Unmanageable terror gives way to a pastoral, idyllic, intimate timelessness minus the hierarchy of age, status or adult control. It has never seemed to me that, in contrast to the entrapment and menace of the shore, the river itself provides this solace. The consolation, the healing properties Huck longs for, is made possible by Jim's active, highly vocal affection. It is in Jim's company that the dread of contemplated nature disappears, that even storms are beautiful and sublime, that real talk—comic, pointed, sad—takes place. Talk so free of lies it produces an aura of restfulness and peace unavailable anywhere else in the novel.

Pleasant as this relationship is, suffused as it is by a lightness they both enjoy and a burden of responsibility both assume, it cannot continue. Knowing the relationship is discontinuous, doomed to separation, is (or used to be) typical of the experience of white/black childhood friendships (mine included), and the cry of inevitable rupture is all the more anguished by being mute. Every reader knows that Jim will be dismissed without explanation at some point; that no enduring adult fraternity will emerge. Anticipating this loss may have led Twain to the over-the-top minstrelization of Jim. Predictable and common as the gross stereotyping of blacks was in nineteenth-century litera-ture, here, nevertheless, Jim's portrait seems unaccountably ex-cessive and glaring in its contradictions—like an ill-made clown suit that cannot hide the man within. Twain's black characters were most certainly based on real people. His nonfiction obser-vations of and comments on "actual" blacks are full of refer-ences to their guilelessness, intelligence, creativity, wit, caring, etc. None is portrayed as relentlessly idiotic. Yet Jim is unlike, in many ways, the real people he must have been based on. There may be more than one reason for this extravagance. In addition to accommodating a racist readership, writing Jim so complete a buffoon solves the problem of "missing" him that would have been unacceptable at the novel's end, and helps to solve another problem: how effectively to bury the father figure underneath the minstrel paint. The foregone temporariness of the friendship urges the degradation of Jim (to divert Huck's and our inadver-tent sorrow at the close), and minstrelizing him necessitates and exposes an enforced silence on the subject of white fatherhood.

The withholdings at critical moments, which I once took to be deliberate evasions, stumbles even, or a writer's impatience with his or her material, I began to see as otherwise: as en-trances, crevices, gaps, seductive invitations flashing the possi-bility of meaning. Unarticulated eddies that encourage diving into the novel's undertow—the real place where writer captures reader. An excellent example of what is available in this undertow is the way Twain comments on the relationship between the antebellum period in which the narrative takes place and the later period in which the novel was composed. The 1880s saw the collapse of civil rights for blacks as well as the publication of *Huckleberry Finn*. This collapse was an effort to bury the com-bustible issues Twain raised in his novel. The nation, as well as Tom Sawyer, was deferring Jim's freedom in agonizing play.

The cyclical attempts to remove the novel from classrooms extend Jim's captivity on into each generation of readers.

Or consider Huck's inability to articulate his true feelings for Jim to anybody other than the reader. When he "humbles himself" in apology to Jim for the painful joke he plays on him, we are not given the words. Even to Tom, the only other friend he has and the only one his own age, he must mask his emotions. Until the hell-or-heaven choice, Huck can speak of the genuine affection and respect for Jim that blossoms throughout the narrative only aslant, or comically to the reader—never directly to any character or to Jim himself. While Jim repeatedly iterates his love, the depth of Huck's feelings for Jim is stressed, underscored and rendered unimpeachable by Twain's calculated use of speechlessness. The accumulated silences build to Huck's ultimate act of love, in which he accepts the endangerment of his soul. These silences do not appear to me of merely historical accuracy—a realistic portrait of how a white child *would* respond to a black slave; they seem to be expert technical solutions to the narrative's complexities and, by the way, highly prophetic descriptions of contemporary negotiations between races.

Consider the void that follows the revelation of Jim as a responsible adult and caring parent in chapter 23. Huck has nothing to say. The chapter does not close; it simply stops. Blanketed by eye dialect, placed auspiciously at chapter's end, held up, framed, as it were, for display by Huck's refusal to comment, it is one of the most moving remembrances in American literature. Then comes the "meanwhile-back-at-the ranch" first line of the next chapter. The hush between these two chapters thunders. And its roar is enhanced by Huck's observation on the preceding page: that although Jim's desperate love for his wife and children "don't seem natural," Huck "reckon[s] it's so." This comment is fascinating less for its racism than for the danger it deflects from Huck himself. Huck has never seen nor experienced a tender, caring father—yet he steps out of this well of ignorance to judge Jim's role as a father.

What I read into this observation and the hiatus that follows Jim's confirmation of his "naturalness" is that the line of thought

Jim's fatherhood might provoke cannot be pursued by the author or his protagonist for fear of derailing the text into another story or destabilizing its center (this is *Huck's* adventure, not Jim's). It invites serious speculation about fatherhood—its expectations and ramifications—in the novel. First of all, it's hard not to notice that except for Judge Thatcher all of the white men who might function as father figures for Huck are ridiculed for their hypocrisy, corruption, extreme ignorance and/or violence. Thus Huck's "no comment" on Jim's status as a father works either as a comfortable evasion for or as a critique of a white readership, as well as being one of the gags Twain shoves in Huck's mouth to protect him from the line of thought neither he nor Twain can safely pursue.

As an abused and homeless child running from a feral male parent, Huck cannot dwell on Jim's confession and regret about parental negligence without precipitating a crisis from which neither he nor the text could recover. Huck's desire for a father who is adviser and trustworthy companion is universal, but he also needs something more: a father whom, unlike his own, he can control. No white man can serve all three functions. If the runaway Huck discovered on the island had been a white convict with protective paternal instincts, none of this would work, for there could be no guarantee of control and no games-playing nonsense concerning his release at the end. Only a black male slave can deliver all Huck desires. Because Jim can be controlled, it becomes possible for Huck to feel responsible for and to him—but without the onerous burden of lifelong debt that a real father figure would demand. For Huck, Jim is a father-for-free. This delicate, covert and fractious problematic is thus hidden and exposed by litotes and speechlessness, both of which are dramatic ways of begging attention.

Concerning this matter of fatherhood, there are two other instances of silence—one remarkable for its warmth, the other for its glacial coldness. In the first, Jim keeps silent for practically four-fifths of the book about having seen Pap's corpse. There seems no reason for this withholding except his concern for Huck's emotional well-being. Although one could argue that knowing the menace of his father was over might relieve

Huck enormously, it could also be argued that dissipating that threat would remove the principal element of the necessity for escape—Huck's escape, that is. In any case, silence on this point persists and we learn its true motive in the penultimate paragraph in the book. And right there is the other speech void—cold and shivery in its unsaying. Jim tells Huck that his money is safe because his father is dead.

"Doan' you 'member de house dat was float'n down de river, en dey wuz a man in dah kivered up, en I went in en unkivered him and didn' let you come in? . . . dat wuz him." Huck says and thinks nothing about it. The following sentence, we are to believe, is Huck's very next thought: "Tom's most well now. . . ."

As a reader I am relieved to know Pap is no longer a menace to his son's well-being, but Huck does not share my relief. Again the father business is erased. What after all could Huck say? That he is as glad as I am? That would not do. Huck's decency prevents him from taking pleasure in anybody's death. That he is sorry? Wishes his father were alive? Hardly. The whole premise of escape while fearing and feigning death would collapse, and the contradiction would be unacceptable. Instead the crevice widens and beckons reflection on what this long-withheld information means. Any comment at this juncture, positive or negative, would lay bare the white father/white son animosity and harm the prevailing though illicit black father/white son bonding that has already taken place.

Such profoundly realized and significant moments, met with startling understatement or shocking absence of any comment at all, constitute the entrances I mentioned earlier—the invitation Twain offers that I could not refuse.

Earlier I posed the question, What does Huck need to live without despair and thoughts of suicide? My answer was, Jim. There is another question the novel poses for me: What would it take for Huck to live happily without Jim? That is the problem that gnarls the dissolution of their relationship. The freeing of Jim is withheld, fructified, top-heavy with pain, because without Jim there is no more book, no more story to tell.

There is a moment when it could have happened, when Jim, put ashore at Cairo, would have gone his way, leaving Huck to experience by himself the other adventures that follow. The reasons they miss Cairo are: there are only saplings to secure the raft; the raft tears away; Huck "couldn't budge" for half a minute; Huck forgets he has tied the canoe, can't "hardly do anything" with his hands and loses time releasing it; they are enveloped in a "solid white fog"; and for a reason even Huck doesn't understand, Jim does not do what is routine in foggy weather—beat a tin pan to signal his location. During the separation Huck notes the "dismal and lonesome" scene and searches for Jim until he is physically exhausted. Readers are as eager as he is to locate Jim, but when he does, receiving Jim's wild joy, Huck does not express his own. Rather Twain writes in the cruel joke that first sabotages the easily won relief and sympathy we feel for Jim, then leads Huck and us to a heightened restoration of his stature. A series of small accidents prevents Jim's exit from the novel, and Huck is given the gift of an assertive as well as already loving black father. It is to the father, not the nigger, that he "humbles" himself.

So there will be no "adventures" without Jim. The risk is too great. To Huck and to the novel. When the end does come, when Jim is finally, tortuously, unnecessarily freed, able now to be a father to his own children, Huck runs. Not back to the town—even if it is safe now—but a further run, for the "territory." And if there are complications out there in the world, Huck, we are to assume, is certainly ready for them. He has had a first-rate education in social and individual responsibility, and it is interesting to note that the lessons of his growing but secret activism begin to be punctuated by speech, not silence, by moves toward truth, rather than quick lies.

When the King and Duke auction Peter Wilks's slaves, Huck is moved by the sorrow of Wilks's nieces—which is caused not by losing the slaves but by the blasting of the family.

> . . . along about noon-time, the girls' joy got the first jolt. A couple of nigger-traders come along, and the king sold them the niggers reasonable, for three-day drafts as they called it, and away they went, the two sons up the river to Memphis, and their mother down the river to Orleans. I thought them poor girls and them niggers would break

their hearts for grief; they cried around each other, and took on so it most made me down sick to see it. The girls said they hadn't ever dreamed of seeing the family separated or sold away from the town. . . .

The thing made a big stir in the town, too, and a good many come out flatfooted and said it was scandalous to separate the mother and the children that way.

Later, when Huck sees Mary Jane Wilks with "her face in her hands, crying," he knows what is bothering her even before he asks her to tell him about it. "And it was the niggers—I just expected it." I think it is important to note that he is responding to the separation of parents and children. When Mary Jane sobs, "Oh, dear, dear, to think they ain't *ever* going to see each other any more!" Huck reacts so strongly he blurts out a part of the truth just to console her. "But they *will*—and inside of two weeks—and I *know* it." Her dismay over the most grotesque consequences of slavery catapults him into one of his most mature and difficult decisions—to abandon silence and chance the truth.

The change from underground activist to vocal one marks Huck's other important relationship—that between himself and Tom Sawyer, to whom Huck has always been subservient. Huck's cooperation in Jim's dehumanization is not total. It is pierced with mumbling disquiet as the degradation becomes more outré. "That warn't the plan"; "there ain't no necessity for it"; "we're going to get into trouble with Aunt Polly"; ". . . if you'll take my advice"; "what's the sense in . . ."; "Confound it, it's foolish, Tom"; "Jim's too old. . . . He won't last"; "How long will it take?"; "it's one of the most jackass ideas I ever struck." But these objections are not enough. Our apprehension as we follow the free fall of the father is only mildly subdued by our satisfaction at the unmanacled exit of the freedman. Tom Sawyer's silence about Jim's legal status is perverse. So perverse that the fact that Huck never speaks of or considers returning to his hometown to carry on with his erstwhile best friend (this time in safety *and* with money of his own) but wants to leave civilization altogether is more than understandable. Huck cannot have an enduring relationship with Jim; he refuses one with Tom.

The source of my unease reading this amazing, troubling book now seems clear: an imperfect coming to terms with three matters Twain addresses—Huck Finn's estrangement, soleness and morbidity as an outcast child; the disproportionate sadness at the center of Jim's and his relationship; and the secrecy in which Huck's engagement with (rather than escape from) a racist society is necessarily conducted. It is also clear that the rewards of my effort to come to terms have been abundant. My alarm, aroused by Twain's precise rendering of childhood's fear of death and abandonment, remains—as it should. It has been extremely worthwhile slogging through Jim's shame and humiliation to recognize the sadness, the tragic implications at the center of his relationship with Huck. My fury at the maze of deceit, the risk of personal harm that a white child is forced to negotiate in a race-inflected society, is dissipated by the exquisite uses to which Twain puts that maze, that risk.

Yet the larger question, the danger that sifts from the novel's last page, is whether Huck, minus Jim, will be able to stay those three monsters as he enters the "territory." Will that undefined space, so falsely imagined as "open," be free of social chaos, personal morbidity, and further moral complications embedded in adulthood and citizenship? Will it be free not only of nightmare fathers but of dream fathers too? Twain did not write Huck there. He imagined instead a reunion—Huck, Jim and Tom, soaring in a balloon over Egypt.

For a hundred years, the argument that this novel *is* has been identified, reidentified, examined, waged and advanced. What it cannot be is dismissed. It is classic literature, which is to say it heaves, manifests and lasts.

1996

Gore Vidal

The author of over two dozen works of fiction, including a number of historical novels engaging various chapters of his nation's past, Gore Vidal (born in 1925) gave Mark Twain a cameo role in his historical novel *1876*. But it is the Mark Twain who emerged a quarter century afterward, the anti-imperialist Twain, who holds particular appeal for Vidal. Like Twain, Vidal has reigned as one of the leading anti-imperialist writers of his era. In scores of outspoken, outraged essays that originally appeared in publications such as *The New York Review of Books* or *The Nation*, Vidal has torn into successive American administrations for what he views as their wrongheaded, blinkered, self-aggrandizing foreign policy. The course of empire, American-style, has long been a topic of concern for Vidal, and his vitriolic wit takes no prisoners. Any attempt to read Vidal's blunt dissent from conventional pieties as anti-American is of necessity derailed by the fact that Mark Twain was there first. As Vidal reminds us in the essay that follows, Twain's *To the Person Sitting in Darkness* was published as a pamphlet in 1901, "a year in which we were busy telling the Filipinos" that "strictly for their own good, we would have to kill one or two hundred thousand men, women, and children in order to make their country into an American-style democracy." Most Americans, Vidal tells us, "were happy to follow the exuberant lead of the prime architect of empire, Theodore Roosevelt. . . . But then, suddenly, Mark Twain quite forgot that he was *the* American writer and erupted, all fire and lava." Vidal's own "fire and lava" eruptions on what Twain called the "Blessings-of-Civilization Trust" have been collected in *The Last Empire* (2000), *Imperial America: Reflections on the United States of Amnesia* (2004), and *United States, 1952–1992* (1993).

Introduction to
Following the Equator and Anti-Imperialist Essays

Both Mark Twain and his inventor, Samuel Clemens, continue to give trouble to those guardians of the national mythology to which Twain added so much in his day, often deliberately. The Freudians are still on his case even though Dr. Freud and his followers are themselves somewhat occluded these days. Yet as recently as 1991, an academic critic tells us that Clemens was sexually infantile, burnt out at fifty (if not before), and given to degenerate reveries about little girls, all the while exhibiting an unnatural interest in outhouse humor and other excremental vilenesses. It is hard to believe that at century's end, academics of this degraded sort are still doing business, as Twain would put it, at the same old stand.

As is so often the case, this particular critic is a professor emeritus, and emerituses often grow reckless once free of the daily grind of dispensing received opinion. Mr. Guy Cardwell, for reasons never quite clear, wants to convince us that Twain (we'll drop the Clemens because he's very much dead while Twain will be with us as long as there are English-speakers in the United States) "suffered from erectile dysfunction at about the age of fifty. . . . Evidence that he became impotent ranges from the filmy to the relatively firm." This is a fair example of the good professor's style. "Filmy" evidence suggests a slightly blurred photograph of an erection gone south, while "relatively firm" is a condition experienced by many men over fifty who drink as much Scotch whiskey as Twain did. But filmy—or flimsy?—as the evidence is, the professor wants to demolish its owner, who, sickeningly, married above his station in order to advance himself socially as well as to acquire a surrogate mother; as his own mother was—yes!—a strong figure while his father was—what else?—cold and uncaring.

No Freudian cliché is left unstroked. To what end? To establish that Twain hated women as well as blacks, Jews, foreigners, American imperialists, Christian missionaries, and Mary Baker Eddy. Since I join him in detesting the last three, I see no need to find a Freudian root to our shared loathing of, say, that imperialist jingo Theodore Roosevelt. Actually, Twain was no more neurotic or dysfunctional than most people and, on evidence, rather less out of psychic kilter than other major figures in the American literary canon.

Twain was born on November 30, 1835, in Missouri. He spent his boyhood, famously, in the Mississippi River town of Hannibal. When he was eleven, his father died, becoming *truly* absent as Dr. Freud might sagely have observed, and Twain went to work as a printer's apprentice. Inevitably, he started writing the copy that was to be printed, and in essence, he was a journalist to the end of his days. Literature as such did not really engage him. *Don Quixote* was his favorite novel (as it was Flaubert's). He could not read Henry James, who returned the compliment by referring to him only once in his own voluminous bookchat, recently collected and published by the Library of America.

Exactly where and how the "Western Storyteller," as such, was born is unknown. He could have evolved from Homer or, later, from the Greek Milesian tales of run-on anecdote. In any case, an American master of the often scabrous tall story, Twain himself was predated by, among others, Abraham Lincoln, many of whose stories were particularly noisome as well as worse—worse!—*politically incorrect*. Our stern Freudian critic finds Twain's smutty stories full of "slurs" on blacks and women and so on. But so are those of Rabelais and Ariosto and Swift, Rochester and Pope and . . . Whatever the "true" motivation for telling such stories, Twain was a master in this line both in print and on the lecture circuit.

Primarily, of course, he was a popular journalist, and with the best-seller *Innocents Abroad* (1869) he made the hicks back home laugh and Henry James, quite rightly, shudder. Yet when the heavy-handed joky letters, written from the first cruise liner, *Quaker City*, became a text, it turned out to be an unusually fine-meshed net in which Twain caught up old Europe and an even older Holy Land and then, as he arranged his catch on the—well—deck of his art, he Americanized the precedent civilization and vulgarized it in the most satisfactory way ("Lump the whole thing! Say that the Creator made Italy from designs by Michael Angelo!"), and made it possible for an American idea to flourish someday.

But Twain was far too ambitious to be just a professional hick, as opposed to occasional hack. He had social ambitions; he also lusted for money (in a "banal anal" way, according to the Freudian emeritus—as opposed to "floral oral"?).

In the great tradition of men on the make, Twain married above his station to one Olivia Langdon of the first family of

Elmira, New York. He got her to polish him socially. He also became a friend of that currently underestimated novelist-editor William Dean Howells, a lad from the Western Reserve who had superbly made it in Boston as editor of the *Atlantic Monthly*. Howells encouraged Twain to celebrate the American "West" as the sort of romanticized Arcadia that Rousseau might have wanted his chainless noble savage to roam.

While knocking about the West and Southwest, Twain worked as a pilot on Mississippi steamboats from 1857 to 1861; he joined the Civil War, briefly, on the Confederate side. When he saw how dangerous war might be, he moved on to the Nevada Territory, where his brother had been made secretary to the governor. He wrote for newspapers. In 1863, he started to use the pseudonym "Mark Twain," a river pilot's measurement of depth, called out on approaching landfall—some twelve feet, a bit on the shallow side.

After the war, Twain began to use life on the river and the river's bank as a background for stories that were to place him permanently at the center of American literature: *The Adventures of Tom Sawyer* (1876); *Life on the Mississippi* (1883); *Adventures of Huckleberry Finn* (1885). He liked fame and money, the last perhaps too much since he was forever going broke speculating on experimental typesetting machines and underfinanced publishing houses. He lived in considerable bourgeois splendor at Hartford, Connecticut; oddly for someone who had made his fortune out of being the American writer, as he once described himself, Twain spent more than a decade in Europe. One reason, other than *douceur de la vie*, was that he was admired on the Continent in a way that he never was, or so he felt, by the Eastern seaboard gentry, who were offended by his jokes, his profanity, his irreligion, and all those Scotch sours he drank. Fortunately, no one then suspected his erectile dysfunction.

Whenever cash was needed and a new book not ready to be sold to the public, Twain took to the lecture circuit. An interesting, if unanswerable question: Was Mark Twain a great actor who wrote, or a great writer who could act? Or was he an even balance like Charles Dickens or George Bernard Shaw? Much of what Twain writes is conversation—dialogue—with different voices thrown in to delight the ear of an audience. But, whichever he was, he was always, literally, a journalist, constantly describing daily things while recollecting old things. In the process, he made, from time to time, essential literature, including the darkest of American novels, *Pudd'nhead Wilson* (1894).

Mark Twain's view of the human race was not sanguine, and much has been made of the Calvinism out of which he came. Also, his great river, for all its fine amplitude, kept rolling along, passing villages filled with fierce monotheistic folk in thrall to slavery, while at river's end there were the slave markets of New Orleans. Calvinist could easily become Manichean if he brooded too much on the river world of the mid-1800s. *Pudd'nhead Wilson* contains the seeds of Twain's as yet unarticulated notion that if there is a God (*What is Man?*, 1906) he is, if not evil in the Manichean sense, irrelevant, since man, finally, is simply a machine acted upon by a universe "frankly and hysterically insane" (*No. 44, The Mysterious Stranger*): "Nothing exists but You. And You are but a *thought*."

The agony of the two boys in *Pudd'nhead Wilson*, one brought up white, the other black, becomes exquisite for the "white" one, who is found to be black and gets shipped downriver, his question to an empty Heaven unanswered: "What crime did the uncreated first nigger commit that the curse of birth was decreed for him?" All this, then, is what is going on in Mark Twain's mind as he gets ready for a second luxury tour, this time around the world.

When one contemplates the anti-imperialism of Mark Twain, it is hard to tell just where it came from. During his lifetime the whole country was—like himself—on the make, in every sense. But Mark Twain was a flawed materialist. As a Southerner he should have had some liking for the peculiar institution of slavery; yet when he came to write of antebellum days, it is Miss Watson's "nigger," Jim, who represents what little good Twain ever found in man. Lynchings shocked him. But then, pace Hemingway, so did Spanish bullfights. Despite the various neuroses ascribed to him by our current political correctionists, he never seemed in any doubt that he was a man, and therefore never felt, like so many sissies of the Hemingway sort, a need to swagger about, bullying those not able to bully him.

In 1898, the United States provoked a war with Spain (a war with England over Venezuela was contemplated but abandoned as there was a good chance that we would have lost). The Spanish empire collapsed more from dry rot than from our military skills. Cuba was made "free," and Puerto Rico was attached to us while the Spanish Philippines became our first Asian real estate and the inspiration for close to a century now of disastrous American adventures in that part of the world.

Mark Twain would have had a good time with the current demise of that empire, which he greeted, with some horror, in the first of his meditations on imperialism. *To the Person Sitting in Darkness* was published as a pamphlet in 1901, a year in which we were busy telling the Filipinos that although we had, at considerable selfless expense, freed them from Spain they were not yet ready for the higher democracy, as exemplified by Tammany Hall, to use Henry James' bitter analogy. Strictly for their own good, we would have to kill one or two hundred thousand men, women, and children in order to make their country into an American-style democracy. Most Americans were happy to follow the exuberant lead of the prime architect of empire, Theodore Roosevelt—known to the sour Henry Adams as "our Dutch-American Napoleon." But then, suddenly, Mark Twain quite forgot that he was *the* American writer and erupted, all fire and lava.

The people who sit in darkness are Kipling's "lesser breeds," waiting for the white man to take up his burden and "civilize" them. Ironically, Twain compares our bloody imperialism favorably with that of the white European powers then abroad in the "unlit" world, busy assembling those colonial empires that now comprise today's desperate third world. Twain, succinctly for him, lists who was stealing what from whom and when, and all in the name of the "Blessings-of-Civilization Trust." But now the American writer is so shocked at what his countrymen are capable of doing in the imperial line that he proposes a suitable flag for the "Philippine Province": "We can have just our usual flag, with the white stripes painted black and the stars replaced by the skull and cross-bones."

In 1905, Twain published a second pamphlet (for the Congo Reform Association), *King Leopold's Soliloquy*, subtitled "A Defense

of his Congo Rule." On the cover there is a crucifix crossed by
a machete and bearing the cheery inscription "By this sign we
prosper."

The soliloquy is just that. The King of the Belgians is distressed by reports of his bloody rule over a large section of black
Africa. Leopold, an absolute ruler in Africa if not in Belgium, is
there "to root out slavery and stop the slave-raids, and lift up
those twenty-five millions of gentle and harmless blacks out of
darkness into light . . ." He is in rather the same business as
Presidents McKinley and Roosevelt in the earlier pamphlet.

Leopold free-associates, noting happily that Americans were
the first to recognize his rule. As he defends himself, his night-
mind (as the surrealists used to say) gets the better of him and
he keeps listing his crimes as he defends them. He notes that his
enemies "concede—reluctantly—that I have one match in history, but only one—the *Flood*. This is intemperate." He blames
his current "crash" on "the incorruptible *kodak*," the "only witness I have encountered in my long experience that I couldn't
bribe." Twain provides us with a page of nine snapshots of men
and women, each lacking a hand, the King's usual punishment.
Twain's intervention was not unlike those of Voltaire and Zola
or, closer to home, Howells' denunciation of the American legal
system—and press—that had found guilty the non-perpetrators
of the Haymarket riots. Imperialism and tyranny for Twain were
great evils, but the more he understood—or thought he
understood—the human race, the darker his view of the whole
lot became, as he had begun to demonstrate in the epigraphs
from Pudd'nhead Wilson's New Calendar at the head of each
chapter of his travel book *Following the Equator* (1897).

In 1895, Twain, his wife, Olivia, and their daughter Clara
started on a round-the-world lecture tour. They crossed the Atlantic; then the United States; then, on August 23, they set sail
from Vancouver bound for Sydney, Australia. For several years
Twain had undergone a series of financial setbacks. Now the
lecture tour would make him some money while a look at the
whole world would provide him with a great deal of copy, most
of which he was to use in *Following the Equator*. At the start of
the tour, Twain seems not to have been his usual resilient self.

"Mr. Clemens," wrote Olivia to a friend, "has not as much courage as I wish he had, but, poor old darling, he has been pursued with colds and inabilities of various sorts. Then he is so impressed with the fact that he is sixty years old." Definitely a filmy time for someone Olivia had nicknamed "Youth."

The pleasures of travel have not been known for two generations now; even so, it is comforting to read again about the soothing boredom of life at sea and the people that one meets aboard ship as well as on shore in exotic lands. One also notes that it was Twain in Australia, and not an English official recently testifying in an Australian court, who first observed that someone "was economical of the truth."

In his travel journal, Twain muses about his past; contemplates General Grant, whose memoirs he had published and, presumably, edited a decade earlier. One would like to know more about that relationship, since Gertrude Stein, among others, thought Grant our finest prose writer. When the ship stops in Honolulu, Twain notes that the bicycle is now in vogue and "the riding horse is retiring from business everywhere in the world." Twain is not pleased by the combined influences of Christian missionaries and American soldiers upon what had once been a happy and independent Pacific kingdom.

They pass the Fiji Islands, ceded to England in 1858. Twain tells the story that when the English commissioner remarked to the Fiji king that it was merely "a sort of hermit-crab formality," the king pointed out that "the crab moves into an unoccupied shell, but mine isn't."

A great comfort to Twain aboard ship is *The Sentimental Song Book* of the Sweet Singer of Michigan, one Mrs. Julia A. Moore, who has, for every human occasion, numerous sublimely inapt verses that never, even by accident, scan. As one reads Twain's own prose, written in his own character, one is constantly reminded that he is very much a stand-up comedian whose laugh-lines are carefully deployed at the end of every observation, thus reducing possible tension with laughter. Of the colonists sent out to Australia by England, Twain observes that they came from the jails and from the army. "The colonists trembled. It was feared that next there would be an importation of the nobility."

In general, Australia gets high marks. Twain and family travel widely; he lectures to large crowds: "The welcome which an American lecturer gets from a British colonial audience is a thing which will move him to his deepest deeps, and veil his sight and break his voice." He is treated as what he was, a Great Celebrity, and "I was conscious of a pervading atmosphere of envy which gave me deep satisfaction."

Twain continually adverts to the white man's crimes against the original inhabitants of the Pacific islands, noting that "there are many humorous things in the world; among them the white man's notion that he is less savage than the other savages." The Freudian critic cannot quite fathom how the Twain who in his youth made jokes about "Negroes" now, in his filmy years, has turned anti-white and speaks for the enslaved and the dispossessed. Dr. Freud apparently had no formula to explain this sort of sea-change.

New Zealand appeals to Twain; at least they did not slaughter the native population though they did something almost as bad: "The Whites always mean well when they take human fish out of the ocean and try to make them dry and warm and happy and comfortable in a chicken coop," which is how, through civilization, they did away with many of the original inhabitants. Lack of empathy is a principal theme in Twain's meditations on race and empire. Twain notes with approval that New Zealand's women have been able to vote since 1893. At sixty, he seems to have overcome his misogyny; our Freudian critic passes over this breakthrough in dark silence.

Ceylon delights. "Utterly Oriental," though plagued by missionaries who dress the young in western style, rendering them as hideous on the outside as they are making them cruelly superstitious on the inside. Twain broods on slavery as he remembered it a half century before in Missouri. He observes its equivalent in Ceylon and India. He meets a Mohammedan "deity," who discusses Huck Finn in perfect English. Twain now prefers brown or black skin to "white," which betrays the inner state rather too accurately, making "no concealments." Although he prefers dogs to cats, he does meet a dog that he cannot identify, which is odd since it is plainly a dachshund. He tries to get used to pajamas but goes back to the old-fashioned nightshirt. Idly, he wonders why western men's clothes are so ugly and uncomfortable. He imagines himself in flowing robes of every possible color. Heaven knows what *this* means. Heaven and a certain critic. . . .

Benares has its usual grim effect. Here, beside the Ganges, bodies are burned; and people bathe to become pure while drinking the polluted waters of the holiest of holy rivers. It is interesting that Twain never mentions the Buddha, who became enlightened at Benares, but he does go into some detail when he describes the Hindu religion. In fact, he finds the city of Benares "just a big church" to that religion in all its aspects. In Calcutta, he broods on the Black Hole, already filled in. The Taj Mahal induces an interesting reverie. Twain notes that when one has read so many descriptions of a famous place, one can never actually *see* it because of all the descriptions that crowd one's mind. In this perception, Twain anticipates the latest—if not the last—theory of how memory works. He also broods on the phenomenon of Helen Keller, born deaf, dumb, and blind; yet able to learn to speak and think. How *does* the mind work?

From India, Twain and company cross the Indian Ocean to Mauritius. Although he often alludes to his lecturing, he never tells us what he talks about. He does note, "I never could tell a lie that anybody would doubt, nor a truth that anybody would believe." We learn that he dislikes Oliver Goldsmith and Jane Austen. As a prose writer, the imperialist Kipling beguiles him even though Twain likens empires to thieves who take clothes off other people's clotheslines. "In 800 years an obscure tribe of Muscovite savages has risen to the dazzling position of Land-Robber-in-Chief." He is more tolerant of the English. But then he is a confessed Anglophile.

Meanwhile, the ship is taking Twain and family down the east coast of Africa. South Africa is in ferment—Boers against English settlers, white against black. Cecil Rhodes is revealed as a scoundrel. But Twain is now writing as of May 1897, one year after his visit to South Africa, and so the outcome of all this is still unclear to him. He sides with the English, despite reservations about Rhodes and company. "I have always been especially fond of war. No, I mean fond of discussing war; and fond of giving military advice." As for that new territorial entity, Rhodesia, Twain remarks that it is "a happy name for that land of piracy and pillage, and puts the right stain upon it"; and he also has Pudd'nhead Wilson observe: "The very ink with which all history is written is merely fluid prejudice."

Finally, "Our trip around the earth ended at the Southampton pier, where we embarked thirteen months before. . . . I seemed to have been lecturing a thousand years. . . ." But he had now seen the whole world, more or less at the equator and, perhaps more to the point, quite a few people got to see Mark Twain in action, in itself something of a phenomenon, never to be repeated on earth unless, of course, his nemesis, Mary Baker Eddy, were to allow him to exchange her scientific deathless darkness for his limelight, our light.

1996

Kurt Vonnegut

Novelist Kurt Vonnegut (1992–2007) was not unhappy when he was referred to as a Mark Twain for the nuclear age—or as the closest thing Americans had to a living heir of Mark Twain. Reportedly he named a son Mark as a gesture to the writer he admired so profoundly and was pleased that his great-grandfather's first name had been Clemens. There were deep affinities between the work of the two writers: Vonnegut, like Twain, was famous for blending satire and science fiction, for raising questions about war that troubled his compatriots, and for using the assault of laughter (often in the form of dark, subversive comedy) to chip away at falsehoods that masqueraded as truths in the world around him. It is not surprising that *A Connecticut Yankee*, a book that looked ahead with ghastly prescience to the meaningless slaughter of a world war, would be a particular favorite of the author of *Slaughterhouse Five* (1969), a book that grew out of Vonnegut's having witnessed the "carnage unfathomable" that the World War II Allied bombing of Dresden created. Few American authors have written anything comparable to the devastating, dystopic apocalypse with which *A Connecticut Yankee* ends. But Vonnegut had, and for that reason, in part, his thoughts on that novel have a special interest for us. Like Twain he was intrigued by the ways in which determinism shaped human existence. Like Twain he was often dumbfounded by the ironies he saw in the world around him. And like Twain in his later years, Vonnegut used the bully pulpit he had acquired as a beloved novelist to berate his country's leadership for what he viewed as wrongheaded foreign policy.

Some Comments on Mark Twain's
A Connecticut Yankee in King Arthur's Court

by Kurt Vonnegut at the Age of Seventy-Two

Novelists in their sunset years commonly find two stories instead of one when reading works of fiction by great writers of the past. The second story is concerned with how the authors felt about themselves and life when they wrote their books. Such autobiographical material is not *between* the lines. It is *in* the lines.

So when Samuel Clemens, alias Mark Twain, says in his preface to this technically flawed world treasure that he is not going to have anything to do in the coming winter of 1889, I am amused by this amalgam of genius and modesty. But I also see a fifty-three-year-old man from nowhere, the self-educated son of nobodies, standing on the rim of a seeming abyss between himself and the years to come. He finds it incredible, in a world with so many universities and sophisticated societies, that he should have been proclaimed an unusually wise and charming person, and a master of the English language. There must be some mistake.

He has flabbergasted himself by writing a novel as comically profound as the masterpiece *Don Quixote*, which is to say *Huckleberry Finn*. How the heck did he do that? He somehow did it five years earlier, and can't imagine ever being that lucky again. So why not quit while he is winning? But he needs money.

He was very tired when he began this book. He felt like an old fighter who has been in the ring too long. Proof? His explanation of how a Yankee got back to the sixth century couldn't be more lame. He got hit on the head. Oh my, my, my. Even less acceptable is the means by which the Yankee persuades Camelot that he is a magician. He, a factory foreman, remembers what an astronomer would not bother to commit to memory, that the only total eclipse of the sun in the first half of the sixth century occurred on the twenty-first of June, A.D. 528, and began at three minutes after twelve noon. And guess how close the Yankee finds himself to that time and date. So he pretends to put out the sun and then bring it back to life again. Oh no, no, no. Please, please, please. One remembers that Twain, in a funny and unforgiving essay, fricasseed poor James Fenimore Cooper for literary crimes not half that bad.

Twain says, again in the preface, that he wrote this book against a deadline, a classic excuse for sloppiness. He ran out of time. But a novel is not a periodical. An author agrees to meet a deadline, the enemy of craftsmanship, for only one reason. He or she wants money as soon as possible. And we indeed know that Twain at this point in his life was ruining himself financially with investments which were injudicious, to say the least.

Despite this book's shaky beginning, though, and the author's less than majestic reasons for writing it in a hurry, it gets better and better, more convincing, as it goes along. Some of the pride and excitement Twain must have felt when creating *Life on the Mississippi* and *Huckleberry Finn*, and maybe *Tom Sawyer*, obviously came back again. What had seemed an abyss had vanished. He was striding cockily straight ahead again! We rejoice! It couldn't have happened to a nicer American.

It did not hurt, surely, that Twain, as depressed as he may have been, had come up with a lulu of a premise. In doing so, incidentally, he, along with Jules Verne in France, was founding the genre we now call science fiction. Time travel! What could a modern man do in order to survive in the England of thirteen hundred years ago? That question set in motion an experiment with ink on paper whose results were bound to be fascinating, results unpredictable even by the author, provided he or she were honest and open-minded, until the end.

I like to think that Twain was both startled and grimly satisfied when he realized that an optimistic, egocentric, shrewd and able technician could only make a bad situation worse by creating and employing the impersonal apparatus of modern warfare. The experiment of this book had in fact already been carried to its logical conclusion with real people when Twain was a young man, which is to say the American Civil War, often called the first modern war. It would be performed again with human beings, not on paper and not with laboratory rats, starting in 1914, the First World War, of course. Twain died in 1910, and so did not live to hear of it, but it wouldn't have surprised him. This book had already forced him to the conclusion, when he was a mere spring chicken of fifty-three, that the human condition was hopeless, no matter what the century.

How pessimistic was he, even without having seen World Wars I and II, and all the high-tech atrocities which followed, and which follow still? He didn't even think highly of peacetime. When he was seventy-four, and he had only one more year of life to go, and a beloved daughter and his closest male friend had just died, he wrote as follows: "I have never wanted any released friend of mine restored to life since I reached manhood."

Quod erat demonstrandum.

1996

Ralph Wiley

Ralph Wiley (1952–2004) was a social and cultural commentator and satirist as well as a pioneering sports columnist. In 1996 he submitted a manuscript—*Dark Witness*, a collection of mordant and hard-hitting essays—to Random House. He had previously published *Why Black People Tend to Shout* and *What Black People Should Do Now*, and he had also co-written a book with director Spike Lee about the making of the film *Malcolm X*. But although *Dark Witness* explored many of the issues related to race and racism that Wiley had focused on in earlier volumes, he did something different here: in addition to including a long chapter on Mark Twain and quoting profusely from Twain in epigraphs, Wiley styled virtually every chapter as a reworking of or response to a specific piece by Twain, a writer he acknowledged as his teacher and inspiration. When Random House insisted that the book needed a subtitle, Wiley suggested "In Homage to Mark Twain." Random House suggested instead "When Black People Should Die." Wiley had already spent his advance, and Random House was unyielding. Finally, reluctantly, he agreed to the subtitle "When Black People Should Be Sacrificed (Again)." But when Wiley gave the book to his friends, he would cross out Random House's subtitle on the title page and write in his own. In 1997 Wiley wrote a screenplay for his good friend Spike Lee: "Spike Lee's *Huckleberry Finn*." In Wiley's script the camera shows viewers scenes as Jim would have understood them, while Huck's voice-over narration conveys Huck's comically limited grasp of what's going on. Wiley had written more than a film script: he had come up with a dramatic new way of reading the book. For example (as Wiley explained in comments on a panel at the American Literature Association): "In Chapter Two of *Huckleberry Finn*, Twain introduces us to Jim by having Tom Sawyer and Huck tiptoeing around him in the dark. Huck: 'When we was passing by the kitchen I fell over a root and made a noise.' Jim 'was setting in the kitchen door; we could see him pretty clear . . . he got up. . . . Then he says, "Who dah? . . . Say, who is you? Whar is you? I know what I's gwyne to do. I's gwyne to set down here and listen tell I hears it agin.' Now who is Jim talking to? Himself? I don't think so. He's talking to the *boys. Sure he saw them. Of course. How could a grown man not see these boys out here making all this noise?* And Twain *means* for us to know Jim saw them. How? 'I fell over a root and made a noise.' So obviously Jim knows. Huck just doesn't know Jim knows. Then, Jim feigns sleep. . . . Jim would have to be a complete idiot to talk out loud about what he's hearing if, indeed, he had any uncertainty whatsoever about what—and who—he'd just heard; he would be silent." Wiley reads this scene as an adult humoring children intent on fooling him; it is a performance with which any parent can identify. Wiley's Jim is sensitive, savvy, and self-aware, a compelling and intelligent father, and a slave seeking his freedom in a racist world determined to keep him in bondage; he plays a minstrel role when that is what a white person expects him to do. Because he sticks to Twain's text so closely, Wiley maintains that his view of Jim is Twain's, too. That Huck has a limited view of Jim should not lead us to mistake that view for the author's. Lee seriously considered the proposed film script but eventually demurred. Wiley, author of ten books and hundreds of articles, died of a heart attack at 52. But as a result of his generous decision to give a scholar permission to publish several scenes from "Spike Lee's *Huckleberry Finn*" for classroom use (which are now available free on the Internet), scenes he wrote have been performed in literature classrooms across the country when *Huckleberry Finn* is taught.

FROM

What's Up with Mad Mark Twain?

You may ask why there are references to Mark Twain in this book—indeed in every book I have inflicted upon an unsuspecting public thus far. I offer you several reasons. The first is the best: fair play. Twain saw clearly, thought clearly and wrote abominably well. He took the language that Americans I know speak and made a beautiful quilt of it, threw it over the whole country and warmed us up—made us a little *too* warm at times. If it's deeply, *really* American, Mark Twain has already written about it—and in such a manner that even today the writing does not cry out for much revision.

And that would be true of the worst of what he wrote. The best, like *Huckleberry Finn*, is so ethereal, knowing, sublime, all-encompassing of American nature as we know it, you sense neither "black" nor "white" was responsible for writing this. Something Else wrote this.

To wit: In *Huck Finn*, Twain-as-Huck, describing his decision to help Jim after the latter has been re-enslaved:

> "I went right along, not fixing up any particular plan, but just trusting to Providence to put the right words in my mouth when the time come: for I'd noticed that Providence always did put the right words in my mouth if I left it alone."

I have been snidely asked if I aspire to be "the 'black' Mark Twain." That aspiration has already been aspirated. I could never be the "black" Mark Twain: Mark Twain is the "black" Mark Twain—and the "white" one, too. I aspire only to be some of the Ralph Wileys, and all any one of us can do in relation to Mark Twain is to point out where the best of him is camped out so that if this book does not move you, you can go off and read Twain, and that is *sure* to work or else the lights are too dim in those rooms where you do your reading. I also am running a deficit owed Twain. He has shown me the beauty in absurdities. Contrast that subversive wit with a Nobel Prize-winning American author of the twentieth century who could draw himself up and haughtily ask, "Who is the Tolstoy of the Zulus?" As if there were no reply. *Tolstoy* is the Tolstoy of the Zulus—unless you find a profit in fencing off universal properties of mankind into exclusive tribal ownership. Apparently, this Nobel Prize–winning author does find profit, and has passed the trait on. His son was editor and advocate of *The Bell Curve*.

Twain put it this way: *"If you pick up a starving dog and make him prosperous, he will not bite you. This is the principal difference between a dog and a man"* (*Puddn'head Wilson's Calendar*). The Nobel Prize is exclusively for humans, then.

Twain demonstrated how well he knew the demarcation between *right and wrong*, knew the boundaries are consistent, the same for all: There is no separate-but-equal category, no territory of right-and-wrong-for-"black"-people. No one, "black" or "white," is exempt because they think they ought to be—otherwise we should all soon be suffering the same exemption. Twain illustrated that the American "white" male cannot only be angry; he can be supremely privileged, yet treacherously just;

outrageously talented, but terribly insight-ridden—and not three out of five at best; a *decent* "white" man who drew upon the true complexity of America without infantile denial—denial that would be funny were it not so pathetic. We should all get down on our knees and thank Providence for Twain, for he paid the deficit owed by giving something money cannot buy. And so if I am going to borrow concepts, pass them off as my property without permission, then they might as well be the very best concepts, taken off a dead man who can't put up much of a wrangle over them and probably wouldn't even if he wasn't dead. I have thought up two or three "original" concepts on my own, but those were heisted, and the better my concept the quicker the bite, it goes without saying without a favorable mention for me. I am not quite dead, as yet. I plan to save on the aggravation of scratching my head bald in search of more original concepts that people are going to palm off as their own without my permission, when some perfectly good Twain is sitting there all available and everything.

Now, if you want to go and call this stealing, or even sacrilege, well, what can I do about that? Hungry eyes are no different from empty stomachs and parched throats. They all are going to eat or drink. At least I am open, fair and fool enough to say that Mark Twain is the only man I would call master, and *mean* it. I say this as a reader and a would-be writer and an African-American. I've read articles, short stories, essays, sketches and novels and scripts for screenplays by writers far and wide, and a precious few of them have moved me to low whistles of awestruck amazement and recognition. I have read great writing and been moved by it, and after all the moving was done the worst effect it ever had was to sentence me to a lifetime of trying to write something good myself. But only after reading much of Samuel L. Clemens, a.k.a Mark Twain, did I think I had possibly gone into the wrong line of work. For within his writing, the recognition was complete, the mastery of the form was total, the lesson finished. He had refined, mastered and retired the form I'd put in thirty years attempting to identify: satire.

Only Shakespeare could be Shakespeare—although Twain did say Shakespeare could be Francis Bacon, maybe to keep up his end of his running feud with the Victorian novelists. Running feuds themselves are irrational: Shakespeare and Twain pointed that out in both life and art. Yet they could not help but be swept up in them, though their circumstances were completely different.

Humanity was what they had in common.

What Americans say when relaxed is based on the tongue Shakespeare wrote in, though it's not the same—not nearly the same, sometimes. The standard is different, and riffs on the standard, the vernacular, idioms and dialects, make it more so. Twain is the Shakespeare of the American standard language—where methods of expressing standards are different.

Shakespeare wrote, "This blessed plot, this earth, this realm, this England—" Can't do any better by it, as far as England is concerned. But we've got a sight more than a plot here in America. We are bigger situated land-wise and have a condition we carry over it wherever we go. This may be one reason why Sam Clemens the reporter was not overly concerned with plot, even of the bookish sort, or so he most deviously claimed. For why seem concerned with plot, a bloody thing requiring many pages, when you can ring the bell at one swoop:

"*I'm told* [*Richard*] *Wagner's music is better than it sounds.*"

And that wasn't even Twain; that is a line from a fellow who looked *up* to Twain, a fellow named Nye who followed along in Twain's way of approaching and saying things; it is the American way.

So Twain took the universal human nature Shakespeare plumbed in a different mode of expression, in language the same but different and threw it in a pot where Americans could get at it. "Our prose standard," he wrote, "was ornate and diffuse; some authority or other changed it in the direction of compactness and simplicity."

It didn't matter if you were "Indians" meeting Marquette and Jolliet, or "white" "black" "nigger" "Chinaman" "Filipino"; it was the manner in which you were called these things that stood for something. It didn't matter who you were when it came to right, wrong and the human proclivity to ignore the difference. That was how he wrote it up, in a voice as subtle, simple, absurd, compact and complex as people he met. He was in a constant state of complaint about these people (remember, Twain went to Europe "on $500 the plumber didn't know I had"), as they so richly deserved, but he loved the land he'd occupied, from the banks of the Mississippi, Missouri and Ohio rivers to the Sierra Nevada to San Francisco Bay to New York City to the meadows of Connecticut. Everywhere the land seemed indescribably beautiful. It was people who made it so incredibly daft. Of course, even the land was up for review every once in a while. Like some land his family owned: *"This Tennessee land had been in the possession of the family many years, and promised to confer high fortune upon us someday; it still promises it, but in a less violent way"* (*Roughing It*).

Many have called me on my annoying admiration for the appropriateness of Twain's intentionally rustic, robust, laconic style; have told me my liking stems not from Twain's execution but from his being "liberal," seeming to tolerate "black" people occasionally. Then again, I have been questioned about my admiration because Twain knew how people had used the word "nigger" and what they meant by it, and when, and who it most reflected on. To me this was subtle craftsmanship of the sweetest, tenderest sort, but it still upset some of the selfsame "black" people Twain supposedly had tolerated a little too well. Mainly, I have been questioned.

I have no answer. If they have read Twain and don't get it, then how am I going to help the situation any? I can only speak of my own shortcomings: *If I could have said it that way first, I would have.* Mark Twain is not master of the school in which I am enrolled—he *built* the school, forced its accreditation, made it known and honored worldwide and kept the admissions policies liberal so that even a wretch like me could get a berth. Not a soft berth, mind you, but in this school who ever has time to rest?

I suppose you could say he was a "divine amateur," as Mr. Arnold Bennett put it back in the roaring '20s. Mr. Bennett himself was a pro's pro writer. He wrote at least twenty-four novels, a clutch of plays, countless essays—the titles of which escape all but the most diligent historians of today. Twain was a self-described "hack journalist"—a hack who happened to be the demiurge of his age; a registrar of humanity more than events; a keeper of times and perpetual human dilemmas and the manner in which they are expressed; a human motion-picture camera already whirring away in a time when no one in his neighborhood knew that technology was just aborning. Twain was more those things than a promoter of "ideology." You know the titles of a few of his books even if you've spent your life heeling it from historians.

Twain wrote *The Innocents Abroad* (1869), with his own frank style struggling to appear from the impenetrable techniques popular in that day; it was Victorian on top but itching underneath, an incorrigible boy in Sunday clothes; this fit the subject of *The Innocents Abroad* like a glove, even if it did not fit Twain. In his next book, *Roughing It* (1872), this definitely Twainlike sentence emerges: "*It was on this wise (which is a favorite expression of great authors, and a very neat one, too, but I never hear anybody* say *on this wise when they are talking*)."

From then on, though he "wrote off in a thousand different directions," as a friend of mine says, Twain's style changed. He wrote what people *said*, and about the differences between that and what they *did*. He also wrote with descriptive beauty such as that displayed at the beginning of Chapter 19 of *Huckleberry Finn*, or with the utter thoroughness of the first 214 pages of *Life on the Mississippi*. He wrote with rectitude, as in Chapters 49 through 51 in *Roughing It*, or in the recollection "A True Story Repeated Word for Word as I Heard It," or "My First Lie, and How I Got Out of It." And he wrote with a brilliance of controlled and telling imagery, never better displayed than in Chapter 12, "Jim Standing Siege," from the never-mentioned story *Tom Sawyer Abroad*. In this sequel to *Huck Finn*, Twain finds a plausible way—plausible, within the absurd burlesque he weaves to hide it—to have Jim, the mild ex-slave, holding a small American flag while striking poses, then standing on his head while *perched on the head of the Sphinx!* as Tom and Huck sail by in a hot-air balloon, getting "effects and perspectives and proportions." No need to go on about it. I've included it in the Notes section. You may go there now and sample some. I'll wait.

. . . Well, *shit*. That is the only word I have available for what I (and others) have been writing in comparison to *that*. *Shit* is a common word, a crude word, but crude is not quite it. What I have written needs a slingshot to get up to crude in comparison to what Twain wrote. His writing reduces mine to precisely that—*shit*. What have I been writing by comparison? Say it all together now. *Shit*. There. It takes a good bit of the sting out of having been bad when you own up and accept it. Yet there is also an American way of saying "shit" that implies excellence. If you say of a book or song or painting or movie or some other attempt at art, "That's the shit!" then that is a high compliment—the highest, really—among certain young American people who can and do talk that way and, even more miraculously, understand each other when they do.

I've spent two books, an aggregate 559 pages, trying to capture an image Mark Twain spends all of *four* pages capturing better—not counting his fifty-page setup. All I can do now is keep trying to live up to Twain's long shadow, to the tradition of that voice. But, just between you and me, I think he has set the bar *too fucking high* for me to do anything but jump under it. I can't touch that bar. I can barely *see* that bar, but that is some consolation, because most people can't see it at all. Twain took a common American expression such as "He'd sell his own mother down the river," a phrase often said admiringly in market-driven America, and get to the root of it, put the pliers to the root, worry it out, and then reconstruct it as the novel *Pudd'nhead Wilson*; or what about when Twain—

Well, no need; the citings could be ceaseless and you haven't got all day. Most authors would like to write one book they might hang their hat on; two qualifies the author for one pantheon or another; three sets you up for retirement. Three great books seems to be the limit for even the most gifted American writers. Consider—Twain wrote *ten* such books. Some are good books you might not get around to because you're busy being knocked cross-eyed by the top five, amazed to find how easily great literature can be swallowed. For not *just me*, Twain's writing is a fine point of art, the literary equivalent of the best blues and jazz, and would be had it no qualities other than a summation of a hidden history, a re-creation of life by the tongue of spoken rhythm, and beauty. Twain raised the "mongrel child of philology": *readability*. He can be read at the end of this century without need of a machete.

My admiration further swells for his repeated reminders of this cardinal truth: That a person, place or thing is dead, praised or said to be regal, doesn't make it classic, royal or better than average. Its actual nature does that. "Real Americans" are the ones who sniff out the difference. Finally, Twain *could get that down aright on paper*. There are wits who can talk, can get a joke when one is loaded up on them, but can't preserve or retell it. Twain wrote—*spoke*—for them because he wrote/spoke in a way they can appreciate—or should be *made* to appreciate.

That here and there in life I traced a path similar to his does not hurt my sense of intimacy with his writings. A slave woman shoos away a dog with "Begone, sah!" circa 1844 in *Huck Finn*, and an electric shock courses through me as I sit book in hand; my own grandmother chased away curs with the similar "'Gone, sah!" in 1964 (a mere coincidence, maybe; to me, some precious links strengthened). In his mid-twenties, Twain went west off the river into northern California and soon was engaged by the press. Then he came east to New York and was soon further engaged by the press. He slung lectures in his spare time. I did some of all that. Beforehand, at the age of twenty-one, Twain struck out from his temporary camp along the Ohio, in Cincinnati, to New Orleans, grubstaked by a fifty-dollar bill he found on a Keokuk, Iowa, street, tantalized by a book he had read that inspired him to plan to sail to South America and bivouac on the Amazon, then bring the wonders of the powder of the coca plant to a waiting world, his way of becoming a captain of commerce. Even you must admit it sounds sort of like me—what you may think you know of me, anyway.

Today, Twain could have watched the movie *Scarface*, and been similarly moved to get rich quick. I've met young men who were. No need to seek verification from them; they are now permanent residents of the quietest neighborhood of all. Fortunes made from cocaine are an unbelievably stupid goal. Young men don't see it because unbelievable stupidity is a young man's primary employment. Twain never made it to the Amazon; the trip was beyond his reach and his means; for our sons, it ain't necessarily so. Circumstance, leveler or booster of youthful ambition, will be accounted for.

Dark Witness: When Black People
Should Be Sacrificed (Again), 1996

Dick Gregory

Dick Gregory (born in 1932) is a social and political humorist and activist whose pioneering candor about race and racism in his topical stand-up comedy routines paved the way for younger satirists like Richard Pryor. When Gregory contracted to write his autobiography (with Robert Lipsyte), the publisher thought it was "getting a humor book," but instead he turned in "a book with hard-core facts about Black life in racist White America" and titled it *Nigger*. The book caused a sensation when it came out in 1964 and has since sold over ten million copies. *Nigger* was prefaced with this note: "Dear Momma—Wherever you are, if you ever hear the word 'nigger' again, remember they are advertising my book." The title of the 2000 memoir containing the text that follows—*Callus on My Soul*—comes from a comment Gregory made in *Nigger*: "Those of us who weren't destroyed got stronger, got calluses on our souls. And now we're ready to change the system, a system where a white man can destroy a black man with a single word. Nigger." Mark Twain was the first "genius of comedy" (as Gregory dubs him) who dared to make the power of this toxic racial epithet central to his satire. Twain "threw it up in the air," Gregory writes, "and I grabbed it."

FROM
Callus on My Soul

After my first night Off-Broadway, one headline read "Dick Gregory Live, He's Back." When I read the reviews, I have to admit that I was relieved that they were good. One paper called me a "genius." I'm funny, but I'm no genius.

There have only been three geniuses in comedy: Mark Twain, Lenny Bruce, and Richard Pryor. Mark Twain was the only one of the three who came out of the madness unscathed. Of course writing is different from standing flat-footed onstage. But he was so far ahead of his time that he shouldn't even be talked about on the same day as other people. Look what he did with his brilliant satire. For the first time in the history of literature a White man talked about a relationship between a Black man and a White boy. Black men didn't even have names;

they were referred to as "nigger." Then he wrote *The Adventures of Huckleberry Finn* in 1884 and talked about "Nigger Jim." Today some people are outraged by that book and they have banned it from many school districts. That's really a shame, because the truth is that Twain was the first writer to refer to us as someone other than a nigger. He attached a name to nigger and made Jim human. Now, we were always human to each other, but Twain's "Nigger Jim" made us human to White folks. They read about Jim and Huck Finn going down the Mississippi River. Nigger Jim was not putting the bait on the hook for Huck—they were fishing together as friends. Twain once wrote an article for *The Buffalo Express* that outraged White folks. It was entitled, "Oh Well, It Was Just Another Nigger." A Black man in Memphis was lynched and then they discovered that it was the wrong man. Mark Twain responded that a bunch of good Christian White folks had lynched a Black man the other day, then found out it was the wrong guy, but so what? It was just another nigger. White folks were outraged. But Mark Twain kept writing and putting a face with the names of Black folks. He was so special that he was born during the appearance of Halley's Comet, which only comes every seventy-five years. When Halley's Comet came again, Mark Twain died that very day.

Almost a century later two other geniuses, Richard Pryor and Lenny Bruce, challenged and strengthened the right to freedom of speech and they both used the stage as their workshop. In order to experience their genius, you had to be there and smell the sawdust. People say that Richard learned from me, and maybe a little of that is true. But Richard Pryor surpassed me in many ways. Richard made it by staying Black. I remember the first time I saw him perform. This White guy came to visit me while I was performing in L.A. He told me there was a new comic in town and that I just had to see him. He also said this new comic would never make it big, because he takes his penis out at the end of each show and shakes it at White folks. This new comic he predicted would never make it big was Richard Pryor. So I went to see Richard for myself and after his show, I went backstage to talk with him.

"Richard," I said, "as a Black father in a racist society, I really have no right to tell you what I am about to tell you. But because this is such a racist country, Black children need to know our Black geniuses. And as long as you end your show like that, they will never know you."

A few years later I was in Atlanta when we passed a theater and I saw all these people standing outside trying to get in. I asked the driver what was going on and he told me that Richard Pryor was in town and had sold out three shows in one night. Over two thousand Black people were still standing outside at the end of the last show. White folks had written him off until he started selling out shows. But after that, they said we'd better bring him downtown. I feel they had written him off because he had stayed Black; he didn't go to the nightclubs to tell anyone's story except that of Black folks and the Black experience.

Until we know more about Richard Pryor, we will never know what made him the comedic genius he is. Perhaps years from now, we will find out what life experiences contributed to making him so brilliant. When Richard started using the word "nigger" in his act, he made it so that every time he said it, it lessened the sting of hearing that word aloud. Richard knew how to play that game—he'd turn every negative thing White folks said about us into a satire and turn the whole thing around. Unfortunately, Richard has been in a wheelchair for years now and he cannot speak very well, because of his M.S.; but his laughter and his ability to make us laugh can never be silenced. If I were a psychiatrist, I would prescribe to Richard the best medicine in the world, laughter. Yep, I would recommend that he get copies of his own tapes and listen to them day and night. He is before his time.

I really took the word "nigger" public in 1963 when I wrote my first autobiography, *Nigger*, with Robert Lipsyte. Dutton Publishing Company thought they were getting a humor book, but they didn't say that in the contract. So I turned in an autobiography. I turned in a book with hard-core facts about Black life in racist White America. Once I had submitted the manuscript and they read what it really was about, they wanted me to name it something humorous to trick White folks into buying it. So Dutton called a big meeting on a Friday and asked me to come back on the following Monday with a humorous title. I went back on Monday and took them the title *Nigger*.

Just imagine a White or Black person walking into a bookstore in New York and saying, "I want a copy of *Nigger*." People were afraid to ask for my book, and bookstore owners were afraid to put it in their stores. Some Black folks would go into a bookstore and say, "I want one of Dick Gregory's what-you-call-it." They just couldn't say the word. And White folks would say, "You named that book a title I just can't say." Or they would complain, saying, "I just can't stand the name of your new book." I didn't hear White folks complaining about the word *nigger* when I was growing up. I only heard them using it. If they had complained about the word *nigger* in the past, there would not have been a need to name my book *Nigger*. Titling my book *Nigger* meant I was taking it back from White folks. Mark Twain threw it up in the air and I grabbed it.

written with Shelia P. Moses, 2000

Ron Powers

Ron Powers (born in 1941), Pulitzer Prize–winning and Emmy Award–winning writer and critic, grew up in Mark Twain's hometown of Hannibal, Missouri. The special sense of connection that Powers has to Hannibal and to Twain has been good for both writers: it has given Powers the material for four absorbing books and it has given Twain the astute and eloquent biographer he deserves. Powers' *White Town Drowsing: Journeys to Hannibal* (1986) took him back to Hannibal as plans for the Mark Twain sesquicentennial were taking shape, and it began a process of interweaving meditations on the world of Twain's childhood and of his own that continued in *Dangerous Water: A Biography of the Boy Who Became Mark Twain* (1999) and in *Tom and Huck Don't Live Here Anymore: Childhood and Murder in the Heart of America* (2001). Far from being a sunlit idyll of innocence, Hannibal turns out to be complex, often dark, and unpredictable—in Twain's day and in our own. Powers' insights into Twain and the world in which he lived, combined with his own gifts as a writer, make his full-length biography *Mark Twain: A Life* (2005) bristle with the energy, economy, and élan of Twain's own prose. In the essay that follows, Powers shines a spotlight on an unjustly neglected work by Twain that bears rereading. "'The War-Prayer,'" he writes, "taken in sum with Mark Twain's other polemic essays of the 1900s, form the Rosetta Stone of dissent from American imperialist folly."

What Hath Happened to "The War-Prayer"?

"What will it take for evangelicals in the United States to recognize our mistaken loyalty? We have increasingly isolated ourselves from the shared faith of the global Church, and there is no denying that our Faustian bargain for access and power has undermined the credibility of our moral and evangelistic witness in the world."

Thus ran a query posed by an evangelical professor of religion

early in 2006.* The "mistaken loyalty" at issue was that of the
writer's brethren—the 87 percent of all American evangelical
ministers who had thrown their influence and Christian authority behind the president and his advisers in their prosecution of
the Iraq war.

The professor's anguish was palpable, yet respectfully phrased;
his moral outrage unmistakable, yet constrained by the rules of
"polite" discourse. "Many of the most respected voices in American evangelical circles blessed the president's war plans," he
went on to remonstrate—reasonably, decorously—"even when
doing so required them to recast Christian doctrine."

A hotter voice lay available, of course, in the archives from a
hundred years past as a model for the dissenting churchman's
diction: a rawer, more headlong voice, a voice less concerned
with comity. A voice more than capable of humbling the reductive, punitive assertion that stains the vast dark side of current
American polemics—such as the assertion of a famous televan-
gelist that "God is pro-war."

"I come from the Throne—bearing a message from Almighty
God!" thunders the counter-voice. And it proceeds to beggar
both the ingratiating timidity, on the one hand, and the pre-
emptive and empty bluster, on the other, of today's enfeebled
debate:

"O Lord our Father, our young patriots, idols of our hearts, go
forth to battle . . . we also go forth from the sweet peace of our
beloved firesides to smite the foe . . . O Lord our God, help us
to tear their soldiers to bloody shreds with our shells . . . help
us to drown the thunder of the guns with the shrieks of their
wounded, writhing in pain; help us to lay waste their humble
homes with a hurricane of fire; help us to wring the hearts of their
unoffending widows with unavailing grief; help us to turn them
out roofless with little children to wander unfriended the wastes
of their desolated land in rags and hunger and thirst. . . ."

These fragments from the heart of Mark Twain's "The War-

*The questioner was Charles Marsh, a professor of religion at the
University of Virginia. Charles Marsh, "Wayward Christian Soldiers,"
New York Times on the Web 20 January 2006, 30 September 2006 <www.
nytimes.com/2006/01/20/opinion/20marsh.html>

Prayer"—the "unspoken part" of the pious minister's prayer for victory made unbearably manifest by the Stranger—contain what is all but missing from contemporary discourse in matters of war, and public policy, the moral destiny of the nation. The sentences are lean, accelerated, cadenced, and charged with imagery. The premise on which their authority depends—in this case, that official and religious cant conceal seeds of their abominable corollaries—is self-evident and irrefutable. They burn like acid through the layers of received wisdom, partisan pleading, and distilled, industrialized non-language that have sabotaged critical thinking—"Support Our Troops" being the supreme, and ubiquitous, soporific.

"The War-Prayer" fully illustrates William Dean Howells's shrewd analysis of what made Mark Twain's diction transformative, even transcendent of its "period": its "bottom of fury," its "indignant sense of right and wrong," its "ardent hate of meanness and injustice." These worthy passions propelled by "his single-minded use of words, which . . . express the plain, straight meaning their common acceptance has given them. . . He writes English as if it were a primitive and not a derivative language, without Gothic or Latin or Greek behind it." Or focus-groups, or marketing, or Rove.

In short: "The War-Prayer," taken in sum with Mark Twain's other polemic essays of the 1900s, form the Rosetta Stone of dissent from American imperialist folly.

So what has happened to it?

Or to frame the question as a new (and still generally "unspoken") prayer: "O Lord our Father—where is thy Stranger with his 'War-Prayer' today? In these our own times of thundering guns and hurricanes of fire and roofless children—the fresh bounties of a God-chosen nation once again explaining its Christian righteousness to the unoffending widows sitting in the darkness of another distant land—whence cometh the fire of thy countervailing talking points?

"O Lord—what giveth?"

The Lord's answer might well be along the lines of, "that dependeth on what your definition of 'happened' is." The piece enjoys incomparably broader cachet today than in Mark Twain's lifetime, when it enjoyed none at all—owing to that famous rejection in 1905 by the *Harper's Bazaar* editor Elizabeth Jordan, out of marketing concerns: she feared that the sketch would offend her female demographic. Published in bowdlerized form in 1923, it received no real attention until the Vietnam era, when war protestors read it aloud in coffee-house protests and mailed it around to one another.

Its re-branding as a kind of pop-cultural museum piece, or gift-shop item, kicked in after that. In 1983, it was tacked, like an amendment rider, onto a PBS adaptation of "A Private History of a Campaign That Failed." Its world premiere as an oratorio took place at the Ulster Choral Society in Kingston, New York, in April 1995, and people came from near. The previous year, it had provided the title of an episode of the science-fiction series "Babylon 5," although Mark Twain's story-line was "tweaked" somewhat: in it, Susan discovers that her ex-lover Malcolm is a member of the Homeguard, a pro-Earth terrorist group; assassination and galactic intermarriage, elements unstressed in the 1905 script, are teased up a little. In the years following America's invasion of Iraq in 2003, "The War-Prayer" has ricocheted through cyberspace, as facile a virtual bumper-sticker for the anti-war Left as are "Freedom is on the march" and "We should invade their countries, kill their leaders, and convert them to Christianity" for the pro-war Right.

All well and good; except that in its very ascension to status as Cultural Treasure, "The War-Prayer"—paralleling the frequent plight of its author—has somehow shed its subversive power as a model for public thought and argumentation.

To be sure, America has hardly lacked for post-Twainian dissenting eloquence: from voices as diverse as John Dos Passos, Mother Jones, Martin Luther King, Woody Guthrie, Adrienne Rich, Bob Dylan, Noam Chomsky, Howard Zinn, Frank Rich, Mollie Ivins, a thousand others. None of these, for all their value (save perhaps for Dr. King, who had his enemies), has equaled Mark Twain's universal renown, combined with his unique bottom of fury, his unique ardent hate of injustice, and with his utter command of American English, unadorned, driving, and warmed up in Hell.

Among our contemporary clergy and progressive political leadership—people for whom "eloquence" is not necessarily a given—it is worse, and at precisely a moment when it needs to be better. Not only has the Left failed to fashion a rhetoric of its own that can stand up to the neo-Kipling bombast of the Right; it has failed to consult the example of the founding father of modern dissent, even though the example is but a mouse-click away.

"When you have prayed for victory you have prayed for many unmentioned results which follow victory . . ."

That is all one needs as a starting-point, really. Upon the hard clear surface of such a truth, one can proceed to erect any number of nubs, snappers, verbal searchlights, shining shafts of truth spoken to power.

But perhaps it is not a failure of imagination alone that has inhibited our would-be paragons of protest from emulating Mark Twain. He himself witnessed the arrival of the true enemies of modern dissent, the dark Twins of Anti-Genius whose presence we now largely take for granted. One twin was Marketing. "I don't think the prayer will be published in my time," the author wrote to a friend after the piece was rejected. "None but the dead are permitted to tell the truth." The other was Official Power. "The half dozen rash spirits that ventured to disapprove of the war and cast a doubt upon its righteousness," reports "The War-Prayer"'s narrator, "straightway got such a stern and angry warning that for their personal safety's sake they quickly shrank out of sight and offended no more in that way."

Given such opposition, it is not hard to understand why "The War-Prayer" remains little more than an entertaining curiosity in our times, as dangerous to emulate as, say, Howard Dean's self-annihilating Scream. As the Prayer's narrator himself admits,

"It was believed, afterward, that the man was a lunatic, because there was no sense in what he said."

Mark Twain Studies (2006)

Michael Blakemore

In 2007 the renowned Australian theater director, actor, and writer Michael Blakemore (born in 1928) directed the world premiere on Broadway of *Is He Dead?*, a comedy Mark Twain had written in 1898, but which had never been produced. Twain's zany, over-the-top, cross-dressing farce, adapted by David Ives, met with great critical acclaim. *Variety* called the play "a ripely enjoyable confection! An elaborate madcap comedy that registers high on the mirth meter and reaches especially giddy comic heights!" The play won or was nominated for a Callahan Award, a Tony, an Outer Critics Circle Award, and four Broadway.com Audience Awards. Blakemore's brilliant direction of the play surprised no one: in 2000 he was the first person to win a Tony for best director of a play (Michael Frayn's *Copenhagen*) and best director of a musical (Cole Porter's *Kiss Me, Kate*) in the same year. Blakemore was also no stranger to farce: he had directed the world premiere of Frayn's ebullient *Noises Off* in England in 1982. Blakemore wrote this essay about how farce works—and how *Is He Dead?* in particular works—several weeks before the play ended its Broadway run. It is published here for the first time.

Is He Alive?

The critics have been so generous about the acting, the design, and the direction of "Is He Dead?" that it may seem a little churlish to complain now about their treatment of the evening's begetter, Mark Twain. They're all agreed that the show is extremely funny. Here's *The Wall Street Journal*: "shriekingly funny—I don't know when I've heard a Broadway audience laugh louder or longer."

Now it may be true that Twain's original manuscript presents serious problems for someone attempting to stage it in the present climate. It rambles over three extended acts, owes much to the theatrical conventions of its own day, and has a cast of over 30. However, it is packed with strong situations, colorful characters, and overflowing comic invention, and it contains at least two quite brilliant scenes which are being performed at the Lyceum Theatre just as Twain wrote them. In one, the hero, disguised as his own sister, tries to convince two maiden ladies of his feminine credentials, and in the other, he attempts to discourage an odious suitor by pretending that his teeth, his hair, one eye, and a leg are not his own. The writing has an almost surreal comic energy and a splendid disregard for any sort of correctness, political or otherwise.

The original manuscript, discovered by Twain scholar Shelley Fisher Fishkin in 2002, has since been published, and I'm not sure that the critics, when they saw the show, really took into account the way that David Ives' adaptation has transformed it. While remaining true to Twain's narrative, principal characters and, above all, tone of voice, he's compressed three acts into two, reduced the cast list to eleven, and brought on stage scenes which Twain was content merely to describe as happening off. The result is a comedy which is constantly on the move, twisting and turning from one incident to the next, and packed with enough material to fuel a dozen farces. To this extent, Ives has made it modern. But it is still a comedy that reminds us there's more than one way we can be made to laugh. Today's stage humor is knowing and informed. It flatters us by suggesting we are clever enough to be in on the joke, and it's a vein of playwriting with a long and illustrious tradition from the Restoration comedies of Congreve through Oscar Wilde and on to Tom Stoppard. However, Twain employs a more direct route to laughter, one where we are literally ambushed by it.

Farce, when it works, is like being at a great sporting event, where we leave our individual selves behind and become one with everyone around us who are likewise bucking about in their seats. It speaks not to who you like to think you are, but to what you suddenly find you have in common with all the people with whom you are sharing the experience. It is the theatre at its most egalitarian, which is perhaps why Twain was drawn towards it. Everyone comes to the party.

However, farce has its difficulties. The most problematic of which is that the complex situations on which the comedy depends often take a long time to set up, and this can test the patience of an audience conditioned by TV. Two of the greatest farcical comedies ever written, the one, American—"The Front Page"—and the other, English—"Noises Off"—solved this by having first acts that engage us by the truthful rendering of character and behavior. In the first, a bunch of jaded reporters sit around the press room of the criminal court building in Chicago waiting upon an execution, and in the second, a company of nervous actors dress rehearse a feeble comedy which they are about to take out on the road. Because the observation in both plays is so acute and funny, one hardly notices the way that explosives are carefully being put in place for comic detonation later in the evening.

Some of the more traditional farces, alas, are a different matter, and I defy any of those critics who adversely compared "Is He Dead?" to its predecessor, "Charley's Aunt," to re-read the latter play and find anything to smile about until well past the half-way mark. Twain may have shamelessly borrowed its central idea—that of a man who is obliged to dress up as a woman—but he makes far livelier use of it. In "Charley's Aunt," the hero puts on female attire to provide a chaperone for a friend who would otherwise be unable to woo his sweetheart. This is tame indeed compared to "Is He Dead?," where a painter of genius is forced into drag to rescue his talent from oblivion and himself from starving to death. The device of cross-dressing is here put to substantial comic use, allowing Twain, along the way, to say things about the shallowness of fashions in art and the absurdity of European notions of rank and royalty. He looks for comedy at its source: the ever-present possibility of tragedy, which, when narrowly averted, becomes funny, and he finds it in his own experience.

As a young man stranded out West and in a state of despair, he had once raised a pistol to his head, only to reconsider at the last moment. This event recurs in "Is He Dead?" when the dejected hero likewise considers doing away with himself. This time round however, it's comedy. Similarly, not long before he wrote "Is He Dead?" Twain had lost a beloved daughter to meningitis and was devastated by grief. A few years later, he's making wild fun of the trappings of mourning and the self-important solemnity of funerals.

Whatever its debt to "Charley's Aunt," Twain's play remains an eccentrically original work. No playwright before him had thought of putting a real person, in Twain's case, Jean-Francois Millet, the most celebrated painter of his day, at the center of a farcical story not one word of which was remotely true. Imagine a playwright today dressing Jackson Pollock in a skirt and submitting him to a string of fictional indignities. Similarly bold is Twain's solution to the tedium of farcical exposition. He begins his play on a note of high melodrama, and within two or three minutes, the audience is up to its neck in a dramatic situation which may be ridiculous, but which is never boring. Audiences enjoy melodrama because it makes for vigorous and immediate storytelling, and because it's reassuring to be told in advance who to love and who to loathe. Nor is melodrama necessarily untrue to life. The handful of people who went to jail in the wake of the Enron scandal (not to mention the hundreds who should've and didn't) were no less greedy, perfidious, and thoroughly wicked than "Is He Dead?"'s sublime villain, Bastien Andre. And were Twain alive, it is not hard to guess what he would have had to say about the perpetrators of the various sub-prime mortgage swindles—indeed, most aspects of our new "Gilded Age" (his expression, by the way). This cast of mind is ever-present in "Is He Dead?", even if most of the time, you're too amused to notice.

When something looks like a dog, wags its tail, pricks up its ears and barks, then it's probably a dog. And when a play makes audiences laugh so much they break the seats, gets funnier as it progresses, and provides wonderful opportunities for a whole company of actors, then it's probably a comedy, and a very good one.

For a second time around, rumors of Mark Twain's death may prove to be exaggerated. The prognosis at the Lyceum Theatre is that he is alive and kicking.

2008

Min Jin Lee

Free Food for Millionaires, the debut novel of Min Jin Lee (born in 1968), met with great critical acclaim when it came out in 2007. In her Korean-American coming-of-age story, money and what it can and cannot buy plays a central role. Her deft attention to commerce and class, to the lures and snares of material goods and how they shape who we are, prompted comparisons to Theodore Dreiser's *Sister Carrie* and Edith Wharton's *The House of Mirth*. As Lee notes in this essay (which is published here for the first time), Mark Twain, too, was intrigued by money-as-character and money-as-chimera. He gave her permission as a writer to probe the seductions of wealth that are so central to the stories she tells. He also helped give her the courage to risk leaving the secure and lucrative career she had as a New York attorney for the unpredictable and financially uncertain job of full-time writer. That decision must have been hard for someone who had grown up in a working-class and immigrant environment, after coming here from Korea with her family at age seven. Unlike the gambles taken by some of Twain's characters, however, Lee's paid off: *Free Food for Millionaires* became a best seller.

Money as an American Character and the Legacy of Permission: Or How Mark Twain Taught Me That It Was Okay to Talk About Money

For years, my immigrant parents ran a dingy wholesale jewelry shop, half a mile from Times Square. They sold nickel silver earrings and bronze bangles to street peddlers and small shopkeepers from the boroughs. On weekends and school breaks, my sisters and I took turns helping out behind the counter. Before I was in middle school, I knew that if a peddler—who carried his folding card table/shop on a shoulder strap—bought six pairs of earrings at 2 dollars a pair, he'd owe my father 12 dollars, and on the streets, he'd have to charge at least 3 dollars a pop to his customer to show something for his day's work. I grew up sorting grimy dollar bills from wrinkled fives, soiled tens and twenties, and in the mornings, I'd go around the corner with a brown paper bag of cash to make a deposit at Manufacturer Hanovers—the precursor of JPMorgan Chase. My freshman year tuition, room and board for Yale College in 1986 was $16,040, and that meant that my parents had to sell a lot of bangles to a great number of peddlers. And that unbelievable sum didn't include textbooks, clothes, allowance, or train fare.

A few months after my debut in Ivy League life, a girl who'd gone to a New England prep school and whose father was a famous lawyer told me in front of a small crowd, "You know, Min, you talk a lot about money."

No one in our group said anything, least of all me. It was the first and last time I had to be told that there was something shameful about discussing mammon in such circles.

After college, I went to law school and then got a job where I made $83,000 a year. After two years, I quit lawyering to write fiction full-time, not that I knew how. I had blown through six-figures for a legal education, so I could not justify an expensive degree in fiction. I went to the public library. I gravitated toward the very good dead writers—19th century Americans and Europeans. Curiously, patterns emerged. A character's inevitable ruin came most often from money. Lily Bart, Emma Bovary, Becky Sharpe, Rosamond Lydgate, Hector Hulot and George Hurstwood—their plots compelled, because she or he couldn't close the purse. Naturally, they couldn't control themselves in other ways either. If being a spendthrift led to your downfall, its opposite fate was the windfall, an inheritance from a distant relation or a wealthy love match that lifted you from your obscure position (see Jane Eyre or Elizabeth Bennet). Later, I read biographies, and, sure enough, authors didn't escape money problems either. Edgar Allan Poe quit college due to gambling debts; Dostoyevsky lost plenty more at the gaming tables; Balzac bought absolutely everything; Zora Neale Hurston died penniless and was buried in an unmarked grave; O. Henry served time for embezzlement, and Oscar Wilde went bankrupt after his jail term.

The one who surprised me was Mark Twain. He wrote about money, but not always like the others. Money was on his mind, which was understandable. He was 11 years old when his father died, and at age 12, he became a printer's apprentice. He tried his hand as a typesetter, writer, printer, steamboat pilot, silver miner, journalist, lecturer, before becoming the archetypal American writer. A self-taught and self-made man, he did things his own way: after declaring bankruptcy at age 59, he later paid off his creditors without having any legal obligation to do so.

For me, what distinguished Twain's fiction was how he used money not merely as a plot mechanism, like the pistol on the drawing room mantel or the coquette's dropped glove, a thing a character controls or not—but as a character in itself. Twain's money as character controls the destiny of his human characters. In three of his greatest money stories, "The £1,000,000 Bank-Note" (1893), "The Man That Corrupted Hadleyburg" (1899), and "The $30,000 Bequest" (1906), the author anthropomorphizes money as an all-consuming, living, breathing force to test love, intimacy, trust, morality, reason, and vanity.

In the "£1,000,000 Bank-Note," a San Francisco mining broker's clerk, Henry Adams, takes his sailboat out for the day but lands in London without a friend or a penny. Adams is pulled off the streets into a gorgeous room where he quickly becomes the object of a wager between two wealthy brothers. Adams is given a letter and a £1,000,000 bank-note to test the premise: Can a poor stranger survive in London with currency of impracticable value? To Adams's surprise, every door is flung wide open for him. Adams says, "Within a week I was sumptuously equipped with all needful comforts and luxuries, and was housed in an expensive private hotel in Hanover Square." At the end of this breezy story, Adams even wins the hand of the well-born English girl Portia Langham, who charmingly turns out to be the stepdaughter of one of the two wealthy brothers.

At the turn of the century when Twain wrote this short story-cum-fable, he was fictionalizing what Americans were beginning to understand—that unimaginable wealth was being created by America's new industrial titans, and that that kind of money was unstoppable in its reach and hegemony. Adams is the accidental buccaneer or fate's arriviste, and what transformed him from a clerk into a millionaire was chance, timing, and the sheer volume of available money. Born in 1835, Twain was born within five years of American multimillionaires John

Rockefeller (1839), Andrew Carnegie (1835), Jay Gould (1836), J. P. Morgan (1837), and Henry H. Rogers (1840). Twain's money shows England—the motherland—that a no-count American matters.

Scene after scene, Adams waves this living piece of paper, and it stuns. The London haberdasher "received it with a smile, one of those large smiles which goes all around over, and has folds in it, and wrinkles, and spirals, and looks like the place where you have thrown a brick in a pond; and then in the act of his taking a glimpse of the bill this smile froze solid, and turned yellow, and looked like those wavy, wormy spreads of lava which you find hardened on little levels on the side of Vesuvius." Credit is extended, and it widens concentrically. What generates permanent smiles is not merit, birth, or position, but the possession of the golden ticket.

For all its appearances, this looks like a jolly story—O. Henryesque and tidy in its nice boy-gets-the-nice-girl-plus-cash ending—but I think Twain is also shouting, unfair, unfair. Because, well, in real life, no one plucks you out of the gutter and hands you a million-pound note to establish your credit history or social pedigree. To wit, the year after this story was published, on the advice of his millionaire pal Henry Rogers of Standard Oil, Twain declared bankruptcy.

In contrast, "The Man That Corrupted Hadleyburg" never pretends to be a feel-good tale.

A self-identified "foreigner" is insulted in Hadleyburg—a town where "throughout the formative years temptations were kept out of the way of the young people, so that their honesty could have every chance to harden and solidify, and become a part of their very bone." To vindicate himself, the injured foreigner delivers a letter and a reward sack of gold weighing over 160 pounds to the home of Mary and Edward Richards. When he arrives, Mary is home alone. Her husband, a bank cashier, is still at work. The poor Richardses are one of the 19 principal couples of Hadleyburg, and they are charged to find the person who once performed a good deed by giving a "ruined gambler" $20, then to reward him with the gold. As in "The £1,000,000 Bank-Note," the letter functions as the starting gun at the races and breathes life into the gold sack. How are we to know who performed this gracious act? The do-gooder made a life-changing valediction to the gambler, and in the sack, a sealed envelope with the original remark will confirm the samaritan's virtue. The Richardses are allowed to pursue the inquiry privately or publicly, but if the latter, the do-gooder's remarks should be submitted in writing to the unpopular Reverend Burgess who will read them out loud in public.

"Hadleyburg" is the undisguised interplay of hubris and hypocrisy. In the first scene, Mary Richards had been waiting for her husband reading the *Missionary Herald* by the lamp, but later that evening, she finds herself dimming the light to caress the sack filled with "the wages of sin" brought to her doorstep by a gambler. Mary "slipped stealthily over and kneeled down by the sack and felt of its ridgy sides with her hands, and fondled them lovingly."

All 19 principals receive the same letter lulling them into believing that each merits the gold, and in front of a national audience—thanks to the Associated Press—Hadleyburg looks the fool when all 19 submit the remark, "You are far from being a bad man: go, and reform." However, only 18 principals' names are read out loud by Burgess. The Reverend has concealed Edward out of gratitude for a past small kindness. It is a small kindness and ironic, because Edward was the only person in town who could have cleared Burgess's name, knowing Burgess to be innocent (his alleged crime is unnamed), but Edward failed to do so for fear of ostracism. In lieu of supporting Burgess publicly, he privately warned Burgess to stay out of town until it was safe to return. Not having heard Edward's name, the foreigner decides to reward the one incorruptible principal not with the gold which was gilded lead, but with its auction value.

The story skewers pride, vanity, xenophobia, racism, hypocrisy, greed, and conformity; the exterior moral is classic Twain. However, his moral has a thorny center, because this is also Edward's story—one of a defeated old man who is good, bad, weak, and wishful for some comfort late in life—someone who is like us.

When the foreigner delivers the checks made out to Bearer in the amount of $38,500 to the Richardses, Twain replaces the seductive sack of gold with the forces of paranoia and guilt. Edward and Mary fret endlessly that Burgess will betray their secret to the town. As in his life, Edward's speech before his death is characterized by ambivalence, and he confesses his guilt while making a groundless charge against the innocent Burgess. The psychologically realistic depiction of Edward's guilt in the last pages is in the vein of Poe's "Tell-Tale Heart" (1843) or Dostoyevsky's *Crime and Punishment* (1866)—authors who'd also been humbled by the coin. Guilt is the emotional manifestation of a crime committed, and though the crime may lie undiscovered, somewhere truth exists—because the criminal knows it does. Edward dies in a feverish hallucination, and his wife soon follows.

For irony, Twain has made the Bearer checks disappear yet resurrects the specter of the demonic sack in the final page: "The last of the sacred Nineteen had fallen a prey to the fiendish sack; the town was stripped of the last rag of its ancient glory." Edward Everyman and his Eve are killed by a sack of gold.

By 1906 when Twain published "The $30,000 Bequest," he was a 71-year-old man who had survived the deaths of his favorite daughter Susy and his wife of 34 years, Olivia. Entering his eighth decade, the author was solvent, esteemed, and honorably lettered—that year, Twain received a doctorate from Oxford University—not shabby for an autodidact from Missouri. Nevertheless, at the beginning of the 20th century, the nation was in the incipient stages of the third worst stock market crash in history—the "Panic of 1907" brought on by President Roosevelt's antitrust measures—and the nation had just emerged from the crash of 1901–3. As a social critic, a close reader of Thomas Carlyle (who termed economics the "dismal science"), and an intimate of Henry Rogers of Standard Oil, Twain would have followed the rise and fall of the nation's fortunes with interest.

In "The $30,000 Bequest", Saladin "Sally" Foster, a 35-year-old bookkeeper, and his "capable helpmeet" wife, Electra "Aleck"—a loving and fiscally responsible couple with two daughters—receive a letter (Twain's starting gun again) from Sally's distant relation, Tilbury Foster. Tilbury (till-he-is-buried—you can almost feel Twain's elbow prodding your gut) is 70 years old and dying. In his will, Tilbury intends to leave Sally $30,000 with the proviso that Sally not inquire about his death or attend his funeral. Tilbury makes the bequest "not for love, but because money had given him most of his troubles and exasperations, and he wished to place it where there was good hope that it would continue its malignant work."

So it does. First, Sally subscribes to the *Sagamore*, Tilbury's local paper, to keep abreast of the obituaries, then the couple conspire madly—Aleck to make the sum grow while Sally schemes to live like a duke. As promised, Tilbury dies, but Sally and Aleck do not hear of it for five years. In the meantime, Aleck "invests" Sally's bequest in real ventures, reaping and piling up vast imaginary gains in her ledger. Now and then, she allots Sally a fraction of her bounty for him to fritter. In their parallel universe, they live in "a sumptuous vast palace which looked out from a leafy summit upon a noble prospect of vale and river and receding hills steeped in tinted mists— and all private, all the property of dreamers; a palace swarming with liveried servants, and populous with guests of fame and power, hailing from all the world's capitals, foreign and domestic." Their real lives are acted out daily without feeling while their hearts and minds are engaged with their lives as billionaires, for soon enough Aleck has earned them "Twenty-four hundred millions, and all safely planted in Good Things, gilt-edged and interest-bearing. Income, $120,000,000 a year." The couple no longer read each other romances at night; the Sabbath is broken; Sally mindlessly filches candles and crockery from his employer; prospective grooms for their daughters are continually cast aside to make room for titled royalty from the Continent.

As they are planning to marry off their elder daughter to "His Royal Highness Sigismund-Siegfried-Lauenfeld-Dinkelspiel-Schwartzenberg Blutwurst, Hereditary Grand Duke of Katzen-yammer," the market vaporizes. "The very next day came the historic crash, the record crash, the devastating crash, when the bottom fell out of Wall Street, and the whole body of gilt-edged stocks dropped ninety-five points in five hours, and the multi-millionaire was seen begging his bread in the Bowery."

Aleck blames herself for not selling—for holding out for five more points when she was already a billionaire on paper. "I am to blame, do not forgive me, I cannot bear it. We are paupers! Paupers, and I am so miserable. The weddings will never come off; all that is past; we could not even buy the dentist, now." Sally the spender refuses to castigate his wife though privately he thought she should have taken (imaginary) profits before the market fell. In a perfectly mixed moment of clarity and delusion, Sally tells his wife: "Cheer up, banish these griefs; we still have the thirty thousand untouched." The characters have lost the plot, but Twain has not.

Aleck and Sally are reconciled and comforting one another when they receive a visitor.

The editor of the *Sagamore* has appeared to collect four years of an unpaid subscription. He lets out that Tilbury Foster has been "in Sheol these five years!" Tilbury died a pauper and left the editor—his executor—a legacy of a wheelbarrow *sans* wheel.

Like the foreigner who avenges himself against the proud people of Hadleyburg with a sack of fake gold, Tilbury avenges his miserable existence with a phantom bequest to a relative who had once curried favor for a relationship with a kinsman who was reputedly well-off. They seem cruel, these agents of fate with their deceptive letters; however, the 19 principals of Hadleyburg and the sensible Fosters were always free to resist. Instead, they ran into the arms of the "fiendish" character—money. In short, they behaved like most people—probably like us.

I once read in a newspaper a math professor saying that lotteries were a tax against the stupid. I bet Twain could have plopped that math professor into a story where he had no choice but to buy a ticket and believe in his luck, because Twain would have sided with the stupid over the smug. The prohibition against discussing money or coveting it was far greater for Twain in his turn-of-the-century Protestant America than in my era of Wall Street bonus babies. If the convention against mammon-speak was a pretense then, surely it is a pretense now. We remain full of shame, envy, pride, lust, greed, confusion, and desire. Especially desire for security, comfort, freedom, respectability—the metaphysical and physical qualities of money and what it can make or destroy. Money bewitches us, breaks us, addles us and scares the heck out of us. Twain knew this inside and out, and I'm glad he did not back down from having his say.

M.J.L.
Tokyo 2009

Roy Blount Jr.

American writer Roy Blount Jr. (born in 1941) is the author of 21 books, most recently an exuberant and quirky excursion into etymology, lexicography, and morasses of meaning entitled *Alphabet Juice* (2008). Born to Southern parents in Indianapolis, Blount went to high school in Decatur, Georgia, and got degrees from Vanderbilt and Harvard before serving a stint in the army. He has reported on the civil rights movement and the Ku Klux Klan; he has covered the Pittsburgh Steelers and Elvis's funeral; he has interviewed public figures from Martin Luther King Jr. to Joe DiMaggio to Eudora Welty to Ray Charles. A contributing editor of the *Atlantic*, he has written articles for some hundred magazines including *The New Yorker*, *Life*, and *Rolling Stone*. Books such as *Crackers* (1979), *Roy Blount's Book of Southern Humor* (1994), *Feet on the Street: Rambles Around New Orleans* (2005), and *Long Time Leaving: Dispatches from Up South* (2007) have cemented Blount's reputation as a deft humorist and a wry commentator on contemporary life. Blount, like Twain, grew up in the South but then made New England his home. And, like Twain, he is an outspoken advocate for the rights of authors (he is currently president of the Authors' Guild). The essay that follows was a July cover story in *Time* in 2008. In our current "golden age of sarcasm," a time when it is not the pundits but "the mocking heads who make something like sense," Blount reminds us that "news in the form of edgy drollery may seem a brave new thing, but it can all be traced back to one source. . . ." "Mark Twain: Our Original Superstar" reminds readers just how remarkably current—and disturbing—Twain's words remain today.

America's Original Superstar

*Mark Twain skewered the powerful, mocked the pious
and helped change a nation*

What, if anything, about this benighted moment of American life will anyone in the future look back on with nostalgia? Well, those of us who have cable are experiencing a golden age of sarcasm (from the Greek *sarkazein*, "to chew the lips in rage"). Jon Stewart, Stephen Colbert, Bill Maher and

Keith Olbermann are digging into our direst forebodings so adroitly and intensely that we may want to cry, "Stop tickling!" Forget earnest punditry. In a world of hollow White House pronouncements, evaporating mainstream media and metastasizing bloggery, it's the mocking heads who make something like sense.

Let not those heads swell, however. News in the form of edgy drollery may seem a brave new thing, but it can all be traced back to one source, the man Ernest Hemingway said all of modern American literature could be traced back to: Mark Twain. Oh, that old cracker-barrel guy, you may say. White suit, cigar, reports of my death have been greatly exaggerated—but he died back in 1910, no? White, male, and didn't he write in dialect? What does he have to do with the issues of our day?

As it happens, many of these were also the issues of his day, and he addressed them as eloquently as anyone has since. The idea that America is a Christian nation? Andrew Carnegie brought that up to him once. "Why, Carnegie," Twain answered, "so is Hell."

What about those Abu Ghraib photographs? In "King Leopold's Soliloquy," a fulminating essay he published in 1905, when he was a very cantankerous 70, Twain imagines the ruler of Belgium pitying himself for the inconvenience of photos showing natives of the Congo whose hands have been cut off by Belgian exploiters. In the good old days, Leopold complains, he could deny atrocities and be believed. "Then all of a sudden came the crash! That is to say, the incorruptible Kodak—and all the harmony went to hell! The only witness I have encountered in my long experience that I couldn't bribe."

Waterboarding? In 1902, American soldiers were involved in a war to suppress rebels in the Philippines, which the U.S. had taken from Spain in the Spanish-American War, then decided to keep for itself instead of granting the Filipinos the independence they thought they had been promised. That outcome enraged Twain. So did "the torturing of Filipinos by the awful 'water-cure.'"

"To make them confess—what?" Twain asked. "Truth? Or lies? How can one know which it is they are telling? For under unendurable pain a man confesses anything that is required of him, true or false, and his evidence is worthless."

Whether Twain was talking about racism at home, the foreign misadventures of the Western powers or the excesses of the era of greed he initially flourished in after the Civil War, his target was always human folly and hypocrisy, which turn out to be perennial topics for further study.

Here he is in *Letters from the Earth*, speaking in the voice of Satan commenting on the strangeness of man's ways: "He has imagined a heaven, and has left entirely out of it the supremest of all his delights . . . sexual intercourse! It is as if a lost and perishing person in a roasting desert should be told by a rescuer he might choose and have all longed-for things but one, and he should elect to leave out water!"

Strong stuff, especially when it's funny. Sometimes unsettling too. But the man who said those things came from America's heart. Mark Twain, who was born Samuel Langhorne Clemens in 1835, grew up on the nation's literal main stream, the Mississippi River, in Hannibal, Mo. Having failed to find a ship that would take him to South America and the fortune he proposed to make from coca, by the age of 23 he had become a Mississippi-steamboat pilot. It was a job he held just briefly, but the memory of the river, its enchantments and dangers, found its way years later into his most powerful book, *Adventures of Huckleberry Finn*. It also found its way into his pen name. Mark Twain, the name he began to write under in 1863, was a river man's term meaning a depth of two fathoms, or 12 ft. (3.7 m).

When the Civil War broke out, Twain may have briefly entertained pro-Union sentiments but at length decided to serve with a ragtag bunch of Confederate irregulars. After a couple of weeks, "hunted like a rat the whole time," he thought better of that commitment and, as Huck Finn did, lit out for the territory. This territory was Nevada and California, where he prospected for silver without luck and practiced scurrilous journalism and general drunkardry with zest.

Twain first came to national attention in 1865, when he published a comical short story in dialect, which was eventually titled *The Celebrated Jumping Frog of Calaveras County*. ("You never see a frog so modest and straightfor'ard as he was, for all he was so gifted.") It appeared in newspapers all across the country, was received as a whole new kind of hilariousness and made him famous. "At the close of the Civil War, Americans were ready for a good cleansing laugh, untethered to bitter political argument," writes Twain's recent, so far definitive biographer, Ron Powers. And at least in this first moment of his fame, that's what Twain gave them.

In the career as an audience-convulsing lecturer that grew out of that first small triumph, Twain would become, as Powers puts it, "the nation's first rock star." We know his voice only from written descriptions of it. It was resonant enough to hold a large lecture-hall audience rapt. He spoke in a slow backwoods drawl, with many strategic pauses. In 1891 he experimented with an Edison dictating machine but concluded that "you can't write literature with it." (He liked to have a human secretary taking notes and laughing in the right places.) But he wasn't the sort of funny man who laughs at his own jokes. In performance and in life, Twain's facial expression—except, presumably, when he was furious, which was often—was deadpan. After Twain's death, the editor of the *North American Review* recalled that he had known him for 30 years and never seen him laugh.

In the first flush of success, Twain began work on a travel book, *The Innocents Abroad*, that would bring him sizable amounts of money. In that book he simultaneously took on the pretensions of Europe and the spectacle of a bunch of comical American tourists, including himself, making a sustained encounter with an Old World that was never quite as impressive as it was supposed to be.

Travel writing was lucrative, but novels were what serious literary men were expected to produce, and from the start Twain longed to be taken seriously, to be regarded as more than "merely" a humorist. So by 1873 he had rolled out his first novel, *The Gilded Age*, which he co-wrote with a Connecticut journalist, Charles Dudley Warner. With that book's title, Twain gave the post-Civil War era, a time of boundless greed and opportunism, the name it still has and that it shares, in some quarters, with the era we seem to be willy-nilly emerging from.

Once Twain found his calling as a writer and lecturer, success came quickly and abundantly. He may have been a critic of the Gilded Age, but he wasn't shy about taking on the trappings of a successful man. When the publishing royalties came pouring in, he built in Hartford, Conn., a big, ornate, financially burdensome house in a style that's been called "steamboat Gothic." It has been fully open to the public since 1974, but recently it has run into serious financial difficulties. A few years ago the group that maintains the house added an expensive visitors' center. Now it can't afford the upkeep, and there's a danger that the house will have to close.

To be honest, it's a spooky place—his favorite daughter died there, ranting and raving—and all the more worth preserving for that. I played billiards there once, on Mark Twain's table, with Garrison Keillor on his radio show. (Radio is a good medium for billiards because you can lie about how many balls you are sinking.) This is not the first time the house has been threatened by debt. That happened in 1891. Back then it was due to Twain's irrational exuberance. He had set up his own publishing company, which flourished for a while but eventually went under. Even before it failed, the Clemenses were compelled to leave the house and go traveling. (In those days, believe it or not, Americans could live less expensively in Europe than at home.) Then their finances got even worse. A marvelous new kind of typesetting machine that Twain had pumped a fortune into had ultimately proved unworkable. Eventually he owed creditors about $100,000, or roughly 2 million of today's poor excuses for dollars.

But Twain declined to let his admirers organize a relief fund. He resolved to make enough money himself, writing and lecturing, to pay back every cent. "Honor is a harder master than the law," he said, sounding considerably more righteous than usual. But it was actually his wife, supported by Henry H. Rogers, an otherwise ruthless Standard Oil exec who had volunteered to manage Twain's money, who insisted he not take an easier way out.

Twain mostly stayed abroad for the rest of the 1890s, establishing his celebrity in Europe and touring the world, making speeches and gathering material for his final, largely acerbic travel book, *Following the Equator*. When he returned to the U.S. in 1900, the Gilded Age was fading, but America was throwing its weight around internationally. Now Twain was not only solvent again but much in vogue—"The most conspicuous person on the planet," if he did say so himself. The renewed snap in the old boy's garters resounded around the world, as he took stands on American politics that, as his biographer Powers puts it, "beggared the Democrats' timidity and the Republicans' bombast."

The Spanish-American War of 1898 had met with Twain's initial approval because he believed that the U.S. was indeed selflessly bringing freedom to Cuba by helping it throw off the yoke of Spain. But the Eagle had also taken the Philippines as a possession, and by 1899 was waging war against Filipinos who were trying to establish a republic. "Why, we have got into a mess," Twain told the Chicago *Tribune*, "a quagmire from which each fresh step renders the difficulty of extrication immensely greater." The contemporary ring of that assessment is heightened by statistics. By 1902, when Philippine independence had been pretty much squelched, more than 200,000 Filipino civilians had been killed, along with 4,200 Americans.

As Twain got older and was beset by personal tragedies like the death of his beloved daughter Susy, his view of mankind grew darker. He once told his friend William Dean Howells that "the remorseless truth" in his work was generally to be found "between the lines, where the author-cat is raking dust upon it which hides from the disinterested spectator neither it nor its smell." But in 1900, when he could no longer stomach the foreign adventures of the Western powers, he came right out and called a pile of it a pile of it. In the previous year or two, Germany and Britain had seized portions of China, the British had also pursued their increasingly nasty war against the Boers in South Africa, and the U.S. had been suppressing that rebellion in the Philippines. In response, Twain published in the New York *Herald* a brief, bitter "Salutation-Speech from the Nineteenth Century to the Twentieth."

"I bring you the stately matron named Christendom," he wrote, "returning bedraggled, besmirched and dishonored from pirate-raids in Kiao-Chow, Manchuria, South Africa and the Philippines, with her soul full of meanness, her pocket full of boodle, and her mouth full of pious hypocrisies. Give her soap and a towel, but hide the looking-glass."

Later that year he published a long essay in the *North American Review*. It was called "To the Person Sitting in Darkness." The title was a biblical reference. The people in darkness were the unconverted, who had yet to see the blessed light. In fact, Twain pointed out, the problem was that they were seeing things too clearly. After years of exposure to Western colonialism, "the People Who Sit in Darkness . . . have become suspicious of the Blessings of Civilization. More—they have begun to examine them. This is not well. The Blessings of Civilization are all right, and a good commercial property; there could not be a better, in a dim light . . . and at a proper distance, with the goods a little out of focus."

The new century did nothing to improve his disposition. In 1901, U.S. President William McKinley was assassinated. His successor was Theodore Roosevelt, McKinley's 42-year-old Vice President, a blustery hero of the Spanish-American War whom Twain regarded as heedlessly adventurous in his foreign policy. "The Tom Sawyer of the political world of the 20th century," he called Roosevelt. Of course, Twain had been a great deal like Tom himself—as a boy, and as a man for that matter—but that was before becoming the conscience of a nation, "the representative, and prophetic, voice of principled American dissent," as his biographer Powers puts it.

Shortly after becoming President, Roosevelt made news by declaring, out of the blue, that "In God We Trust" should be removed from U.S. coins because they "carried the name of God into improper places." Twain responded, in conversation with Carnegie, that "In God We Trust" was a fine motto, "simple, direct, gracefully phrased; it always sounds well—In God We Trust. I don't believe it would sound any better if it were true."

Religiosity prevailed in Twain's era but not in his heart. Though one of his closest friends, Joseph Twichell, was a minister, Twain derided religions—Christianity, in particular—and the notion of a benevolent deity. His strongest written sacrileges were not published, however, until well after his death. He was a more interesting disbeliever in some ways than today's Bill Maher or Sam Harris or Christopher Hitchens, who readily dismiss religion as inflammatory nonsense. Twain, who was full of inflammatory nonsense, could appreciate the indigenous blessednesses he encountered around the world. Stopping in Benares, India, "the sacredest of sacred cities," Twain discovered that "Hindoos" venerate flower-garlanded phallic stones with enormous gusto, which led him to muse on the durability of the impulse to believe. "Inasmuch as the life of religion is in the heart, not the head," he observed, religions are hardy. "Many a time we have gotten all ready for the funeral" of one faith or another, "and found it postponed again, on account of the weather or something."

What put Twain off about religion was its bossiness and its alignment with corrupt community values that people—those standing to profit—insisted on calling a higher power. The very expression "moral sense" made him curl his lip. He denounced his own conscience, which frowned upon his anarchic instincts, his love of enjoyment, and made him feel guilty and rebellious.

The pivotal moment in *Huckleberry Finn* is when Huck decides not to do what his conscience tells him is right, to turn in "Miss Watson's Jim" as a runaway slave. Instead, he decides to abide by his personal affection for Jim, although the upshot will be, according to all he has been taught, eternal damnation for violating the norms of society and its view that a slave is the rightful property of its owner.

As Twain became increasingly angry over the years, less the jester and more the Jeremiah, there was grumbling in some quarters that he had been better when he was funnier. (You could call this the Woody Allen problem.) The New York *Times* accused him of "tumbling in among us from the clouds of exile and discarding the grin of the funny man for the sour visage of the austere moralist."

The *Times* had a point. As a social critic, Twain was most enjoyable when he followed his natural humorous tendency to denounce folly and iniquity in all directions. This is what he was doing in *Following the Equator* when he wrote, "All the territorial possessions of all the political establishments in the earth—including America, of course—consist of pilferings from other people's wash. No tribe, however insignificant, and no nation, howsoever mighty, occupies a foot of land that was not stolen. When the English, the French, and the Spaniards reached America, the Indian tribes had been raiding each other's territorial clothes-lines for ages, and every acre of ground in the continent had been stolen and restolen 500 times."

Try rallying a cause with that. Then there's the long essay Twain produced in 1901, "The United States of Lyncherdom." This is not a single-minded polemic. It registers the horror of lynchings but also undertakes to empathize with people who attended them. Their motivation, Twain argued, is not inhuman viciousness but "man's commonest weakness, his aversion to being unpleasantly conspicuous, pointed at, shunned, as being on the unpopular side. Its other name is Moral Cowardice, and is the commanding feature of the make-up of 9,999 men in the 10,000 . . ."

As a remedy, Twain proposed, tongue in cheek, that sheriffs might be dispatched to communities where a lynching was about to take place. If they could rally enough citizens to oppose the hideous deed, that would make the anti-lynching position the new conventional wisdom that everyone would flock to conform to. But a problem—where to find enough sheriffs? Why not draft them from among the Christian missionaries spreading the malady of Western civilization in China? (Missionaries were a favorite target for Twain.) In China, he told his readers, "almost every convert runs a risk of catching our civilization . . . We ought to think twice before we encourage a risk like that; for, once civilized, China can never be uncivilized again . . . O compassionate missionary, leave China! come home and convert these Christians!"

There is something upsetting, off-balancing, about "The United States of Lyncherdom" that has kept it alive all these years. It's against lynching, all right, but it seems to take more of an interest in being against righteousness. It makes you wonder whether you yourself, possibly, or let's say your grandmother, might have appeared, smiling, in a photograph of a lynch mob. And just as you're about to block out that queasiness, Twain slams in a snippet of what a particularly despicable lynching (in Texas, as it happened) was like. Oh, God. (The man was slow-roasted to death over a coal-oil fire.) And then, when he starts taking off on the missionaries? I don't know that I want to express this opinion. But there's no getting around it: it's funny.

Not only was "The United States of Lyncherdom" politically incorrect, it still is. It blames one of the most shameful aspects of American history on moral correctness, the herd mentality that prevailed among Americans who regarded themselves as right thinking. Twain decided that the country, or at least his readership, was not ready for that essay. It wasn't published until 1923, when Twain's literary executor slipped it, hedgily edited, into a posthumous collection. Not until 2000 did it appear in its original form, and then in an obscure, scholarly publication. It takes a genius to strike the funny bone in a way that can still smart nearly 100 years later. The nation's highest official accolade for comedy is the Kennedy Center's Mark Twain Prize for American Humor, which will be awarded this November to the late George Carlin—another man whose commentary grew bleaker and more biting in his last years. But old Mark, unvarnished, might be too hot for cable, even, today.

Time, 2008

Bronze relief portrait of Mark Twain by Barry Moser, 1985–86.
Pennyroyal Press.

SOURCES AND
ACKNOWLEDGMENTS

INDEX

Sources and Acknowledgments

Great care has been taken to locate and acknowledge all owners of copyrighted material included in this book. If any owner has inadvertently been omitted, acknowledgment will gladly be made in future printings.

George Ade. "Mark Twain as Our Emissary" in *Century Magazine*, 81 (December 1910), pp. 205–6.

W. H. Auden. "Huck and Oliver" in *The Listener* (London) (October 1, 1953), pp. 540–41. Copyright © 1953 by W. H. Auden. Reprinted by permission of Curtis Brown, Ltd.

Thérèse Bentzon. From "Les Humoristes Américains: Mark Twain" ("The American Humorists: Mark Twain") in *Revue des Deux Mondes*, 100 (July 15, 1872), pp. 313–15. Translated by Greg Robinson.

Yan Bereznitsky. From "Mark Twain on the Bed of Procrustes" in *Literaturnaya Gazeta* (Moscow) (August 18, 1959), p. 4. From "The Question Is Significantly More Profound: A Letter to Charles Neider" in *Literaturnaya Gazeta* (Moscow) (December 12, 1959), p. 5. Translated by Robert L. Belknap. In Charles Neider, *Mark Twain and the Russians: An Exchange of Views* (Hill & Wang, 1960), pp. 13–15, 19–24.

Michael Blakemore. "Is He Alive?" Published here for the first time. Copyright © by Michael Blakemore. Printed by permission of the author.

Roy Blount Jr. "America's Original Superstar" in *Time* (July 14, 2008), pp. 48–53. Copyright © 2008 by Roy Blount Jr. Reprinted by permission of the author. Originally published in *Time* magazine.

Jorge Luis Borges. "Una Vindicación de Mark Twain" ("A Vindication of Mark Twain") in *Sur* (Buenos Aires) (November 1935), pp. 40–46. Translated by Geoffrey O'Brien. Copyright © 1935 by Maria Kodama. Reprinted by permission of The Wylie Agency, LLC.

David Bradley. Introduction to *How to Tell a Story and Other Essays*

(Oxford University Press, 1996), pp. xxxi–lix. Copyright © 1996 by David Bradley. Reprinted by permission of Oxford University Press, Inc.

Sterling Brown. From *The Negro in American Fiction* (Washington: Associates in Negro Folk Education, 1937). Reprinted as *The Negro in American Fiction* (New York: Argosy-Antiquarian, 1969), pp. 67–69.

Livia Bruni. From "L'Umorismo Americano: Mark Twain" ("American Humor: Mark Twain") in *Nuova Antologia* (Rome) (February 16, 1905), pp. 696–709. Translated by Patricia Thompson Rizzo.

David Carkeet. From *I Been There Before* (Harper & Row, 1985), pp. 55–63. Copyright © 1985 by David Carkeet. Reprinted by permission of the author.

Jesús Castellanos. From "Mark Twain" in *Los Optimistas* (Madrid, 1910), pp. 115–20. Translated by Edward M. Test.

G. K. Chesterton. "Mark Twain" in *T. P.'s Weekly* (London) (April 19, 1910), pp. 535–36.

Bernard DeVoto. From Introduction to *The Portable Mark Twain* (Viking Press, 1946), pp. 13–30. Copyright © 1946, 1968, renewed 1974 by The Viking Press. Used by permission of Viking Penguin, a division of Penguin Group (USA).

E. L. Doctorow. Introduction to *The Adventures of Tom Sawyer* (Oxford University Press, 1996), pp. xxxi–xxxviii. Copyright © 1996 by E. L. Doctorow. Reprinted by permission of International Creative Management, Inc.

Theodore Dreiser. "Mark the Double Twain" in *English Journal*, vol. 24, no. 8 (October 1935), pp. 615–27. Copyright © by Theodore Dreiser. Reprinted by permission of The Dreiser Trust, Harold J. Dies, Trustee.

T. S. Eliot. Introduction to *Huckleberry Finn* (Chanticleer Press, 1950), pp. vii–xvi. Copyright © 1950 by The Estate of T. S. Eliot. Reproduced by permission of Faber and Faber Ltd.

Ralph Ellison. "Twentieth-Century Fiction and the Black Mask of Humanity" in *Confluence* (1953). Reprinted in *Collected Essays of Ralph Ellison*, ed. John F. Callahan (Modern Library, 2003), pp. 81–99. Copyright © 1995 by John F. Callahan. Used by permission of Modern Library, a division of Random House, Inc.

Eduard Engel. From "Mark Twain: Ein Amerikanischer 'Humorist'" ("Mark Twain: An American 'Humorist'") in *Magazin für die Literatur des Auslandes*, 98 (1880), pp. 575–79. Translated by Valerie Bopp. From "Mark Twain" in *Geschichte der englischen Litteratur von den Anfangen bis zur Gegenwart. Mit einem Anhang: Die nordamerikanische Literattur* (Leipzig. 1897), pp. 65–68. Translated by Valerie Bopp.

Maks Erik. From "Sholem Aleichem and Mark Twain: Notes on the Eighth Anniversary of Sholem Aleichem's Death" in *Tog* (Vilna) (May 23, 1924, and May 30, 1924). Translated by Zachary M. Baker.

Leslie Fiedler. "Come Back to the Raft Ag'in, Huck Honey!" in *Partisan Review*, 15 (June 1948), pp. 664–71.

Edward Field. "Mark Twain and Sholem Aleichem" in *Stand Up, Friend, with Me* (Grove Press, 1963), pp. 72–73. Copyright © 1963 by Edward Field. Reprinted by permission of the author.

Hamlin Garland. "Mark Twain's Latest" in *Boston Evening Transcript* (January 10, 1890), p. 6.

Henry Gauthier-Villars. From *Mark Twain* (Paris, 1884). Translated by Greg Robinson.

Mike Gold. "Twain in the Slums" in *San Francisco People's World* (1959). Reprinted in *Mike Gold: A Literary Anthology*, ed. Michael Folsom (International Publishers, 1972), pp. 306–8.

Dick Gregory (with Shelia P. Moses). From *Callus on My Soul* (Longstreet Press, 2000; Dafina Books, 2003), pp. 255–58. Copyright © 2000 by Dick Gregory. All rights reserved. Reprinted by arrangement with Kensington Publishing Corporation, www.kensingtonbooks.com.

Ángel Guerra. From Prólogo: *Mark Twain, Cuentos Escogidos* (Prologue to *Mark Twain: Selected Tales*) (Madrid 1903). Translated by Edward M. Test.

Lafcadio Hearn. "Mark Twain on the Mississippi" in *New Orleans Times-Democrat*, 20 (May 1883), p. 4.

Theodor Herzl. From "Mark Twain in Paris." Written in 1894; first published in 1903. Reprinted in *Mark Twain Quarterly* (Winter 1951), pp. 16–20. Translated by Alexander Behr.

Hal Holbrook. Introduction to *Mark Twain's Speeches* (Oxford University Press, 1996), pp. xxxi–xlii. Copyright © 1996 by Hal Holbrook. Reprinted by permission of Oxford University Press, Inc.

William Dean Howells. "Mark Twain: An Inquiry" in *North American Review*, 172 (February 1901), pp. 306–21.

Johannes V. Jensen. "Mark Twain" in *Politiken* (Copenhagen) (April 23, 1910), p. 5. Translated by Jan Norby Gretlund.

Chuck Jones. From *Chuck Amuck: The Life and Times of an Animated Cartoonist* (Farrar, Straus & Giroux, 1989), pp. 34–36. Copyright © 1989 by Chuck Jones. Reprinted by permission of Farrar, Straus and Giroux, LLC.

Erica Jong. Introduction to *1601 and Is Shakespeare Dead?*: 'Deliberate Lewdness' and the Lure of Immortality (Oxford University Press, 1996), pp. xxxi–xl. Copyright © 1996 by Erica Jong. Reprinted by permission of the author.

Helen Keller. "Our Mark Twain" from *Midstream: My Later Life* (Doubleday, Doran & Company, 1929), pp. 47–69. Copyright © 1929, 1957 by Helen Keller. Reprinted with permission from the American Foundation for the Blind.

Rudyard Kipling. "An Interview with Mark Twain" in *The Pioneer* (Allahabad) (March 18, 1890). Reprinted in *From Sea to Sea* (Doubleday, Page & Company, 1913), pp. 167–81.

Andrew Lang. "On the Art of Mark Twain" in *The Critic* (London), 16 (July 25, 1891), pp. 45–46.

Lao She. From "Mark Twain: Exposer of the 'Dollar Empire.'" Speech delivered in 1960. *US–China Review*, 19 (Summer 1995), pp. 11–15. Translated by Zhao Yuming and Sui Gang (with J. R. LeMaster).

Min Jin Lee. "Money as an American Character and the Legacy of Permission: Or How Mark Twain Taught Me That It Was Okay to Talk About Money." Published here for the first time. Copyright © 2010 by Min Jin Lee. Printed by permission of the author.

Ursula Le Guin. Introduction to *The Diaries of Adam and Eve*: Reading Young, Reading Old (Oxford University Press, 1996), pp. xxxi–xli. Copyright © 1996 by Ursula K. Le Guin. Reprinted by permission of the author and the author's agents, the Virginia Kidd Agency, Inc.

David Ross Locke. From "New Books" in *Toledo Blade*, 21 (September 1869), p. 1.

Lu Xun. From "A Short Introduction to 'Eve's Diary,'" preface to Mark Twain, *Eve's Diary* (Shanghai, 1931). Translated by Gongzhao Li.

Norman Mailer. "Huck Finn, Alive at 100" in *The New York Times Book Review* (December 9, 1984), pp. 1 and 36–37. Copyright

© 2009 by the Estate of Norman Mailer. Reprinted by permission. All rights reserved.

José Martí. From "Escenas Norteamericanas" ("North American Scenes") in *La Nación* (Buenos Aires) (sent November 27, 1884, and published January 11, 1885). Translated by Edward M. Test. Reprinted in José Martí: *Obras Completas*, volume 1 (Havana, 1946), pp. 1575–79. From "Escenas Norteamericanas" ("North American Scenes") in *La Nación* (Buenos Aires) (sent January 13, 1890, and published March 12, 1890). Translated by Rubén Builes and Cintia Santana. Reprinted in *Obras Completas de Martí*, volume 40 (Havana, 1942), pp. 113–22.

H. L. Mencken. From "Mark Twain" in *The Smart Set* (October 1919), pp. 138–43.

Toni Morrison. Introduction to *Adventures of Huckleberry Finn* (Oxford University Press,1996), pp. xxxi–xli. Copyright © 1996 by Toni Morrison. Reprinted by permission of International Creative Management, Inc.

Kenzaburō Ōe. From "An American Traveler's Dreams—Huckleberry Finn Who Goes to Hell") in *Sekai* (September 1966). Translated by Hiroaki Sato. Copyright © 1996 by Kenzaburō Ōe. Reprinted with permission of The Wylie Agency LLC.

George Orwell. "Mark Twain—the Licensed Jester" in *Tribune* (London) (November 26, 1943), pp. 14–15. Copyright © 1968 by Sonia Brownell Orwell and renewed 1996 by Mark Hamilton. Reprinted by permission of Houghton Mifflin Harcourt Publishing Company.

Ron Powers. "What Hath Happened to 'The War-Prayer'?" in *Mark Twain Studies*, 2 (2006), pp. 31–34. Reprinted in *Journal of Transnational American Studies* (2009), pp. 1–4. Copyright © 2007 by Ron Powers. Reprinted by permission of the author.

John Seelye. From *The True Adventures of Huckleberry Finn* (Northwestern University Press, 1970), pp. v–xii. Copyright © 1970, 1987 by John Seelye. Used with permission of the University of Illinois Press.

George Bernard Shaw. Letter to Samuel L. Clemens (July 3, 1907) in *Bernard Shaw: Collected Letters, 1898–1910*, ed. Dan H. Lawrence (Dodd, Mead & Company, 1972), pp. 696–97.

George Soule. "Mark Twain Protests" in *The New Republic*, 9 (November 18, 1916), p. 8.

Abel Startsev. From *Mark Twain in America* (Moscow, 1963; revised edition, 1985). Translated by Katya Vladimirov and Nina Yermakov Morgan.

Wallace Stegner. "Yarn-Spinner in the American Vein" in *The New York Times* (February 10, 1957), pp. 1 and 25. Copyright © 1957 by Wallace Stegner. Reprinted by permission of Brandt & Hochman Literary Agents, Inc.

Marina Tsvetaeva. "Books Bound in Red" in *Evening Album* (1910). Translated by Yuri Tretyakov.

Mark Twain. "Memoranda: An Entertaining Article" in *Galaxy* (December 1870), pp. 876–78.

Gore Vidal. Introduction to *Following the Equator and Anti-Imperialist Essays* (Oxford University Press, 1996), pp. xxxi–xl. Copyright © 1996 by Gore Vidal. Reprinted by permission of Oxford University Press, Inc.

Kurt Vonnegut. "Some Comments on Mark Twain's *A Connecticut Yankee in King Arthur's Court* by Kurt Vonnegut at the Age of Seventy-Two" (Oxford University Press, 1996); pp. xxxi–xxxiii. Copyright © 1996 by Kurt Vonnegut. Reprinted by permission of Oxford University Press, Inc.

Robert Penn Warren. "Last Laugh" in *The New Yorker* (June 12, 1978), p. 34. Copyright © 1978 by Robert Penn Warren. Reprinted by permission of William Morris Endeavor Entertainment, LLC on behalf of the author.

Ralph Wiley. From "What's Up with Mad Mark Twain?" in *Dark Witness: When Black People Should Be Sacrificed (Again)* (One World/Ballantine Books, 1996), pp. 30–39 Copyright © 1996 by Ralph Wiley. Used by permission of Ballantine Books, a division of Random House, Inc.

Grant Wood. "My Debt to Mark Twain" in *Mark Twain Quarterly*, 2 (Fall 1937), pp. 6, 14, and 29.

Editor's Acknowledgments

The Mark Twain Anthology would not have come into being without the generous help of many people. I am grateful to Harold Augenbraum, Executive Director of the National Book Foundation, for having suggested this project in the first place, and my agent, Sam Stoloff, for his help in seeing it to fruition. I am indebted to

Mary-Louise Munill and the Interlibrary Loan department at Stanford University as well as to my research assistant, Allen Frost, for their invaluable help. I also owe a debt of thanks to Robert H. Hirst, General Editor of the Mark Twain Project at the Bancroft Library, and Neda Salem of the Mark Twain Project for their generous assistance.

I am grateful to all of the scholars who provided translations: Zachary M. Baker, Valerie Bopp, Rubén Builes, Jan Norby Gretlund, Gongzhao Li, Nina Yermakov Morgan, Geoffrey O'Brien, Patricia Thompson Rizzo, Greg Robinson, Cintia Santana, Hiroaki Sato, Edward M. Test, Yuri Tretkakov, and Katya Vladimirov. I would particularly like to thank several of my fellow Founding Editors and Advisory Board members of the *Journal of Transnational American Studies* who helped me think through the transnational dimensions of this project, helped me identify primary sources and connect with some of the translators, and, in three cases, did the translations themselves: David Bradley, Alfred Hornung, Tsuyoshi Ishihara, Shirley Geok-lin Lim, Gongzhao Li, Nina Yermakov Morgan, Greg Robinson, Werner Sollors, Takayuki Tatsumi, and Yuri Tretkakov.

Although most of my research for this book took place in libraries, archives, and online, there are several cases in which personal contact with an author was an important source of material that is in a headnote. I was privileged to meet Kenzaburō Ōe in Austin, Texas, in 1996, where he confirmed my sense that *Huckleberry Finn* had played a key role in the genesis of his first novel, and wrote an inscription to that effect in a book of his I had brought for him to sign. I also had the pleasure of meeting the late Abel Startsev when he made a trip to New York in the 1990s; our talk over lunch underlined for me just how hazardous a business it had been to write about American literature in the Soviet Union. I was pleased to have the opportunity to interview the late Ralph Ellison in 1991; comments he made in that interview appear in the headnote in this book. And my insights into the late Ralph Wiley's work come from the many conversations we had in person and on the phone from 1997 until his death in 2004—conversations about Mark Twain, the satirist's craft, and race and racism in America (including a three-hour conversation we had with Spike Lee in his Brooklyn office when Lee was considering shooting the script Wiley had written for him, "Spike Lee's *Huckleberry Finn*"). I had the honor of working with director Michael Blakemore when I guided Mark Twain's play, *Is He Dead?* (adapted by David Ives), to Broadway, and was with him as he finished the essay that appears in this book, in which he shares his insights into the dynamics of comedy and farce. Essays in this book by David Bradley, E. L. Doctorow, Hal Holbrook, Erica Jong, Ursula Le Guin, Toni Morrison, Kurt Vonnegut, and Gore Vidal began as pieces that I commissioned as editor of *The Oxford Mark Twain*. If I had not met Min Jin Lee at a conference at Columbia University in 2008, I doubt I would have been able to persuade her to write the lovely essay she wrote expressly for this book.

Others who drew my attention to useful materials, provided constructive feedback, or offered a range of encouragement and support include: Alyce Boster, Colleen Boucher, George Bugli-arello, Guido Carboni, Mark Dawidziak, Chiyuma Elliott, Carol Plaine Fisher, Bobby Fishkin, Jim Fishkin, Joey Fishkin, Tom Free-land, Roland Greene, Jan Hafner, Susan K. Harris, Nigel Hatton, Andrea Herrera, Josef Jarab, Nick Jenkins, Matt Jockers, Michael Keller, Carol Lawrence, Steven Lee, Jim Leonard, Dagmar Logie, Kevin MacDonnell, Eric Martinsen, Mario Materassi, Robin McClish, Monica Moore, Susan Napier, Hilton Obenzinger, David Palumbo-Liu, Nelia Peralta, Patricia Parker, Carla Peterson, Gillis Plaine, Arnold Rampersad, Lin Salamo, Jennifer Summit, Thomas Tenney, Mark Woodhouse, and Martin Zehr. I could not have completed this project without the superb collections of the Green Library at Stanford University and the Bancroft Library at the University of California at Berkeley. I am also grateful for courtesies extended to me by the Pequot Library in Fairfield, Connecticut, and the Ganett-Tripp Library at Elmira College as I worked on this book.

My work was greatly enriched by key bibliographic studies: Roger Asselineau, *The Literary Reputation of Mark Twain from 1910 to 1950* (Paris: Librairie Marcel Didier, 1954); Louis J. Budd, ed., *Mark Twain: The Contemporary Reviews* (Cambridge: Cambridge University Press, 1999); Stuart Hutchinson, ed., *Mark Twain: Critical Assessments*, 4 vols. (Robertsbridge, U.K.: Helm Information, 1993). Also useful were Frederick Anderson and Kenneth M. Sanderson, eds., *Mark Twain: The Critical Heritage* (London: Routledge & Kegan Paul, 1971); J.C.B. Kinch, ed., *Mark Twain's German Critical Reception, 1875–1986: An Annotated Bibliography* (Westport,

Conn.: Greenwood Press, 1989); and Robert M. Rodney, ed., *Mark Twain International: A Bibliography and Interpretation of His World-wide Popularity* (Westport, Conn.: Greenwood Press, 1981).

My greatest debt is to the man who set all this in motion. Only an author as rich and complex as Mark Twain could have generated such excitement and interest on the part of so many stellar writers over such a long period of time. It is a privilege to be able to honor his memory with *The Mark Twain Anthology*.

Index of Works by Mark Twain

"About Smells," 142–43

Adventures of Huckleberry Finn, xv–xxi, 5–6, 47, 78, 81–82, 92–93, 95, 114, 116. 122, 134, 136, 141, 143, 147, 149–50, 155–56, 176, 178–80, 182, 184, 190–92, 195–96, 200–5, 209, 211, 213–14, 216–17, 221–25, 228–52, 258–63, 267, 269, 276, 286, 296–97, 302–13, 317–25, 333, 349–51, 362, 365, 380–81, 386, 391–92, 394, 399, 408–19, 423, 432–33, 435–37, 441, 443, 446, 469, 474

The Adventures of Tom Sawyer, xvii, 4–5, 31, 35–36, 40, 67, 72, 93, 95, 115–16, 122, 136, 147, 150, 153, 155, 178, 182, 184, 190, 192, 196, 200–5, 216, 220, 234–35, 242–43, 319, 346–50, 363–71, 399, 423, 433

The American Claimant, 182, 284

"Aurelia's Unfortunate Young Man," 25–26

Autobiography, xxi–xxii, 73, 143, 184–87, 190, 194, 211, 220, 272, 277–82, 384–85

"The Awful German Language" (*A Tramp Abroad*), 30–31, 37–40, 47, 85

"The Californian's Tale," 272

Captain Stormfield's Visit to Heaven. See Extract from Captain Stormfield's Visit to Heaven

"The Celebrated Jumping Frog of Calaveras County," 24–25, 56, 59, 103, 135, 150, 217–18, 222, 273, 374, 469–70

The Celebrated Jumping Frog of Calaveras County, and Other Sketches, xvii, 14

Christian Science, 132, 184, 383, 385, 399

"The Chronicle of Young Satan," 137

"Comments on the Killing of 600 Moros," 280

"Concerning the Jews," 100

A Connecticut Yankee in King Arthur's Court, vi, xvii–xviii, xxv–xxvi, 1, 41, 47–48, 53–54, 61–65, 78, 80, 87, 93–95, 114, 131, 136, 149, 188, 209, 212, 224, 287, 351, 399, 431–33

"The Curious Republic of Gondour," 142

"The Czar's Soliloquy," 190

[Date, 1601.] Conversation, as It Was by the Social Fireside, in the Time of the Tudors, 143, 181, 183, 188, 193, 210, 386, 389–92, 394

"A Day at Niagara," 271

"A Defence of General Funston," 468–69

Diaries of Adam and Eve. See Extracts from Adam's Diary and Eve's Diary

"A Double Barrelled Detective Story," 184

Eve's Diary, xxiv–xxv, 169–70, 173–75, 184, 397–407

Extract from Captain Stormfield's Visit to Heaven, 145, 184

Extracts from Adam's Diary, 397–407

"Fenimore Cooper's Literary Offences," 100, 361, 432

Following the Equator, 89, 99, 102, 143, 284, 383, 385, 420, 426–30, 472, 474–75

The Gilded Age, xvii, 24, 58, 93–95, 122, 190, 192–93, 196, 209, 218, 223, 470

"His Grandfather's Old Ram" (*Roughing It*), 273, 376

A Horse's Tale, 272

"How I Edited an Agricultural Paper Once," 56, 106–7

"How to Tell a Story," 273, 334, 359–61

Huckleberry Finn. See Adventures of Huckleberry Finn

"In Defense of Harriet Shelley," 100

The Innocents Abroad, xvii, 4, 13–24, 26–27, 30–36, 39–40, 42, 51–53, 58, 80, 87, 89, 94, 98–99, 103, 108–12, 118, 122, 136, 150, 178, 184, 188, 190, 192, 216, 224, 317, 378–79, 422, 441, 470

Is He Dead? 454–57

Is Shakespeare Dead? 165–66, 386

"Jim Baker's Blue-Jay Yarn" (*A Tramp Abroad*), 273, 401

Joan of Arc. See Personal Recollections of Joan of Arc

"The Judge's 'Spirited Woman'," 56

"The Jumping Frog." *See* "The Celebrated Jumping Frog of Calaveras County"

"The Killing of Julius Caesar 'Localized'," 26

King Leopold's Soliloquy: A Defense of His Congo Rule, 2, 184, 425–26, 468

Letters, 374, 385

Letters from the Earth, 143, 211, 380–81, 384–85, 469

Life on the Mississippi, xvii, 4, 30, 39, 42–46, 72, 99, 111, 120, 136, 162, 176, 192, 205–6, 208, 210, 216, 234, 271, 273, 399, 423, 433, 441

"Little Bessie," 143

"The Man That Corrupted Hadleyburg," 183–84, 188, 237, 460–63, 465

Mark Twain in Eruption, 211, 384–85

"My First Lie, and How I Got Out of It," 381, 385, 441

"My Late Senatorial Secretaryship," 58

The Mysterious Stranger: A Romance, 137–50, 174, 181–84, 187–88, 192–94, 220–22, 271, 327. *See also* "The Chronicle of Young Satan" and "No. 44, The Mysterious Stranger"

"No. 44, The Mysterious Stranger," 137, 424

"Old Times on the Mississippi," 42, 222. *See also Life on the Mississippi*

"The £1,000,000 Bank-Note," 85, 272, 460–61

"Only a 'Nigger'," 446

Personal Recollections of Joan of Arc, xvii, 41, 94–95, 114, 147, 149, 183–84, 188, 190, 192, 214, 206, 216, 327–28, 399

"Political Economy," 135

The Prince and the Pauper, xvii, 41, 94, 116, 188, 190, 192, 216, 275, 399

"The Private History of a Campaign That Failed," 222, 452

Pudd'nhead Wilson. See The Tragedy of Pudd'nhead Wilson

"A Reminiscence of the Back Settlements," 142

Roughing It, xvii, 28–29, 40, 42, 44, 52–53, 58, 61, 87, 94, 98–99, 111, 122, 136, 153, 178, 190, 205–8, 271–73, 317, 330–31, 376, 399, 440–41

"A Salutation-Speech from the Nineteenth Century to the Twentieth, Taken Down in Short-Hand by Mark Twain," 285, 294, 472–73

"Seventieth Birthday Dinner Speech," 378, 382

1601. See [Date, 1601.] Conversation, as It Was by the Social Fireside, in the Time of the Tudors

Sketches, New and Old, 24, 56, 87, 142

Speeches, 374–85

"Stirring Times in Austria," 100

"The Story of the Bad Little Boy Who Didn't Come to Grief," 56, 105, 107

"The Story of the Good Little Boy Who Did Not Prosper," 105, 107

"The $30,000 Bequest," 272, 460, 463–65

Three Thousand Years Among the Microbes, 143

"To My Missionary Critics," 380

To the Person Sitting in Darkness, xvii, xxii, 88, 205, 285, 380, 420, 425, 473

Tom Sawyer. See The Adventures of Tom Sawyer

Tom Sawyer Abroad, xviii–xix, 441

The Tragedy of Pudd'nhead Wilson, xviii, 2, 182, 197–98, 215–16, 225, 380, 424, 437, 442

A Tramp Abroad, xvii, 8, 30–31, 36–40, 47, 52–53, 85, 99, 118, 136, 143, 147, 149–50, 216, 272–73

"The Treaty with China," 284

"A True Story, Repeated Word for Word as I Heard It," 8, 87, 196, 441

"The United States of Lyncherdom," xxii, 380, 475–76

"The War-Prayer," xxii, 139, 143, 285–86, 373, 449–53

What Is Man? xvii–xviii, 148–49, 181–84, 187–88, 193–94, 208, 220, 424

"What Paul Bourget Thinks of Us," 361–62

This book is set in 10 point Janson, a faithful re-creation of a seventeenth-century Dutch typeface designed by Nicolas Kis. The display type is Bodoni Condensed. The paper is acid-free and meets the requirements for permanence of the American National Standards Institute. The binding material is Pearl Linen, an aqueous-coated cloth made of 100% cotton fabric and manufactured by ICG/Holliston, Tennessee. Composition by Dedicated Business Services. Printing by Malloy Incorporated. The Smyth-sewn binding and ribbon marker were added by Dekker Bookbinding.

THE LIBRARY OF AMERICA SERIES

The Library of America fosters appreciation and pride in America's literary heritage by publishing, and keeping permanently in print, authoritative editions of America's best and most significant writing. An independent nonprofit organization, it was founded in 1979 with seed money from the National Endowment for the Humanities and the Ford Foundation.

1. Herman Melville, *Typee, Omoo, Mardi* (1982)
2. Nathaniel Hawthorne, *Tales and Sketches* (1982)
3. Walt Whitman, *Poetry and Prose* (1982)
4. Harriet Beecher Stowe, *Three Novels* (1982)
5. Mark Twain, *Mississippi Writings* (1982)
6. Jack London, *Novels and Stories* (1982)
7. Jack London, *Novels and Social Writings* (1982)
8. William Dean Howells, *Novels 1875–1886* (1982)
9. Herman Melville, *Redburn, White-Jacket, Moby-Dick* (1983)
10. Nathaniel Hawthorne, *Collected Novels* (1983)
11. Francis Parkman, *France and England in North America*, vol. I (1983)
12. Francis Parkman, *France and England in North America*, vol. II (1983)
13. Henry James, *Novels 1871–1880* (1983)
14. Henry Adams, *Novels, Mont Saint Michel, The Education* (1983)
15. Ralph Waldo Emerson, *Essays and Lectures* (1983)
16. Washington Irving, *History, Tales and Sketches* (1983)
17. Thomas Jefferson, *Writings* (1984)
18. Stephen Crane, *Prose and Poetry* (1984)
19. Edgar Allan Poe, *Poetry and Tales* (1984)
20. Edgar Allan Poe, *Essays and Reviews* (1984)
21. Mark Twain, *The Innocents Abroad, Roughing It* (1984)
22. Henry James, *Literary Criticism: Essays, American & English Writers* (1984)
23. Henry James, *Literary Criticism: European Writers & The Prefaces* (1984)
24. Herman Melville, *Pierre, Israel Potter, The Confidence-Man, Tales & Billy Budd* (1985)
25. William Faulkner, *Novels 1930–1935* (1985)
26. James Fenimore Cooper, *The Leatherstocking Tales*, vol. I (1985)
27. James Fenimore Cooper, *The Leatherstocking Tales*, vol. II (1985)
28. Henry David Thoreau, *A Week, Walden, The Maine Woods, Cape Cod* (1985)
29. Henry James, *Novels 1881–1886* (1985)
30. Edith Wharton, *Novels* (1986)
31. Henry Adams, *History of the U.S. during the Administrations of Jefferson* (1986)
32. Henry Adams, *History of the U.S. during the Administrations of Madison* (1986)
33. Frank Norris, *Novels and Essays* (1986)
34. W.E.B. Du Bois, *Writings* (1986)
35. Willa Cather, *Early Novels and Stories* (1987)
36. Theodore Dreiser, *Sister Carrie, Jennie Gerhardt, Twelve Men* (1987)
37a. Benjamin Franklin, *Silence Dogood, The Busy-Body, & Early Writings* (1987)
37b. Benjamin Franklin, *Autobiography, Poor Richard, & Later Writings* (1987)
38. William James, *Writings 1902–1910* (1987)
39. Flannery O'Connor, *Collected Works* (1988)
40. Eugene O'Neill, *Complete Plays 1913–1920* (1988)
41. Eugene O'Neill, *Complete Plays 1920–1931* (1988)
42. Eugene O'Neill, *Complete Plays 1932–1943* (1988)
43. Henry James, *Novels 1886–1890* (1989)
44. William Dean Howells, *Novels 1886–1888* (1989)
45. Abraham Lincoln, *Speeches and Writings 1832–1858* (1989)
46. Abraham Lincoln, *Speeches and Writings 1859–1865* (1989)
47. Edith Wharton, *Novellas and Other Writings* (1990)
48. William Faulkner, *Novels 1936–1940* (1990)

49. Willa Cather, *Later Novels* (1990)
50. Ulysses S. Grant, *Memoirs and Selected Letters* (1990)
51. William Tecumseh Sherman, *Memoirs* (1990)
52. Washington Irving, *Bracebridge Hall, Tales of a Traveller, The Alhambra* (1991)
53. Francis Parkman, *The Oregon Trail, The Conspiracy of Pontiac* (1991)
54. James Fenimore Cooper, *Sea Tales: The Pilot, The Red Rover* (1991)
55. Richard Wright, *Early Works* (1991)
56. Richard Wright, *Later Works* (1991)
57. Willa Cather, *Stories, Poems, and Other Writings* (1992)
58. William James, *Writings 1878–1899* (1992)
59. Sinclair Lewis, *Main Street & Babbitt* (1992)
60. Mark Twain, *Collected Tales, Sketches, Speeches, & Essays 1852–1890* (1992)
61. Mark Twain, *Collected Tales, Sketches, Speeches, & Essays 1891–1910* (1992)
62. *The Debate on the Constitution: Part One* (1993)
63. *The Debate on the Constitution: Part Two* (1993)
64. Henry James, *Collected Travel Writings: Great Britain & America* (1993)
65. Henry James, *Collected Travel Writings: The Continent* (1993)
66. *American Poetry: The Nineteenth Century*, Vol. 1 (1993)
67. *American Poetry: The Nineteenth Century*, Vol. 2 (1993)
68. Frederick Douglass, *Autobiographies* (1994)
69. Sarah Orne Jewett, *Novels and Stories* (1994)
70. Ralph Waldo Emerson, *Collected Poems and Translations* (1994)
71. Mark Twain, *Historical Romances* (1994)
72. John Steinbeck, *Novels and Stories 1932–1937* (1994)
73. William Faulkner, *Novels 1942–1954* (1994)
74. Zora Neale Hurston, *Novels and Stories* (1995)
75. Zora Neale Hurston, *Folklore, Memoirs, and Other Writings* (1995)
76. Thomas Paine, *Collected Writings* (1995)
77. *Reporting World War II: American Journalism 1938–1944* (1995)
78. *Reporting World War II: American Journalism 1944–1946* (1995)
79. Raymond Chandler, *Stories and Early Novels* (1995)
80. Raymond Chandler, *Later Novels and Other Writings* (1995)
81. Robert Frost, *Collected Poems, Prose, & Plays* (1995)
82. Henry James, *Complete Stories 1892–1898* (1996)
83. Henry James, *Complete Stories 1898–1910* (1996)
84. William Bartram, *Travels and Other Writings* (1996)
85. John Dos Passos, *U.S.A.* (1996)
86. John Steinbeck, *The Grapes of Wrath and Other Writings 1936–1941* (1996)
87. Vladimir Nabokov, *Novels and Memoirs 1941–1951* (1996)
88. Vladimir Nabokov, *Novels 1955–1962* (1996)
89. Vladimir Nabokov, *Novels 1969–1974* (1996)
90. James Thurber, *Writings and Drawings* (1996)
91. George Washington, *Writings* (1997)
92. John Muir, *Nature Writings* (1997)
93. Nathanael West, *Novels and Other Writings* (1997)
94. *Crime Novels: American Noir of the 1930s and 40s* (1997)
95. *Crime Novels: American Noir of the 1950s* (1997)
96. Wallace Stevens, *Collected Poetry and Prose* (1997)
97. James Baldwin, *Early Novels and Stories* (1998)
98. James Baldwin, *Collected Essays* (1998)
99. Gertrude Stein, *Writings 1903–1932* (1998)
100. Gertrude Stein, *Writings 1932–1946* (1998)
101. Eudora Welty, *Complete Novels* (1998)
102. Eudora Welty, *Stories, Essays, & Memoir* (1998)
103. Charles Brockden Brown, *Three Gothic Novels* (1998)
104. *Reporting Vietnam: American Journalism 1959–1969* (1998)
105. *Reporting Vietnam: American Journalism 1969–1975* (1998)
106. Henry James, *Complete Stories 1874–1884* (1999)

107. Henry James, *Complete Stories 1884–1891* (1999)
108. *American Sermons: The Pilgrims to Martin Luther King Jr.* (1999)
109. James Madison, *Writings* (1999)
110. Dashiell Hammett, *Complete Novels* (1999)
111. Henry James, *Complete Stories 1864–1874* (1999)
112. William Faulkner, *Novels 1957–1962* (1999)
113. John James Audubon, *Writings & Drawings* (1999)
114. *Slave Narratives* (2000)
115. *American Poetry: The Twentieth Century*, Vol. 1 (2000)
116. *American Poetry: The Twentieth Century*, Vol. 2 (2000)
117. F. Scott Fitzgerald, *Novels and Stories 1920–1922* (2000)
118. Henry Wadsworth Longfellow, *Poems and Other Writings* (2000)
119. Tennessee Williams, *Plays 1937–1955* (2000)
120. Tennessee Williams, *Plays 1957–1980* (2000)
121. Edith Wharton, *Collected Stories 1891–1910* (2001)
122. Edith Wharton, *Collected Stories 1911–1937* (2001)
123. *The American Revolution: Writings from the War of Independence* (2001)
124. Henry David Thoreau, *Collected Essays and Poems* (2001)
125. Dashiell Hammett, *Crime Stories and Other Writings* (2001)
126. Dawn Powell, *Novels 1930–1942* (2001)
127. Dawn Powell, *Novels 1944–1962* (2001)
128. Carson McCullers, *Complete Novels* (2001)
129. Alexander Hamilton, *Writings* (2001)
130. Mark Twain, *The Gilded Age and Later Novels* (2002)
131. Charles W. Chesnutt, *Stories, Novels, and Essays* (2002)
132. John Steinbeck, *Novels 1942–1952* (2002)
133. Sinclair Lewis, *Arrowsmith, Elmer Gantry, Dodsworth* (2002)
134. Paul Bowles, *The Sheltering Sky, Let It Come Down, The Spider's House* (2002)
135. Paul Bowles, *Collected Stories & Later Writings* (2002)
136. Kate Chopin, *Complete Novels & Stories* (2002)
137. *Reporting Civil Rights: American Journalism 1941–1963* (2003)
138. *Reporting Civil Rights: American Journalism 1963–1973* (2003)
139. Henry James, *Novels 1896–1899* (2003)
140. Theodore Dreiser, *An American Tragedy* (2003)
141. Saul Bellow, *Novels 1944–1953* (2003)
142. John Dos Passos, *Novels 1920–1925* (2003)
143. John Dos Passos, *Travel Books and Other Writings* (2003)
144. Ezra Pound, *Poems and Translations* (2003)
145. James Weldon Johnson, *Writings* (2004)
146. Washington Irving, *Three Western Narratives* (2004)
147. Alexis de Tocqueville, *Democracy in America* (2004)
148. James T. Farrell, *Studs Lonigan: A Trilogy* (2004)
149. Isaac Bashevis Singer, *Collected Stories I* (2004)
150. Isaac Bashevis Singer, *Collected Stories II* (2004)
151. Isaac Bashevis Singer, *Collected Stories III* (2004)
152. Kaufman & Co., *Broadway Comedies* (2004)
153. Theodore Roosevelt, *The Rough Riders, An Autobiography* (2004)
154. Theodore Roosevelt, *Letters and Speeches* (2004)
155. H. P. Lovecraft, *Tales* (2005)
156. Louisa May Alcott, *Little Women, Little Men, Jo's Boys* (2005)
157. Philip Roth, *Novels & Stories 1959–1962* (2005)
158. Philip Roth, *Novels 1967–1972* (2005)
159. James Agee, *Let Us Now Praise Famous Men, A Death in the Family* (2005)
160. James Agee, *Film Writing & Selected Journalism* (2005)
161. Richard Henry Dana, Jr., *Two Years Before the Mast & Other Voyages* (2005)
162. Henry James, *Novels 1901–1902* (2006)
163. Arthur Miller, *Collected Plays 1944–1961* (2006)
164. William Faulkner, *Novels 1926–1929* (2006)

165. Philip Roth, *Novels 1973–1977* (2006)
166. *American Speeches: Part One* (2006)
167. *American Speeches: Part Two* (2006)
168. Hart Crane, *Complete Poems & Selected Letters* (2006)
169. Saul Bellow, *Novels 1956–1964* (2007)
170. John Steinbeck, *Travels with Charley and Later Novels* (2007)
171. Capt. John Smith, *Writings with Other Narratives* (2007)
172. Thornton Wilder, *Collected Plays & Writings on Theater* (2007)
173. Philip K. Dick, *Four Novels of the 1960s* (2007)
174. Jack Kerouac, *Road Novels 1957–1960* (2007)
175. Philip Roth, *Zuckerman Bound* (2007)
176. Edmund Wilson, *Literary Essays & Reviews of the 1920s & 30s* (2007)
177. Edmund Wilson, *Literary Essays & Reviews of the 1930s & 40s* (2007)
178. *American Poetry: The 17th & 18th Centuries* (2007)
179. William Maxwell, *Early Novels & Stories* (2008)
180. Elizabeth Bishop, *Poems, Prose, & Letters* (2008)
181. A. J. Liebling, *World War II Writings* (2008)
182s. *American Earth: Environmental Writing Since Thoreau* (2008)
183. Philip K. Dick, *Five Novels of the 1960s & 70s* (2008)
184. William Maxwell, *Later Novels & Stories* (2008)
185. Philip Roth, *Novels & Other Narratives 1986–1991* (2008)
186. Katherine Anne Porter, *Collected Stories & Other Writings* (2008)
187. John Ashbery, *Collected Poems 1956–1987* (2008)
188. John Cheever, *Collected Stories & Other Writings* (2009)
189. John Cheever, *Complete Novels* (2009)
190. Lafcadio Hearn, *American Writings* (2009)
191. A. J. Liebling, *The Sweet Science & Other Writngs* (2009)
192s. *The Lincoln Anthology: Great Writers on His Life and Legacy* (2009)
193. Philip K. Dick, *VALIS & Later Novels* (2009)
194. Thornton Wilder, *The Bridge of San Luis Rey and Other Novels 1926–1948* (2009)
195. Raymond Carver, *Collected Stories* (2009)
196. *American Fantastic Tales: Terror and the Uncanny from Poe to the Pulps* (2009)
197. *American Fantastic Tales: Terror and the Uncanny from the 1940s to Now* (2009)
198. John Marshall, *Writings* (2010)
199s. *The Mark Twain Anthology: Great Writers on His Life and Works* (2010)
200. Mark Twain, *A Tramp Abroad, Following the Equator, Other Travels* (2010)
201. Ralph Waldo Emerson, *Selected Journals 1820–1842* (2010)
202. Ralph Waldo Emerson, *Selected Journals 1841–1877* (2010)
203. *The American Stage: Writing on Theater from Washington Irving to Tony Kushner* (2010)

To subscribe to the series or to order individual copies,
please visit www.loa.org or call (800) 964.5778.